"Bring the power of God's Love more fully into your daily life."

PROPHET DEL HALL

Spiritual
Keys

For a More
Abundant Life

Editors: Del Hall IV, Lorraine Fortier

Assistant Editors: Lynne Hall, Molly Comfort, Paul Nelson

"Keys in Action" story introductions written by Del Hall IV

Cover Design by Del Hall IV
Cover Image by shutterstock.com

Copyright © 2022 F.U.N. Inc.
All rights reserved.

ISBN: 978-1-947255-10-4

Spiritual Keys

For a More Abundant Life

PROPHET DEL HALL

"The days of any religion or path coming between me and my children are coming to an end" saith the Lord

DECEMBER 29, 2013

Table of Contents

Appendix

Foreword

   Would you like to break free from worries, fears, anxieties, feelings of unworthiness, endless mind chatter, self-destructive habits, or other negative tendencies? These Spiritual Keys can help you break free from the narrow human state of consciousness and really start living your life, living from the perspective of the real eternal you. You are an eternal spiritual being — an individualized piece of the Holy Spirit, personalized through lifetimes of experience within a temporal, physical embodiment. It is quite an accomplishment to break free from the human consciousness and operate more as your true spiritual self — an eternal child of God. It is through my father's great love, wisdom, patience, and absolute trust in God that he has guided those of us at the Guidance for a Better Life retreat center to manifest more of our Divine nature and bring more of God's Love into our lives. He has done this, in part, by introducing us to, and helping us learn to live, a set of Divine spiritual principles — or what we call "Spiritual Keys." These Keys have helped many find true happiness, love, peace, freedom, and more. Now he is pleased to offer them to you. The keys to a more abundant life are in your hands.

   Del Hall IV

Introduction

Thank you for reading my book. My motivation for writing this book is to share some of the Spiritual Keys that have so improved the lives of my students at Guidance for a Better Life retreat center in Virginia, USA. Through my Keys to Spiritual Freedom Study Program I gently introduce individuals to God's eternal teachings over time in just the right order and right amount. As part of the program students each receive personal mentoring, teaching discourses, guided spiritual exercises, and opportunities to participate in group discussions. The growth of many of these individuals has been quite remarkable. The degree of peace, joy, clarity, wisdom, self-respect, purpose, confidence, freedom, and love, both received and demonstrated, in their lives has increased dramatically.

Many, if not most, started my mentoring program quite "un-free," being controlled or limited by some of the following negative aspects of life: fear, worries, self-doubts, anger, lack of purpose, harmful habits, loneliness, feelings of unworthiness, guilt, and only a superficial level of joy and peace in their hearts. The eternal teachings of God bring true freedom and truly change lives for the better. I have personally witnessed these transformations and the many ways God has so blessed the students that come to Guidance for a Better Life retreat center; now it is time to bring these sacred teachings to others.

For thirty years I have mentored individuals in how to successfully build an abundant life of love based upon a foundation of absolutely knowing God is real, He is alive and active, and loves you dearly. This foundation of certainty is built over time through experiences that only a true Prophet of God can deliver. Along the way God's teachings and principles for an abundant life are introduced. I call these principles "Spiritual Keys." These Keys are not just mental concepts, they are living guideposts to be practiced and integrated into daily life. It takes time to fully understand and "live" each Key, and many Keys depend upon and work best only when other foundational Keys have first become operational and are being consistently applied in daily life.

Although the principles that lead to an abundant life seem simple intellectually, it takes time to truly understand and appreciate their profound nature. It also requires guidance, structure, and proper pacing to effectively integrate these new ways of viewing and living into daily life. This is what I hope to accomplish for you by adapting my Keys to Spiritual Freedom Study Program into this distance-study offering.

So much I share is based upon personalized counsel I provide through face-to-face interactions during our retreats, and it is challenging to effectively translate this important dynamic into written text. However, I truly wish to share as best I can, with a prayer that this book will bless those whom I may never meet personally. This is why I have included study guidance throughout to help you as much as possible. I have also added many stories written by my students that illustrate the use and effectiveness of the Spiritual Keys. My hope is these actual examples of the "Keys in Action" will inspire you to embrace these eternal truths and principles and open you to the possibility for a more abundant life they hold.

I have set the pace of this book to incrementally build a larger view of what an abundant life looks like, how to achieve it, and what is possible in your relationship with the Heavenly Father. As you read further into the latter sections, the value and importance of the seemingly simple foundations established in the early steps will become increasingly clear. The pace set will also give you the time to absorb a dramatically higher view of life, freedom, and love. The real eternal you may begin to feel excitement and hope and rejoice at what you discover, but the intellectual side of you might struggle with such a magnitude of change. In addition to the study guidance I provide throughout, I include suggested rest periods — to increase the probability you make it to the climactic and stunning end of this book. I truly want the eternal truths found herein to be digestible, understandable, and empowering. These seemingly simple principles and truths lead to a freedom few ever experience while living here on Earth in a physical body. I so very much want to help you recognize your true eternal self and develop your profound potential as a beloved child of God.

Love and Blessings,
Prophet Del Hall

Definition of Spiritual Keys

Spiritual Keys are like nuggets of spiritual truth that provide a road map to a richer and fuller life. They are a set of Divine principles, which help us make better decisions in all areas of our lives. Spiritual Keys, if understood and integrated into daily life, can help us build a more abundant life. The Keys are like seeds that if watered and nurtured will bloom into something profound and bear "fruit" in your life and the lives of those you love.

These Keys can also bring us closer to God and His Prophet, which is the foundation of an abundant life. Some Keys tune us into the Divine so we can receive guidance or experience God's Love directly. Other Spiritual Keys are like spiritual laws, and like the law of gravity they work whether one knows of them or not. Being aware of these is a huge advantage. Some Keys bring spiritual wisdom. Other Keys help us travel through life more smoothly and in balance, while helping us avoid unnecessary troubles and challenges. Many of these Keys help us to grow in our ability to both give and receive love.

Some Keys seem extremely simple. Readers may sometimes feel they already understand and use certain Spiritual Keys. Often this is not true. ALL Keys have deeper meanings and use than the simple English words used to describe them. The deeper use and meanings are gained through study, prayer and contemplation, life experiences, and online discourses from Prophet. The shared stories of the "Keys in Action" will also greatly improve the understanding and value of the Keys. It is best to be humble and respectful regarding ALL Keys. They are ALL very powerful spiritual tools and profound truths that can greatly benefit one's life!

The profound nature of the Keys will further reveal itself when you start to see how the Keys work together in combination with other Keys. This is because individual Keys do not stand alone and independent of other Keys. Part of the secret of each Key is how it relates to, affects, or impacts other individual and groups of Keys. This is perhaps the most important concept to understand regarding the Keys, they are like a living ball of wisdom that work together best.

Prophet Del Hall

Keys to Spiritual Freedom Study Program

In this book I will introduce the Spiritual Keys in the same general order as I do at my retreats. This next section provides some necessary context by giving an overview of our "Keys to Spiritual Freedom Study Program." Having this background will help you better understand the overall structure of the book and the progression of the sections I patterned after our retreats.

Over the years I have been guided to share the Spiritual Keys in the order that is best for spiritual growth. At Guidance for a Better Life retreat center my son, Del Hall IV, and I developed a program of five retreats for new students, from Step One to Step Five. At each retreat I introduce a new set of Keys. The new Keys introduced build upon the Keys from the previous retreat. I provide an in-depth discourse on each of the new Keys and also review the Keys taught at prior retreats. Introducing the Keys in this order and reinforcing them as I do works well and provides a gentle and complementary transition between the five Steps. Also, because some Keys are not particularly effective without understanding and using the earlier Keys shared, it is best to allow some time to practice and integrate each set of Keys into your life before continuing on with the next Step and learning a new grouping of Keys.

The "Keys to Spiritual Freedom Study Program" is designed to be completed in as soon as two years, but no more than four years, as there is a certain pacing I find necessary for students to gain the most benefit. At my retreat center each student's progress is reviewed after completing Step Five. If they are accepted for additional spiritual mentorship, and it is in their heart to continue, students may attend advanced level spiritual retreats.

To help you more fully appreciate how the Spiritual Keys work in everyday life, I have added for this publication a special "Keys in Action" section at the end of each Step. I include stories written by my students that demonstrate a particular group of Keys in practice. I picked these stories because they cover the Keys introduced in that particular Step pretty well. Most, if not all the stories, have additional Keys you will not have learned about yet. That should not be a problem though; in fact, it will introduce you to upcoming Keys a little early. When you do read about those Keys later on in the book, you will already have a feel for them in practice. It is difficult to share any story written by my students that does not have several Keys involved. Remember, in the "Definition of Spiritual Keys" I mentioned how the Keys complement and support each other. You will also find I added some Study Guidance at the end of each story I believe will assist you in receiving more clarity from that reading.

After completing the Keys shared in Step Five you will find the Step Six Keys. These Keys are lightly discussed during my retreats, when appropriate throughout the previous Steps, but once a student enters the advanced program they are shared in greater detail and provided in written form. You will also be exposed to Step Six Keys when reading the "Keys in Action" stories I provide after each Step. It is difficult to separate out those Keys from the stories as they all work together. This will actually be beneficial to you by getting an early introduction.

At any time while reading this book you may choose to enhance your study through a variety of offerings including my online YouTube videos, podcasts, and other books. All of our offerings can assist you in understanding the various topics in this book. These additional study aids also provide a break from reading, giving more time to relax and absorb the beautiful new view of life being shared and is now within your reach.

Step One: Tools to Recognize Divine Guidance

There is a deep well of spiritual light, love, and guidance to draw from as you go about your life. You are never alone — the Voice of God is always with you trying to help guide you through the challenges of life and manifest more joy and happiness. The problem for most folks is life is busy and full of distractions making it hard to "hear" those gentle whisperings or "see" the Hand of God. The first step in learning to confidently follow Divine guidance is being able to recognize it in the first place. Divine guidance comes in countless ways, from the dramatic to the very subtle; we call this the "Language of the Divine." This section will provide Spiritual Keys, which will help you tune in and listen for this guidance and become more aware of the many ways God is reaching out to you. Very much like "teaching a man to fish" versus "handing him a fish," these Keys are focused on giving you the tools to pursue and ultimately receive guidance and insights directly from the Divine.

The following Keys will be introduced:

Soul and Self

Our real and eternal self is called Soul. As Soul we are literally an individualized and eternal piece of God's Voice, the Holy Spirit. More specifically, the Holy Spirit is made of God's Light and Sound, which is actually God's Love. **As Soul we are made in the image of God.** As an individual and uniquely experienced Soul you have free will, intelligence, imagination, opinions, clear and continuous access to Divine guidance, and immortality. **As Soul we have an innate and profound spiritual growth potential, way beyond the spiritual growth of what our physical selves alone can accomplish.**

Soul is eternal, with no beginning or end. When living on Earth Soul needs a physical body to reside within. One might call our physical bodies "earth suits" for Soul. While our physical body eventually wears out, Soul never wears out, but moves to higher worlds after leaving a particular physical body permanently. <u>We do not "have" a Soul, we "are" Soul that has a body. This is a major change in consciousness and it takes time to absorb, accept, and eventually live this core truth. Experiencing yourself as Soul is the essential foundation for extraordinary spiritual growth.</u>

Soul innately wants a relationship with Its Maker, God. Soul is destined to eventually become part of God's team as a coworker with God (a servant of God) through God's Prophet. Singing HU (an ancient name for God and when sung becomes a love song to God) and other spiritual exercises nourish and strengthen Soul. **As Soul gains strength over the mind we begin to operate more as Soul, then Soul influences our decisions and choices for the better, thus growing both closer to God and creating a more abundant life while here on Earth.**

When operating as Soul we have a higher spiritual consciousness than our physical self. **When we speak of our higher self, we are referring to Soul. With the help and guidance of God's Prophet, Soul has an unlimited potential to grow into higher and higher states of consciousness.** When we stay spiritually nourished, receiving our daily spiritual bread, and recognize our true selves as

Soul, we make better choices in life. Then both our daily life improves and our relationship with God grows. The spiritual wisdom we gain during our earthly incarnation can be taken to the other worlds when we translate. As Soul we can keep our relationship with God and God's Prophet in the next world. We can take our spiritual progress and wisdom with us.

When we speak of our lower self, or little self, we are referring to our physical body and physical mind. Compared to Soul our lower self is very limited and mortal. **As Soul we have access to far more wisdom and intelligence than even the smartest physical mind. Our goal is to allow Soul to influence our daily behavior and decisions.** This brings abundance, joy, peace, clarity, and love. Only Soul can explore the Heavens or visit the Abode of God with Prophet, not the temporal physical self.

Before we fully operate as Soul we must better understand our lower self. Prophet, and the use of the Spiritual Keys and other tools to be given, will help us truly know our lower self over time. **All our fears, anger, vanity, excessive attachments, lusts, greed, self-doubts, loneliness, and worries are of the lower self,** NOT SOUL. We are not our defilements; they are only a part of our lower physical selves. Their control over our lives can be greatly reduced or removed by understanding and using the Spiritual Keys being offered and with the guidance of Prophet. For us to more fully recognize ourselves as Soul we need help to remove or lessen the negative passions of the physical mind.

Soul is that part of us made in the image of God, that knows God best, is selfless, wants to bless others, and can more truly, fully, and deeply love their neighbor and God, as we have been commanded to do. Soul has been around forever. Being created long ago it has developed wisdom and experience way beyond intellect. Soul knows what is best for us, better than the mind. Soul is very receptive to the Holy Spirit because it is made from an individualized piece of the Holy Spirit. **When Soul and our mind work together in the way God intended our life blossoms. The Spiritual Keys will lead to Soul and the lower self working together the way God intended, and abundance will follow!**

Study Guidance: The secret to grow spiritually and bring the power and abundance of God's Love into your daily life is to not only grow your lower physical self spiritually but **also to grow and strengthen your eternal self** — Soul. Accepting that they "are Soul" that "has a physical body" is the true foundation for my students' exceptional growth and spiritual experiences and potentially could be for you too. **You do not "have" a Soul, you "ARE" Soul.** For now, just keep that concept gently in your mind until later in this book.

Gratitude

When we are grateful our heart opens, and we become more aware of, and receptive to, Divine guidance. **This is because the Divine speaks to our hearts, our higher self Soul, more than, but in addition to, our minds. This is why nourishing Soul is so very important.**

When we are grateful we relax. Our creativity increases when relaxed, thereby helping us find solutions to life's challenges.

A grateful heart attracts abundance. When we are grateful for someone or something it <u>blesses us</u>. **The one who is grateful is the one who is blessed.** When we are grateful for the gifts and blessings from God, God offers even more blessings. When we do not recognize the blessings we ALREADY have, additional blessings slow in coming or in being recognized.

By each day reflecting on things we are thankful for, we begin to develop an attitude of gratitude. Grateful people are happy! Ungrateful and self-centered people are never truly happy. Being grateful focuses our attention outside of us. True happiness has less to do with the amount of "stuff and possessions" we have and more to do with practicing an **attitude of gratitude. This attitude can be developed over time. Focus on what you do have and be grateful.**

As we think of all of the things we are grateful for, realize they are **ALL gifts of love from God, delivered by the Holy Spirit**. Our very life is a gift from God to be thankful for. We exist because God loves us!

Gratitude is a form of, and an expression of, love. It is the foundation, the cornerstone, and the secret of love. Gratitude is best demonstrated, just like love is best demonstrated.

Gratitude for the teacher nourishes the relationship and may grow into appreciation once we understand the magnitude and value of the gift, then into reverence.

One can never truly advance very far spiritually without gratitude, but fortunately you can grow into being a more grateful person if it's not something that comes to you naturally.

Study Guidance: Even being grateful for something as seemingly simple as a morning cup of coffee will help you build this very important attitude for spiritual growth. **Developing an attitude of gratitude is very important for learning to recognize God's guidance, Love, and blessings, because it OPENS your heart, which makes you more receptive. In other words, an open heart helps in recognizing God's guiding Hand in your daily life.**

Recommended Spiritual Exercise: A good way to develop an attitude of gratitude is to keep a journal of things you are thankful for each day, however simple, little, or small.

HU

HU is an ancient name for God, and when sung, it becomes a love song to God. It is not really a word; it is a sound vibration which originates from the Abode of God — the twelfth Heaven. HU has been around literally forever, way before the English language was created, or any earthly language. It is pronounced like the word hue.

When we sing "HUUUUUUUUUU" we become more receptive to allowing the Divine to help purify the lower self. The lower self, the physical mind and body, need help with the negative passions of the mind. These passions include anger, fear, greed, vanity, excessive attachments, worry, feelings of unworthiness, loneliness, etc. Singing HU brings the potential to experience God's Light and Sound, which purifies the mind and body and reduces these negative passions over time. This is much more effective than spending too much time focusing on the passions themselves. HU can also bring clarity, strength, healing, health, and protection. The Divine determines the gift to be received, although we can ask for specific help, guidance, or clarity.

Singing HU UPLIFTS our consciousness, which enables us to experience a higher and wider view of life. From a higher view we may more fully recognize truth. The truth might be about us, about the Divine, about a situation we are involved in, or clarity about someone else. From a higher view we have the opportunity to make better decisions. **HU OPENS US to be more receptive to truth and other spiritual help being offered.**

When we sing HU it brings spiritual nourishment to us, especially to our real selves, Soul. If we sing HU every day it brings us our "daily spiritual bread." This builds spiritual stamina, like going to a physical gym daily builds physical strength. Soul needs daily nourishment just as our physical body needs food.

HU can be sung out loud or silently. **When singing HU we are sending love and gratitude to God, to our Heavenly Father, unencumbered by words.** God hears and recognizes our every HU, so we focus on each individual HU we sing. The quality of our voice is not as important as our intent to send love and gratitude. You do not have to "feel" the love first before expressing love to God in a HU, the love is expressed in trying to sing the best HU you can.

It is good to set time aside daily for our relationship with God. One way to do so is by singing HU. It **demonstrates to God** you want to draw closer to Him. The Divine will respond either during the HU, shortly after the HU, in a dream, an awake dream (see glossary), or in some other way, whether we recognize the response or not.

When we are fearful, upset, or in grief, sing HU aloud or silently. Doing so often brings peace. **When we experience peace we can hear Divine guidance more clearly.** If in trouble sing HU, and it may bring clarity to the situation. When we see a situation clearly we can make better decisions. Singing HU brings us spiritual strength too, which also helps us make better decisions.

Singing HU is a pure prayer. It is not asking for anything or telling God what to do but sending Him love and gratitude. The love we send comes back to us in some form or fashion. **The extra love we send to God goes to other Souls we may know and to Souls we may never meet. So singing HU not only blesses us but blesses others.**

After singing HU for a few minutes or up to fifteen or twenty minutes, sit still and quiet for a while and **just listen with your heart.** Over time and with practice you will recognize the Divine response. It may come as a feeling or experience of deep peace, clarity on something important to you, a healing of some type, a feeling of renewed strength, a comforting, an experience of literally perceiving and recognizing the Holy Spirit in the form of God's Light or Sound, or even an experience of Prophet taking you, as Soul, into the higher worlds of God. Early on you might not recognize a return of God's Love, but **you will be building spiritual strength and nourishing Soul,** two important foundations. When you read the "Keys in Action" stories you will know what is possible in time, do not give up. Even if you only relax during your HUUUUUUUUs it is well worth your time and effort.

Study Guidance: Prayer is personal communication with God and is an extreme privilege. God hears every prayer from the heart whether or not we recognize a response. Singing from the heart an ancient name of God, HU, is the foundational prayer that activates and glues the Spiritual Keys together. Without singing HU regularly the effectiveness of the Keys is very much diminished. Also, without the spiritual nourishment gained when singing HU, Soul will not be as active and as effective in life, and this is of major importance for the potential extraordinary growth you will see is possible as you continue to read. All the blessings of our Heavenly Father come through His Grace. The practice of singing HU makes you much more receptive, the only way possible at times, to receive this Grace. Without HU you cannot accept the profound level of God's Love that will be revealed to you in this book. **Much like Gratitude, singing HU also opens our hearts to God's Love and Grace. Learning to accept God's great Love for us is the cornerstone of this book.**

Recommended Spiritual Exercise: Singing HU (*HUUUUU…*) pronounced "hue" serves as a tuning fork with the Holy Spirit that brings you into greater harmony with the Divine. Start by thinking of something you are grateful for, then sing HU. I recommend singing HU fifteen to twenty minutes each day. After singing it is best to give God time to respond. I recommend sitting in silence for five to ten minutes after singing HU. This can bring love, joy, peace, clarity, and raise you to a higher view of a situation when upset or fearful.

Throughout the day you can sing HU silently or out loud for a few minutes at a time. This brings spiritual nourishment similar to snacking on physical food throughout the day and keeps you more in tune with the Holy Spirit.

Discernment

Discernment is to distinguish between those thoughts, words, deeds, and actions, which contribute to spiritual freedom, abundance, and growth and help you accomplish your own personal priorities and goals, and those which do not and are a waste of your time and effort. Good discernment also includes deciding what to focus on and even the thoughts we allow into our consciousness. For example, negative thoughts about ourselves are very unhealthy and can be personally destructive. Self-discipline, restraint, and discernment are interrelated. **Good discernment is using our free will, given to us by a loving God, wisely. Making right choices leads to both freedom and love and demonstrates gratitude for the gift of free will.**

Soul has a higher level of discernment than any physical mind. Spiritually nourishing Soul by singing HU will begin to improve the choices we make in life. Deciding to be nourished as Soul by the Holy Spirit may be one of the best decisions one can make. Asking Prophet, a concentrated aspect of the Holy Spirit, for guidance and clarity on the inner (spiritually, not in the physical) will also improve our decisions. **When we combine Divine guidance with our own improved discernment, we create a life with an abundance of God's Love.**

Good discernment will reduce the problem of self-indulgence. Self-indulgence often leads us to unhappiness, problems, complications, and entanglements and also slows our spiritual growth. Deep down we do not respect ourselves when we are self-indulgent. When we practice discernment we build respect and confidence in ourselves, grow spiritually more mature, and create a better life for ourselves and loved ones. Good discernment in our decision making can stop potentially stressful situations before they occur.

Knowing your long-term goals, and making certain decisions AHEAD of time greatly improves the chance of using discernment and staying true to your goals and priorities. For example, if a decision is made to be faithful to a spouse before a temptation or passion arises, there is less chance of doing something you will regret because the decision has ALREADY been made to remain faithful. Other examples of making decisions before emotional and physical temptations arise could be not stealing, not using drugs, not watching inappropriate adult material, and not cheating your employer. One cannot be on God's team on a high level if they do not have good discernment. God needs to know we will make the right choices before we are given more spiritual authority. Making decisions when you are "clear," and not based upon short-lived emotions such as passions, fear, and excitement, can lead to better discernment and less regret. Now temptations are no longer so tempting.

If you are clear on your goals, a lot of choices are essentially already made. Generally, avoid making important decisions when out of balance, angry, fearful, stressed, lacking sleep, or emotionally worked up in any way. Discernment means knowing what is right and having the strength to do what is right. Initially one might need lots of willpower to make good decisions for themselves, but as they grow spiritually, the earlier temptations are no longer controlling their lives so much. The desire to do things that are not so good for us lessens with spiritual growth and a relationship with the Divine, until we no longer even want those things in our lives.

Study Guidance: It should be self-evident that good choices can lead to good results in life. Bad choices can derail an otherwise beautiful life. Perhaps the most important use of discernment is to use your free will to use the Keys, such as Gratitude and HU, to help the Holy Spirit nourish Soul and for you to draw closer to God. The Spiritual Keys in this book can make that decision a reality.

Note on Negative Passions of the Mind: I mentioned the negative passions of the mind in my Introduction and in the Keys Soul and Self, HU, and Discernment. These passions include fear, anger, guilt, worry, lust, greed, excessive attachments, and vanity. Although you may already know these passions are not beneficial, I want to explain specifically why they are detrimental to spiritual growth and true freedom.

One of the benefits of the Keys Gratitude and HU is that both Keys can open your heart. You have learned that you are more aware of and receptive to the Holy Spirit when your heart is open. The passions: fear, anger, guilt, and worry tend to close our hearts, thereby reducing our ability to "hear" the Divine communication that is always available to us, rather than helping us toward our goal of improving our Divine communication. Guilt can be beneficial for a <u>very short</u> period of time if one learns a useful lesson, takes responsibility for their actions, and then quickly gets over and moves past the guilt. Holding onto guilt whether one is conscious of it or not serves no purpose and is very damaging to one's overall wellbeing and spiritual development.

As Soul you are made from an individualized piece of God's Holy Spirit, therefore you are a Divine child of God. Lust is anything that controls us, such as beer, chocolate, drugs, excessive focus on sex, money (greed), etc. As Soul, a Divine being, to be controlled by something like beer or drugs does not make sense, you are so much more. To be controlled by such things means you lack freedom from them. One of the benefits of spiritual growth is freedom from allowing such things to control you.

Excessive attachment to anything tends to blind us to our options. Being excessively attached means we are entangled or "tied up" in something and that makes us less free; less free to use our creativity as Soul to find solutions to a challenge we may face, see our options in a situation, or recognize opportunities or choices that may benefit us. It takes some experience and discernment to determine when our attachments have become excessive. Both vanity and excessive attachment make us less receptive. With vanity we feel we already know what we need, or are so "full of ourselves" there is little or no room for new perspectives or suggestions, therefore we are less willing to truly listen and be receptive. With excessive attachment, we are less receptive because many times we are attached to a certain outcome or way we think things "should be," and we are unwilling to accept other possibilities or trust what God wants for us or others in a particular situation.

One may never completely remove these negative passions from life, but any reduction of any of them is improvement. If one of them has you "by the throat," and it is reduced to only occasionally flaring up, not flaring up as bad or for as long, that is progress. Over time, if the Spiritual Keys are integrated into daily life, these passions usually reduce to a point where they no longer "control" an individual.

All these passions negatively affect our decision-making skills and our ability to use our free will wisely, which is an example of discernment. Try to never make important decisions when under the influence of these negative passions. Becoming aware of when you are under their influence is part of coming to know thyself (Key Soul and Self). This is an essential part of one's continued spiritual growth and development.

Attitudes and Thoughts

Our thoughts have power! What we imagine has much more impact on our life experiences than our willpower. What we **expect** in life does more to determine our experiences than what we do. When we understand the power of this Spiritual Key we become more discerning about what we think and imagine. What we think can solidify into a future situation to bring a positive or negative impact to our life.

Imagination is a mental faculty that is a gift God granted Soul. This gift allows Soul to picture in thought. When Soul adds picturing, desire, and expecting of a certain outcome, it has the power to manifest. As we grow spiritually we need to be even more discerning of our thoughts.

The Divine never gives us a challenge greater than our ability to find a solution. Keeping that attitude increases our chances of finding a solution because we can truly imagine a solution exists, thereby activating our creativeness. **A high level of creativeness comes from Soul, and when Soul is nourished, an overall increase in finding solutions in life is the benefit.** An attitude of defeat decreases our creativity.

The power in our life to create comes from the Divine source and is manifested by our THOUGHTS. In your thoughts imagine you already have that which is desired; visualize yourself from the goal already achieved or state of consciousness desired. Placing emotions into this desired state adds strength and power to the creative attitude. Therefore having fear of something adds a very strong negative emotion. For example, imagine walking on a narrow log to cross over a dangerous stream. If your focus is on the fear of falling rather than safely crossing the stream it is likely you will fall. **Negative thoughts are very strong. This reinforces the need for discernment on what we choose to think about or focus upon.**

What we think of ourselves can be helpful or very destructive. It is important to always remember we are Soul created because God loves us. In time these words will ring even more true. Thinking God could NOT love you or forgive you is very negative and is an untrue thought. This one negative attitude could negate much of the other Spiritual Keys found in this book. Thoughts of unworthiness are very strong because they are negative. Imagine how you would feel if God really does love you. **He absolutely does! You are worthy of God's Love no matter your past!!!!**

As we grow, make better decisions, and improve our ways, we need to take new mental pictures of ourselves to replace the old view we carried. It is difficult to move forward if we keep visualizing and thinking we are still our former selves.

Strong negative emotions, such as fear, victim consciousness — one of being in a "pity party," and lacking of gratitude, adversely affect our attitude and thoughts and our spiritual growth. For example, the real eternal you, as Soul, is made from a piece of God's Holy Spirit. As you more fully accept this truth, how could you ever be a victim of anything, even if it seems so logically. How could you be a victim of a can of beer, a comfort food, or of another person? Never allowing a victim consciousness is very important in your goal of spiritual growth. **An attitude of being a victim robs one of spiritual strength and control over one's own life.**

Investing too much time and energy focusing on our problems can make them even stronger in a negative way. Spending some energy and time on the things going well in our life can give us a needed break. Often when we take a break from problems and relax a solution is more likely to come.

A "can do attitude" inspires us to look deeper for solutions to life's challenges. Even when a "can do attitude" seems illogical, the attitude and thought of "I cannot" is more dangerous and is like putting ourselves in a prison where we are weakened, reducing our ability to find solutions. **Keeping the attitude that there is ALWAYS a solution in every situation strengthens us. Knowing there is always a solution helps one trust and be patient.**

An **attitude of gratitude** helps one more fully recognize the blessings of God in their daily life. Some blessings must be recognized to be accepted. When we more fully see the Hand of God in our lives, we more fully accept that God and Prophet want to help us and truly love us, just the way we are.

Study Guidance: The primary point of this Spiritual Key is that our attitudes and our thoughts do have a major impact on us, whether in a positive way or in a negative way. What we EXPECT in life has a profound impact on us, sometimes more than our efforts and actions. Learning to use discernment in what we think and focus on can greatly improve our life, strengthen the positive view we have of ourselves, influence our peace and balance, and even impact our relationship with God.

Spiritual Growth

There is ALWAYS more when it comes to spiritual growth. One never knows all there is about God's ways, God's truths, or the worlds of God. Even God's Prophets continue to grow in their ability to live God's truths daily.

Understanding spiritual truths (Spiritual Keys) is a never-ending quest. There is always more clarity, deeper and wider understandings, and new ways to integrate spiritual truths into daily life. It's our responsibility to keep looking for the "more" and to replace what we "think" we know with an actual experience of truth. **To grow spiritually we must be willing to replace our misunderstandings with more accurate realizations.**

We must be open to discover ever new and wider understandings of spiritual truths and how each truth relates to and interacts with other truths. Each new experience or spiritual discourse has the potential to add additional depth of clarity and understanding. Those with the attitude of excitement for their spiritual path and for spiritual growth will do well, versus those who are afraid to step up and grow because they're afraid of taking a chance at being wrong.

To reform a truth is to remove misunderstandings or defects of understanding. This makes the truth of actual operational value. If a truth is not understood to a point where it can be integrated into daily life, then it has little actual value for our spiritual growth. Worse, a partial understanding of God's truths can be harmful to further growth.

To transform a truth is to change its form or outward appearance. To truly understand a spiritual truth we must recognize it in different and various ways and situations. Sometimes a truth is hidden within a larger situation or in combination with other truths, in ways hard to recognize. So just being able to recite a truth does not make it of great value to the seeker.

Being receptive to a qualified guide is necessary. Over time the building of trust and love for God's chosen Prophet is necessary to reach one's true potential spiritually. Making an effort to "water the seeds" of insights and instruction given by Prophet helps growth. Nourishing Soul by singing HU daily, with love and gratitude and not in a rote way, helps growth. Service to God leads to growth. Leaving open the possibility that you do not fully understand a teaching or lesson from Prophet makes one more receptive. During contemplations ask Prophet where to focus. Abiding in Prophet throughout the day greatly improves growth. Being willing to let Prophet take you a little beyond your comfort zone helps improve receptiveness and growth.

Staying excited about God's ways and the adventure you are on is a must. Remaining motivated over a long period of time is also necessary, as is truly wanting a personal loving relationship with the Heavenly Father, more than just having stimulating experiences. **If your desire for God is sufficient and you do your part and let Prophet do his part, then God's Grace will make it so. Having a living teacher and guide greatly facilitates spiritual growth.**

Spiritual growth builds upon earlier lessons. Make an effort to remember and truly lay hold of those lessons. **One of the first things to remember is that as Soul you have an innate and profound spiritual growth potential given to you by God Himself. He wants you to grow to the level where you can be safely guided Home to Him.**

Study Guidance: Understanding, using, and integrating the Keys into daily life is an important way, and maybe the only way, to grow to one's highest potential. Later in this book the importance of letting a Prophet of God be your guide will be introduced. This will be very clear by the end of the book as you complete your reading of the one hundred and thirty-five stories found in the "Keys in Action" sections. We will cover the Spiritual Key of God's Prophet in Step Three. For now, relax about fully grasping or accepting the concept of Prophet and keep moving forward to the fifteen stories I share with you next.

Step One Keys in Action

After each of the stories you read in the "Keys in Action" sections of this book, I help you recognize the Keys in each story by providing you a Keys summary. First, I list the Keys found in the story that you have already studied. Then I list the Keys in the story that have not yet been studied but will be covered in later Steps. Some Keys are nearly interchangeable, such as God's Love and God's Grace found in Step Three, so they may be confusing. To help clarify this for you, when a Soul "feels," recognizes, or experiences God's Love, I call that Key, God's Love. When a Soul is invited into the Heavens, to one of God's Temples of Learning, receives a healing, or receives past life information, I call that Key an example of God's Grace. Both the Keys God's Love and God's Grace are gifts of His Love, but I treat them as separate Keys as it is helpful for you to see the difference, albeit subtle, in the ways God's Love may be shared with us.

It is possible I missed listing a Key found in a story, so if you notice one I did not list, good for you. I hope by listing the Spiritual Keys found in each of the first one-hundred stories you will better recognize the Keys in Action and receive more clarity on how the Spiritual Keys work together.

He Held My Hand

The HU SONG is one of the greatest gifts we could pass on to you. Singing HU will strengthen your connection to Spirit regardless of what path you are on. Many of the phenomenal experiences and realizations shared in this book occurred, in part, due to singing HU.

Back in August I went to a HU sing at the Guidance for a Better Life retreat center. HU is a love song to God. There were about eighty people there, a lot whom I had never met before. Del, the Prophet of God, came in and explained the song and where it originated from. Then he began to sing HU and everyone followed.

The sound of everyone singing HU was just so beautiful, it was the most people I have ever sung with. As we were singing I became very relaxed. With my eyes closed as I continued singing I started to see these small lights, some blue and some white. Then I saw a door and in the door was a rectangle of bright white light shining through. Being somewhat new to this experience, I could feel myself get anxious and the door was gone.

I sat back, relaxed and continued to sing HU. The door with the white light appeared again. I stayed relaxed, then I felt a hand take mine and we walked to the door. I did not feel any anxiety or nervousness this time. We walked to the door and it opened. Inside was the brightest white light I have ever seen, it just filled the area.

Standing in the doorway and still holding the Prophet's hands, I began absorbing this beautiful white light. It was not only warm, but more than that I felt this overwhelming presence of peace. We just stood there and never said a word.

When I sing HU at home, I thank God for giving me such an experience that I can visit over and over again.

Written by Steven Lane

Keys in this story: HU, Gratitude, Soul (Steve, as Soul, went into the inner spiritual worlds with Prophet to the door of light. The Light was an aspect of God's Holy Spirit, and seeing it is experiencing God's Love. Steve experiencing the overwhelming presence of peace is also a gift of God's Love)

Keys not yet studied: God's Prophet, God's Love

The Healing Power of HU

HU is an ancient name for God that can be sung quietly or out loud as a love song to God. Singing HU raises you up and opens you up spiritually making you more receptive to receive God's Love and healing. Those that have been singing HU for many years in their daily contemplations know there is always more to experience and learn about HU.

The HU was shared with me about fourteen years ago by my aunt and uncle. The first time I sang it in a group, I wept. It awakened something inside of me. My heart was opening to express pure love to God, and I now know that it was the eternal part of me, Soul, crying tears of joy. I cherish singing HU and have grown to sing it faithfully many times throughout the day. Each time I feel refreshed, more at peace, and more grateful. Sometimes as I sing I am aware of a blessing or an experience and sometimes I am not. Over the years I have received a lot of healing when singing HU.

This summer at a weeklong retreat at Guidance for a Better Life I experienced a profound healing while singing HU. During an opportunity to have alone time at the retreat I hiked to Vision Rock (rock outcropping on retreat center property with a stunning view), sat down, and sang HU. I did not ask for a healing nor did I even know I needed one. I just prayed to give all my love to God and be receptive to whatever and however it came back. I invited Del, the Prophet, whom I trust immensely, to join me spiritually. We met in my inner vision, and to my surprise we traveled in our Soul bodies above space and time into past and future lives. I had an amazing experience and a healing that penetrated into the past, present, and future all at once. I was shown all the areas of my lives where there had actually been love, but it had not been recognized. I was also shown God's Love flowing into areas that truly were devoid of love. It was both a retroactive and future-reaching healing. To say my past, present, and future received healing during an out of body experience might be much for some to accept, but nonetheless it is true. My spiritual guide, the Prophet, is authorized to do this, and it was the singing of HU that opened me up to receive this blessing.

It is humbling and exciting to know that I cannot grasp the full measure of God's Love, Grace, and Mercy, nor do I need to. This healing showed me that giving my love to God via singing HU came back to me a thousand times over. It is difficult to put words to this healing and what it means to me. It is changing my life for the better and even changing the lives of people around me.

The HU continues to reveal more to me as I grow in my ability to receive God's blessings. I may never comprehend its value completely, but my heart knows that no matter what I go through in life, God's Love can open me to Divine blessings. I know it was the singing of HU that raised me up to a higher level where my spiritual guide could bless me. This blessing would not have been possible without the many years of conditioning my guide spent preparing me for that healing. Without the guide, singing HU alone could not have taken me on the journey of healing I experienced.

I learned from this experience that we all have wounds we may or may not be aware of from this life and even past lives. We all carry a burden equal to our measure. They affect the way we view the world, the choices we make, and our ability to give and receive love. My experience while singing HU gave me more compassion for others and myself. I have always appreciated HU, but now I understand more of its incredible healing power.

Written by Tash Canine

Keys in this story: HU, Soul, Gratitude (cherish)

Keys not yet studied: Receptive, God's Prophet, Prayer, God's Grace (blessings/healings), God's Love

God's Healing Love

God's Light and Love give us life — we are never without them.
We were created from and continue to be nourished and sustained by
God's Light and Love. However, when we take steps to draw closer to
God we can experience them in ever-greater magnitudes. There is no
ill that the Light of God cannot soothe.

One morning I awoke early feeling quite poorly with a headache accompanied by nausea. Since I worked the afternoon shift I decided that there was sufficient time to allow the sick feeling to go away on its own, instead of taking medication. Several hours passed without any relief. I decided to prepare for a short nap with a spiritual practice that brings me peace and comfort. I opened my heart and expressed love and appreciation to my creator by singing HU, then went to sleep. HU is a love song to God that was taught to me by the Prophet Del Hall, my spiritual teacher.

While I was asleep I had a dream of being bathed in a beautiful and comforting golden light. Upon awakening the symptoms of my illness were completely gone. Gratitude for the healing Light of God's Love overtook me while I realized how much I am loved and cared for.

The Prophet has taught me how to fortify my awareness of the connection that exists between my creator and me. He has helped me to recognize that the personal love connection I have with the Divine is the most precious bond I will ever have.

Written by Bernadette Spitale

Keys in this story: HU, Gratitude

Keys not yet studied: God's Love (Golden light is God's Love directly from God), God's Grace (given dream and healing), God's Prophet

An Eternal Love Song to God

Love is like breathing... there is a giving out, and a receiving in. If you are longing to know the love of the Lord seek first to give love. For it is in the expressing of love that you will gain love.

It was a late summer evening. Our day had been filled with wonderful discourses about the Love of God based on our personal experiences. Earlier that day, I had witnessed the Divine give a healing, through Its Prophet, for a pain which another Soul had carried for lifetimes. I was blessed to listen to the Living Word as It flowed through my teacher. Yet there was more. My heart was brimming with gratitude and appreciation for my teacher, the God-ordained Prophet, Del Hall. The mantle which God has bestowed upon him is evident to us, his devoted students. Time and time again we have witnessed and experienced the Love of God flow through him.

At the time, I had been attending classes at Guidance for a Better Life for about five years. Being in the presence of Del had conditioned me to accept more of God's Love, and also to give more love. To me, the blessing of being able to love God is grace in itself. To be able to express this love is a gift upon a gift. Before we began to sing HU, our love song to God, we thought of things we were grateful for. We had the opportunity to really cherish one or two of them. Sometimes, I have found that my list could just keep going, but Del has taught me that by sometimes focusing on just one blessing I come to really treasure and recognize its value in my life. My husband and I had recently found out I was pregnant with our first child, and for this my heart was bursting with love and appreciation.

As the crickets' song echoed throughout the woods around us and the birds found their evening perches, Del's voice began our love song. HUUUUUUUU. Putting words to and describing the beauty of this song is difficult. It is beautifully simple, yet profoundly touching. And singing it in a large group of fifty or so Souls, like I was that night, is a special gift. That night my heart sang with a depth that I had not yet experienced before. My fellow classmates' songs really touched me, it was as if their love and the love of Prophet was lifting me higher, inspiring me to sing with more love too. Have you ever loved something so much it actually felt like your heart was stretching? This was one of those times for me. As I sang HU, I felt as if I was going to burst with love. With all my heart and everything that I am, I longed to express my love to the Lord. I longed to be able to give back even a fraction of the Love I had received throughout that day and my life, to pass on some of the blessings I had received. I knew I was heard by God. God knows us and knows our hearts. Knowing this is glorious. And so with each out breath, came love for the Lord. In that moment, I could have sung forever. As Soul we are eternal beings. Our life experiences and the blessings we have day to day will one day pass, yet the eternal will remain. Through God's current Prophet, I have come to connect with the eternal, and that evening, I experienced some of my own eternal nature as Soul loving God.

While singing HU in the stillness, I heard songs within songs. In the song, I heard stillness within stillness. We sang in this world for about twenty minutes, but in essence we sang for eternity, reaching closer and closer in love to our Lord. I experienced Heaven on Earth that summer night. I am truly grateful. Love is like water; it needs to flow and have an outlet. If you feel stale, find a way to give love, no matter how small the act seems. I promise you it will bless your life.

Written by Molly Comfort

Keys in this story: HU, Gratitude, Soul

Keys not yet studied: God's Prophet, God's Love, God's Grace (healing)

Gift of a New Life

Separation from God and your Divine qualities causes pain of the heart. Many people lead "good" lives but still do not have a "deep peace." It is only when we close the gap and knowingly live a life connected to Spirit that we truly flourish.

Throughout my life I have felt an unfounded doubt and fear that I may not be good enough or able enough to succeed in this life. My life has been blessed by being raised in a loving family that provided me with a good secure home. My parents were supportive of my endeavors and never lost faith in me even during the trying adolescent years when I sometimes did not make the best decisions. I grew into a challenging and satisfying career that provided me with a good income and married a wonderful loving woman who gave me a daughter whom I love dearly. There were many trying times, but things always worked out for the best even when it took time and hindsight for me to realize it.

I have a successful blessed life but still felt fear and doubt and lacked a deep inner peace, until I experienced the healing power of the Love of God. I was introduced to the HU, a love song to God, in 2002 by Del, and throughout the years with his outer and inner guidance I was being conditioned to be released from the fears I carried for many lives. By singing HU daily, offering my love to God, the Love of God raised my awareness to a level that I was able to accept His healing.

Part of the realization that I was given is that I have not been doing it alone. He has always been with me, guiding me, and providing me with the ability to meet any challenge. I am so loved that I have never been given more than I can handle through His Love and guidance. Each and every life experience is an opportunity to learn, grow, and strengthen my personal relationship with God. Knowing this, my fear and doubt has diminished. A deep peace now fills my being along with the prayer to manifest His Love with every moment of my life. Thank you Lord for the blessings I have been given and continue to receive.

Written by Terry Kisner

Keys in this story: HU, Gratitude

Keys not yet studied: God's Grace (gift of deep peace, and healing of fear and doubt), Prayer, God's Prophet, God's Love

Prayer Averts Health Problem

Dreams are one of the many ways Spirit can communicate with you. Cultures for thousands of years have looked to their dreams as a source of Divine guidance. They are not simply residual mind junk from your day. An "awake dream" is communication from Spirit that occurs when you are awake, which is also known as a "sign," "coincidence," or "synchronicity." It is when you, the observer, feel there is more to an experience than the surface meaning. The following story illustrates just this. It also shows that our prayers are heard, but it is up to us to recognize the answer.

About twelve years ago, shortly after I moved to Virginia, I noticed that my overall health was declining. I found myself more and more tired, moody, and irritable. I had wondered if a food I was eating could be causing my symptoms, but I was unable to determine the exact cause. After several unsuccessful months of trying to figure out what was going on I received some help from Spirit that changed my life.

One evening after work I decided to make pancakes and eggs for dinner. After mixing up the pancake batter I let it sit for a moment, and I sat myself on the couch to rest. I relaxed for a moment then began singing HU to express my love for God. I asked God to please help me figure out what was going on with my body. After a few minutes I got up to make my pancakes. As I walked into the kitchen, the box of pancake mix fell off the counter, and its contents spilled on the floor. Cleaning up the mess I wondered, "What is going on, boxes of pancake mix don't just jump off the counter?" As I picked the box of pancake mix off the floor the ingredient list was turned towards me. In big bold letters the word WHEAT seemed to be highlighted and almost jumping off the box. Kneeling on the floor with this box in my hand, staring at these bold letters I wondered, "Maybe I'm allergic to wheat. Is this an answer to my prayer?"

A few days later I followed through on the insight I had been given. I started looking for a doctor, and after being tested for several allergens, she concluded I was indeed allergic to wheat. During the testing she also found that I had high levels of lead in my blood. After I eliminated the allergens from my diet and cleansed the lead out of my body, my health improved greatly. I am very grateful to have been given this awake dream, which led to a major improvement in my health.

Written by Mark Snodgrass

Keys in this story: HU, Gratitude

Keys not yet studied: Prayer, God's Grace (answer to prayer leading to a healing)

A Child of God is Born

*Sometimes God pulls back a curtain allowing us to experience the
spirituality of a situation. The following is a beautiful testimony
of witnessing the sacredness of childbirth. It is at this moment that
Soul enters the body and a new adventure begins.*

How grateful I am for my children, three gifts that God has
bestowed upon my wife and I. What were once happy "additions" to
the family are now integral parts that I would not want to imagine
our lives without. Each of my children's births was a precious and
sacred moment, but it was the birth of my eldest child that gave me
a glimpse into the divinity that was clothed in each little bundle of
joy.

The morning my eldest child was born, I stood in the delivery
room experiencing all the nervousness and excitement of a first-time
dad-to-be. My mind raced forwards and backwards as the moment
crawled nearer and nearer.

Because I was at the front of the bed, ready to offer sips of water
and cold washcloths to my wife, I could see everyone else in the
room. Several people, including the doctor, head nurse, and various
other nurses and assistants popped in and out. Time seemed to slow
to a freeze, and I watched, with this sort of detached viewpoint, a
panorama of the other people there.

There was what I can only describe as a reverent anticipation
bubbling up in the room. Everyone — it seemed like a lot more than
the three or four individuals there — seemed riveted on this sacred
moment. There was an overwhelming reverence for Soul permeating
the air. A spark of God was about to don another body, take Its
knocks, learn Its lessons, and continue on Its journey home to the
Heart of God. I believe each person there, whether conscious of it or
not, was recognizing Soul — the Divine spark about to be housed in
a tiny little body — but also which lived in each other and in
themselves. Each in his or her own way recognized that the source
of this spark of life was God.

While my wife, the doctor, and several nurses prepared for the imminent birth, a young nursing assistant stood in the middle of the room unconsciously rocking back and forth, in a slow cadence to some distant rhythm only she could hear. She hugged herself instinctively, as if rocking an invisible baby in her arms. It was hard to say if she was imagining comforting the baby about to be born or herself. Maybe both.

When my son finally arrived, I moved into position to "catch" him. I witnessed a ball of glowing light so intense and brilliant it became hard to see anything else. I immediately recognized this Soul as someone I had loved dearly before. Watching Soul enter the body was breathtaking. The doctor and nurses helped guide his tiny body into my arms. I was holding him when he took his first breath in this body, before surrendering him to my wife's welcoming embrace. The recognition between mother and son seemed apparent as well.

In my years at Guidance for a Better Life, Del has repeatedly led me to experiences that have shown me there is so much more to us than just our bodies — much more than just the parts we can normally see. I believe I witnessed a glimpse of that in my son as he was being born, a glimpse into the Divine essence of our being, which is born into this world to learn, to love, and to attempt to pick up the trail back to Its eternal Home.

Written by Chris Comfort

Keys in this story: Gratitude, Soul (ball of glowing light)
Keys not yet studied: Reverence, God's Prophet

Singing HU With My Granddaughter

Man needs reminding, but Soul does not forget the sound of HU,
an ancient name for God that can be sung in loving gratitude. What a
joy to witness someone experience it for the first time in this life.

It was a beautiful summer day and my granddaughter and I were swinging on the swing under the poplar tree in my backyard. At the time she was twenty-one months old. She was sitting on my lap as we were swinging, just looking around the backyard and enjoying the day and that moment in time.

My heart was full of appreciation and love for the time I was spending with her. Any time with this beautiful little "gift from God" is a special gift for me. If you are a grandparent you know what it is like to hold a grandchild! I began singing HU, a love song to God, to express my appreciation. Immediately and swiftly she turned around to look at me. I knew she recognized the ancient sound of HU. Her true self, Soul, recognized this sacred sound. I asked her if she remembered the HU and she said, "Yes." I asked her if she would like to sing HU and she replied, "Yes." I started to sing HU and the sweetest voice began to sing it as well. We both sang HU for a while, expressing gratitude and love for God.

My heart, which was already full of appreciation, was opened more and filled with more gratitude and love. Sharing HU, which is so precious to me, with my granddaughter was such a joy. Her innate recognition and sweet singing of this beautiful love song has no words. We were encompassed in love.

Written by Renée Dinwiddie

Keys in this story: HU, Gratitude (appreciation), Soul

Keys not yet studied: God's Love (encompassed in love)

Gratitude Transformed My Day

If you feel your heart closing for any reason, making the conscious choice to take a moment, sing HU, and focus on gratitude can help open it back up. This is no small thing. Your day will be fundamentally different if your heart is open versus closed. God speaks to and delivers His blessings to an open heart.

One recent morning I made a special effort to get out of the house early. I planned to stop at a large home improvement center on the way to work. I love to walk the long aisles of lumber and hardware, happily imagining all the things I could build with them. I see not just stacks of lumber, but future sheds and snug homes for my animals. I also see other projects to enrich the lives of my wife, Diane, and me. My intention that morning was to check out aluminum fascia and soffit for a project I had in mind. I had about fifteen minutes or so to spend in the store.

I was greeted by a friendly store employee who directed me to the aisle where he thought I would find the aluminum soffit and fascia. There I found the same products in vinyl but not aluminum. I spent about ten minutes fruitlessly searching for either the aluminum or someone else to help me. I was aware time was running out and felt some irritation creep in; it was about time to go on to work. On the way out I encountered the same helpful man who had originally sent me to the wrong location. He still wanted to help. Although skeptical, I decided to give it one more try. I followed him to another location where he thought we might find the aluminum. It was not there either, but we did encounter another employee who informed us the aluminum I sought was only available by special order. I thanked the first man who had twice tried to help me, wished him a good day, and left for work. I knew it would be tight, time-wise.

As I drove to work I was aware that I was a little irritated over the lost time. I did not want to arrive at the school where I work under the influence of irritation, so I chose to sing HU, a love song to God, to improve my mood and perspective. I also listened to an audio of a large group of students singing HU at Guidance for a Better Life. At the beginning of the recording Del Hall, God's Prophet, suggests we think of something for which we are grateful. This would open our hearts to better express our love for God when singing HU. He reminds us "Gratitude is the secret of love." Del has taught me to sing HU and practice gratitude. He has shown me to see and appreciate how these and other spiritual teachings transform lives. My life is richer and happier for it.

Hearing the physical voice of Prophet, God's distributor of blessings and grace, triggered a wave of gratitude for the countless blessings in my life. Hearing HU opened my heart more and more as the song continued. Each remembered blessing was connected to still more blessings. I thought of my growing love and appreciation for Prophet. I savored the love of my family, friends, and pets. I was on my way to my new job. The job is literally an answer to a prayer to work in just that school. I gratefully considered the attitude of gratitude that sweetens my life. Gratitude transforms day, upon day, upon day; a result and gift from implementing Del's teachings. So Del's seemingly simple, yet very profound, suggestion to think of something I was grateful for released a cascade of remembered blessings. My earlier irritation was gone. I felt a sense of joy and gratitude for the day I was about to experience. I could not wait to get to school and see the kids and teachers.

Blessings were everywhere I looked. As I drove I saw more clearly the beauty of nearby farms and distant mountains. I took notice of the horses and cows in the pastures and the mist on the hazy mountains. I actually arrived at school a few minutes early since I sailed through several intersections on green lights, something else to be grateful for. I gave further thanks for my relocation to Virginia. I arrived at work with a lighter step and a smile on my face. Gratitude made a profound difference in my interactions with others that day. Through the attitude of gratitude I experienced each moment as a gift to be savored. I saw each person I encountered as a fellow Soul on their own life adventure. A few moments of gratitude transformed my whole day. This ongoing gift of living with a sense of gratitude is changing my entire life. Gratitude allows me to see God's blessings more clearly and for what they are, gifts from our loving

Heavenly Father. I know I am blessed with a life of lasting abundance.

Written by Irv Kempf

Keys in this story: HU, Gratitude, Soul, Attitudes and Thoughts. (irritated and then joy)

Keys not yet studied: Prayer, God's Prophet, God's Love (recognized blessings)

My Priorities Bring Peace

We must make time to connect with God every day to stay nourished. It matters not how busy "life" gets. If we do not, things fall apart. The following is an excellent testimony on the need for daily spiritual bread.

Whenever I get started on a new project, I jump into it wholeheartedly. I develop a type of tunnel vision and focus only on the task ahead. This can be a good attribute in some ways, allowing me to get a lot done in a short amount of time, but it is also a detriment in other ways as I become so focused on the task at hand, I lose sight of the big picture. Some time back we started a new project at work. We had a really tight deadline and a lot to accomplish. As is my habit, I started pouring more and more energy into the project, sometimes working up to twenty hours a day trying to catch up and get ahead of the problems that kept cropping up. It seemed the harder I tried, the further behind we were. This pace kept up for several weeks, and I was becoming pretty exhausted.

A very important part of my spiritual practices is spending quality time with Divine Spirit. I set aside time each day to tune in, communicate, and develop a stronger, richer, and deeper relationship with God and God's Voice, the Holy Spirit. This time is essential to keep me in balance, keep my priorities in focus, and reconnect in a meaningful way with the Source of all existence.

As I started working more and more hours, and trying harder and harder to pull this project together, I spent less and less time on my spiritual pursuits. I prayed every day and recognized the presence of the Divine in many of the events of the day, but I was not spending that quality time with Divine Spirit necessary for me to grow stronger in my relationship. I could not sit idle for long. Very soon the relationship grew weaker as I focused on temporal things and not on spiritual things.

One night I had a very strong and clear dream. In that dream I felt the presence of the Prophet next to me. We were going to look at a house I was going to move into. The house was very run down. I could not get into the front door as it was in disrepair. Entering the house through the back, the inside was just as bad as the outside. Sheetrock was pulled down, the wiring was poor. All in all, it was in bad shape.

When I awoke I contemplated on the meaning of the dream. The dream spoke of the condition of my spiritual life. If I did not make some changes, my spiritual home (life) was going to look like that old, broken down house. The house was not suitable for truly living. Truly living for me is spoken of in the Bible as a "more abundant life." It is a life rich and full, strong in the relationship with the Holy Spirit. Seeking first that relationship is what allows one to truly experience all the blessings that God wants to share with us. Focusing on worldly impermanent things, as I was doing, and was demonstrated in the dream, produces the opposite.

That day, I set aside time for God. I found a quiet place and sang HU, a love song to God. HU is a pure expression of your love to God and a way to give thanks for your blessings. It is not asking for anything, it is not seeking anything from God. It tunes you into Spirit, and brings greater harmony with the Divine. I sang HU for awhile and then suddenly I received a great gift from God. All the weight and tension that I did not even know I was carrying fell off my shoulders. I felt a warm inrush of love, joy, and peace. I saw with clarity what I had been missing. The love and joy that was downloaded to me was an incredible blessing and healing. I shared those blessings with the Divine in gratitude. I expressed my gratitude for the blessings, my gratitude for the insight and clarity, and my gratitude for the dream that brought me back to my true priorities.

Written by Paul Nelson

Keys in this story: HU, Gratitude, Discernment (Paul used information from his dream to make a decision to be better nourished spiritually)

Keys not yet studied: Proper Focus, Prayer, God's Prophet, Contemplation, God's Grace (weight and tension replaced with love, joy, peace, clarity, and the dream given), Consistency (time each day), Personal Effort (to make correction), Balance and Detachment

Love Thyself

You are here on Earth to become more refined in your ability to give and receive love. Of the two, more seem to struggle with receiving, especially when it is from ourself. Regardless of how you "feel," the fact remains — you are worthy.

When I first came to Guidance for a Better Life I was shy and self-conscious, full of anxiety and guilt, carrying a sadness around with me as my own. I felt unworthy of God's Love based on a false mental view of myself. It took many experiences to break through this, to realize I was looking at myself from my mind, instead of viewing myself as Soul, my spiritual side, my true self. Slowly, I quit beating myself up as much and began accepting that I am worthy of God's Love. I am not the mistakes I blew all out of proportion. I learned to forgive and love myself.

An inner experience at Guidance for a Better Life, during a spiritual exercise that included singing HU, helped me to see this truth more clearly. Del, the Prophet, took me on a journey to a Temple of God, known as a Temple of Learning. It was beautiful beyond description and filled with God's Love. In the center, a beam of Light was shining on an open book on a pedestal, God's Book. Prophet encouraged me to read from it. I stepped into the beam and read "Love Thyself with all Thy Heart and Soul."

I knew I could no longer beat myself up or judge myself so harshly. I also realized that I could not truly love God until I could love Its creation, me, Soul, a particle of Its Holy Spirit. This is helping me accept a profound truth, "Soul exists because God loves It." My existence, every breath, every moment of life, is a gift from God to be cherished.

I am grateful to Prophet for being with me every step of the way on my journey of growth and discovery, for his guidance, protection, and truth. It is by accepting Prophet's hand, and the relationship that followed, that has allowed me to move from a limited and miserable view of myself to the boundless one of Soul. Surrendering my old ways of thinking, many based on half-truths and falsehoods, gives me the freedom to pursue a life of abundance.

Written by Gary Caudle

Keys in this story: HU, Soul (traveled into the Heavens to a Temple of Learning with Prophet), Attitudes and Thoughts (Gary held negative thoughts of unworthiness, then learned to accept God really loves him)

Keys not yet studied: God's Prophet, Living without Doubt, God's Grace (both being invited to a Temple of Learning and being given "Love Thyself" a healing to accept that God loves Gary), God's Love (felt inside the temple)

A Letter of Healing

*When we close our hearts in an attempt to avoid pain in one area
of our life, it ends up limiting the amount of love we can give and
receive in all areas of our life. No matter the reason, if our heart is
open — it's open, if our heart is closed — it's closed. It is a package
deal. Thank God the Prophet knows this and can gently help us to
heal all areas of our life.*

This is my experience of the beginning of the healing between
my father and me. Little did I know at the time that it was the
beginning of so much more. My father's and my relationship had
been strained and stressful since a very early age of my life. My
father had some mental health challenges, and our family life and
environment was volatile much of the time. I knew my dad loved
me, but the way I responded and reacted to him and most situations
was to close down.

I was attending a weeklong retreat taught by Del, the Prophet. Del
suggested to the class to write a letter of love and appreciation to
someone as a healing exercise. At that time in my life I had been
avoiding any contact with my father even though he would
sometimes reach out to me.

I started to sing HU, a love song to God, to try to open my heart
toward my father. I also asked Prophet on the inner for help in
writing my letter. After singing HU and with Prophet's help, I was
able to open my heart and think of my dad in a new and more truthful
way. I was gifted with recognition of the love he had for me and the
ways he had shown that love through the years. I was now open to
expressing appreciation and acknowledging the things he had done
for me. Things that before this exercise I was never able to express
to him or even myself. I also was able to apologize for my actions I
knew had caused him sorrow and pain and that I also held guilt
about.

Del told us we did not have to mail the letter, but I did. It was the
first time I had lovingly reached out to my dad in many years. It
seemed on the surface to be a simple exercise, but it had a deep and

healing effect on me, my father, and our relationship. Over time I began to realize just how deep. By writing this letter with Prophet there was a healing in me. I softened and my heart opened more. Before this letter I had thought that by closing my heart I was keeping out the pain, but actually I was limiting the amount of love I could give and receive in ALL areas of my life. On one level this was a simple exercise, but through Prophet, the Hand of God was involved in this experience, and it was profound. Del, as the Prophet of God is authorized to speak for God, so when this exercise was suggested God was involved.

My dad told me he received the letter and appreciated it, resulting in a beautiful change in our relationship. One might think it was because of the outer letter, and some of it was. However, most of the healing came from deep within, which only God can do. The change that occurred was not only in my relationship with my father; the blessings of this healing also changed my relationship with my children, husband, friends, and the way I relate in life. I am so appreciative of my relationship with Prophet; the ripples from that healing continue to affect all those I come in contact with.

Written by Renée Dinwiddie

Keys in this story: HU, Gratitude

Keys not yet studied: God's Prophet, God's Grace (gift of clarity of her Dad's love and gift of healing her heart)

More Freedom Less Worry

*When we are overly attached to the decisions our loved ones make
it puts a "cloud" over our love for them. They are a child of God first,
and as such they will never be alone. Learning to love them in a
relaxed, peaceful way will help improve your relationship.*

It came as an unexpected surprise when my adult daughter decided to attend a HU Sing during her impromptu visit with us one weekend. Two weeks prior, before any of us were aware she'd be visiting, Prophet — my spiritual teacher and inner guide — appeared to me in what I can now say was a prophetic dream. In this dream he explained my daughter had contacted him about an upcoming retreat, indicating in some way she wanted to surprise me.

I felt fortunate to be among those in attendance at the HU Sing that day, and sharing the experience with my daughter made it much more special. The moment I closed my eyes and began singing HU I saw her as a baby securely cradled in the arms of the Divine. I recognized her as Soul — a beautiful, glowing bundle of light and sound. My heart overflowed with an overwhelming sense of gratitude. Different moments from her life began to play out after that, allowing me to experience each one from the perspective of knowing the Hand of God has always been with her and always will be. A higher truth was evident: Although she is my daughter in this lifetime, she belongs to God and has always been in the loving arms of her Heavenly Father. The peace and trust I felt in this moment can hardly be put into words. Being totally in the moment and aware of the Presence of God, I experienced detachment from worldly concerns of every kind. Divine love filled my heart and I felt free; free to simply love.

Prophet took me on a personal journey into the higher worlds and it changed me. The experience was tailor-made to bring me peace, trust, and a greater understanding of love, as it is in Heaven. Through this experience I was able to recognize my two grown children as adults, which has positively affected how I interact with them. I am less emotionally attached to their decisions and free of the expectations I once carried of being invited to weigh in on their decisions. I now have room to enjoy their presence and relate to them as treasured friends; precious Souls I am blessed to share this life with as we each make our way home to God.

It is a profound gift to savor the experiences of life together, unfettered by the emotional entanglements I once mistook for love. I am grateful to Prophet for showing me a higher, purer way to love, one that allows me to care in a relaxed and peaceful way.

Written by Sandra Lane

Keys in this story: HU, Soul, Gratitude, Spiritual Growth

Keys not yet studied: God's Prophet, God's Love (God's Love for her daughter, love filled Sandra's heart), God's Grace (gift of clarity, gift of dream, gift of peace and trust, journey into the higher worlds), Balance and Detachment

The Process of Freeing Me

Prophet leads his students through the process of awakening to their true eternal selves, Soul. This is done through experiences in both the waking and sleeping states. He gently peels back the layers of untruth and removes blocks to God's Love, truth, and ways. The result — an abundant life.

My inner and outer relationship with God's true Prophet has been the key to unlocking what has held me back, perhaps for lifetimes, from real freedom, joy, deep peace, security, balance, and knowing God loves me, personally, as He loves each of us, personally. One of the first retreats I took at Guidance for a Better Life was on wilderness skills. Though we were engaged in much physical work, Del Hall began to teach to all who would listen, profound lessons as the Divine came through him. He did not force teachings on us; it is his nature to see the blessings in all life, and he shares what comes through him freely. He suggested we pay attention to dreams while we were at the retreat. He had found many of his students were able to remember some interesting dreams while on the property that helped them in their lives. If we wanted to, we could ask for dreams that night.

My dreams were usually long and seemed senseless, but I asked for a dream that night because there was something about Del. Everything he said, and even when he did not say anything, was genuine, truthful, and motivated by love of truth. I listened to him, and he quenched a thirst I did not know I had. My thirst was not related to the physical labor of practicing wilderness skills, it was Soul's thirst for Its freedom and for God's truth.

I was given two short dreams that very night. In one, Del was holding me up in the air. We hovered over a dumpster, a big orange dumpster. Orange is a predominant color of the Causal plane (second Heaven) of God's Worlds, where karmic patterns from lifetimes are stored along with other past life records. Del put things in that dumpster for me, things I did not need. I asked if I could help. He said no, not yet. He said there were three locks that he knew how to undo to put things in the dumpster, and I did not know how to open those locks yet. Through that dream I was allowed to see God's own true Prophet, Del Hall, in one of the roles he fulfills from God, that of Redeemer. The Redeemer, as a vehicle for God, can lift individuals closer to spiritual liberation.

In the other dream my boss from many years ago, a librarian, was in a birdcage, with the door closed. It symbolized the "lower self" side of me in that cage, not the librarian. The Dream Master, another role or aspect of the Prophet, blessed me with this truth about myself. However, my subconscious mind, trying to protect me, toned it down by censoring it through the symbols of the librarian in the birdcage — so as not to alarm me. I was not free to live as my real self, Soul, yet. God sends the Prophet, as Redeemer, to help Soul help itself be free.

God endows each of us with a truth detector (see Glossary), which is a vital attribute of Soul. My truth detector recognized the Voice of God coming through Del, and I would return to the retreat center for more living waters to quench my spiritual thirst. I began to learn of Spiritual Keys that could unlock my heart and begin the process of freeing me of worry, fear, vanity, guilt, lack of confidence; the whole slew of the human consciousness experience was wearing me down and tearing me up. Del taught HU, which is a love song to God, a prayer to God. HU is sung directly to God. Soul begins to awaken and be tuned to God's "channel," instead of the channel of the mind. HU, sung on a fairly regular basis, was one of the first Keys to unlock my heart so Divine attributes like love, peace, trust, balance, and joy could flourish and begin to edge out the things I did not need anymore.

Del encouraged us to think of something we were really grateful for before we began to sing HU. Gratitude is another Key that opened my heart more. Thinking of one thing I was grateful for led to another, and another, and another. A more open heart is more receptive to Divine guidance. Prophet can place so many blessings from God in a grateful heart, such as love, clarity, peace, joy, and more.

HU and Gratitude prepared, conditioned, and purified me enough; so I could consciously meet with Prophet, be taught by him on the outer and inner, and develop a growing relationship of trust and love. This relationship is the jackpot Master Key! Over time and with focus, these Keys become a way of life. I continue to appreciate them even more: HU, Gratitude, and my relationship with Prophet.

When I followed Del's suggestion and asked for a dream at that early retreat at Guidance for a Better Life, in effect letting the Divine know I was interested, I began a process of becoming a more active participant with the Hand of God in my life. Not just one area of my life would be improved, but all areas. With the help of Prophet and with deeper appreciation, I look back and see I have always been in the Hand of God throughout my life. So have you. I continue to ask for dreams and am so grateful for them; for they reach me, teach me, and are reflections of Soul's life in the planes of God's Worlds. Each of us has our own personal, individualized syllabus from God. How sweet it is to become more conscious of the love and freedom God has in store for you!

Written by Martha Stinson

Keys in this story: Soul and Self, HU, Gratitude

Keys not yet studied: God's Prophet, God's Love (Martha received love), God's Grace (peace, trust, joy, clarity, and dreams), Receptive, Living Without Doubt (knows always been in the Hand of God)

Simple Secret to a Better Life

Sometimes the life and love we seek is right in front of us, yet we are blind to it. One of the things that may be blocking our view is a lack of gratitude. Your life will become so much better when you learn to recognize and be more grateful for the blessings you already have.

Growing up I was anxious and frequently upset. My mind was full of negative thoughts focusing on worries and what I lacked more than the good in my life. I know I felt grateful at times, but it was fleeting and inconsistent. This was normal to me. I did not know another way of living existed, yet I yearned to be happy. This negative outlook became the most apparent at special occasions. Times I should be celebrating tended to be my saddest moments. When I graduated college, instead of being happy I accomplished four years of schooling and did well, I was wracked with worry over the future and sobbed that night feeling lost and alone. Vacations were awful because, of course, I was there, and without life's usual distractions, the incessant clamor of my negative thoughts would overwhelm me.

This all changed after meeting Prophet and becoming his student at Guidance for a Better Life. I began to learn spiritual truths that when utilized made life a joy to live. I experienced God's Love for me personally and learned I am Soul, a child of God, and not all my fears, anger, and negative attitudes. For the first time in my life I had love in my heart. I was more alive than I had ever been.

A couple years passed and I met and married Mark, the love of my life. He lived in the beautiful home he built with his own hands. I had a job I enjoyed and friends I loved, yet I was miserable. I had not gotten serious about attaining self-discipline over my mind and its negative attitudes. I was spoiled and selfish still focusing more on what I did not have. Eight short months after our marriage had begun it was in danger of being over. I started fights when there was no reason to and actually began to place more importance on the amount of money I brought home than the love between Mark and I. I had never intended this, yet it was happening. My thoughts and attitudes were ruining my life.

It was the truth given to me by Prophet that would ultimately change everything. He told me I was not grateful. He also told me I could change and could become grateful. I had a choice, and the ball was in my court. If I did not change and start applying the spiritual truths I had learned, the door to the life I wanted would close, perhaps forever. The spiritual truths are like keys and the Spiritual Key of Gratitude, like any key, has to be used. Keys do not open doors by themselves.

Shortly after receiving this truth I was home on the weekend with Mark, and we were driving to the dump. It was a bright and sunny day, yet the warmth did not touch me. My heart felt closed, and Mark and I were silent as we drove. Moments later a wave of love like a breath of fresh air flowed into my heart. I felt free. I began to feel grateful for the sunny day, being with Mark, and my life. Gratitude for many things began to fill my heart, and I laughed out loud thinking, so this is gratitude, the secret of love!

The difference between my grateful heart and the cold emptiness of being closed down moments before was so drastic, like night and day. I know this was a gift from God to get me started in the right direction. Not only was I going to the dump physically, but spiritually I was dumping the old way of living and embarking on a future brighter than I could imagine. This made it absolutely clear that gratitude was a lifeline for me, and this became written in my heart.

After this life-changing moment, progress was at first slow and mechanical. I paid attention to my thoughts and attitudes and began to make conscious choices about what I would allow myself to think about. I also started a gratitude journal, which I wrote in throughout the day. This kept me focusing on the good and happy things in life. Eight years later, Mark and I are enjoying a beautiful love-filled marriage. We are a real family now. I do not have to try to be grateful. I thank God that this way of thinking is part of me. There are times when I get grumpy or down, and I still will start counting my blessings, which produces a quick change in attitude. Gratitude opens my heart and fills me with love. This pushes out fears, doubts, and negative attitudes that are harmful to me.

The truth is my life was always beautiful and the love was there, but it was my uncontrolled negative thoughts and attitudes that kept me from feeling it. I did not need to change my husband, my job, or make more money. Everything I ever wanted and more was right there. I just needed to truly recognize and appreciate it.

Written by Carmen Snodgrass

Keys in this story: Gratitude, Discernment, Soul and Self, Attitudes and Thoughts

Keys not yet studied: God's Prophet, Truth is Love, Receiving God's Grace (gift of the wave of love), Cause and Effect, Balance and Detachment, Peace of Mind and Heart, Growth of Consciousness, God's Love

Step Two: Understanding Divine Guidance

Step Two continues to help you become more familiar with the many ways God communicates with His children daily. You will gain confidence in your ability to "hear" accurately, as it is quite common early on to not know if insights are coming from the mind or from the Divine. This section will help you better understand what Spirit is trying to communicate and give you the confidence to follow it. With this skill, something you as a child of God innately have, there is no challenge in life you cannot get through. It will also help you recognize, on a very personal level, how much God loves you. Once you begin to develop fluid communication with the Divine, you will not only be more equipped to receive daily guidance, but will also be more open to God's truth in general. This can lead to profound spiritual growth and help with understanding the mysteries of God and self.

The following Keys will be introduced:

Receptive

1. Having the quality of receiving, taking in, or admitting.
2. Able or quick to receive knowledge, ideas: a receptive mind and heart.
3. Willing or inclined to receive suggestions, offers, input with favor.
4. Being open and responsive to the Divine gifts.
5. Willing to grow in trust of the Divine and Its agents.

The Love and blessings of God and His Prophet are available to all who are receptive. Having a grateful heart can open one to being more receptive. When one has a grateful attitude they more often and more clearly see blessings in their life and the lives of others. An ungrateful person becomes increasingly more closed and less able to recognize the good of life. Ungrateful people are very difficult to help or teach spiritually.

Being receptive is the responsibility of each individual. For God or His Prophet to "make" a person receptive would be violating that person's free will. For Prophet to violate another's free will would be breaking spiritual law, and he will never intentionally do so. One can be receptive to either positive or negative influences; practice Discernment when deciding what you are receptive to and allow into your life. Prophet will provide tools to help a seeker be receptive to the Divine, but the student must decide to use the tools provided. Being in the presence of God's Prophet often opens certain individuals to be more receptive to the Holy Spirit.

Having a sincere and prolonged desire for God's Love and truth may increase your receptiveness. The Three-Part Prayer, which helps you recognize God's blessing being delivered by Prophet throughout the day can develop trust. (The Three-Part Prayer will be introduced in Step Three) Developing trust in God's Prophet often increases receptiveness.

God enables and authorizes His Prophet to lift individuals to a higher spiritual view of life and to share the Love and Light of God. The more receptive an individual becomes the higher and the sooner Prophet lifts an individual student. The Spiritual Key HU, if sung daily can nourish Soul, open the heart, and clear the mind, it is one of the most effective ways for an individual to become receptive to God's blessings and teachings. Prophet can help you become more receptive to God's Love, truth, and Grace but only to the degree you are receptive to him.

Sometimes one is more receptive when they hear something they already agree with but not so receptive to new concepts. The way or style Prophet delivers a teaching can also influence receptiveness. Some people can only receive a certain type of love and truth but are less receptive when not given in their preferred way. Some have difficulty being receptive to correction. **All the above limitations can slow spiritual growth. Over time Prophet can help remove all the limitations of receptiveness if one's desire and effort is sufficient.**

An individual may pray to be more receptive to the Divine in all Its forms. One can also make a conscious decision to be receptive! **If one is truly receptive, they respond to guidance. They take the input, and they do something with what they received.**

Study Guidance: Being receptive is being willing and able to accept HELP! For some this is hard, because accepting help is actually accepting LOVE. Over time most can grow in their ability to become more receptive. Soul is naturally better than the mind at this, so staying spiritually nourished is important. The more receptive one is to the Divine, the smoother life can be.

Remembrance

1. Retained mental impression; memory.
2. The length of time over which recollection or memory extends.
3. State of being remembered; commemoration: to never forget there is a God who created and loves you, and you are His child, Soul.
4. Something that serves to bring to mind or keep in mind some place, person, event, memento.
5. To retain memory of blessings of love or friendship freely given.

One of the most important Keys to continued spiritual growth is remembrance. **To be successful on the path home to God, over a long time, one needs to build a high level of trust and love in their relationship with God and God's chosen Prophet. Keeping a daily journal of blessings you recognize can help with remembrance and build trust.**

As you implement some of what you receive in this book, you will begin to more fully recognize God's Hand in your life. As you develop more gratitude, sing HU, and more fully open your heart you may experience peace, clarity, joy, less worry, fear, and loneliness, or experience more or new forms of love. **This growth will likely continue if an effort is made to remember these gifts of love and beneficial change. Keeping a journal is helpful for remembering and reviewing these gifts.** Those who come to Prophet's retreats will have experienced spiritual blessings most could only dream of having! By remembering most of the blessings and experiences given through Prophet an individual builds trust. Then if difficult times come and a student becomes confused, the trust of the teacher and his ways, which were built over time, can help tremendously.

The more one remembers God's blessings in their life, the more gratitude and appreciation builds in their heart. Gratitude and appreciation further open an individual to be more receptive.

This openness creates upward spiritual momentum, trust, and growth. Remembrance also demonstrates gratitude for our blessings. Without remembering our blessings we cannot have lasting gratitude.

Really laying hold of a lesson or Spiritual Key by taking the time and effort to understand it increases our ability to remember. Without accepting, understanding, and **remembering** a truth it is not possible to integrate that truth into our daily life. To benefit from a truth of God it must be made operational. Just knowing God's ways and truths is not enough. **Without actually living God's ways we are less free and have a less abundant life.**

Spiritual growth builds on earlier lessons, so the more advanced lessons require one to understand and remember the basic lessons they have learned and experienced. As you read and study the Spiritual Keys, make time to go back and review the earlier Keys. **The earlier Keys will begin to be better understood after reading the later Keys and help with remembrance. Studying the Keys is an iterative process.** I also suggest you read our books and watch our videos; they will reinforce and remind you of what you have read in this book. They will also help you with recognizing and remembering how the Spiritual Keys work together. For those who come to Prophet's retreats, keep a journal of experiences at each retreat and review your notes. Regularly attend retreats where we review earlier lessons, sing HU together, and contemplate on your experiences. Write letters to Prophet (if you attend retreats) sharing your experiences and insights to receive feedback from him.

Remembrance helps avoid repeating the same mistakes. Remembrance is active, not passive. Remembrance helps build and maintain your spiritual foundation and momentum. Remembrance helps build trust, gratitude and appreciation, and may improve receptiveness. You can pray for remembrance.

Some important truths to always remember: God did not retire two thousand years ago, He is still active in our lives and continues to share higher truths and more of His teachings through Prophets He has ordained; we exist because God loves us; your true eternal self is Soul, as Soul we live forever, as Soul we can visit our

Heavenly Father with His chosen Prophet...... there is always more to learn about the nature of God, His ways, and His truths.

Study Guidance: The reason to receive and learn the eternal teachings and ways of God is to LIVE them daily, which brings an abundance of love, clarity, peace, wisdom, joy, and growth; while reducing the negative aspects of life such as worry, fear, loneliness, anger, and guilt. One needs to use discernment to remember at least the foundational teachings, or they cannot be integrated into daily life. Remembering to receive daily spiritual nourishment, "our daily spiritual bread," is critical for success.

Understanding Change

Conditions and circumstances in the physical worlds are in flux and cannot be relied upon to be stable. Continents, countries, towns, our health, our spiritual consciousness, friends, relationships, jobs, our views, etc. are all subject to change. Change and instability are part of the worlds of time and space; **therefore one should not be surprised by change, but instead learn to adapt and be supple with change.**

The mind is often uncomfortable with change, but Soul is comfortable and experienced with change. **The more we operate as Soul the more relaxed and comfortable we are when faced with change in our lives.**

To grow in our spiritual consciousness requires change. Without change we cannot grow spiritually or in any other area of life. To make a relationship or marriage better requires change. To grow more capable in our jobs requires change. To improve our health may require a change of diet, exercise, stress level, environment, etc. Change can be good!

Becoming more open and receptive to God and His Voice, the Holy Spirit, requires change and brings change. Every time we sing HU we open ourselves to purification and potential positive change. Every Spiritual Key, dream, or awake dream we make an effort to understand brings potential change. **These changes may be small individually but, in the aggregate, can be profound. The whole point of this book is to bring profound and POSITIVE personal change.** For your life to go from good to great requires change. Developing the absolute knowing and trust that God and His Prophet truly love you and want the best for you can greatly reduce the stress that some changes in life may bring.

Learning to become the cause in life may bring change toward some personal stability. (Cause and Effect is a Spiritual Key found in Step Four) Each visit or contemplation with God's Prophet, if receptive, brings potential change and growth. Staying close to Prophet is the best way to prepare for and embrace change.

To grow and develop as a person requires change. Life in the lower worlds, below the fifth Heaven, often throws us curves, challenges, and changes that are unwelcome. These changes are part of the constant interplay between the positive and negative forces. If one is under the care of God's Prophet, these unhappy experiences that challenge us can result in stretching us in growth beyond what only pleasant experiences can bring. God has set up a system where every experience can make you better and stronger if you learn from it. From the fifth Heaven all the way to the twelfth Heaven one finds stability. More on this topic later.

The teachings of and a relationship with God's Prophet have the potential to bring a CORE stability of peace, wisdom, and love that transcends all earthly changes and instability. **God's eternal ways and teachings do not change and His Love for you does not change. There is stability and strength found in having a loving personal relationship with God and His Prophet.**

Study Guidance: Life is a parade of changes and a movement from one state of consciousness to another. Do not be surprised by change, it is part of life. The more one is attached to something the more difficult they will find change. Staying close to Prophet and keeping Soul nourished can improve one's attitude toward changes in life.

Suggested Spiritual Exercise: Reflect upon changes in your life that have been very positive and good. This may improve your attitude toward change.

Contemplation and Meditation

Meditation is a passive spiritual exercise where one first tries to still the mind. Once the mind is still the practitioner hopes something spiritual comes into their consciousness. In more advanced meditation one hopes God-Realization comes to them, and they become "one with God." One never becomes one with God! We can become one with God's Spirit, Voice, or essence; the Holy Spirit, Eck, or the Light and Sound, all being different names for the same thing. Generally in this type of exercise the best one can hope for is an experience on the third Heaven, called the Mental plane.

The Mental plane is controlled by the negative power, which is often called the Devil or Satan. He uses illusion to misdirect and confuse individuals, so one's experience may be suspect using meditation. In most meditations the focus is generally on self.

Meditation can be a good start and help calm one's mind, which is a benefit for most everyone. It also relaxes the physical body adding some health benefits. Developing the self-discipline to meditate regularly is a positive.

Contemplation is more active, like Soul is active, and has specific purpose and focus. It is not so concerned with "feelings" but with insights, clarity, understandings, and spiritual nourishment. Its focus is on God, more than self. Before we sing HU we may gently focus on an intent or topic we would like clarity on, if it is Thy Will. We might wish to meet with Prophet spiritually and let him decide the experience. Then we surrender the intent and send love and gratitude to God by singing HU, whether or not we receive an insight on the intent we had at the beginning.

By singing HU we are drawing close to God, receiving spiritual nourishment, receiving protection, being purified, increasing our creativity, strengthening our bond with the Holy Spirit, and praying. Our focus is on God more than ourselves, though we always benefit. **An important part of contemplation is to make time to LISTEN to God after singing HU.** We usually do not expect to literally hear a voice, but rather we may have an inner visual or experience of some kind, receive "a nudge," or even perhaps a knowingness.

During contemplation we can have an experience beyond the third Heaven, all the way to the Abode of God on the twelfth Heaven, if appropriate and if escorted by Prophet. We might experience peace, receive clarity on a discourse of Prophet's or other personal matter, experience the Holy Spirit in the form of Light and Sound, be taken to one of God's Temples of Learning, or receive health insights, etc. It is best to surrender the outcome of each contemplation to God, let Him decide what is best. Sending love and gratitude to God is far more important than receiving something back, although there is almost always a response, whether recognized or not.

With practice you will become more confident and trusting in your understanding of the inner communication that results from contemplations. Those who come to Prophet's retreats will receive guidance and help in understanding what they receive in contemplations. The one hundred and thirty-five stories in this book can help the reader better understand and recognize contemplation experiences. All our books and videos can help both students and readers become more confident in trusting and understanding their own personal experiences.

After contemplation one is more open, sensitive to, and receptive to the Holy Spirit and Prophet. THIS IS OUR GOAL! If one sings HU daily they become increasingly more open, sensitive to, and receptive, even for extended periods of time after the contemplation. For example, sing HU in the morning for about twenty minutes before starting your day. Then every few hours throughout the day sing a short HU out loud or silently. Doing this makes you very aware of and alert to Divine guidance throughout much of the day. Eventually your entire day becomes one of contemplation. Now you have virtually constant communication and guidance from the Holy Spirit all day. This is what we want so much, and it can be achieved with sufficient personal effort and consistency.

Study Guidance: Contemplation is a form of prayer and a wonderful way to draw closer to God, while also nourishing and strengthening Soul. **Contemplation is a beautiful way to develop**

two-way communication with the Divine. Contemplation can bring revelation and guidance from above all day long and into the night! Singing the ancient name of God, HU, is a most effective prayer and contemplation.

Growth of Consciousness

Individuals are born into the general state of consciousness of their family and surroundings. This may include the ability to learn enough to get along and even make a living to provide for oneself. An individual consciousness is that state of awareness lived in daily. One part of this state involves the sense organs, the physical awareness relayed by the physical senses. The other part of one's daily state of awareness is independent of physical senses and involves one's spiritual awareness. It takes spiritual effort to go beyond basic survival and gain higher states of both physical and spiritual consciousness. Each individual has a different state of consciousness, but there are general levels that can be recognized.

Human Consciousness is the general state of those on Earth. It is primarily a social state that involves the negative passions of the mind: fear, anger, worry, self-doubt, unworthiness, greed, lust, and vanity. The negative power, Satan, often controls individuals through these passions. This state has little true freedom or true spiritual connection or understanding.

Cosmic Consciousness is an early stage of enlightenment. It involves controlling the mind and intellectual senses. This is a large part of Hinduism and Buddhism. Psychic realization is similar but of a lower nature. It involves mind powers and psychic powers and abilities, **which are unstable**. This is not real spiritual illumination but an early stage, or facet, of spiritual growth. There are many facets of spiritual growth.

Soul Consciousness, also called self-realization, is found on the Soul plane, the fifth Heaven. It is recognizing and beholding oneself as Soul, not male or female, or any other "labels" or "identities," or any other aspect of the dualistic lower worlds. One can have the experience of Soul Consciousness when taken to the Soul plane by Prophet yet not be fully established in that state. Once one accepts and recognizes they are Soul, that has a body versus a body that has a Soul, many possibilities for growth of consciousness open up. For example, eternal life, spiritual travel into the Heavens, and past lives now make sense.

Spiritual Consciousness is the awareness of the Holy Spirit, the inner presence of God's essence and the inner form of God's Prophet, most of the time. A living relationship and closeness to the Holy Spirit in thoughts and actions is a daily relationship and a recognition that Prophet is always with you, wherever you are. If receptive and open Prophet blends with and shares his consciousness, injecting spiritual energy that activates and quickens our once-dormant potential. Travel in the higher Heavens of God with Prophet is now almost effortless. Now one is conscious that God is a reality.

God Realization happens at the Abode of God, His Ocean of Love. Over time and with many travels to the Abode of God with Prophet one KNOWS the reality of God beyond all faith and earthly teachings. Often personal experiences of God's Love, Mercy, Grace, Light, truth, power, wisdom, and His personal recognition as a beloved child become a solid foundation for living an abundant life of love, truth, and service. Now one begins to know from experience something of the Heavenly Father and understands deeply the Father knows and loves them personally.

God Consciousness is beyond physical senses. It is a view of, understanding of, and experience best left for future discussions. This is the consciousness that Prophet will eventually share with those truly devoted to God's truth, ways, and path.

One's consciousness can vary throughout the day. The goal is to have our baseline state move upward. **Some indications that our consciousness is moving upward:** an attitude of gratitude, consistency in doing our spiritual exercises, a desire for and receptiveness to truth about oneself, willingness to share the eternal teachings, devotion, trust, and love for the teacher, attainment of clarity and precision of truths, being more interested in what God thinks about something rather than what other people think, showing up to retreats, making the effort to understand and remember spiritual gifts, operating more as Soul, reduction and control of negative passions of the mind, demonstrating through our actions and choices that these teachings and this opportunity are sacred, walking in peace and being the cause rather than the effect more of the time, doing better at giving and receiving love, and making a personal effort to reach a deeper understanding of the Spiritual Keys, etc. **Often others recognize our growth better than we do, because we are not focusing that much on ourselves.**

To change to a higher consciousness is one's goal under the Prophet's guidance. There is a high level of correlation between one's relationship with God's Prophet and one's consciousness. Higher views of life, "levels of consciousness," beyond cosmic consciousness can only be attained through teachings, guidance, mentorship, and spiritual travel into the Heavens with Prophet. One generally does not build a higher and wider consciousness directly. It is built by building a loving and trusting relationship with God's Prophet and through service to God.

It sounds contrary, but if too much direct effort is made on growing one's consciousness rather than through service and in building a relationship with Prophet, it often backfires due to self-indulgence. **Excessive focus on self is a sign of the lower human consciousness, not of someone with a higher spiritual view.** Someone with a higher spiritual view thinks of others with love and respect. For example, the first commandment is to love God with all your mind, heart, and Soul; and the second commandment is to love one's neighbor as yourself. Certain aspects of a spiritual consciousness can only be attained by working as a team with God's Prophet. This can be achieved whether or not one ever meets Prophet in the physical. More on this topic in Step Three.

Study Guidance: Spiritual growth is a growth in one's consciousness, which is a change to a higher and more accurate view and understanding of life. It is not accomplished directly, but by following the guidance of Prophet, such as staying consistently spiritually nourished and integrating the Spiritual Keys into daily life. As one's consciousness improves, their relationship with the Divine becomes more certain and many of the lower negative passions fall away, bringing more freedom, recognized and accepted experiences of God's Love, and an overall abundance in life.

Step Two Keys in Action

Peace in My Heart

When facing a challenge in life it can be easy to fall into worry and lose our peace. The problem is when we lose our peace, we lose our clarity too. It then becomes harder to confidently and clearly see the next step to take, which leads to more worry and uncertainty, resulting in a downward spiral. The solution is to focus on what matters most — our relationship with God. It is when we seek first the Kingdom, all things, including His peace, can be added unto us.

Have you ever wished for some peace in your heart, to have a break from worrying about what the future may bring? I was in such a situation a few years ago when I was looking for a new job. I had attended college classes at night one year after another, so I could be licensed for a new career as a teacher. Then there was a window of opportunity to find a job while the spring hiring season lasted, and there was stiff competition for jobs in the area where I live. I was starting to feel stressed about the prospect of moving to a different county or significantly increasing the length of my daily commute should I not find a job close to home. Every weekend was time when I could be writing a cover letter or completing an application, but today there was an opportunity to do something different. I had a chance to sing HU at an event hosted by Guidance for a Better Life at a nearby conference center. This was something I did not want to miss.

At the conference center the large group gathered and sang HU for a while. The beautiful sound of many voices singing together reverberated throughout the room. We sat in silence once we stopped singing, and I was immersed in gentle waves of Divine love. I then became aware of a blessing that was within the love. I recognized it as the peace of the Lord. The peace set my mind at rest and my heart at ease. It was not the same as the peace I had experienced relaxing in the shade after a day of work in the hot sun or going fishing alongside a mountain stream while on vacation. I had experienced that sort of peace as a young man, but it often would leave me when it was time to go back to school and, as I grew older, when it was time to be back at work on Monday morning. This peace was deeper.

As it filled me, I was freed to be content in the moment with no concern about what the future might bring or whether I would find a new job. It was peace from the Divine; a precious gift I was intent on cherishing as long as I could.

I was also gifted with clarity. I could see clearly how when I feel myself start to lose peace in my heart it is essential to look at the direction I am heading in; I might be heading in a direction that is not where my heart is leading me. I knew in such a situation I would want to put the brakes on, listen more intently to the inner guidance within me, and be willing to change course if need be. I knew I did not want to do anything that would take me away from this beautiful, peaceful state I was dwelling in.

When the group had an opportunity to share our experiences from the HU Sing, I was amazed by the incredible variety of blessings that were shared. Each person who shared their experience had received a blessing that was tailor-made and unique for them. When I had the chance to share, I said I had been blessed with peace in my heart. Del, who was hosting the event, responded by saying how God knew what I was going through as I searched for a new job, and how I needed some peace. I left the conference center feeling happy, refreshed — at peace with myself and the world around me.

The gift I received is one that keeps on giving. Years later I have revisited the experience of the HU Sing and have been blessed by remembrance of how I do not want to do anything that causes me to lose peace. Remembering my experience helps me to have clarity about decisions I am faced with today and to choose wisely. The day at the conference center is one in a long string of blessings throughout the years. There have been many other times since the HU Sing when I have sung HU, and the Divine has responded by giving me exactly what I needed. I am so grateful and continue to be amazed our prayers are heard.

Written by Roland Vonder Muhll

Keys in this story: HU, Gratitude, Remembrance, Discernment (going to HU Sing)

Keys not yet studied: Peace of Mind and Heart, Prayer, Proper Focus, Receiving God's Grace (gift of peace and clarity), God's Prophet, God's Love (gentle waves)

Gift of Surrender

The truly strong are those who know how to surrender. Not in the worldly sense of quitting or giving up, but of turning their spiritual growth over to Spirit and trusting not only the outcome, but the path taken to get there. Putting ourselves into "His Hands" contributes to a life of abundance because He knows us even better than we know ourselves.

The heat of the day was waning into a beautiful summer evening as the cool mountain air refreshed us with its breeze. We were gathered as a group in the field by the cabins where we sat in a circle. Prophet sat in the twelve o'clock position. It was the beginning of our annual weeklong summer retreat. We were there to invite the Divine into our hearts and to give permission for It to teach us in whatever ways would be best for our spiritual growth. We sang several holy names, each one bringing a different experience or feeling: a vastness, a feeling of spiritually opening up near the top of my head, and a sense of movement and flow. Then we sang Prophet's name. This brought a different, more personal feeling; one of love and affection, the sweetness of a relationship that has been growing naturally over the years.

Prophet gave us an opportunity to say a personal prayer, if we wanted. We could surrender the coming week to Divine Spirit to whatever degree we were comfortable. God knows what is in our best interests for spiritual growth, but He will not violate our free will. It is important to consciously choose to open our hearts and be willing to receive His blessings. I wanted to make the most of this week, so I surrendered as fully and completely as I could. In doing so I was saying, "Lord I trust you to bring exactly what I need during this retreat and in whatever manner and style you choose. I know you know what is best for me."

We began to sing HU, a love song to God. The sound from the group was so beautiful. HU resonated in my ears and vibrated through me. I felt an energy coming down from above, then I saw it. It was a white-hot, intense light. I felt love emanating from it. We began to sing a bit more softly. There was a swirling motion inside the beam of light. I noticed flecks of this white light coming off as it swirled around. As these pieces of light came off they turned golden, piece by piece, each one containing enough Divine love to move a mountain, heal a broken heart, bring joy, or whatever was needed. Just then the wind picked up. I was grateful for the coolness it brought. I saw the golden flecks of light being carried away. Tailor-made gifts of God's Love each destined for a specific Soul, exactly what they need, just when they needed it.

As for me, I was basking in love. The beam of light Prophet brought into our circle was pulsating with life and love, blessing us all. The days ahead were to be savored. Having the opportunity to be taught directly by the Prophet of our time is a rare gift. These would be some of the most precious and spiritually fruitful days of my life, as every retreat on the mountain has come to be, because I surrendered.

What I have come to know about surrender, through my personal experiences during these retreats, is very different from what the world thinks of it. Surrender is not an act of giving up, it is giving over. Giving over guidance and direction of my spiritual affairs to the Divine. Surrender is not the mark of a loser, but of one who gains a life of abundance and may experience the glories of Heaven on Earth. Surrender is not a sign of weakness but one of wisdom, courage, and strength. It is through surrender that Soul wins. It is through surrender you become a refined instrument of God and can be a vehicle for Spirit to bless others. It is through surrender you are freed. It is a gift to be treasured, a jewel with many facets, each beautiful in the way it reflects the light of Divine love with which it was given to us. Done willingly and joyfully, surrender brings an even greater appreciation for the sacred privilege of being allowed to surrender to God. Under Prophet's loving guidance I have been shown these things, and I wish to share these blessings with you.

Written by Lorraine Fortier

Keys in this story: HU, Gratitude, Spiritual Growth, Soul, Receptive (trusting the Lord and surrendering)

Keys not yet studied: God's Prophet, Prayer, God's Love (experiencing God's white and golden Light and basking in love), Spiritual Strength

I Am Soul, Light and Sound of God

There are certain "Core Truths" we teach at our retreats. Not only are they taught, folks actually get to experience them. One of the most important of these truths is "You do not have a Soul" rather, "You are Soul." This seemingly simple switch in perspective can set you free.

Many years ago, my father and spiritual teacher, the Prophet, shared a simple yet profound Divine truth with me and a class of students at Guidance for a Better Life. He shared with the group that we are Soul that has a body. Not what we had commonly thought — that we are a human body that has a Soul. He went on to give an example that it would be like identifying with ourselves as our cars — not as the driver, the animator, on the inside. Our "cars," our physical bodies, will wear out over time, but the real "us," Soul, will carry on and can get new "cars," physical bodies, for the next leg of our spiritual journey.

This simple, yet profound truth lifted a veil of illusion and opened the doors for so many wonderful possibilities and opportunities. Hearing and knowing that we are Soul meant that we are eternal. We are a Divine spark of God. We are children of God, created out of the Light and Sound of God, and our potential for spiritual freedom, growth, and love is infinite.

Our bodies are a gift from God, to be respected and cared for, but it is not who we are, nor does it limit our connection with the Divine. As Soul we can be taught by an inner and outer spiritual guide. Together with our guide we are free to explore God's amazing inner worlds, the various Heavens, in dreams and contemplations.

In one such contemplation, after singing HU, I found myself as Soul with my spiritual guide on an inner plane. We were on the beach at a vast and beautiful ocean. The golden light from the sun was shining down on us — it was warm and comforting. It bathed us in waves of love, peace, joy, security, and more. It was the Divine Light of God. The freedom and boundlessness of experiencing a moment purely as Soul is something that was never possible in my human body. I was able to feel absolute stillness and activity all at once and an indescribable strength in experiencing the real me. I felt free from the weight of the world and loved by God beyond my wildest imagination.

Our true home as Soul is the Heart of God. Thinking about that reality consciously reminds me who I really am at my core and brings with it so much peace. I may have a challenging day at work, but knowing I am Soul and not alone keeps a "bigger picture" and the "eternal view" present in my mind and heart. The events in daily life are less able to consume me when kept in perspective. As Soul I know that God has prepared me with everything I will ever need for my spiritual journey.

When I heard my father say, "I am Soul," I knew I was hearing truth. Over many years and through many experiences the truth revealed that night has sunk in deeper and deeper. The Divine has blessed me with personal experiences that solidified the knowingness in my heart. Even still, I know there is so much more to discover regarding the truth that we are Soul.

Written by Catherine Hughes

Keys in this story: HU, Soul, Growth of Consciousness, Contemplation

Keys not yet studied: God's Love (felt waves of His Love, experience of white and golden light), God's Grace (being welcomed at God's Abode — Ocean experience will make sense later in this book), Truth is Love, Spiritual Strength, Living Without Doubt, God's Prophet (guide)

Through the Eyes of Soul

*Whether physically young or old, we are all first and foremost Soul
— eternal spiritual beings. We are all children of God. When Soul
tunes in spiritually it has a higher view regardless of the physical age
of the body Soul resides in.*

The room was filled with more than just physical bodies seated in chairs, but Souls that love God. Looking down the rows everyone seemed appreciative to be in Prophet's presence. The annual clean-up weekend preparing Guidance for a Better Life retreat center grounds for a new year was just wrapping up. We gathered together as Del was about to lead us in singing HU. I always enjoy this opportunity as the group expresses to God the love and gratitude in our hearts.

As I sat down I looked around at the beautiful scene in that room and over at my family with a smile on my face, expressing the joy and gratefulness in my heart. I reflected on the gift of being there together. My husband and I attend retreats offered by Prophet Del Hall on a regular basis. This is where we learned about HU, which is also an ancient name for God. In turn we taught it to our three children and sing it at home, but on this day we would all be participating in singing together at the retreat center.

Prophet led the HU song, and our voices followed in unison, sending love to God, wave after wave as individuals and as a group. There was an immediate response from God. His beautiful Light and Love filled the room and flowed beyond. It showered down to all in attendance and created a brightness spanning throughout the space. I could feel the sound reverberating in my heart and being. This living Light and Sound of God, His Voice, seemed to draw out and showcase Divine qualities as I overflowed with joy, gratitude, and love. This beautiful cycle of giving God love and appreciation, and then receiving His Love continued with no perception of time, until Prophet ended by saying, "Thank you."

As the group dispersed I stood outside by the edge of the building holding my three-year-old son. He kept poking his finger at a wooden post in front of us. His face looked puzzled as he continued this direct and deliberate movement. When I asked what he was doing he said, "What is that Mom?" Chuckling and slightly confused by his question I said, "It is wood. It is part of the building." Still displaying a perplexed look he said, "Hmm… wood, yeah. But this isn't a building, it is a light castle." I was taken aback. Everything stood still in that moment. I was amazed my son could see what I knew to be true based on my own experiences and those shared by others over the years at the retreat center.

In that moment we were both seeing through Soul's eyes, not our physical ones. We had just sung HU with open hearts in the presence of God's Prophet tuning in to Spirit, and there was a higher view before us. We were raised up to see it. My son saw clearly. He was seeing truth. He was experiencing that building as what it really is — not an illusion, but God's Light. And it is everywhere. We just need to look through a new lens. At the same time I was seeing him as Soul, maybe for the first time. It was more personal than seeing others as Soul. This was my own child, and it made an impression. Just as quickly he was back to acting like a little boy and talking about other things, but in that window of a moment my view changed.

He is my son, but really he is Soul first. I knew that, but I experienced it and that changed something. My view, perception, and interactions were different. This experience brought out a desire in me to be more aware of demonstrating for my children how I am led by Prophet and love God. They are each a child of God I am blessed to care for in this life. I am privileged to guide, nurture, encourage, and help them find their way. It is not simply my job to "take care of them" in providing food, clothing, shelter, and supervision, but I am entrusted to love and guide them. I am their mother, but first and foremost they are each a child of God on loan to me to raise. Regardless of their age, they are Soul first. These messages sank into me so much deeper that day.

That one small interaction held layers of lasting truth and lessons I still think about today. With that new image of my son, I recognized my goal to be clear and focused, so I may be the best teacher I can for my children. I want to model for them to the best of my ability, and I can when I am led by Spirit. We simply need to accept the

Divine help and guidance that is always available to Soul; just like my little one did that morning, seeing our real surroundings through the eyes of Soul. God's Love is everywhere. Prophet wants to show those willing and ready.

Written by Michelle Hibshman

Keys in this story: HU, Gratitude, Soul, Growth of Consciousness

Keys not yet studied: God's Prophet, God's Love (filled the room), Give Love First, God's Grace (son seeing "light castle"), Truth is Love (seeing truth)

Child of God — Really

You are so much more than your temporal physical body. You are Soul, an eternal child of God, created out of the Light of God. Many find this hard to believe but nonetheless, it is true. Beneath our shortcomings as humans, we are spiritually magnificent. The more you allow the Prophet to let you experience, know, and identify with your true self, Soul, the more the "earthly baggage" will lose its grip.

We gathered at the Guidance for a Better Life retreat center, ready to sing HU. Del explained the HU and then said that you might know intellectually that you are a child of God but not fully understand what exactly that means, how sacred and special that really is. In time and with spiritual experience you may gain true understanding. I thought I knew what it meant to be a child of God but wondered if I was about to learn more.

During the quiet time after singing HU, I flew rapidly through a narrow dim tunnel and came out at God's Ocean. I recognized this as the twelfth Heaven, one of the very high Heavenly Worlds. I was distinctly aware that I was Soul. Instead of a body, I was my true self, a ball of light. I sparkled with pure rays of white light. Within my light was nothing dark or negative. I knew intuitively that it would be impossible for anything negative to stick to Soul.

When I had exited the tunnel, I escaped the bodies that cover Soul and disguise the perfection of God's creation. The disguise is so good that it even fools us. Anger, fear, worry, and their relations are not Soul. We are not our defilements or our mistakes. We are children of God, perfectly created with virtually limitless potential. As I looked out at the water I recognized sparkles in it made of the same light as me. God created Soul out of Itself, in Its image, Its own Light. Yet I also recognized that God is much more than Soul could ever be, even if Soul's potential was fully realized.

I was not alone. Prophet brought me there and remained beside me. As a ball of light he embraced me, his light enveloping mine. Within him, I felt closer to God, with all that God knows and sees at the Prophet's fingertips. I cannot find my way home alone. I need a guide, the Prophet, to show me the way.

As I opened my eyes following the HU, the world looked different. I knew deeper than before that I am Soul, a child of God. Beneath our human coverings is Soul, my true self and yours. We are both, you and I, one of God's glorious creations. Sing HU, look within, and ask the Prophet to show you your true self. A grand adventure awaits!

Written by Jean Enzbrenner

Keys in this story: HU, Soul, Growth of Consciousness

Keys not yet studied: God's Prophet, Prophet's Inner Presence (his light enveloping her), God's Grace (gift of love to be invited to His Abode — God's Ocean, the twelfth Heaven)

Nourished in the Light of God

Tuning in with Spirit during prayer is one of the best ways for you, Soul, to receive nourishment. One of the purest prayers is singing HU, an ancient name for God, as an expression of love and gratitude to God. Singing HU alone is wonderful, but there is truly something glorious about joining with a multitude to do so. The following is an experience from one of the group HU sings we hosted on the mountain.

While attending a "HU Sing" at Guidance for a Better Life, I had an experience in the Light and Sound of God, which is a more definitive name for the Holy Spirit or Voice of God. I have been a student there since 2005. In this time I have seen this Light many times and heard the Sound in various ways. I know that it is only by the Grace of God that I am able to have these experiences. Each experience builds on the next, and I realize these precious gifts are not random. There is a very personal nature to my experiences and how love is expressed to me.

As Del led us in singing HU, I listened to his voice, and the voice of many Souls expressing their love and gratitude to God. I began to perceive a growing ball of blue light in my inner vision (third eye or spiritual eye). The blue turned to intense white light, and I had a sense of floating, as if weightless. My teacher was with me, as the inner guide now, and we began to rise up inside of this light. Before long I was bobbing as if I was on a raft in an ocean. The nourishment of this light came in waves. In the light, I experienced wisdom, peace, love, joy, and boundlessness. I was a part of a living sea of God's Light and Sound. I was cleansed, cared for, and uplifted in this presence.

There was texture to this light and sound. It was not static but alive. It came from a living God, and I became more alive in this experience. I know more of my true nature and some of the nature of God as a result. A deep realization spoke to my heart, and I knew it as the Voice of God. "I love you — I love all my children — You are a part of my living essence."

These words opened me even more to love, and I prayed never to take this experience, or any of my experiences, for granted. Part of me knows that language and words cannot truly convey my experience, and how it continues to deepen my realization of God and of my true self. I am transformed by the solid foundation of knowing, not just believing, that a living, loving, and merciful presence does exist, and that we exist because of the endless love It pours out. This continues to inspire me to discover and rediscover my Divine gifts and live them out loud. That is why I share this.

My story is not about how loved I am, but how loved we all are. We are never alone. There was a time in my life when I felt alone. I did not know or perceive this Light and Sound, this loving presence. I only discovered it, as I said, by the Grace of God, and the spiritual tools and truth I learned at Guidance for a Better Life. This has made it possible for me to know that God is real. Its Light and Sound nourishes, animates, and sustains all creation.

My heart tells me that God wants to feed all of us, but we must open our "spiritual mouths" to accept this nourishment. Singing HU is one way that is available to all, regardless of our spiritual path, or where we are in our relationship with God.

Written by Tash Canine

Keys in this story: HU, Soul, Gratitude, Growth of Consciousness, Receptive (open "spiritual mouths")

Keys not yet studied: God's Prophet, God's Love, Prophet's Inner Presence (blue light), Spiritual Food, God's Grace (invited to Abode of God, experienced wisdom, peace, love, joy, boundlessness, cleansed, cared for, uplifted, blue and white light of God), Prayer, Living Without Doubt

Truth Uncovered

You are so much more than your physical body or any of the labels you could place on yourself. You are first and foremost Soul, an eternal spiritual being created by God with love. If you are blessed to experience this truth firsthand for yourself, you will truly know God loves you just the way you are.

Sometimes we have an experience with God that is pivotal to our growth, a precious moment we hold sacred in our hearts we will never forget. A moment that transforms us so much we can never see ourselves the way we were before that precious experience. This story is one of those moments for me.

It was the Step Three Building Divine Relationships retreat of 2013. I had been having some inner struggles with self-doubt, self-acceptance, and wondering if God really could love me the way I was. I didn't even know if I loved me just the way I was. We sat in the Beach House, the name given to our sacred classroom. It was evening, and even though the wind was blowing cold outside it was warm inside, and there was a comforting feeling inside the classroom. Del, the Prophet, offered us the opportunity to be blessed by the Divine and join him for a spiritual experience. As I sat with my eyes closed Prophet led us in a HU song to God. I began to feel lighter, and as I surrendered to the Divine, I felt God's pure Love pouring into me and filling me with attributes such as strength and a trust not only in Him, but in myself as well.

I was standing in a huge column of God's Light and Love. I felt completely safe and secure bathed in this love. Prophet showed me myself. I looked how I know myself to look when I look into the mirror; I saw my physical body. Prophet shared with us that we could shed our outer body, our "earth suit," in the same fashion we would take off a garment of clothing. Prophet helped me shed this outer sheath like a jacket, and I watched it fall away from me. Then without pausing he brought me up to the first Heaven, also referred to as the Astral plane. The part of myself I could now see looked like the physical body I knew as myself, but it was lighter, glowed more, and had a translucency my physical body did not have.

While I did not see Prophet at that moment, I was acutely aware of his strong presence and knew it was only with his guidance and help I was being raised in consciousness to other planes to higher and higher Heavens. I have read in scripture, 2 Corinthians 12:2 KJV, where Saint Paul spoke of "a man caught up to the third Heaven," and this was what I was being given the opportunity to experience for myself. Prophet brought me to the second Heaven, the Causal plane, and on the way up I shed my Astral body and watched it fall away, revealing my Causal body, which was even lighter and brighter than my Astral body had been. We continued our upward journey in this beam of God's Light, and as we raised up to each Heaven I shed each corresponding body: my Astral body, my Causal body, my Mental body, and finally I shed my body from the Etheric plane to reveal my true self, Soul. I was a blindingly bright ball of God's Light and Sound.

Prophet asked us to look at our true self. I saw something so beautiful, so pure, and so refined. My brightness and light was astoundingly breathtaking. This is how God made me, this is the real me! I felt no worries, no fears, no concerns, nor insecurities as I basked in this moment of truth experienced. An overwhelming knowing came over me and sank into my heart; God truly does love me. I knew God Himself was placing this truth directly into my open heart: God loves me just the way I am. I looked at myself, and I loved what I beheld. How could I not love such a precious, beautiful Soul? How could I not love something God uniquely and purposely made? I then understood that those garments, those light bodies from each Heaven of God covered up my true self, Soul. These light-bodies, layer over layer, had hidden from me the most beautiful truth of all, that I am Soul. This experience completely shattered the previous perception I had of myself.

I wish I could fully convey to you how precious and amazing it was to see myself in my true form as Soul. It was liberating, it was strengthening, and it was awe-inspiring. It freed me from the restrictive confines of how this physical world dictates to me daily that I am a woman, a wife, a mother, a daughter, a worker, and a washer of sippy cups. I am no longer bound by some idea of who I am based on my appearance, or what I do, or my physical belongings. These physical trappings cannot even touch the sacredness of my true Divine nature.

I am so eternally grateful to have been given such a loving gift, to see with clarity how limitless and breathtaking my true self is as Soul. I now have a new image of myself. No wonder I had a hard time loving myself; I had never truly experienced the real me. Do you desire to experience your true self?

Written by Ahna Spitale

Keys in this story: Soul and Self, Gratitude, Growth of Consciousness, HU

Keys not yet studied: God's Prophet, Prophet's Inner Presence, Spiritual Strength, God's Love, Truth is Love, God's Grace (her experiences in Heavens)

I Am Light and Sound

A core truth you will come across in our writings time and time again is that you do not have a Soul, rather... you are Soul that has a body. You are an eternal spiritual being within a temporal earthly embodiment. This seemingly simple switch in perspective can have a monumental effect on how you see yourself.

I returned home one Sunday evening in 2014 from a winter weekend retreat with a strong desire in my heart. I wanted to let my love for the eternal spiritual teachings consume me in every area of inner and outer life, and with a willingness and commitment to go to a whole new level in my spiritual journey. Prophet's words during the weekend were etched in my heart, "Immerse yourself in It" (meaning Divine Spirit and the ways of the eternal). "Let your excitement for these teachings spill out. If you have the eye of the tiger in you, let it loose." His words reverberated in me and brought a boldness and confidence going forward, exploring the inner worlds with him in new ways, being open to new opportunities to share the love and wisdom in these teachings with others, and approaching my time spent in contemplation, dreaming, and reading with creativity and renewed purpose.

The night after I returned from this retreat I spent time in contemplation just before bed and lovingly sang, "Prophet." Prophet is my beloved inner and outer teacher, God's ordained representative on Earth who is here to show us how to have a more personal relationship with our Heavenly Father and guide us home to Him. From personal experience I know him as the embodiment of the Holy Spirit, the Light and Sound of God, who physically manifests the fullness of God's Love, wisdom, and other glories of the Divine, and the one who can help us manifest this same Divine nature that is in all of us. After singing Prophet's name, I sang HU, an ancient name for God. I imagined breathing in light and sound, the Breath of God. I breathed in deeply, holding it a little then slowly breathing out as I sang, sending love back to God freshened and enriched with light and sound each time. I was suddenly inspired to say, "I am light and sound." Soul is made of light and sound, a part of Divine Spirit, a "spark" of God. A big growth area over the years has been learning to accept I am Soul, but in this moment even that was holding back the fullness of the truth I was hungry for, "I am light and sound." Wow, that was a bold statement! But, that was what was in my heart so I sang it aloud, a little shy and hesitant at first and then with more and more confidence. These words resonated at a deep level. By stating this truth more directly, I identified with my true nature more than I ever had before.

I was taken by Prophet to an inner spiritual Heaven where I stood next to a brilliant beam of flowing light and sound. I knew this beam as an aspect of the inner Prophet. I felt myself as a "strand" of this beam but separate and distinct as I stood next to it. I then saw an aspect of God Himself there with us, one I knew personally and loved with everything I am. I continued to sing HU. The air I breathed came direct from God. His breaths came into me and became my breath that felt like a river coursing through me. I then

94

saw His breath was also giving life to the beam. His breath became the beam itself. As I continued to send love to God by singing HU, I moved closer and closer to the beam of God's Light and Sound until I was inside of It. It began then to flow through me. My perception of this grew slowly until I could feel a steady flow of Divine Spirit running through my being. I could still feel myself, but I no longer felt separate. I was inside of It, and now I was aware that It was inside of me, flowing continuously, filling me with life and love. I was available to be used for Divine purpose and to be a blessing to others, a willing distributor of God's Light and Sound. Every breath I took connected me back to the Source of all that I saw and knew.

After this inner experience, I remained in quiet contemplation a little longer then went to bed, asking Prophet to guide me as we continued to explore the inner worlds while my physical body slept. When I awoke, I lay in that sacred space and could still feel the light and sound running through me. It brought expanded awareness and insights on the experience itself, dreams from the previous night, interests in daily life, and some home projects that were important to me. These insights gently flowed into my consciousness and then moved along in the river of Divine Spirit that ran through me. I am light and sound! What an incredible gift not just to say these words but to know them from real experience! I was so filled with appreciation and love that I got up after a time and wrote this amazing experience in my journal so I would always remember it.

Prophet blessed me with this gift of love not only to help me more fully manifest my Divine nature, but so I may share it with others. You too can sing this, for it is true for you. You are Soul. You are light and sound. Sing the name "Prophet" and ask his help in getting to know the real you. I guarantee you will like what you see!

Written by Lorraine Fortier

Keys in this story: HU, Soul, Contemplation, Attitudes and Thoughts, Growth in Consciousness, Gratitude

Keys not yet studied: God's Prophet, Prophet's Inner Presence, Personal Effort, Blending with God's Voice, Proper Focus, God's Love, God's Grace (whole experience of being taken into Heaven)

I Feel Right With God

Dreams are so much more than simply images. They are not just a television set on the back of our eyelids projected by the mind that we passively watch. They are memories of our active experiences in the greater worlds of Spirit and one way that God can teach and bless us. Sometimes a dream might contain a profound truth and leave no visual memory but rather, a knowingness. Do not discount these.

It was early March, and I could hear the cold biting wind outside nipping at the windows of the log cabin we were staying in. I was in that cozy place between the dream world and the world where my physical body lay resting. I tried to gently go over my dream so I could record it in my dream journal. Eyes still closed, I continued to stay in that space, savoring it. No images of the adventures I had had drifted into my consciousness, just a feeling. A deep solid as a rock, sink-your-teeth-into kind of feeling. As I rubbed the sleep from my eyes and pulled my dream journal closer to write, I lay there stumped. I had no words to write. I could not remember any details of the experience I had just left.

Journaling my dreams is one way I demonstrate gratitude for the sacred experiences I have been given, so pulling my pen cap off I began to write. "I don't remember my dream, but I woke up feeling right with God." I climbed down the ladder to the main cabin area, and after a warm breakfast of home cooked oatmeal we gathered at the table for class. We began our small class by sharing our dreams from the night before with our teacher Del Hall.

Soon it was my opportunity to share. I felt a little sheepish thinking I did not have much to share with the group. Del listened with full attention as I shared not remembering my dream but waking up and feeling right with God. Del's eyes smiled as he said, "One of the most important aspects of a dream is what God is trying to communicate to us." He continued, "Most people would love to wake up feeling right with God." I sat there jaw slightly dropped. "I feel right with God." The gravity and magnitude of those seemingly simple words slowly sunk in. My heart overflowed with love. I was immediately glad I had spoken up and shared my dream and even more grateful to Del for personally helping me to understand the gift of love I had been given.

To this day I cherish that dream. I often revisit that moment where I remember being snuggled warm in my sleeping bag and nestled in God's Heart. That feeling so lovingly placed in my heart continues to bless me and provide me with spiritual nourishment, bringing me comfort and strength when the storms in life make the surface waves choppy, and I seek something solid under my feet.

Back in the cabin at Guidance for a Better Life, Del's discourse on dreams continued as we learned how to become more fluent in the "Language of the Divine," to better understand the subtle inner communication we all have. Del taught us many things that morning such as sometimes all we remember when we wake is a sound or a color. At other times we wake with just a feeling or a knowing that a personal message from God was placed directly in our hearts. I felt a week's worth of learning and truth was imparted into our hearts in the following hours, and before we could blink it was time for lunch.

Sitting around that table, warmed by the steadily burning fire in the wood stove and the truth in Del's words, I learned the importance of trusting my experiences. I learned the importance of having a teacher to personally help me understand the blessings I have been given. Especially when it is a "simple dream," like waking up feeling right with God.

Written by Ahna Spitale

Keys in this story: Gratitude, Remembrance

Keys not yet studied: God's Prophet, Spiritual Food, Spiritual Strength, Truth is Love, God's Grace (gift of the dream and the feeling)

Skills to Cope With Depression

*We all face challenges in life, which are ultimately opportunities
for growth. During these times we can actually forge a deeper
relationship and appreciation for God. One key is to not lose sight of
the Hand of God that is available. Those that ask God for help and
also do their part will ultimately come out stronger, versus just
"make it through."*

About two years ago my life changed. Everyone goes through changes, but this was one of those major turning points for me. I had recently moved with my husband and two young children to a town where we did not know anyone. The move required that I leave a job I really liked and enjoyed. Then we had our third child. To me this was a whole lot of change in a very short period of time.

I thought I had prepared for these changes. I am not complaining, I have a very good and happy life. I knew all these changes were blessings, but I was struggling. I was experiencing some level of baby blues or postpartum depression, and all the changes added to how I was feeling. This concerned me because I knew depression. I had been depressed at earlier times in my life and did not want to go there again.

Between my personal history and experience from my previous job I had some tools and skills to manage this issue. In the past I did my best to just "make it through" those tough times, but this time was different because I knew the Hand of God was working in my life. I have been blessed to experience God's Love in so many ways. Over the years I have built a loving and trusting relationship with God's Prophet, the Hand of God, so when I recognized my situation I now knew how to more than just "make it through." This time I knew I had help available. I asked for help and accepted that help. I listened and followed the Divine guidance given to me with love and compassion. I knew His comfort. I knew that even in the moments when I felt alone that I am never alone. Prophet is with me every moment. He helped me have the strength to do my part: to wisely use the tools and skills I had been taught in the past, and to truly know I could do it with him. So this time my experience with depression really was different, and I am forever grateful.

I kept praying for help and continued attending retreats at Guidance for a Better Life. That is where I originally learned about God's Prophet and the importance of our relationship. Everything continued to build toward a good outcome. The inner guide, the inner part of Prophet, and I spent time in scripture, reading spiritual books, putting love into everything we did throughout the day, and being grateful. Together we sang HU with my baby even in those tired, weary, early weeks and so much more. I paid attention to my dreams and used those late-night feedings awake with the baby as an opportunity to write them down and say, "Thank you." The Prophet nudged me to speak up for myself and take care of myself. He encouraged me to step out of my comfort zone and join activities and social groups where I met wonderful, welcoming people in the community.

God responded to my prayers by guiding and helping me daily. Life was enjoyable and not a struggle. I had faith in Him, and in turn He helped me have faith in myself to keep going forward. I came out better than ever, and feel I have a stronger and deeper relationship with Prophet than I even had before. My life was good, but now I was appreciating it more. My sacred relationship with Prophet makes my life abundant, and it is continually growing.

Instead of spiraling down and retreating into depression like I had in the past, I stepped out, survived, and then thrived with my focus on God's Love. Things were not distorted as they had been before in that same space and frame of mind because the Prophet helped me to see clearly from a higher view, as Soul. That higher view helped me to appreciate the gifts of God that were everywhere around me. My heart was open and filled with love, which gave me the opportunity to enjoy loving and caring for my family again. I allowed love in, so I could give it out to others, and was shown a deeper understanding of giving and receiving love. I am very thankful for the blessing to walk with Prophet daily and to give and receive God's Love. It has changed my life.

Written by Michelle Hibshman

Keys in this story: Understanding Change, Gratitude, HU, Soul

Keys not yet studied: God's Love, God's Prophet, Spiritual Strength, Personal Effort, Prayer, Cause and Effect (relationship with Prophet changed the effect of depression), Prophet's Inner Presence, Spiritual Food

My First Glimpse of Soul

Our true identity as Soul is hidden behind our earthly packaging and Its shortcomings. We are so much more than our physical bodies and minds; we are Soul, eternal spiritual beings created out of the Light and Love of God. Being able to accept and live this truth is a cornerstone to spiritual freedom. It is one of the first things Prophet teaches and helps his students experience for themselves.

The first time I visually saw my true and eternal self, Soul, I was surprised. In my ignorance I thought I knew what Soul would look like. I was at a special weeklong retreat at Guidance for a Better Life. In a contemplation led by Prophet Del Hall, I was taken out of my body spiritually. The contemplation was an active experience where I was allowed to see and know real truths, God's truths.

It was pleasantly dark all around me; at least that was what I was aware of. I knew Prophet was by my side. I was given a special mirror that would show me what I looked like spiritually as Soul. I thought I would see a soft white orb of light. I spiritually raised the mirror up to eye level and looked. I saw a flash of dazzling, brilliant light. It was so vibrant! It was so much brighter than the glint off a diamond in the sun. In that instant I experienced some of my God-given qualities of life, motion, and beauty all at once.

Prophet thank you so much for that first glimpse of the real me, Soul. It was so far removed from the angry, confused person I thought I was. I thank you Prophet for the truth that I can operate and see with Soul's viewpoint, a much higher and more peaceful view of life. I do not have to live every day in the human consciousness of anger, fear, guilt, and unworthiness. I can now recognize and learn to live with love from a higher spiritual view!

I work in a hospital emergency department. Driving home from a long shift last week I was reveling in the remembrance of a discourse Del, the current Prophet, gave about the truth of Soul. As I drove I was in a sea of God's Light and Sound. This Divine light and love flowed all around, and Its beauty inspired a subtle and deep joy within my heart. I was filled with love. At that moment I was experiencing that as Soul, I was an individualized part of this light and sound, the very Essence of God. I appreciated knowing you Prophet, the one who speaks truth and shares God's Living Word with Soul. It is such a privilege to know you Prophet and know the reality of God.

Written by Carmen Snodgrass

Keys in this story: Soul, Gratitude, Growth of Consciousness, Remembrance, Contemplation

Keys not yet studied: God's Prophet, Truth is Love, God's Love

Captain's Chair

God created us to live our lives from the higher dynamic viewpoint of Soul, not the lower rigid mental state. Until our mind is on board with this arrangement and takes a backseat to Soul, it will throw quite a fuss. No better is the difference between mind and Soul and the battle for top dog illustrated than in this testimony.

Our family had just finished a delicious evening meal and were enjoying some quality time together in the living room. I had settled into my chair, put my feet up to relax after a day at work, and was enjoying watching our two-year-old daughter play. My wife and I began to share our day when our daughter got up from playing, came over, and told me to get up out of my chair.

I explained to her I was enjoying sitting in my chair. She then got very animated and put her hands under my legs trying her best to lift me out of my chair and said, "Up Daddy!" I firmly told her this was my chair, and I was not moving. She then began to cry and throw a tantrum screaming "My chair Daddy." My wife and I looked at each other with disbelief and a slight smile for this was an exceptional two-year-old moment, even for her, and not her normal behavior. I did not know why, but felt a strong urge to stay firm no matter what she did and stay sitting in my chair. I knew it was best for her. I proceeded to explain to her this was Daddy's chair, but she could sit with me if she liked. She screamed louder, and the tears were running down both sides of her now-flushed red cheeks as she stood there crying and screaming over and over, "Get up Daddy, it is my chair, get up Daddy, it is my chair. Get up Daddy, it is my chair." After about five minutes of this behavior there was no sign of letting up, so my wife took our daughter for a bath to calm her down.

This caught my attention for this was over the top behavior even for a two-year-old child. I was left with a sense of peace. I had a knowing that being firm in my attitude, that I was not going to get up no matter what, was best for all involved. Our daughter got her bath, calmed down, and we all went about our evening.

A few weeks later Prophet was helping me and a group of students understand more about our true nature as Soul. A smile came across my face as the memories of my daughter's behavior a few weeks earlier came rushing into my consciousness. I was given the clarity to see how it tied into our conversation, and it reminded me of a spiritual truth Del has taught me over the years. Soul belongs in charge of our mind and not the other way around. Soul belongs in the captain's chair of our life. We are Soul, the spiritual adult in the relationship with the mind. It is much like the loving relationship between a parent and a child.

The mind, we call the "lower self," is much like a two-year-old and was never designed to run our life. The mind is very limited and is the source of our frustrations, fears, anger, worries, self-doubts, vanity, excessive attachments, and a variety of other ailments. It does not like change, gets overwhelmed, and is generally closed to ideas outside of itself. These are all traits of the mind but not of Soul. The mind is good at balancing our checkbooks and taking care of our daily tasks, but it is very limited when compared to the boundlessness of Soul.

Soul is creative, resilient, happy, peaceful, and cherishes freedom. It also has clarity, a can-do attitude, access to wisdom, and is generally open to new ideas. Soul has a higher spiritual consciousness than the mind, thus better equipped to run our lives. Soul is free to travel the Heavens, has a greater capacity to give and receive love, and Its potential for growth has no limits.

When we begin to be more spiritually nourished, Soul grows stronger in our life. We begin to make better choices and decisions that benefit us and those we love. Some of the things that help Soul grow stronger are singing HU, reading scriptures, paying attention to dreams, spending time with Prophet, and learning to recognize and be grateful for the blessings in life.

When Soul begins to get stronger the mind may start to protest. At first it feels threatened and does not want to give up sitting in the captain's chair. The lower self has been used to being in charge of our life and has grown to like telling us how things should be. Initially the mind does not like the idea of Soul being in charge and will protest, yell, and scream, much like a two-year-old throwing tantrums to get its way. When Soul gains enough strength it takes charge of the mind and takes Its rightful place in the captain's chair of our life. This is what is best for us, and what is best for our little-self.

Our true self, Soul, is designed by God to be in charge of the mind. Soul has a higher view of life, sees more clearly, and is receptive to God's Love, truth, and guidance. As Soul we are more relaxed, peaceful, joyous, loving, wise, and creative. God actually created the mind to be subservient to Soul; an instrument to be used by Soul to achieve Its purpose during Its sojourn on planet Earth. This experience is a reminder to me that I want to live my life with Soul in charge of the lower self. I want to be nourished as Soul daily and feed it the spiritual food it needs to grow stronger and stay strong, because this is my Divine nature — Soul. It is the true expression of myself as God created me.

Thank you Prophet for giving me this experience and for helping me manifest my Divine nature and the dreams of my heart.

Written by Mark Snodgrass

Keys in this story: Soul and Self, HU, Receptive, Understanding Change, Gratitude, Remembrance, Discernment (better choices)

Keys not yet studied: God's Prophet, Spiritual Strength, God's Grace (given clarity), Spiritual Food, Connecting Spiritual Events

The Love You Always Wanted

*The experience of meeting an aspect of God is profound and deeply
personal; it fills you with God's Love and leaves you lacking nothing.
The idea of partaking in a spiritual journey home to God might be hard
for some to believe. It is, however, truly possible if you have a spiritual
guide who is authorized to show you the way.*

The experience of God is like nothing in this world. It can shatter
your limitations, transform your heart, and change your life. It can
give blessings far beyond what you ever thought to ask for. It can fill
you with love; the love you had always hoped for, but never knew
for sure was really out there. The experience of God can do all this
and more. I have been blessed to see the Face of God many times.
These Divine experiences were made possible by the guidance of the
current living Prophet of God, Del Hall of Virginia. Years of Del's
guidance led me to see God face-to-face. The following paragraphs
describe one such experience and the Divine impact it has had on my
life.

It was a clear Sunday morning at Guidance for a Better Life, and
a group was gathered in the building we call the Beach House. The
group took their seats, and we prepared to sing HU, an ancient love
song to God. Del led us in a sacred and beautiful opening prayer, and
we began. The harmony of praiseful voices filled the room. Gently
my awareness shifted from my physical body sitting in the Beach
House to my spiritual side, Soul, the real me. As Soul I was aware
of being on the shore of a vast ocean of love and mercy with Prophet.
We knelt on the sand in reverence, then approached the sparkling,
golden waters of God. As we entered the water God's Love
permeated my very being. It was refreshing and nourishing. Peace
and contentment filled me as I drank deeply. Then a tremendous
white light appeared over the waves. It emanated the intense yet
nurturing Love of God, for this was no ordinary light but an aspect
of God Himself. With Prophet's help I opened myself to be as
receptive as possible to this experience of God. Slowly, a face
appeared in the light. A face that radiated the most profound love,

wisdom, and power one could imagine. As the eyes fell upon me, it felt almost like I was melting into God's pure Love and truth.

Basking in God's mighty Presence, old misunderstandings of God, life, and truth crumbled away. More room was made in my heart for accepting love and truth. An extraordinary feeling of blessedness and gratitude flowed through me. What gift had I been given? Was it even possible to put into words? I knew this much — God's gaze gave me a greater capacity to love, to serve Him, and to accept truth.

Afterwards, as I sat contemplating what had just happened, I saw the Face of God again, but this time it was not directed at me. He was pouring His golden Light and Love all over our beautiful blue planet. I know His Love is gently marinating our planet, preparing, and nurturing Souls for a great upliftment that is to come.

I feel so blessed to have been given this glorious experience and many like it. God's Love is the love so many seek yet do not know where or how to find. It can be found through His current living Prophet. He can guide you home to God, as he has done for me and many others.

Written by David Hughes

Keys in this story: HU, Soul, Receptive, Contemplation, Gratitude, Spiritual Growth

Keys not yet studied: God's Prophet, God's Love, Prayer, God's Grace (going to the Abode of God)

I Heard Heavenly Music

Within the Heavenly realms the Voice of God, or the Holy Spirit, manifests itself in a wide range of spiritual light and sound. Often the color of the light, or in the following case the sound heard, is a road map of sorts to which Heavenly plane Soul is on. God delivers His Love to Soul via the light and sound, so to experience the Voice of God in any form is a profound blessing.

Throughout my spiritual studies I had oftentimes read about the beautiful sounds that can be heard on the various spiritual planes of existence. In my heart I desired that I might have an experience of hearing Heavenly music, but it was not forthcoming until just recently. On June 7, 2015 many gathered in singing HU, a love song to God, in the presence of Prophet Del Hall. I began by letting go of all external distractions. I prayed to become a perfect vehicle for God's Love, all the while opening my heart to allow a continuous stream of God's Love to flow through it with each wave of HU.

There was a sense of being lifted up spiritually higher as we continued to send love out to the unseen worlds. We had been singing for about ten minutes when, within the sound of those singing HU, I distinctly heard the sound of a flute. Elated about the blessing of hearing the sound of the fifth Heaven, the Soul plane, my heart soared with love as I sang to my Heavenly Father. More sound came into my awareness; it was of violins, the sound that originates on the eighth Heaven. I now had personally been blessed to experience the Holy Spirit, God's Voice, as both Light and Sound!

I was allowed to experience these sounds in order that I might testify to the reality of Soul's ability to travel in worlds beyond what the physical eyes can see. I also know that to experience God's Light or Sound is a special gift of love. Since I was singing in the presence of the Prophet of God, there was a plus factor at play that one will only know by direct experience.

In appreciation of and gratitude for the blessings!

Written by Bernadette Spitale

Keys in this story: HU, Receptive (effort to open her heart), Soul, Gratitude

Keys not yet studied: God's Prophet, Prayer, God's Grace (gift of experiencing God's Light and Sound), God's Love (experiencing God's Light and Sound is experiencing His Love)

Happiness and Self-Control

God has given us the gift of being able to choose our state of consciousness. This choice is made daily by our thoughts, actions, and attitudes. The choice of whether to focus on things that close our hearts or open them is ours. What a sacred responsibility and opportunity.

Several months ago God, through His Prophet, gave me a dream that really helped me. I dreamed I was asleep, and in the dream I woke up and went downstairs to find the two main doors in our house were open a crack. I felt uneasy about this. Were they open all night? Was someone in the house? Were they left unlocked? I awoke with a slight uneasiness lingering inside.

I knew this dream was significant, but I was unsure of what Prophet was teaching me. I decided to take this into contemplation. This is a most amazing way to receive insight from the Divine. I started by singing HU, a love song to God, with the intent to understand the dream better. I realized while singing HU the doors were symbolic of areas in my life that were gateways to negativity. After singing HU I sat quietly and asked Prophet to help me see areas where I was allowing negative influence into my life and consciousness. Prophet showed me I had been allowing thoughts of unworthiness to linger within me. These were subtle thoughts of doubting I was worthy of love and not drawing clear boundaries of what I would allow myself to think about. This was due to sloppy thinking and not staying nourished spiritually.

I began to sing a special prayer, "Prophet loves me. I am worthy of Prophet's love. I accept Prophet's love. I love you Prophet!" I felt my heart begin to fill with love. I felt relief from the doubt I had allowed into my state of being. With this doubt removed more of God's Light and Love could then come into my heart! A discourse from Prophet then flowed into me. It is my privilege and responsibility to safeguard what I allow into my consciousness. My consciousness is like my home. I want it to be warm and inviting to God and His Prophet. I want love in my home, and I want it to be a safe welcoming place for my loved ones.

Then Prophet showed me the other open door in the house was anger. Just the night before I felt anger over something, and I noticed how that anger bled into another issue. I began getting upset about things that were fine! It happened so fast. Prophet gave me clarity to see how quickly I can go down an unproductive road when I get angry. Having the feeling was not the problem, but focusing on it and dwelling in that state was like leaving an open door for more negativity to enter. It is important for me to have self-control in this area, and I appreciated this lesson from Prophet. This is not the first time Prophet has made me aware of this particular passion of the mind.

Prophet explained there could be other areas to be watchful of, but the main point was to be aware of my thoughts and remember it is a God-given gift to be able to choose what to focus on. My life is full of God's Love, and that is what I want to focus on. Staying spiritually nourished by spending quality time with God's Prophet is key. It is because of my relationship with Prophet that I am able to live a life of more freedom than I used to. I have the freedom to truly be happy. Thank you, Prophet!

Written by Carmen Snodgrass

Keys in this story: HU, Contemplation, Attitudes and Thoughts, Discernment, Growth of Consciousness

Keys not yet studied: Proper Focus, Truth is Love, Spiritual Food, God's Prophet, God's Grace (her dream giving her clarity), God's Love, Prayer

Step Three: Building Divine Relationships

The most important and profound spiritual truth is that you are never alone. As a spiritual being, created out of the Light and Love of God, you are connected to God spiritually via the Light and Sound of God, or the "Voice of God." God's Prophet, who is a conduit for God's Light and Love on Earth, is here to help you make and nurture this connection. God always has a Prophet on Earth to help teach and lead His children Home. This might be hard for some to understand or accept, but nonetheless it is true. This section is an opportunity to begin the pursuit of this truth for yourself. Ultimately God wants a personal relationship with each and every one of us. This truth and the reality of this statement will become exceedingly clear later in my book. As the current Prophet I am here to help you make your relationship with God a reality, and if you have one already, make it more beautiful than you ever dreamed possible.

After reading Step One through Step Three I suggest reflecting upon how you are digesting the first three steps. If you have struggled or feel you have what I call "Spiritual Indigestion," perhaps take a break from moving forward for a while. There is no rush! Remember, at my retreats where I personally mentor each student, I take about four months to introduce Step One through Step Three and a minimum of two years to introduce the first five steps in total. If you are spiritually well nourished by singing HU daily, you can grow in accepting God's teachings quite rapidly. However, the mind is slow to accept change and often, if pushed into change too fast, revolts. Hence, spiritual indigestion. You will get so much more out of this book by going at the pace that is right for YOU and ensuring the real, eternal you stays well nourished by using the tools and suggestions I provide. Part of spiritual growth is knowing thyself. Socrates, the classical Greek philosopher, said essentially the same thing when he said "Man, know thyself." As I wrote in the Definition of the Spiritual Keys:

"Individual Keys do not stand alone and independent of other Keys. Part of the secret of each Key is how it relates to, affects, or impacts other individual and groups of Keys. This is perhaps the most important concept to understand regarding the Keys, they are like a living ball of wisdom that work together best."

Therefore, some practice of foundational Keys is required to comfortably move forward. This practice nourishes Soul and gives the mind time to adjust to new, and usually foreign, views of life. Deciding when to move forward is your choice, but remember the Key Discernment.

The following Keys will be introduced:

Spiritual Strength

To have access to the Kingdom of Heaven and God's direct Love requires spiritual strength. One can develop the needed strength under the guidance of God's Prophet. **The number one way to build spiritual strength is by regularly and consistently doing the spiritual exercises given by Prophet.** Regular and consistent spiritual exercises provide daily spiritual nourishment to strengthen Soul and will also help you begin to develop self-discipline and focus. Self-discipline, proper focus, proper practice, and prolonged determination are important aspects of strength.

Daily contemplations bring relief, truth, and insights where the mind and intellect cannot. This builds trust in the inner communications and strengthens the relationship with the inner Prophet (a concentrated aspect of the Holy Spirit). **Reading scripture** builds wisdom of God's truths, which is a foundation of spiritual strength. In time a desire and receptiveness for truth grows deep in one's heart; this also builds strength.

Challenges and the trials of life can build strength if one recognizes and takes responsibility for their thoughts and actions that caused or contributed to the event. Sometimes the Divine puts a seeker into difficult situations to build strength, activate creativity, and grow more confident in self and in their relationship with Prophet. Creativity, an attribute of Soul, is an aspect of strength.

The STRENGTH of one's relationship with God's Prophet is the key to entering and traveling the Kingdom of Heaven. The depth of trust, love, and willingness to serve others as a coworker with Prophet is a vital aspect of spiritual strength. One's loyalty to God's teachings and the courage to stand up for the ways of God when under pressure are a measure of strength. One must be conditioned to build spiritual strength. Spending time with Prophet's longtime students, reading Prophet's books, watching his videos, listening to his podcasts, or being in his presence can condition one to be desirous of truth over illusion. Being receptive in the presence of Prophet brings clarity and strength. In this world it takes real strength to follow TRUTH, and truth leads to God's Love and true freedom. Those fortunate to experience Prophet's love and follow his guidance will one day experience God's true Love.

Having resilience, the ability to bounce back quickly and recover one's spirit, focus, and priorities from setbacks is an aspect of strength. And, when ready, **making a sacred commitment** to one's spiritual path is an aspect of strength. Making a commitment to one's path is liken to marriage versus dating. Once married one's focus is less scattered and can be concentrated upon one's commitment. This extra focus through the choice of commitment adds strength. With proper focus and nurturing, a relationship with Prophet can be strengthened in love, trust, and commitment over time, becoming a spiritual marriage, one of abiding in Prophet and allowing him to abide in you.

Having positive thoughts and attitudes about oneself adds strength; whereas having negative thoughts of self greatly weakens. Having clear purpose and goals, and the focus and self-discipline to achieve them, adds strength. Doing what needs to be done, even if afraid, builds confidence and strength. Having a "can do" attitude adds strength. Resisting temptations can build spiritual stamina and strength. Setting boundaries with ourselves and others adds strength and protection. Taking responsibility for our lives brings freedom and adds confidence and strength, whereas having a victim consciousness weakens and limits. Being more concerned with what God thinks about you than what people think or say about you is a sign of strength. Remembering you are loved, and will always be loved, by God and Prophet gives strength.

If you truly desire spiritual strength, but lack certain aspects of strength, **pray for what you lack.** God, through His Prophet, can provide the necessary strength until you become stronger. Prophet desires you to accomplish your spiritual goals and is here to assist in every way as you grow. **Reliance on the teachings, truth, and love of God is our real strength.**

Study Guidance: The more you understand, accept, LIVE, and rely upon the truth and teachings of God the more fortified and strengthened you will become. **Climbing the "spiritual mountain"**

to go all the way Home to our Heavenly Father with His Prophet is very possible, as you will read later in my book, but it takes internal spiritual fortitude and strength. Being nourished as Soul daily is a must, because only Soul can travel the Heavens home to God.

Receiving God's Grace

God's Grace is very real and can work wonders in our lives and in our understanding of His teachings and ways. His Grace is of vital importance in manifesting our highest spiritual potential and in creating the most abundant life.

Generally, grace does not come to us just because we desire to have it. Generally, God does not violate the free will He gave to us, so drawing close to God is an exercise of OUR free will and is in a sense giving God permission to share His Grace. God's Grace is an exercise of His free will. **A wonderful way to draw close to God is having the discipline to sing HU daily and consistently do our other spiritual exercises. Singing HU makes you more able to recognize and receive His Grace.**

To have grace lift us up to a higher view of life we must first make some effort of our own. **To be teachable requires one make the effort to lift their consciousness to where the teachers are.** Jesus shared the same when he told his followers, "Come to me and be lifted up." That statement shows that some effort on our part is required before being lifted up to a higher view by the Grace of God.

All spiritual experiences are gifts of love given through God's Grace! These gifts of love might include healings, clarity, wisdom, peace, joy, direct experiences with God's Love, spiritual travel into the Heavens, gift of dreams, protection, and even being led to this book, etc. Each and every gift is tailor-made and unique for each individual. If your desire for God is sufficient and you do your part, God's Grace will make it so. **Walking in accord with the ways of God will ensure His Grace continues to flow into your life.**

God's Love for His children, Souls, is not optional in the sense that we exist because He loves us. If God did not love us we would not exist. **His Grace is optional in the sense He does not have to share His Grace.** Without His Grace we cannot make our way home to Him. God delivers much of His Grace through His chosen Prophet. God's Grace allows Soul to meet, recognize, and be taught by His Prophet. God's Grace gives Soul the desire for the Heavenly things in life. When our sufficient personal effort, proper focus, and loving relationship with Prophet are combined with God's Grace, we can achieve our highest spiritual goals.

Study Guidance: God will always love you, but **His Grace is optional.** Your efforts, an exercise of your free will, may be a catalyst for God's Grace. Singing the love song to God, HU, prepares and conditions you to receive God's Grace. However, all the blessings received are a result of His Grace, not the HU itself. God's Prophet has the privilege to deliver much of God's Grace, in the name of, and on behalf of the Heavenly Father.

God's Prophet
The Master Key

There is always a Prophet of God residing in the physical world. Each of these Souls in a physical embodiment is chosen and raised up by God. Former Prophets have prepared and conditioned the soon-to-be Prophet over multiple lifetimes. God ALWAYS has one primary Prophet at any given time in history. This is a long and unbroken line of God's Prophets. Prophets' words and teachings come directly from God, our Heavenly Father. **Prophet is the Master Key that unlocks the deeper meanings hidden within all the other Keys.** He activates and unleashes their value by helping you integrate and make them operational in your life.

In the Bible Jesus said he would ask his Father to send a comforter. "And I will pray the Father, and he shall give you another Comforter that he may abide with you forever." John 14:16 KJV The original Greek word used for Comforter was "Paraclete." Paraclete implied an actual physical person who helps, counsels, encourages, advocates, comforts, strengthens, and sets free. "Comforter" **is only one aspect** of the original meaning.

God had Prophets before Jesus and Christianity and will continue this line of teachers. The Bible includes historical accounts of many Prophets prior to Jesus. Some Prophets are extra-special spiritually, such as Jesus who was also the Father's Son. Each of God's Prophets has a special mission given to them by God. Each usually has the highest God Consciousness on Earth during their time. God's Prophet is given spiritual authority directly from God. This authority includes, but is not limited to, sharing God's Light and Sound and taking Souls into the Heavens, to God's Temples of Learning, and Home to God Himself. It also includes teaching God's eternal truths, speaking on behalf of, healing, protecting, and passing on the blessings and Grace of God.

All of God's Prophets are also here to lift up Souls in consciousness, as high as possible for each individual Soul. God wants His children to know His ways and His Love. He sends

Prophets to teach His ways and truth, and for those who are ready, bring them HOME.

There are two aspects of God's Prophet, an inner spiritual Prophet and an outer physical Prophet. The inner Prophet can teach us through dreams, intuition, spiritual travel, inner communication, and his presence. The outer Prophet also teaches through his discourses, written word, videos, and his presence. Having an inner and outer teacher brings great benefit and tremendous opportunity to grow. Prophet is always with us spiritually on the inner. Prophet points to and glorifies the Father.

The Role of God's Prophet

An introductory understanding of God's handpicked and Divinely trained Prophet is necessary to fully benefit from reading this book. God ALWAYS has a living Prophet of His choice on Earth. He has a physical body with a limited number of students, but the inner spiritual side of Prophet is limitless. Spiritually he can help countless numbers of Souls all over the world, no matter what religion or path they are on — even if that is no path at all. He teaches the ways of God and shares the Light and Sound of God, which is the Holy Spirit. He delivers the Living Word of God. Prophet can teach you physically as well as through dreams, and he can lift you into the Heavens of God while still living to grow in wisdom and love. He offers protection, peace, teachings, guidance, healing, and love.

Each of God's Prophets throughout history has a unique mission. One may only have a few students with the sole intent to keep God's teachings and truth alive. God may use another to change the course of history. God's Prophets are usually trained by both the current and former Prophets. The Prophet is tested and trained over a very long period of time. The earlier Prophets are physically gone but teach the new Prophet in the inner spiritual worlds. This serves two main purposes: the trainee becomes very adept at spiritual travel and gains wisdom from those in whose shoes he will someday walk. This is vital training because the Prophet is the one who must safely prepare and then take his students into the Heavens and back.

There are many levels of Heaven, also called planes or mansions. Saint Paul once claimed to know a man who went to the third Heaven. Actually it was Paul himself that went, but the pearl is, if there is a third Heaven, it presumes a first and second Heaven also exist. The first Heaven is often referred to as the Astral plane. Even on just that one plane of existence there are over one hundred sub-planes. This Heaven is where most people go after passing, unless they receive training while still here in their physical body. Without a guide who is trained properly in the ways of God a student could misunderstand the intended lesson and become confused as to what is truth. The inner worlds are enormous compared to the physical worlds. They are very real and can be explored safely when guided by God's Prophet.

Part of Prophet's mission is to share more of what is spiritually possible for you as a child of God. Few Souls know or understand that God's Prophet can safely guide God's children, while still alive physically, to their Heavenly Home. Taking a child of God into the Heavens is not the job of clergy. Clergy have a responsibility to pass on the teaching of their religion exactly as they were taught, not to add additional concepts or possibilities. If every clergy member taught their own personal belief system no religion could survive for long. Then the beautiful teachings of an earlier Prophet of God would be lost. Clergy can be creative in finding interesting and uplifting ways to share their teachings, but their job is to keep their religion intact. However, God sends His Prophets to build on the teachings of His past Prophets, to share God's Light and Love, to teach His language, and to guide Souls to their Heavenly Home.

There is ALWAYS MORE when it comes to God's teachings and truth. No one Prophet can teach ALL of God's ways. It may be that the audience of a particular time in history cannot absorb more wisdom. It could be due to a Prophet's limited time to teach and limited time in a physical body on Earth. Ultimately, it is that there is ALWAYS MORE! Each of God's Prophets brings additional teachings and opportunities for ways to draw closer to God, building on the work and teachings of former Prophets. That is one reason why Prophets of the past ask God to send another; to comfort, teach, and continue to help God's children grow into greater abundance. Former Prophets continue to have great love for God's children and want to see them continue to grow in accepting more of God's Love. **One never needs, nor is there a good reason, to stop loving or accepting help from a past Prophet in order to grow with the help of the current Prophet. All true Prophets of God work together and help one another to do God's work. Departed Prophets cannot teach physically, in the physical, because they do not have a physical body. This is why it is both necessary and beneficial having a Living Teacher.**

All the testimonies in this book were written by my students at the Guidance for a Better Life retreat center. It is here that the nature of God, the Holy Spirit, and the nature of Soul are EXPERIENCED under the guidance of a true living Prophet of God. God and His Prophet are NOT disparaging of any religion of love. However, the more a path defines itself with its teachings, dogma, or tenets, the more "walls" it inadvertently creates between the seeker and God. Sometimes it even puts God into a smaller box. God does not fit in any box. Prophet is for all Souls and is purposely not officially aligned with any path, but shows respect to all.

YOU can truly have an ABUNDANT LIFE through a personal and loving relationship with God, the Holy Spirit, and God's ordained Prophet. This is my primary message to you. Having a closer relationship with the Divine requires understanding the "Language of the Divine." God expresses His Love to us, His children, in many different and sometimes very subtle ways. Often His Love goes unrecognized and unaccepted because His language is not well known. The testimonies in this book will show you both the "Keys in Action" and some of the ways in which God expresses His Love. It is my hope that in reading this book, you have begun to learn more of the "Language of the Divine." The stories span from very subtle Divine guidance to profound examples of experiencing God up close and very personal. **After reading this book I hope you will know your relationship with God has the potential to be more profound, more personal, and more loving than any organized religion on Earth currently teaches, however good and true.**

If you wish to develop a relationship with God's Prophet, seek the inner side of Prophet, for he is spiritually already with you. Few are able to meet the current physical incarnation, and most people do not need to meet Prophet physically. Gently sing HU for a few minutes and then sing "Prophet" with love in your heart and he will respond. It may take time to recognize his presence, but it will come. The Light and Love that flows through him is the same that has flowed through all of God's true Prophets. A more abundant life awaits you.

Study Guidance: Accepting that God always has one of His chosen, trained, and spiritually empowered Prophets on Earth is, for some, difficult to accept due to fear or misunderstanding. Perhaps viewing this truth in another, but familiar, way might help: **For God so loves the world that He never leaves us alone waiting for help, but He always ensures one of His Prophets is available for those who desire to learn more of His ways and truths and are longing to come Home to Him, Our Father.**

The challenge is finding God's Prophet, then determining if the Prophet is true, raised up and ordained by God, or just someone calling himself a prophet. This is where having learned to trust your heart can greatly help you to know the truth. You, as Soul, will resonate with truth. Some may claim to be a true Prophet of God, but that does not make their claim credible. Interestingly, there are two-hundred and twenty-seven verses in the KJV of the Bible about Prophets, **most about God's true Prophets.** Less are about false Prophets, and those references are mostly in Revelation. Today many people who hear the word Prophet automatically assume a FALSE prophet. Just because false prophets may exist does not change the magnificent gift of love God gives the world: God will still ALWAYS have one of His true Prophets available for those receptive and those not deceived.

Prophet, The Spiritual Master Key, is involved in almost every one of the one-hundred and thirty-five stories found in the "Keys in Action" sections of this book. Perhaps those testimonies will help you consider accepting the ultimate gift of God's Love, His Prophet. **Those who have developed a loving relationship with God's**

Prophet "know that their relationship with Prophet is the Key to everything good."

Spiritual Exercise: To reach out to Prophet sing HU for a while and then softly sing "*Prophet, Prophet, Prophet, Prophet…*" for a while. In time you will learn to recognize his response. One of the ways to recognize Prophet's response to this spiritual exercise is seeing a flash of blue colored light. Other ways might include the feeling of peace, warmth, comfort, or experiencing spiritual light.

Note: Perhaps now is a good time to go to "My Father's Journey" in the appendix on page 469 to read about Del Hall's long journey to become God's Prophet.

Three-Part Prayer

The "Three-Part Prayer" can become a way of life that improves one's relationship with Prophet and solidifies the truth that God Loves YOU. One's relationship with Prophet is the key to spiritual growth and an abundant life. That is why God always has one of His Prophets on Earth. Being in the inner or outer presence of Prophet can also bring spiritual nourishment. **The primary purpose of this spiritual exercise however, is to help you savor and recognize God's Love being demonstrated throughout the day.** The love can come in many different ways and since Prophet is the primary deliverer of God's Love and blessings this exercise will help you recognize both God's Love for you, and the daily presence of Prophet. **A secondary purpose of this exercise is to develop gratitude for your blessings.**

Nightly prayer:

1. Reflect upon all the things you are grateful for from today. Accept that they were all gifts of love from God given and delivered through His Prophet. This serves as a reminder that Prophet was with you all day.

2. Ask Prophet for a dream or any experience that will help your relationship with Prophet grow.

3. Tell Prophet you will be receptive. This means you will be watchful and receptive for the answer to this prayer for the next few days. As you begin to recognize Prophet's response you will know you are heard by him. This begins to develop an inner communication with Prophet you can rely upon.

You may start doing this spiritual exercise/prayer at night before falling asleep. Over time and with a little effort this "Three-Part Prayer" will begin to be done throughout the entire day. You will begin to more quickly recognize blessings such as protection, comfort, life going more smoothly, and guidance. In other words, you will more quickly recognize the "Hand of God" in your life. It will become easier to see your blessings from God being delivered through His Prophet. This has the potential to build a strong, loving, trusting, and sacred relationship with Prophet, while also helping you to realize you are never alone. It is also a reminder that Prophet is always with you and there for you. Remember, **Prophet is a concentrated aspect of God's Holy Spirit, and being in and recognizing this special presence is uplifting and beneficial in many ways. The benefits of building a relationship go beyond any Prophet's individual personality.**

Study Guidance: To more fully accept the blessings from God, you have to recognize them in the first place. To recognize Prophet delivering God's blessings throughout the day can help build a loving and trusting relationship with God's Prophet, **if that is your desire**. Those who do have such a relationship with Prophet truly know it is the Key to everything good in life.

Spiritual Protection

God takes care of and protects His own. If you follow the teachings of God that Prophet shares, you automatically have a certain amount of Divine protection. As a coworker with Prophet you are on God's team. As such, you do not have to ask to be taken care of or your needs to be fulfilled; a follower of God's ways receives without needing to ask. **However, it is important and still your responsibility to use good judgment and discernment to avoid confrontations, situations, certain people, and entanglements that could lead to problems.**

When one is a serious student of God's Prophet they receive protection and guidance. However, the negative power Satan does what it can to keep people away from God and His teachings. That is one of his jobs and purpose. **Satan has little actual power over you, but he is a master of using deception and trickery to make you think he is in charge or has power over you.** Sometimes Satan uses people such as psychic workers or others to stir up emotional waves and disturbances. This causes hardships, which can infect the mind and body. Stay away from these types of people and situations; they are being used by the negative power to slow or block your spiritual growth, often by putting a wedge between you and Prophet.

Using discernment to avoid unnecessary interaction with such people and putting your faith in God's Prophet offers protection. If you believe someone is sending you negative energy, a psychic attack, try one of the following spiritual exercises:

1. Imagine a large mirror around you that faces away and toward the sender of negative energy. Imagine any negativity being reflected back to the sender. The negative energy will be deflected away from you. The Divine will decide if the energy is just deflected or goes back to the sender, not you.

2. Visualize God's white Light completely surrounding you and protecting any harm from coming to you. Know Prophet is within

the light with you. Picture him in his physical form smiling and offering you his hands to hold onto.

3. Imagine you are surrounded by a golden bubble of God's Love and protection.

Knowing and speaking scripture out loud can provide protection, confidence, comfort, and remind you of your priorities. In extreme situations state firmly out loud: "I belong to God, I choose Prophet, I reject Satan, I am yours God, I am on God's team." Repeat this, or a version of this, many times if you feel you are under a negative attack from Satan; it is very effective.

Protection does not mean challenges and lessons of life are removed. Some situations are allowed to happen to build strength, learn a lesson when we are the "effect," or to work off karma (The Key Cause and Effect and the Key Karma will be covered in Step Four). Remember you are never given more than you can find a solution for if you are willing to stretch and grow. Try to recognize this protection during events and challenges.

Study Guidance: Once again, staying spiritually nourished will help improve your decisions, thereby reducing the chance of making poor decisions that lead to unpleasant or compromising situations. If you are following the ways of God with Prophet you do not need to worry excessively about protecting yourself. However, it is always good to be alert rather than naive.

Reverence

1. Attitude of deep respect tinged with awe, more than gratitude and appreciation.
2. Outward manifestation; act of demonstrating through actions.
3. Demonstration of deep respect; being receptive, remembering the blessings given, using the spiritual tools available.
4. One should have reverence for God, His ways, path, truth, and His chosen Prophet.
5. Have reverence for oneself as SOUL, you are a child of God.

Soul innately has reverence for the ways of God! It is the mind that lacks the ability to truly revere both God and our true identity, Soul. Over time an individual under the guidance of God's Prophet will begin to operate more as Soul, their true eternal self. As this transition takes place one will begin to notice gratitude evolving more into appreciation and then into reverence. Reverence for God and His ways, truth, and path will come with spiritual growth. Reverence for God's Prophet is demonstrating reverence for God. With true reverence one's spiritual view and understandings will take a giant step forward. **Reverence is experienced!**

To truly experience reverence one must be operating as Soul, which is not a likely possibility when one first gets onto the path. So start with being grateful for the teachings and experiences given. Find gratitude for Prophet being willing to guide and assist, instruct, correct misunderstandings, and share the ways of God with you. Over time gratitude will evolve into appreciation of the teachings. **Appreciation means you are starting to understand the VALUE of the spiritual experiences and lessons given that add abundance in your life.**

One cannot make oneself have reverence for God's teachings or His Prophet. The ability to experience reverence is a gift from God, **but one can learn and practice gratitude.** Relax, there will come a time when every fiber of your being will want to fall to your knees in front of God and give thanks for your very existence! **This is when you become the most receptive and can be taught the innermost secrets of God.** You are the limiting factor to what God can reveal to you. Until one operates more fully as Soul, experiencing true reverence is unlikely.

There is no rush; again, relax and practice gratitude. Gratitude is best demonstrated through your actions, such as staying consistently nourished, reading Prophet's books, watching his videos, and by studying and reviewing the Spiritual Keys. **Often your actions most clearly express your priorities!**

Study Guidance: Reverence is a profound experience of Soul. This experience is a gift from God and will happen in due time. Start with developing an attitude of gratitude, and remember gratitude is best when it is demonstrated through your actions.

God's Love

Knowing for certain that God exists and truly loves you is the most solid foundation upon which to build one's life. No matter what life brings, knowing God's Love for you brings the ability to persevere. Knowing God loves you just the way you are, and will ALWAYS love you, provides the ultimate security in one's life.

One of the main reasons we incarnate on Earth is to learn to both give and receive love in its many forms. For many people accepting love from another person can be difficult, let alone from their Heavenly Father. After thirty years of providing spiritual mentoring, I have found that early on most of my students were better at giving love rather than receiving love. It has taken years for some to be comfortable accepting love, even though deep down they want love. For example, if a person has a hard time accepting a compliment, it is often a sign they have a difficult time accepting love from another person. Imagine how much more love is available from God. To repeat, **one of the main reasons we incarnate on Earth is to learn to both give and receive love in its many forms.**

There are different levels of knowing God's Love. One's foundation on this path and in daily life is more solid the more certain they are in knowing God's Love and in their ability to accept it. Scripture that assures us of His Love is one type of knowing. However confident in the truth found in scripture, this level of knowing is a mental concept. **Learning to recognize God's Love in one's daily life goes beyond a mental concept into personal experiences.** (Remember the Three-Part Prayer) Experiencing love is more "solid" and brings certainty in one's knowing more than reading about it or being told that God loves you.

Many of the Spiritual Keys condition one to be able to recognize and accept more love: Singing HU daily, the Three-Part Prayer, Gratitude, God's Prophet, Receptive, Contemplation, Prayer, Spiritual Food, Prophet's Inner Presence, and Blending With God's Voice all help one grow in the ability to accept Divine love. Additionally, Prophet's suggested and/or guided spiritual exercises provide opportunities to actually recognize, experience, and accept

God's Love for oneself. Over time and with many experiences given in just the right order and amount, one grows stronger in the ability to accept love. Eventually Prophet takes those Souls he personally mentors into the Heavens, where the love of God is concentrated at God's Temples of Learning, and even to the twelfth Heaven, the Abode of God Himself. Now one experiences God's Love up close and very personal, and it is far beyond any mental concept.

To have the Heavenly Father tell one face-to-face that He cherishes them is the ultimate experience and assurance of His Love. Prophet can only take Soul, not one's physical body, to God's Abode for such an experience. Now one has the most solid foundation and certainty of God's Love to build a life upon. For many people the above discussion may be difficult to accept. Later in this book you will have the opportunity to read more about these types of experiences and explore what is possible.

One of the most important teachings of God's Prophet is that God loves every Soul He created. **We literally exist because God loves us!** This core truth is so important for Souls to accept that it is woven into nearly all Prophet's teachings. All my books, videos, and podcasts demonstrate this over and over again in countless ways.

In all the years I have mentored people I have noticed many have a deep feeling of being unworthy of love, and especially of God's Love. It often takes years of help for those feelings to dissipate. God helps me find and understand the root of those feelings of unworthiness, but I also find it so sad. I absolutely KNOW God loves each of us, His children, at a level none may ever be able to fully grasp or comprehend. **The good news is that those feelings can be removed and then God's Love is eagerly accepted.**

Study Guidance: It takes time and effort to more fully accept just how much the Heavenly Father truly loves you. **This is one of the most important and primary roles of God's Prophet!** Many of the Spiritual Keys condition you to give and receive more love in general, and help you recognize and accept more of God's Love specifically.

Spiritual Exercise: Look for a small area in your life that is an example of not being able to accept love, such as not being able to accept a compliment or finding it difficult to accept help, and start there. Practice growing in those areas, stretching a bit with each opportunity. It may not seem like much, but it's cumulative, and it will make a difference in your life.

Step Three Keys in Action

An Awakening

We can experience the Light of God in the waking state or, like in the following example, the dream state. Either way, our initial experiences with the Light are often to "wake us up" from our slumber and inspire us to make the journey home to God. It is the Love of God that draws us home.

A little over ten years ago I attended my first retreat at Guidance for a Better Life called "Wild Edible Plant Weekend." I did not know at the time how much this choice would transform my life in beautiful abundant ways. All I knew was that I was looking forward to spending a weekend in the mountains away from the everyday humdrum of city life. Upon arrival I felt something special about this place. Peace had entered my heart, and I enjoyed the beauty that surrounded me. On the surface this was just a wild edible plant class, but I felt something deeply spiritual stir within me that weekend.

After the class I had a vivid dream of flying down the gravel road that leads to the retreat center. I saw Del, who I now know is a true Prophet of God, and his wife Lynne, sitting on a bench outside their home. As I flew towards them they stood up, and I saw beautiful white light shine around them. The light was stunning and would have been too much for human eyes, but through the eyes of Soul I found this light welcoming and nurturing. I said, "I don't know why I am here," and they replied, "Well, we are glad that you came." This was the Light of God shining through them to me, and the love, Divine love, I felt flowing from them awakened the true me, Soul, a Divine spark of God.

This dream was a gift of love from God through His Prophet to help me "wake up" spiritually. The spiritual tools Del has taught me for the past ten years have allowed me to accept my divinity as Soul and make God a reality in my life. This precious and sacred gift of knowing from experience that my Heavenly Father loves me and has sent His Prophet to show me my way Home is something I cannot keep to myself. My heart sings to be an instrument of God to give and receive Divine love so other Souls, like you perhaps, may awaken to your Divine nature as well and truly know God loves you and that His Prophet is here to help show you your way Home.

Written by Shanna Canine

Keys in this story: Soul, God's Prophet, God's Love (shared by the inner Prophet), Gratitude

Keys not yet studied: Prophet's Inner Presence

Meeting My Husband in a Dream

Often we are given the "eyes to see" at the perfect time in our journey through life. There is no sense in losing sleep just because we did not recognize it earlier. Trust that God's timing is perfect, and He knows when we are ready to accept the blessing He has to offer.

Have you ever had the experience where more is shared and understood by looking someone in the eyes than by any words exchanged? I was given a dream in which I do not recall any words being spoken, but what was said through a glance altered my life more than any other dream I have had. During a dream over ten years ago my teacher, the Prophet, introduced me to my future husband. While I had known Chris as a fellow student at Guidance for a Better Life for almost five years, our conversations had remained casual, nothing more. We both had been in prior relationships and had not seen more than a friendship and a common love of the retreat center between us.

In the dream the Prophet was standing before me looking at me with so much love. He knows me so well, has known me forever,

136

and wants what is best for me and to see me truly happy. With love in his eyes Prophet stepped to the side and allowed me to see who stood beside him. Chris stood there with love in his eyes. At this silent introduction Prophet brought us together in this life. I knew in that unspoken moment that we had loved each other many times before. What was shared without any words was, "Here is someone whom you love and someone who loves you dearly too."

Shortly after this dream Chris and I went on our first date. This dream has become part of our history: ten years and three beautiful children later. But our story did not begin with my dream, it began many lifetimes ago. The dream gave me a remembrance of what once was and a premonition of what could be, all in the eyes of the Prophet and my future husband. And while I did not decide to marry him based on this one dream, it was definitely the threshold that opened my eyes to recognize him as the man I love. It was an opportunity to grow in our love for God by learning to express Divine love with each other once again.

As eternal beings, the love connections we share with our loved ones span space and time. The love that builds and grows in one lifetime leads to the next. It creates bonds of love that transcend beyond the confines of the physical world. The Divine reconnects us with those we love as a gift of love. We are given opportunities to heal past hurts and celebrate the joy of life together.

It is by the Grace of God I was given this opportunity to be with my beloved Chris. Thank you Prophet for knowing me so well and introducing me in a dream to the man whom I have loved so many times before and whom I dearly love now. It is a gift that has made me truly happy.

Written by Molly Comfort

Keys in this story: God's Prophet, Soul (in dream), God's Grace (giving Molly clarity of loving Chris before), God's Love (reuniting Chris and Molly), Remembrance

Keys not yet studied: Truth is Love, Prophet's Inner Presence, Karma

Shackled to Ball and Chain

*Your ability to grow spiritually is directly proportional to your
ability to accept truth. This can be more difficult when it is about
yourself and not flattering. However, if you wish to be freed of the
things holding you back you have to first be able to accept they are
there. The truth can then set you free.*

About a year and a half ago, I had a life-changing healing by
God's Grace. For several months I had been in a funk. I knew
something was off, but I did not know what it was or how to fix it. I
wanted to make changes in my life — switching jobs, moving, etc. I
was caught up in thinking only about myself, and my actions were
reflecting my self-indulgence. Spiritually, I was lazy and acting like
a juvenile. I was spinning my wheels spiritually and felt like I was
stuck. When you stop moving forward spiritually, you cannot stay
in one place, you tend to slide backwards; that is exactly what I was
doing. I was allowing negative thoughts into my consciousness, and
these were turning into a self-fulfilling prophecy.

During a retreat at Guidance for a Better Life my teacher lovingly
pointed out to me how I had allowed my foggy thinking to get me
"into a real pickle." He gave me a lot of truth about myself, and with
God's help I was able to hear the truth and begin to accept it. The
clear truth from my teacher was an answer to a prayer that had been
in my heart. Even though I was not fully aware of how much of a
mess I had created with my negative thoughts, I knew I needed help
from the Divine and God read my heart.

After class was over for the evening, I walked down to the pond
and sat on a bench. I sang HU for a while and begged for the Divine
to help me learn this lesson, see more clearly, and begin moving
forward spiritually again. I wanted to overcome this "hiccup" and
put it in the past. When I stopped talking, I then spiritually saw a
shackle around my neck with a long chain and a ball attached to it. I
saw the bright white Light of God around me, and then it became
more intense and focused. It looked like a laser beam. The laser
beam of God's Love burned through the shackle that was around me,

and I was released. I surrendered whatever the ball and shackle represented to the Divine and knew I had been given a gift from God. If I were to focus on that shackle and feel bad for whatever it was it would have been counterproductive and self-indulgent.

I still do not know to this day what the shackle was, and I am fine with that. By the Divine Grace of God, I was free. God read my heart and also heard my prayer that night. I am no longer caught up by my foggy thinking and am spiritually growing and moving forward again.

Thank you God for hearing all of my prayers and answering those in my best interest.

Written by Michelle K. Reuschling

Keys in this story: Attitudes and Thoughts, God's Prophet (teacher), Receptive, HU, God's Love, God's Grace (provided healing), Gratitude

Keys not studied yet: Truth is Love, Prayer, Personal Effort

Prayer to Find a Job

Many times our prayers are heard, and answered, but we miss taking the steps needed to make them a reality. The Divine will guide us in the direction to answer our prayers, but we will never get there if we cannot "hear" the guidance. It pays, literally — in the following story, to learn how to listen to those gentle whisperings.

I had a sincere prayer in my heart to find a new job and I expressed this in prayer to God. I realized it would not happen without some effort on my part, so I polished my resume and applied for a couple jobs in the area I was interested in living. After receiving some mild interest from one company, and some weeks passing by, I decided to apply to a few more positions. I got a call one Tuesday from a company requesting a one-hour phone interview. The company was located four hours from my home, but it just so happened I was going to be traveling to that area the upcoming weekend, so I was available for an on-site interview. To me an in-person interview was much better than a phone interview. The Divine was already helping! I have come to learn from Prophet that apparent "coincidences" are not just luck or by chance, rather they are blessings from the Divine. The timing to my interview was one such blessing.

After confirming a meeting time, I started preparing for the interview. I prayed to God for help and sang HU to get in tune with the Divine. What questions should I be prepared to answer? What questions do I ask of them? I researched the company and the position. I anticipated some of the questions that I might be asked, and I rehearsed my responses the best I could, but the possibilities were endless. All through this process I felt Del, the Prophet, guide me to very specific questions.

The morning of the interview I sang HU, invited Prophet to be with me, and surrendered the outcome. This was very comforting because I trusted the outcome would be perfect regardless if it resulted in a job offer or not. The hiring manager explained this was a time for them to get to know me and for me to learn if this was a position that interested me — this was precisely the insight I received during my preparation! As the interview progressed, I was asked ten questions, and of the countless questions that could have been asked in an interview, I had rehearsed and prepared for every one of the ten. Prophet had prepared me for those exact questions, an answer to my prayer. The interview conversation flowed naturally, and everyone seemed to be at ease. This experience is one of the many over the years that have confirmed my prayers are heard! God loves us and wants us to live happy and abundant lives, in all areas of life.

Written by Chris Hibshman

Keys in this story: HU, God's Prophet (shared God's Love by preparing Chris for the interview), God's Love

Keys not yet studied: Prayer, Personal Effort, Connecting Spiritual Events

Divine Healing After Divorce

Within the Heavenly realms exist spiritual temples. Places where the truth of God is kept pure, safe from the polluting minds of men. With the proper guide you can spiritually travel to these sacred temples to gain in wisdom, understanding, or in the following case, to receive healing. The price of admission — an open heart.

Divorce can be a difficult experience that may take one a while to work through on different levels. For me it took time and was a process of grieving, healing, and learning to let go. Divine Spirit helped me work through this difficult period in a positive and constructive way by giving me many dreams and other inner experiences. They helped me to keep my heart open, be fair and honest when interacting with my former husband, and sincerely wish him well in his life ahead.

A major healing came while I was at a three-day day spiritual retreat at Guidance for a Better Life. Del, my spiritual teacher who is a true Prophet of God, was guiding us on an inner experience where we were blessed with a sacred opportunity. We were spiritually taken to visit one of the spiritual Temples of Learning that exist in the vast inner worlds of God. These temples are a place where Souls can go to learn, be healed, gain insight, or have other experiences that help them in some way, but one can only get there if taken by an authorized agent of God.

As Del guided us to the temple in our Soul bodies, I noticed a sense of lightness like I was flying. I trusted him, so although this was like exploring new spiritual territory, I did not hesitate to follow. I arrived in what looked like a large rotunda with many arched windows and velvet tapestry. Light streamed into the room from all directions. It was not ordinary physical light, it was the Light of God that illuminated the temple. There was a podium that looked like it should hold a holy book, but instead there was a fountain on it. My former husband was there, he cupped his hands, took water from the fountain and poured it over his head. I looked down at his ankle and heard four links of a chain that had been there fall to the floor. I went to the fountain and did the same, taking some of its living water and poured it over my head. He helped me dry my face, and we agreed all was as it should be as we journeyed separately on our own paths. I said goodbye to him as we left.

This occurred nearly four years after our divorce. God knows us better than we know ourselves. Although outwardly I had gone on with my life, I was still attached at some level and afraid to let go. This experience was a healing one because afterwards, I felt as if I was able to release something I was holding onto. The chain links falling to the floor made me think that perhaps past life karmic ties between us may have also been undone as well. I do not think I could fully comprehend all that happened, but I know the magnitude of the blessings were awesome. I felt freedom and strength and had courage to move on. The healing waters of the fountain, an aspect of Divine Spirit, originate in the Abode of God, the source of God's unlimited Love and Mercy. It was truly out of God's great Love and bountiful Grace and Mercy that this miraculous healing could take place when I was ready, and it was through the Prophet that this became so.

I treasure this sacred experience, and the very real impact it had on my life. This was an important turning point for me. I am ever grateful for Prophet's inner and outer spiritual guidance that helped resolve the situation in a way that was mutually beneficial to my former husband and me. I am so appreciative of the ways he helped me keep an open heart, soothe the pain, guide me through the grieving process, and let go of unnecessary entanglements. Being able to finally move forward with confidence and being at peace with the past was indeed a very precious gift. Thank you!

Written by Lorraine Fortier

Keys in this story: God's Prophet, Soul (traveled to temple), God's Love (Holy water and temple light), God's Grace (healings), Gratitude, HU (before traveling to temple)

Keys not yet studied: Balance and Detachment, Karma, Prophet's Inner Presence

I Am Free to Be Me

*One of the greatest attributes Soul has been created with is the
ability to communicate with God. Having this constant lifeline of love
and guidance as you go through your day can make life a joy to live.
All Souls have the potential for this communication, but it must be
nurtured. Similar to when learning a new language, it takes time and
is much easier when you have a teacher who is fluent.*

Lately I have been looking back in my life and realizing the hand
of the Divine and Its loving presence has been with me all along.
The presence of an inner guide or inner teacher has been right there
with me guiding and protecting me all through my life. As I grew in
strength spiritually, I began to recognize and notice the Divine
presence of the Holy Spirit in every incident and aspect of my life!
God has a plan custom designed just for ME!

I first learned about the constant presence of the Prophet during
retreats at Guidance for a Better Life. I learned the Voice of God,
Holy Spirit, was working through him! It was astounding to know
God knows my every thought and prayer! At first I was very weak
at this recognition. It was like making a commitment to exercise, to
get in physical shape. I worked with the skills I learned at the retreat
center, very weakly at first. As the weakness faded the inner part of
the Prophet's presence grew stronger. As His presence grew stronger
I began to have one-sided conversations with the Divine, my side at
first! Over time I talked to God and began to LISTEN. Now as I
listened to the inner guidance I could hear suggestions coming
through, solutions, and long sought answers. Sometimes when I first
awaken I will receive an insight to a question I asked the night
before.

I learned and became skilled at recognizing how my sleeping and
awake dreams were customized to help me understand an answer to
a prayer. They were alerting me to a solution I was seeking.
Sometimes a seemingly random conversation was of importance,
even a license plate word would be of significance, a clue to what I
had asked. I grew to understand even the timing of an answer was of

great value. I was now ready to hear Divine guidance, which of course, was in my best interest, always knowing I still had free will to choose.

The confidence I have now, the knowingness, the really knowing with all my heart God hears me is a gateway to a life filled with love and freedom to be just me! It is a comfort beyond all measure. I will ask you this; what if God knows you so well that He knows your every thought and prayer? What if He hears and knows your every word and deed? How would you live your life? Would you live it differently? Would you be grateful to know how very much you are loved and guided?

I know God loves me just the way I am or I would not exist. And to recognize He hears and knows me so personally, better than I know myself, and really cares how my life progresses is a very extraordinary gift. The blessings in my life are endless since I woke up and recognized the loving presence of the Prophet in my life and the personal closeness we have developed together.

I love my life!

Written by Nancy Nelson

Keys in this story: Spiritual Strength, God's Love, Gratitude, Growth of Consciousness

Keys not yet studied: Prophet's Inner Presence, Prayer, Living Without Doubt, Connecting Spiritual Events, Personal Effort (she made a commitment to practice the skills she learned at retreats)

Truth Accepted Set Me Free

The truth can truly set us free. But first we must be fortunate enough to be in the presence of someone adept at delivering the truth — no matter what that truth might be. Secondly, we must be able to accept the truth — even if it takes time. There is no way to move beyond the things that are holding us back and grow spiritually if we cannot accept truth.

The idea of being a blessing to others captivated my heart during a winter retreat at Guidance for a Better Life. At the time I was often tense and uptight and took myself a little too seriously. I suffered from a deep insecurity that often manifested as thinking a little too highly of myself. In covering up the low opinion that was underneath I often pushed away the very love I craved; certain deep down that I was unworthy.

That weekend I was given a life-changing gift from Prophet. A healing from God delivered by Prophet is incredibly personal. It is delivered precisely and perfectly in the way that fits us best in that moment. Whether it is delivered gently or sharply does not diminish the love that accompanies it. That weekend Del spoke to me very directly. He did not sugar coat it nor soften it. He said what must have been obvious to everyone but me — that when it came to love, I was in my own way.

To the human consciousness correction can often be scary, something to avoid at the very least. It is a precious gift to have a living Prophet, a teacher who can correct mistaken concepts about love, encourage adjustments in our attitudes, and point out passions of the mind that limit not only our freedom but also our ability to give and receive love — one of Soul's main joys in life! The Bible verse about truth setting us free is very real! A correction of even a small fraction can pay huge dividends down the road of life and can be not only life altering, but occasionally lifesaving.

That weekend I did not hear the blessing and love that came with those words. Yet Prophet had seen a small opening and adeptly planted a seed. Despite my inability to hear it at that time the message was still delivered. A short time after I got home from the retreat a remarkable thing occurred. That little seed began to grow and a wonderful insight blossomed. What had seemed muddled now became clear. I saw the love behind the correction. It was not done to make me feel or look bad, it was done to help free me. It was exactly the answer I needed, but I had not recognized the form it took. I falsely believed love was always supposed to come in a soft and gentle manner. Yet here I was, after a few words that were direct and to the point, happier and freer for it.

I now saw love from a new perspective. Love is like breathing. It flows in, and like a breath of air it must flow out again. In looking back with a little bit clearer perspective at how I was "breathing," it seemed to me I was making myself hyperventilate! Wasn't breathing, like giving and receiving love, often best when it is natural and relaxed — when I was not focusing on the fact I was doing it?

Del has often said that he craves the truth no matter what. The first time I heard that I was shocked. "But what if it makes you look bad?" I thought to myself. It took me years to see the wisdom in his words. It has inspired me to consciously seek and embrace truth whenever it graces my life. The experience at this retreat was a big step toward accepting more truth, not from the skeptical, vain perspective of the mind but from the mature viewpoint of Soul. Over time, with the Prophet's help, guidance, and continued correction, the healing and insight from this experience transformed my initial reluctance into an innate appreciation and desire for God's truth.

Written by Chris Comfort

Keys in this story: God's Prophet, Receptive, Growth of Consciousness, Soul, God's Love (delivered through Prophet), Gratitude

Keys not yet studied: Truth is Love

Blue Light Brought Peace

We are not alone. God loves us and always has a living Prophet here on Earth to help, teach, protect, and comfort us. Ultimately — to lead us home to God. This Divine Guide can appear to you as a blue light in your inner vision or in the physical itself. Either way, it is joyous proof of being loved and not alone.

When I first moved away from home it was a very stressful time. I was in a totally new area and everything was unfamiliar. The stresses of moving, plus my first college classes, were taking a toll. I was having a hard time finding a new balance, so I prayed for help.

One night I was sitting in my dorm room working on homework. Out of the corner of my eye, I saw a brilliant flash of blue light. It was accompanied by a profound sense of peace. From the spiritual teachings I had received at Guidance for a Better Life, I knew this was no ordinary light, it was the Light of God; referred to in so many spiritual scriptures. The Light of God is one of the special ways in which God communicates to us. The blue light in particular indicated the presence of a high-level spiritual guide, Prophet. His presence also brought the profound sense of peace, the peace that I had been so hungry for and had prayed for.

Twenty-four hours later, I stepped foot on the property of Guidance for a Better Life for another weekend retreat. I know the Prophet used the blue light to prepare me to get the most out of the weekend. This retreat was the beginning of a whole new leg of not only my spiritual journey, but my life! It brought joy and balance back into my life. Now I know that a spiritual guide is always with me, an ever-present source of comfort, guidance, protection, and inspiration.

Written by David Hughes

Keys in this story: God's Prophet, God's Love (His Light and peace), Spiritual Growth

Keys not yet studied: Balance and Detachment, Prophet's Inner Presence (blue light), Prayer, Connecting Spiritual Events, Living Without Doubt

Dream Before the Dream

Soul incarnates into the physical world over many lifetimes to learn more about giving and receiving love. The wide variety of experiences we have (which depends a lot on the role we play in that particular life) help us to grow in consciousness and become more spiritually mature. The lifetimes when we are fortunate enough to be in Prophet's physical presence our opportunity for spiritual growth is exponential.

When I first started attending classes at Guidance for a Better Life in 1998 I lived in North Carolina and in another state of consciousness. I had a tendency of residing in victim consciousness along with a poor attitude. After nearly a year without taking any classes at the school, my then significant other suddenly was offered a job in Charlottesville, Virginia, and we moved shortly afterwards in the spring of 2003. Over the next number of months I would run into several students from the school, and I always knew when they had just been up to a spiritual retreat. The Light of God shone brighter in their eyes.

The first ten months after the move I worked various temporary jobs, many in the financial planning arena. After one of the temporary jobs ended abruptly, I found myself doing some deep soul searching. I surrendered on the inner and made a commitment to take responsibility for my spiritual growth and not let it be governed by my significant other. It was a pivotal time for me. In response, the Divine gave me several potent dreams over the next several days.

One Wednesday night I attended a book discussion and talked afterwards with one of the students from the school. I shared a dream with him. He told me about an upcoming class that following weekend and encouraged me to call the school. I was hesitant; it had been a long time since I had been in touch. Yet, I got strong inner guidance to call Thursday evening, and by Friday evening I was back up at the school! I was welcomed with so much love. I felt like the prodigal daughter!

Early in the weekend we sang HU as a group, a beautiful love song to God, and surrendered the weekend to the Divine. This gathering took place under a starry blanket of clear sky, out in the field by the log cabins. Del suggested we "raise up" in consciousness as Soul and look down at our physical bodies below. I could see our small group in a circle as Soul, each a beautiful glowing ball of light. I found myself getting very excited as this was what had transpired in my dream earlier in the week! I was living my dream!

Later in the weekend I had an opportunity to share my experience and my dream in class. Del "casually" asked me about another dream the night prior to this dream, but in that moment I could not recall it. It piqued my curiosity though, so I looked back through my dream journal. Sure enough, there it was… a most beautiful dream with Del in it! From this I gained a much deeper appreciation of Del's role as a spiritual teacher ordained by God (Del was ordained by God in 1999 but not yet His Prophet until 2012). Del could teach and guide us in our everyday lives on the outer and could also come and work with us on the inner. Through the guidance of the Holy Spirit he can be aware of both!

In this dream Del and I were examining a huge collage, an exquisitely beautiful tapestry on the wall of various hues and textures. He commented that it was impressive, I replied saying it included all aspects of my life. The weave was quite stunning and could be representative of all the lifetimes I have lived as Soul, with each lifetime a unique patch: as a whole, a very lovely tapestry. Over lifetimes I have had the opportunity to live a full spectrum of experiences, including living in various countries of the world, both as female and male, all races and colors, and in a variety of walks of life… an amalgam of life on Earth that brought lessons of living. Now through God's Grace I have the opportunity to be guided by and be in the presence of a God-ordained teacher. What an amazing journey and opportunity of lifetimes!

Throughout lifetimes Prophets of God, including Jesus as the Son of God, have been wayshowers to guide us back to God, our Father. It is a very precious gift to be guided back to God. God waits patiently, and if need be for lifetimes, until we exercise our free will and choose to draw nigh to Him. Just that quick we are welcomed back and lovingly blessed. My life is infinitely better and abundantly blessed by accepting the invitation offered. God and His Prophet love us each dearly and want to develop a close personal relationship. Doing so will transform your life!

Written by Jan Reid

Keys in this story: Attitudes and Thoughts, Soul, Spiritual Growth, HU, God's Grace (being guided by His Prophet), God's Prophet, God's Love (seen in my students' eyes and their presence), Discernment (Jan's decision to return for more growth), Gratitude, Receptive (Jan came back much more receptive and teachable)

Keys not yet studied: Prophet's Inner Presence (in her dreams)

The Prophet Shows His True Self

There are times when the curtain of "reality" is pulled back and we are allowed to see things as they truly are. We will never be shown more truth than we can handle at any given moment. So trust in God's perfect timing that you will "see" when the time is right, and remember — there is always more.

During one of my first retreats at Guidance for a Better Life I was blessed to see the light and love of the Prophet. I was listening to him as he was speaking with another student, and he began to turn into light. His arms and legs began to glow, and then his torso began to change. I watched in amazement as his whole body turned into a ball of light. I was seeing the Prophet as Soul, as his true self. He then turned to face me; I could feel so much love coming through the light he was sending to me. I began to look around the room and noticed no one else seemed to be reacting to this. Everyone was looking directly at the Prophet, but no one appeared to see what I was seeing. This was a gift especially for me.

I turned to my girlfriend, who is now my wife, and she was also showing no reaction to what was happening. I leaned over, whispering, and asked if he did this all the time. She just smiled at me with a knowing look in her eye. Prophet stayed in his Soul body until just before the end of the session. That is when his appearance returned back to his physical body.

After this I learned that Prophet can teach students in many ways. He can teach each one of us individually while at the same time teaching the group as a whole. However he teaches, we all receive the lessons that are right for us. I am so grateful to the Prophet for sharing his light and love with me. (At that early retreat Anthony believed it was Prophet's light and love, however, Prophet was sharing God's Light and Love)

Written by Anthony Allred

Keys in this story: God's Prophet, Soul, God's Grace (to recognize God's Prophet more fully) God's Love (light and love of God shared by Prophet) Receptive (or would not show him), Growth of Consciousness

Keys not yet studied: Prophet's Inner Presence

God, I Love You

Many people would love to know with confidence God loves them. Sadly, many do not. On the other side of the coin — there are folks who would cherish knowing that God receives the love they send in prayer. Singing HU answers both these prayers of the heart.

About twenty years ago HU was first shared with me by my teacher Del, now a God-ordained Prophet. I was stunned. Here was a simple, direct way to send my love to God in a very real and pure way. It was a revelation to me. Not only was God alive, but He loved me. And now I could express my love to Him and He could hear it. It had been a dream of mine my entire life to be able to just once tell God directly that I loved Him. This was a prayer come true.

The HU is something I now sing daily. Whether at home or in the car to and from work, quietly or out loud, it has grown into an integral way of communicating with and nurturing my personal relationship with the Divine. There is also something special about singing HU with a group of people and something different about singing it at Guidance for a Better Life. Here is an experience I had singing HU at the Guidance for a Better Life retreat center.

I am sitting in a room of about fifty people. We sing HU, a love song to God. It's a collage of sound that soon builds in strength and depth and intent with every wave. The harmonies are absolutely blissful. At times the angelic voices around me seem to number in the thousands. At other moments it feels very small and intimate, like it is just God and us. The love is so overwhelming; I do not want to stop. How beautiful it is to hear.

After a while longer, we stop singing, but it does not feel like it has ended. The HU still reverberates. In my heart, I know I am heard. I know I am loved. Thank HU.

Written by Chris Comfort

Keys in this story: HU, God's Love, Growth of Consciousness, Gratitude (thank HU), God's Prophet, Remembrance (twenty years

and still remembers his experience)

Keys not yet studied: Prayer, Personal Effort, Cause and Effect, Spiritual Food, Consistency (daily HU)

Blessed to Be a Witness

Being at the hospital offering love and support to a loved one is a blessing. In the following story the author was not able to be there physically but was taken spiritually by Prophet for a visit. The blessings of God's Love she witnessed went way beyond a single hospital room.

Several years ago my heart was heavy. I had recently found out someone I care about very much had cancer. It had been a long and trying time to get to the diagnosis. Once it came, the doctors very quickly recommended surgery as the best course of action.

I wanted to be there for her, but it was not feasible at the time. My thoughts were with her and her immediate family throughout the entire process. I had a desire to help however I could, so I made family phone calls, coordinated efforts, and sent care packages, but I felt there was more I could be doing. I knew I could pray, so I did.

A couple days after her surgery, I attended a retreat at Guidance for a Better Life. Prophet Del Hall led the group in singing HU, a love song to God. As we sang, God's Love rained down in golden drops of light like a shower washing over me, and I felt so much love. I saw my loved ones at the hospital in and around her bed. I stood next to Prophet in the recovery room and noticed it was filled with Divine love that felt comforting and protecting. My heart smiled with gratitude to know his presence was there. My prayers were answered, and I was blessed with the added gift to actually recognize it. Even though I could not be at the hospital physically during that time, I was able to be there spiritually as Soul, which brought me comfort and peace. I did not know what lay on the journey ahead, but I know she and her family were not alone during that difficult time.

As the experience continued Prophet said, "Let's go," and turned to exit the room. I followed, and as we walked down the hall I saw beams of light gently flow from him to each open doorway. Prophet was passing along God's Love to each person and family. Love, comfort, healing, peace — whatever was needed was individually provided as different manifestations of God's Love from that light. These are such beautiful gifts of God's Love through His Prophet. I watched in awe, seeing in a way I had not before, blessed to witness this sacred act and grateful that Prophet bestows these gifts from God.

This experience was a gift on so many levels. Whether they know it or not, my loved ones were blessed. God's Love filled that room in whatever form they needed — love, comfort, peace, strength, and more. I was fortunate to see it and was comforted knowing Prophet was with them. My prayer was answered to be with them and express my love. At the same time I was able to witness Prophet distributing God's Love to many Souls at the hospital. What a beautiful sight to behold.

God loves us and sends His Prophet to help us. I am blessed to have his inner guidance and outer teachings. They help me experience such things and learn the "Language of the Divine" to understand the blessings. I am so grateful for that. It has changed my life and is available for you too.

Written by Michelle Hibshman

Keys in this story: God's Prophet, God's Love (golden drops of light and God's Love to others in the hospital), HU, Gratitude, Soul, Growth in Consciousness (Michelle's view of Prophet)

Keys not yet studied: Prayer, Prophet's Inner Presence

Witnessing the Voice of God

The experiences we are blessed to have with God, the Prophet, and the Holy Spirit build our trust in the Divine and provide "food for Soul." If they are not only written in our journals, but rather etched in our hearts, we can relive them multiple times, and they will continue to provide spiritual nourishment.

The Prophet is a Divinely inspired teacher who speaks the Word of God. I have witnessed numerous sacred experiences over the years that have solidified my trust in him. Prophet has guided me through my life, and because of this my life has become so abundant with joy, love, clarity, truth, and so many more of the glories of God. Out of all the experiences I have had that have built my trust and faith in the Prophet, this is one that really stands out.

I was blessed to see, with my physical eyes, Prophet speaking as the Voice of God, speaking the true Word of God. I watched as he spoke during a retreat at Guidance for a Better Life, and I saw what I can only describe as the Light of God flowing straight from his mouth. With each word he spoke a beautiful golden light streamed directly from his mouth. The Word of God was manifesting. I blinked my eyes a few times to make sure I was seeing clearly. This was amazing; I could actually see the Light of God physically coming from Prophet's mouth as he was speaking the Word of God.

Reliving this experience continues to amaze me. I am so grateful to have been blessed with an experience similar to those written about in scripture. Being witness to this has fortified my loving relationship with the Prophet.

Written by Emily Allred

Keys in this story: God's Prophet, God's Love (God's Light and Love and wisdom coming out of Prophet), Remembrance, Growth of Consciousness (Emily's view of Prophet), Receptive (or would not show her), Gratitude

Keys not yet studied: Living Without Doubt

Love: My Heart's Desire

*Many overly identify with their earthly human side and forget they
are Soul, a child of God. There is something truly special beneath all
your physical struggles and mental hang-ups. You are not your
shortcomings — you are not your defilements. You are Soul. At your
core you want to serve God and will find the greatest happiness
through giving and receiving love. Fortunately, the opportunities
to do this are endless.*

Many years ago I watched a friend bring her husband a cup of
coffee while he was busy at work. It was a simple act, but profound
in the lessons and insights it has brought me over the years. Back
then, I had a very different perspective on this than I do today. At
the time I saw it as subservient; a duty expected of a woman by a
man. I wondered why he did not get his own coffee. My view was
coming from a low level, so condensed and narrow it distorted
everything, like wearing a pair of broken glasses. I had reduced
something done out of love to a gender thing and, in my ignorance,
could not see the beauty and selflessness demonstrated in this act.

I carried a lot of unhappiness and pain of the heart back then
because this way of living and experiencing life left little room for
love, and it separated me from God and my own Divine nature. We
are so much more than male and female, skin color, religious
affiliation, age, or any other physical or social label. We are Soul!
Eternal beings, created by God and endowed with Divine qualities,
and we are here to learn to give and receive love. From this view of
Soul a boundless expanse exists. When we open our hearts to God's
Love it lifts us to a higher view, and a whole new world of unlimited
possibilities and love awaits. We begin to see the infinite ways love
can be expressed, and appreciate all the ways it may come back to
us, even in something as seemingly small as a cup of coffee. The size
and packaging of the love that's delivered does not make it any more
or less significant. Love is love. Any act motivated by love, big or
small, is special.

Divine love fills my heart and uplifts every aspect of my life
today. It may come directly from an inner experience or through

family and friends, work, laughter, pets, singing of birds, the sunrise… all life. It brings me joy being able to share this love with others. This is my heart's true desire. I am happiest being in service to God and giving of myself, whether it is through compassion or charity to a stranger, listening to a friend, or spending quality time with family. Love is best when demonstrated.

God's Love, Grace, and spiritual guidance through Del, a true Prophet of God, has helped me grow from seeing through "broken glasses" to having the clarity of Soul. In fact, when I first met Del and started attending his retreats at Guidance for a Better Life back in 1995, I did not even know I had a distorted view of love. I was not aware of the ways this was affecting me, and every relationship I had, or how much it was limiting the joys and happiness of life. I did not know the real me, and I certainly did not know what would truly make me happy deep down.

Having the privilege of being Prophet Del Hall's student for the past twenty-five years has brought me this wisdom. It has changed my life and continues to do so, in countless, beautiful, and profound ways. This opportunity is available to you too, and if you wish, Prophet can help you discover your heart's desire.

Written by Lorraine Fortier

Keys in this story: Soul, God's Prophet, Growth of Consciousness, God's Love, Understanding Change, Remembrance (the way she used to be) Gratitude, Attitudes and Thoughts (big change over the years)

Keys not yet studied: Peace of Mind and Heart, Balance and Detachment

Heart of a Child

Our children may be physically young, but as Soul they are just as old as us. They too have access to the higher truths of God and in many ways have less mental hang-ups between themselves and the recognition of those truths. It would be a beautiful thing if parents could help their children grow into the responsibility of adulthood while maintaining a childlike openness to God.

It really is amazing to be a dad to my young children, especially from the perspective of a student at Guidance for a Better Life and Prophet Del Hall. There are truths that have taken me twenty years to learn, that my children know instinctively. They know there is a living God who loves them unconditionally and who communicates with them daily. They know giving is a key to happiness. Witnessing this on a regular basis has blessed me and fills me with a childlike sense of wonder as these Souls play and grow, fuss and argue, and otherwise figure out their way in this physical world. They amaze me daily. One day they will say something that blows me away and the next moment they will act very age-appropriate, like crying because their favorite pajamas which have been worn for the past three days need to be washed, and all the alternative jammies are "just not the same!"

One night at bedtime when my eldest son Liam was two and a half, he called out for me. Often he wanted an additional "one last hug," or he was not quite ready to go to sleep and was trying to coax another bedtime story out of me. I entered his room, which was decorated with a hand-painted mural of an Octopus' Garden, with a friendly eight-legged sentinel watching over his sister's crib. Liam lay on his back with a far-off gaze on his face. He said something in a strong but quiet voice. I was not sure I had heard him correctly so I moved closer and asked him to repeat what he had said. "Prophet is in my heart," he said simply, his hand over his heart in testimony.

His face transcended the moment, the setting of his bedroom, and our roles as father and son in this lifetime. There was an ancientness about him that contrasted with his youthful countenance. He did not speak to me as my son, or as a cute little boy, or even as a human. He spoke to me as Soul, the Divine essence created by God and placed in these physical bodies for the simple purpose of growing in Its ability to give and receive love. There was reverence in his soft voice that melted away my fatigue and the various concerns of my long day. I leaned over and listened intently. "Feel Daddy," he said moving my hand over his chest. "Right here. Feel it?"

Divine truth poured out freely as I witnessed this beautiful Soul connect the Divine and eternal presence of Prophet with his very heartbeat. This was not something I had taught him. He was not regurgitating something he had overheard his parents say. This was truth he brought with him, as Soul, into this body and was simply connecting it to his immediate reality: God is alive and is always with us — as close as our heartbeat — in the form of His chosen Prophet. As Soul, we all know this. When you slow down and listen with the heart of a child, you too can hear the beating of God's Love for you.

Written by Chris Comfort

Keys in this story: God's Prophet, Soul, God's Love, Reverence

Keys not yet studied: Prophet's Inner Presence, Living Without Doubt (Liam is certain Prophet is always with him)

Step Four: Prophet Shares Spiritual Keys

This section is another opportunity to grow spiritually and learn to live life with more balance and harmony. I share Spiritual Keys that will help you more fully manifest your divinity and find more joy in life. These Keys will begin to unlock the door to the Kingdom of Heaven. During this Step God's truths will continue to be revealed. The Keys in this section will provide "seeds," that if nurtured may build an even stronger relationship with the Divine.

The following Keys will be introduced:

Cause and Effect

There are two areas where we need to understand the principle of cause and effect. First, are we spiritually mature and free to be the cause in our daily lives or not really free because we are the effect of others' moods, thoughts, attitudes, or actions? The second area of cause and effect is related to karma. Karma is a spiritual accounting system used by the Divine to account for good actions and not so good actions. Karma influences the lessons we are given in life that help us grow spiritually mature. It determines why we incarnate in a certain family, are male or female, rich or poor, generally healthy or not, live in a more free or wealthy country or poor or restrictive nation.

Let's begin with the first aspect of cause and effect. **As we grow and mature spiritually one of our goals is to become the cause more often than the effect.** For example, let's say we are in a really good and happy mood on our way to school, work, or a family gathering. When we arrive everyone is depressed, unhappy, angry, fearful, agitated, or generally in a low mood. Do we join them in their misery or stay in our happy and joyful mood? If we remain happy in spite of their low mood, we have not allowed ourselves to become the EFFECT. We are free from their moods having a negative effect on us. In fact, if we remain happy, they might begin to feel better, which would be us becoming the CAUSE; even if they do not, we are still the cause of our own happy and joyful state of being.

What if we lose our happy and joyful mood to be like them, in a low mood? If so, we allow their influence to affect us in a very negative way. This would make us both a less mature and less free spiritual being. We not only harm ourselves but lose an opportunity to potentially be a blessing to others by setting a positive example.

Let's say a friend of ours is complaining about their spouse, only focusing on negative thoughts. We join in listing bad attributes of not only their spouse, but now add our spouse into the conversation. Pretty soon we are deep into a "pity party." We start thinking maybe we should leave our spouse. We both go home and begin horrible arguments with our spouses. We have become the EFFECT of our friend's attitude.

What if we had pointed out to our friend some good qualities of their spouse during the rant? The conversation might have gone in a much different direction. When we had gone home we might have felt more love for our own spouse, thereby avoiding the horrible argument. In this example we have become the CAUSE. We not only blessed ourselves and our spouse but potentially blessed our friend and their spouse.

When we are the CAUSE the Divine can use us to potentially bless others. We say potentially used to be a blessing because the other persons do not have to follow our example, but they might choose to. We are now becoming a spiritual coworker. We also have more balance and stability in our own life. **We are exercising our free will when choosing to be the CAUSE, thereby learning to make conscious choices.** Learning to make conscious choices is a form of freedom and the real value of the Key of Cause and Effect. Staying spiritually nourished is an important prerequisite for making conscious choices.

Sometimes we are the effect, for example: of the weather, of political/world events, of people, of driving in heavy traffic, or of other situations not in our control. In these examples we might be the effect physically, but we can still be free internally to be the cause in other ways. **We are still free to choose how we will react to such situations and free to choose what our thoughts and attitude will be. Being spiritually nourished improves our chance of using good discernment and of making the best decision.**

The more attached we are to a certain outcome, the more likely we will become the effect. Detaching from and surrendering the strong desire for a certain outcome frees us from being the effect, regardless of the final outcome.

Examples of cause and effect: drawing close to God, God will respond — staying spiritually nourished, Soul is strengthened — give love freely and love will be returned in some form (Key in Step Six) — prayer, God will respond — gratitude, heart opens — Sing HU a love song to God, will raise you up to a higher view and make you more receptive to the Holy Spirit — study and integrate the Keys into daily life, you will grow spiritually and more fully recognize God's Love.

Study Guidance: The real value of understanding cause and effect is in learning our decisions have consequences, both positive and negative. **A loving God gave us free will, learning to use that free will in the most positive way adds abundance to our lives and the lives of others.**

Karma
(Spiritual Accounting)

Karma is basically an accounting of our actions. Some of our actions in this life, and in past lives, cause harm to or help other Souls or ourselves. This accounts for what we think of as good and bad karma. Those actions then create rewards or retributions. A very simple example is when a parent rewards a child for doing something considered good and when a child receives a penalty for doing something the parent finds not so good. Over time if a parent is fair and consistent the child develops responsibility. The child becomes an emotionally, mentally, and physically well-balanced, happy, mature adult. **In the case of karma, the Divine is impartial, totally fair, and consistent over lifetimes helping Soul to mature spiritually.**

For example, if we were wealthy in a prior life but were abusive to the poor, the Divine might have us reincarnate into a poor family to learn a lesson. If we have unresolved issues with prior family members we might incarnate into another life together to work out the karma created. In an opposite situation, if we have a strong love bond, we might be very blessed to have another physical life together. The Divine makes those decisions for most Souls. These are examples of the karmic kind of cause and effect.

Karma is a blessing to us, not a bad thing. It teaches us responsibility for our actions and thoughts. Most of the lessons of living, both pleasant and unpleasant, involve karma. Some of the circumstances we find ourselves in are due to our actions, attitudes, and thoughts from lifetimes ago. Other circumstances, situations, pleasant and unpleasant moments are due to our daily actions, attitudes, and thoughts. For example, we have a strong burst of anger that sends out negative energy, it might create a consequence for us. We might now miss having a pleasant experience that was on the way to us, or perhaps our new daily karma results in the inconvenience of a flat tire.

Over time, usually a very long time and over many lifetimes, we begin to learn our thoughts and actions have consequences and we will be held accountable. **Accountability is part of the purifying of the lower self and of Soul, which is necessary to become a mature spiritual being. It is a blessing to be held accountable in all areas of life.** As we grow into higher states of consciousness the time between the cause and then the effect of our actions lessens. This is an advantage to our growth because we more quickly see the consequences of our actions by connecting the two events.

When the Prophet accepts us under his care and teachings he takes our karmic records. Prophet now administers our cause and effect. This is of great value and blessing for us! For example, he can help us pay off old karmic debts on the inner during dreams; often this way is much easier on us. For example, let's say we burned down a neighbor's home in a past life. The Divine might have your home burn down in this life to repay the debt. Prophet might instead choose to give you a dream where your house burns down and you wake very upset. Although the dream was uncomfortable, it is far easier repayment than your physical house burning to the ground. One way or another debt must be repaid. Prophet can even hold back repayment until we are stronger. Or, if we are ready, he can help us pay off the old karma quicker. This helps us to move past these old lessons and make room for new and higher spiritual lessons.

Nothing in life is really free! We must work for everything. People who live off others will eventually have to repay the debt in some way or form at some time, whether in this life or another. The principles of karma applies to individuals, groups of people, cities, and countries. Leaders of countries are held accountable for their actions. There is no free ride, nor would a spiritually mature Soul want a free ride. **God uses karma to create mature Souls here in the lower worlds.** He sent us into these lower worlds from the high spiritual Heavens to learn to think of, care for, and love other Souls, and to become responsible for our actions. It is a gift to grow spiritually mature; karma is actually our friend and helpful to our spiritual goals.

Study Guidance: Good karma brings spiritual seekers to Prophet to learn the eternal ways of God. **Karma is a form of purification, not punishment.** Love trumps Karma. Make the effort to pay attention to the things that come into your life, both positive and negative, and contemplate on whether it's connected to a recent thought, action, or attitude. As we begin to better see how our thoughts, actions, and attitudes affect our life and those around us, we will be inspired to make better choices. Do not overthink karma or try to earn good karma. Stay spiritually nourished, balanced, and under the wing of Prophet and most of your decisions will be okay.

Balance and Detachment

To stay in balance while living in a physical body is quite a challenge. When we allow ourselves to become out of balance emotionally, mentally, or physically, we can become drained of energy, lose focus, are less happy, and make poor decisions. We also affect negatively those around us. **A certain amount of stress and strain is part of living, but our goal is to minimize or at least reduce the wild ups and downs in our life.**

Balance is a form of peace, and when we are at peace our communication with the Divine is clearer. Our goal is to grow toward twenty-four hour a day communication, where we are always open to Divine guidance and love. Strong attachment to things of this world generally causes much stress and strain. We can enjoy our physical possessions but not be overly attached to them. If they are damaged or lost we do not want to fall into an unbalanced mood. We will lose all our physical possessions when we translate to the higher worlds at the end of this physical incarnation. We can only take our spiritual growth and the love of those closest to us to the other side, not our stuff.

Often our stress is directly related to something we are attached to being a certain way or to a specific outcome. For example, we are attached to getting a high grade on a test in school the following day, so we end up stressing and worrying all night. If we have done all we could to study and get ready for the test, why stress and lose sleep worrying about the next-day test? Why not detach from the outcome of the test and get a good night's sleep? Being attached at this point to the outcome of the test is a poor use of your energy, thoughts, or emotions.

If we are attached to a very specific way we think this world should be, or how our country should be run, and things go differently we may get upset and thrown out of balance. It is okay to care about world events and do what we can, but it is best for our own balance to not become attached to outcomes. We have opinions and care but view physical life from a higher view and remain detached. **We take the long view and focus our priorities on our**

spiritual growth and the Kingdom of Heaven. The negative side likes to use world events to get people all worked up and induce fear and indignation.

There are an endless number of things, situations, and events that can frustrate us in our daily lives and throw us out of balance. It is okay to care about those things but best to stay detached from allowing them to greatly affect us. We cannot control the world, other people or their opinions, the weather, or most things outside of us, but we can control how we react and respond. To be attached to things outside of ourselves is not a good use of our energy. **It is a full-time job and takes most of our effort and attention living our own life.**

Entanglements are a form of attachment. When we allow ourselves to become entangled in someone's situation we are less free. It is okay to assist or help another when they ask for help or guidance, but best to help without becoming entangled or ensnared into their problem. Doing so then makes their problem our problem. When we become entangled in others' situations it is like we are caught in a snare or net, making the situation more difficult and creating our own mental confusion. We can learn to detach from others' problems and not become entangled while still helping and caring. **We can be clearer and more discerning when we stay above the fray, therefore being more helpful and loving, without endangering ourselves or losing freedom.**

How do we detach from the decisions, mistakes, and actions of our loved ones? We love them from a higher spiritual view! For example, our adult child decides to travel the world, go to a trade school, or start a career rather than attend the college we think they should attend. Realize they are God's child first and have their own lessons, karma, and own personal syllabus home to God. Perhaps trust that they ARE following their personal lesson plan. If things do not work out well for them, trust it was a needed growth opportunity. **Higher spiritual love allows others the room to grow in their own way.**

How do we detach from situations involving a loved one, such as a spouse, during a very serious health challenge? **We probably DO NOT detach.** We simply cannot let go of our strong attachment to a certain desired outcome during these difficult situations. As we grow spiritually we find our heart does trust the Divine at these times, and that helps. **Some experiences in life will always be difficult, but truly trusting God can help us from having a complete meltdown, or help us more quickly recover from one.** By detaching from things we can and trusting in God where we cannot detach, we hope to never go completely off the deep end of life no matter the circumstances we find ourselves in.

There are ways to stay in balance that have little to do with detachment. For example, let's say we have been inside at our computer for several days writing a book or doing other inside activities. Perhaps the weather has been rainy or foggy for days. We start to feel off, unusually tired, or in a down mood. We could go for a long walk, work outside in our yard, or go to the gym to feel much better and get back in balance. **This is an example of balancing mental activity with physical activity.**

If we spend too much time watching television, listening to loud music or other loud noises, hanging out with certain people, doing physical work, being over stimulated, or focusing on our job we can get out of balance. Even too much of a good thing can negatively affect our goal of maintaining balance. **We learn to develop a balance between work activities and relaxing activities, and time in peaceful or stimulating environments.**

We feel what we feel and do not deny our emotions, but we do not live by or make decisions based upon our emotions. A large part of staying in balance is control of, or lessening of, our negative emotions. Emotions such as fear, anger, worry, lust, vanity, or greed can easily throw us out of balance and create serious problems for us. Singing HU regularly and developing an attitude of gratitude help control these strong emotions. **Developing a loving relationship with Prophet can actually reduce the stranglehold effect these passions of the mind can have over Soul. In time Prophet guides us to spiritual healing of even the worst passions.**

Study Guidance: Is there an area in your life you feel out of balance in, or an outcome you are overly attached to? The first step in getting back into balance is to be aware you are out of balance in the first place. Living in balance is a "moving target." What looks and feels like balance today may be different for you tomorrow, depending on countless variables. Learning to stay in balance in life is a sign of spiritual maturity and growth. **Strong attachments and strong emotions can blind us to our options and throw us out of balance.** Staying in balance helps us recognize the difference between what is important versus urgent. **When living in balance, a reduced stress state, you better "hear the whisperings of God."**

Economy
(Best use of Resources)

Economy is the efficient, effective, and careful management of our resources, including our time, energy, focus, finances, and physical, mental, and emotional health. Who does God want to be in charge of these valuable gifts of resources? And who benefits the most by good stewardship of our resources? The answer to both questions is of course, us! Practicing Economy brings certain freedoms.

The Spiritual Key of Economy has a huge effect on living a more abundant life, both physically and spiritually. For example, some people with modest incomes have far less financial stress and strain than those making large incomes. They are able to provide for the things they need and want by using their income wisely. Less stress also leads to clearer communication with the Divine, which can bless all areas of our life.

We all have the same twenty-four hours in a day. Some people say they do not have time to HU or contemplate on spiritual topics daily, or to exercise, enjoy a hobby, or take vacations, etc. By using our resource of time wisely we can make time for the things we truly value.

Getting the most use out of our resources is a sign of spiritual maturity and wisdom. **God has given us everything we have in life. Using these resources wisely shows gratitude and respect to God, even glorifies God.** Conversely, wasting our gift of resources shows a lack of understanding for who is providing them. Everything we have is on loan from God.

When we wisely use our gifts we have more self-respect and feel better about ourselves. However, balance is needed in the area of economy. For example, we come home from work and decide to relax. That might be the wise choice! Or, we decide to treat ourselves with a purchase that is just for fun and not really practical, that might be a wise decision. Practice balance in the management of resources. Economy does not imply austerity or martyrdom.

Our time is on loan from God. Use it wisely and give some of it back to God through prayer, reading scripture, and the study of His ways. When God sees us being good stewards of the resources He loaned to us, often more resources come our way.

Study Guidance: Good use of our resources takes a certain amount of discernment and self-discipline. Self-control in one area of life often bleeds into other areas to benefit us. Being a good steward of our resources both benefits us and demonstrates gratitude to God for our blessings. Practicing economy gives us real control over our lives.

Peace of Mind and Heart

This Spiritual Key is closely related to the Spiritual Key Receptive. The more peace one has, the more receptive to Divine communication they will be. A functioning and operational relationship with aspects of the Divine (God, Prophet, Soul, and the Holy Spirit) requires clear, accurate, and fluid communication. Any relationship is improved with good communication.

Being receptive to Divine guidance, love, and truth improves communication. **Having a core of peace in one's heart and mental calmness creates the necessary conditions for being able to clearly receive and understand Divine guidance.**

For example, suppose you are observing the reflection of a landscape on a totally calm and smooth lake surface. You can make out in great detail the terrain on the far side of the lake, so precise that it is no different than looking directly at the terrain. The lake's reflection is as clear as if it is a polished mirror. This is an example of clear and precise communication due to a peaceful heart and mind, just like the calm and smooth lake surface. Now imagine a wind creating lots of disturbances on the lake surface. Notice the ripples on the water disrupting the image of the terrain on the far side of the lake. Now the image is unclear. The wind creating disturbances is like trying to receive clear guidance from the Divine with a lack of peace. **Having stress, worry, anxiety, anger, or fear reduces the clarity of communication due to lack of peace.**

Sometimes when we most need guidance we also lack peace. Over time many of these Spiritual Keys allow us to maintain peace even under difficult circumstances: singing HU, knowing God's Love, trusting and loving Prophet, Spiritual Protection, Spiritual Strength, Balance and Detachment, Prophet's Inner Presence, Gratitude, Prayer, etc. often bring peace. Over time, with mentoring and combining some of the Keys with a growth of consciousness, one can learn to keep a core peace under most every circumstance. **This skill is very important in receiving Prophet's guidance clearly, no matter the situation in which one finds themselves.**

Study Guidance: There is a direct correlation between clear communication with Prophet and the amount of peace in your heart and mind. Thinking of something you are grateful for and singing HU often brings the necessary peace. **Our goal is to build a core peace deep inside that never leaves us, even if surface stress, or waves, come and go throughout the day.** Knowing God will love you always no matter what, that as Soul you are immortal, and that Prophet loves you and is always with you is important in building such a core peace.

Step Four Keys in Action

Gift of God's Peace

To be truly present in the moment, conscious of the inner presence
of Prophet and fully aware of God's Love for you, brings a peace that
surpasseth all understanding. All these gifts come from having a
conscious relationship with God's Prophet, the greatest blessing of all.

I recently had the privilege of attending a one-day retreat at Guidance for a Better Life titled "Recognizing Divine Guidance." At this retreat God's chosen Prophet, Del Hall, shared precious Spiritual Keys and tools to help us recognize Divine guidance in our lives. Prophet shared that the whisperings of God in our lives demonstrates God's Love for us. Understanding the whisperings of God helps to teach the ways of God, which can "lead to a more abundant life with less road blocks or detours." On this particular day one of the ways I was blessed to recognize God's Love for me was through an experience I had during a HU Sing.

HU is an ancient name for God and love song to God. Singing HU is a beautiful way to express love and gratitude to God. Del shared that singing HU tunes a person in to the Divine and opens us to God's Love. Singing HU can raise us up to higher levels spiritually. He also taught me that thinking of something I am grateful for in life opens my heart and is good to do before singing HU. I took the opportunity to express gratitude to God for the gift of my wife and for the blessing of being present at this retreat with Prophet and many other beautiful Souls.

As I sang HU I focused on each one as an expression of my love for God and was touched by an amazing and sacred gift: that God created Soul, our true selves, with the capacity to give and receive Divine love. As we sang HU I began to feel spiritually lighter as my heart filled with God's Love. This reminded me of Prophet sharing how singing HU "uplifts our consciousness" and "brings spiritual nourishment." Through my spiritual eye I began to perceive God's Light in white and gold colors flowing through Prophet to the group as a whole and to each person individually. I had the impression each person was receiving a personal gift of love from God through His Prophet.

During the quiet time after singing HU I was blessed with an opportunity to be with the inner presence of the Prophet. I looked into his eyes and heard the words, "Just be." Physically I felt my shoulders relax, and I cherished "just being" in this moment with Prophet. A deep peace bloomed in my heart, and I recognized this peace as a personalized gift of love from God through His beloved Prophet. This gift of peace woven from God's Love for me also brought the sense of a deeper trust in God and His Prophet. One of the pearls of wisdom Del shared during the retreat was that recognizing Divine guidance "helps build trust in God being there for you." I am incredibly thankful and blessed to know this is true from personal experience, for never in my life has this been more apparent than in recognizing, nurturing, and appreciating the sacred gift of having a conscious relationship with the Prophet of our times. I am truly grateful God always has a living Prophet here to teach us through personal experience about our true and Divine nature as Soul, and to guide us on our wondrous journey home to the Heart of God.

Written by Shanna Canine

Keys in this story: God's Prophet, HU, God's Love, Soul, Gratitude, Receptive, Attitudes and Thoughts (excellent), Growth of Consciousness (deeper trust in God and Prophet), God's Grace (experiencing God's Light and given peace)

Keys not yet studied: Proper Focus (on relationship with Prophet), Prophets Inner Presence

My Daughter Born By Spirit

*Many times we are overly attached to a particular outcome or way
of doing something without even knowing it. The more attached we
are the more we tie God's Hands in delivering His blessings. When we
truly let go the situation can be born anew.*

I am blessed to be the mom of three amazing and beautiful girls.
Eleven years ago, this journey of motherhood began. I loved being
pregnant with my first child. Excitement, anticipation, worry, and
joy all coexisting while we awaited her arrival. Being holistically
minded, it was my deep desire to have a natural childbirth. My
loving husband and I prepared as much as we possibly could, reading
a plethora of books, and taking every birthing class offered in our
area.

The big day was finally approaching. On June 7th, at 2:15 PM my
water broke, and with it some complications arose. I was admitted
to the hospital before labor truly began. A natural birth was still on
the table, but as time ticked on the possibility was looking less likely.
I relied on the HU, one of my best spiritual tools to keep me calm. I
felt peace and knew all would be fine. Five hundred miles away my
sister-in-law was also waiting with anticipation. She kept checking
in to see how labor was progressing. We went through the entire next
day and still no baby.

Exhausted at this point I gave in, and they administered drugs to
speed up labor. I finally yielded and accepted an epidural for the
intense pain that labor brings on. On the evening of June 8th true
labor was finally setting in. My sister-in-law went to bed that
evening with us in her thoughts. She had a dream, and in that dream
she saw a brilliant blue light gently push the baby from my womb.
Meanwhile back at the hospital, at the exact same moment, I looked
at my husband and said, "I need help, I need help, and I truly
surrender!"

I felt a sudden and noticeable warmth in my womb and instantly
had a rush of stamina. On June 9th at 2:15 AM, exactly thirty-six
hours to the minute of my water breaking, we gazed eyes upon our

sweet baby girl. It was the Light of God that touched my baby and helped her come into this world. Even though earlier in the day I sang HU, and I felt peace, I still had an attachment to the way I wanted things to work out. I was not even aware of my attachments until I verbally surrendered the outcome. My sister-in-law's dream confirmed what I was feeling in those same moments. In my hour of need God heard my cry and gave me one of the greatest joys of my life — my daughter.

Written by Kate Hall

Keys in this story: HU, Balance and Detachment (Kate surrendered her attachment), God's Love, Cause and Effect, Gratitude, Receptive (Kate was more receptive when she surrendered her desired outcome to God)

Keys not yet studied: Prayer (when Kate asked for help God took it as a prayer), Connecting Spiritual Events (asking for help and immediate comfort) Proper Focus (when Kate focused on delivering the baby over the "desired way" of delivering), Prophet's Inner Presence (blue light)

Hiking With Mom in Heaven

It is a sacred opportunity and blessing to visit with a loved one who has passed away. Because we are personally known and loved by God, sometimes God will answer additional prayers of the heart during these reunions. In the following example the author had the chance to experience the trip he had wanted to take with his mother.

My mother passed away at age eighty-eight. She had a strong faith and often spoke joyfully about going to Heaven when her time came. In fact, she specifically requested my three brothers and I sing at her funeral the old hymn, "When We All Get to Heaven."

She had been widowed at age fifty-five when my father had a massive heart attack. She never remarried. She continued to teach elementary school for ten more years and then retired to enjoy a life of volunteer work and traveling. Upon returning from one of her trips to Ireland, she said she wished I could have been there to hike with her in the beautiful countryside. I wished I could have been there too!

The last few years I watched her body decline, but as Soul, she remained her delightful, joyful self. As she needed more and more help with daily living we spent more and more time together. The bond between us grew through many weeks of cancer treatments and hospitalizations. When she breathed her last breath, it was bittersweet. I know she is finally where she longed to be, and yet I miss her.

Soon after her passing I was blessed to be at Guidance for a Better Life. A group of students and Del, the Prophet, were singing HU, a love song to God. During the silent time after singing, Del appeared spiritually in front of me on the inner and took me to see my mother! She was standing in a beautiful green meadow. The day was unusually bright and clear, with a hint of cool breeze. Mom's appearance was just as it was in her middle adult years, still with the natural color in her hair. She was wearing brightly colored clothes and sunglasses and had a big smile. She was so happy to see me and I was so happy to see her. She beckoned me with her arms to come walk with her. We hiked along together through the meadow and up a light brown dirt trail up into the surrounding hills. As we went higher we saw the beauty of the meadow from above. It was more beautiful than I could ever imagine Ireland to be. We spoke no words, sharing love and joy in our hearts to be hiking there together, fulfilling our wish from many years ago.

When my awareness returned to the room where I was sitting, I was glowing with love and gratitude for Del for taking me there. What an amazing gift! I now know for sure mom really is happy and well, and that she still loves me dearly.

My brothers and I looked forward to singing joyfully at her memorial service, "When we all get to Heaven, what a day of rejoicing that will be, when we all see Jesus, we'll sing and shout the victory!"

Written by Paul Harvey Sandman

Keys in this story: HU, Soul, God's Prophet, Gratitude, God's Grace (the gift of visiting his mom)

Keys not yet studied: Prophet's Inner Presence, Prayer (Paul's wish to hike with his mom in Ireland)

Pink Healing Spiritual Light

It's a wonderful thing to be able to feel — to experience the emotions of living life here in the physical. However, if we let our emotions take charge they will run us ragged. The Light of God can help set us free by bringing us into balance with an emotional healing. Like all healing though, we must first truly be receptive for it to last.

The quality of my external life, a reflection of my emotional instability, reached a point where it had become unbearable. As a result of past mistakes in behavior and thought patterns I was full of remorse, guilt, and self-loathing. Thankfully, there was a light that still burned brightly deep inside the murky overlay of negativity I had heaped upon my true self. Soul is a spark of the Divine, which when allowed to burns brightly and fervently with God's Love.

By grace I was led to Guidance for a Better Life and its founder, Prophet Del Hall. He steadily, skillfully, and carefully helped me chisel through the layers of untruth I was living to reveal a life of hope and worthwhile pursuits through which I would find peace and satisfaction. As I followed Prophet's spiritual guidance and made change a priority, the truth I encountered slowly reformed and transformed me from the inside. My spiritual senses were becoming more refined.

One especially surprising gift of healing spiritual light came to me several years ago while I was readying myself for sleep after a long workday. It was a soothing pink glow that shone all about my bedroom. I blinked my eyes in amazement thinking there was something wrong with my vision. The light remained for several minutes. I closed my eyes in contemplation and said a prayer of thanksgiving for this emotionally healing light of the Astral plane.

I am now aware that the gift of love I received that night was not a singular event. It was the catalyst for the repair of my emotional body, and the healing process still continues to heal emotional wounds, as I'm prepared and ready to release them. My heart overflows with gratitude to God for the freedom that I now enjoy. My intention is to continue to follow the spiritual guidance of Prophet, so that I will become all that I am born to be as a child of the Almighty.

Written by Bernadette Spitale

Keys in this story: Receptive, Attitudes and Thoughts (negative at first), Soul, God's Prophet, Gratitude, God's Grace (gift of healing and led to Prophet), Contemplation, Growth in Consciousness, Understanding Change

Keys not yet studied: Proper Focus (changed her priorities), Truth is Love (truth she encountered guided her to a better life), Prayer

Confident in My Decision

Our mind and emotions are part of who we are in this world, but they are not the eternal spiritual side of us. Soul is, and it is Soul that has a direct line of communication with the inner Prophet. This relationship brings us the clarity to make decisions we can have peace with instead of decisions solely based on emotions.

My sister and I live several hundred miles from one another and seldom have the opportunity to spend time together as we once did. As a gift for my forty-ninth birthday she invited me to travel as her guest on a trip out West — a trip that would involve meeting one another at a connecting airport before traveling to our final destination. As much as the thought of having this time together appealed to me, I did not want to jump into it blindly.

An aspect of my spiritual education at Guidance for a Better Life has taught me the importance of maintaining balance in all areas of my life, and that doing so goes hand in hand with living an abundant life. Few things threaten our balance more than allowing our emotions to dictate our decisions. And while the mind is a useful tool, Soul, our true Self, resides above the influence of both logic and feelings. From Its higher viewpoint better decisions can be made.

In addition to considering the impact on my home life, work, health, and finances, I looked to the inner Prophet for help in the decision-making process. The help I had asked for came to me in the form of a dream. In it I found myself in a brightly lit airport on one of the inner spiritual Heavens. I had just gotten off a plane when to my surprise, I spotted my sister seated in a waiting area up ahead. I looked forward with joyful anticipation to surprising her as I approached. Her face came alive with a beautiful smile as she stood to greet me. Our meeting was a happy one. The peace and clarity I awoke with left me with a knowingness in my heart it was okay to go. The decision turned out to be a sound one, and the trip was full of blessings for each of us.

I have learned the basis for sound decisions ultimately rests on whether we have peace in our heart. A true Prophet of God has the unique ability, through dreams, contemplation, and other forms of inner communication, to show us the truth in our own heart from the viewpoint of Soul.

Written by Sandra Lane

Keys in this story: God's Prophet, Balance and Detachment, Soul, God's Love (received peace and clarity), Contemplation (looked to inner Prophet), Peace of Mind and Heart, Cause and Effect (received clarity by not making an emotional decision on her own), Discernment (wanted to make a conscious choice)

Keys not yet studied: Prophet's Inner Presence, Personal Effort (made the effort to look to Prophet)

Building Divine Relationships

Regardless of how far we've come on our spiritual journey — there is always more. Nowhere is this more evident than in the amount of God's Love available for us. It is infinite, and as we are able to accept even more it will be showered upon us.

Guidance for a Better Life offers a five-part Keys to Spiritual Freedom course of study. The third retreat in this series is titled, "Building Divine Relationships" and is taught by Prophet Del Hall. Divine relationships can be with God, the Voice of God (sometimes called the Light and Sound of God or the Holy Spirit), God's Prophet, or with Soul — your true self. Under Prophet Del Hall's loving guidance I had an experience at this retreat that could easily be the highlight of a lifetime. It is one I will never forget that held great significance and helped me gain a greater capacity to love.

Before singing HU, Prophet asked us to think of something we were grateful for specifically from that day, and then to ask for an experience of some type that would help me build my relationship with the Divine, and then promise to be receptive to whatever blessings I was given. This prayer Prophet brought to us was given to him directly from God. It has become known as the Three-Part Prayer. I began by being grateful for something that happened early in the day at home and my thoughts just flowed from one moment to the next. Without intending to do so, I ended up going through my day, step by step, and saw God's Hand in everything I did, and I felt gratitude for it all. We began singing HU, and an amazing experience followed. After singing HU it took me a while to take it all in. I had a hard time finding the words to describe what had happened.

In my journal I wrote: *"Oh my gosh — LOVE. My heart is just bursting and overflowing with love. It began in my heart, love pouring out so strong, fueled by the gratitude I felt every step of my day — I couldn't just stop at one thing. The love flowed out of me to you Dear God, but it was unlike anything I had ever felt before. A kind of dam broke, a wall or resistance of some type was cleared by your Grace and love poured out of me. It felt strong, beautiful, and uplifting. Your Divine Spirit beckoned me closer with Its Heavenly music, eventually engulfing me into the sound. I felt love, indistinguishable now whether coming out of me to you Lord, or from you to me. It was our love, the love of our relationship. I may have experienced this in a very real way before, but perhaps I am feeling it in a more true sense tonight as whatever hurts or pains I had numbed myself to were healed, and the protective walls I had built around my heart crumbled in the light of your security, comfort, and magnificent Love. I cried and cried the most beautiful tears I have ever felt. It was almost hard to breathe because the feeling of awe from the beauty of it took my breath away. As I write, even now, the tears keep flowing. 'Rapture' is the word that is in my heart. This love I feel is incredible! It has been there, but not like this. The love in me has been strong and very much there, building all these years, but now it is flowing, and I can feel it more than ever tonight. Oh my gosh — the tears just keep coming. It is amazing. Thank you!!!"*

This incredible experience took me by surprise. It helped me build upon my Divine relationships in part by showing me the depth of what was already there and then taking me even further with realizations that followed. I know to my core that I love God and have felt it. I know God and His Prophet love me, and I have felt and experienced this love in many beautiful ways, and yet the degree and intensity of what I felt in this experience knocked my socks off. There truly is always more... wow! It is not random, of course. I see a seamless progression over time from retreat to home to retreat, and a continuous flow of God's Grace and Love through truth, insights, healings, experiences with the light and sound, direct interaction with aspects of the Divine, and being blessed moment to moment with added clarity, purification, and more being in Prophet's presence. My heart is filled with gratitude and appreciation for God's Prophet, and the life of abundant love he has brought me to living.

Written by Lorraine Fortier

Keys in this story: Receptive, God's Prophet, Gratitude, HU, God's Love, God's Grace, Spiritual Growth (there is always more), Spiritual Strength (experiences like this strengthen the love and trust toward God and Prophet), Three-Part Prayer

Keys not yet studied: Living Without Doubt, Spiritual Food, Blending with God's Voice

Thankful I Shared

The greatest hindrance to accepting our initial experiences with the Light and Sound of God can sometimes be ourselves. We let our mind, which is fearful of change, cause us to doubt. It is during times like these when it is key to have a teacher who understands the "Language of the Divine."

During my first three-day spiritual retreat at Guidance for a Better Life, Del encouraged us to participate in a relaxing sit exercise. During this sit exercise we were instructed to go find a place to sit outside, relax, and enjoy being in the mountains. I found a spot in the woods on a large smooth rock. After I got comfortable, I began to think of something I was grateful for to help open my heart. I then sang HU for a while. When I was done singing HU, I asked the Prophet to show me Divine love. I looked around at my lush green oasis in the woods. I felt a wave of peace wash over me. I felt myself melt into the rock as I listened to the flowing stream rush by, the birds chirping around me, and the occasional call of a bullfrog. Directly in front of my field of vision was a twinkling orange light. I began to sing "Prophet" silently to myself several times. As I was singing "Prophet," I heard bells ringing. Soon after this, the sit exercise came to an end.

I went back up to the school for class. As time passed before I shared the experience with the group, I began to mentally talk myself out of the experience. I began to physically justify the light I saw as spotlights mounted outside of the school someone must have happened to turn on. Since this was my first spiritual class at the retreat center, I thought that I was too new at this to experience the Divine Light of God. Boy was I wrong!

I felt multiple nudges from the inner Prophet that I should share my experience with the group. Since I was not sure if I had actually experienced something, I felt a good bit of hesitancy. After hearing many other individuals share their experiences during the exercise, I finally decided to share my experience with the group. When I shared, I received so much clarity on my experience. I learned that I was actually at the second Heaven during my experience. The calling card that I was at this Heaven was the color orange and the tinkling of bells. These colors and sounds that I thought I had made up or misconstrued as a physical light were actually God responding to me! By opening my heart and singing a love song to God, God responded by telling me "I am loved by God." Had I not shared this experience with Del, I may have easily talked myself out of this Divine blessing, this gift of love from God. I may have missed that God not only heard me, but responded to me. The purpose of this exercise was to have God through His Prophet show us Divine love. Sometimes the response from God may be so subtle we are not even aware of it. Thank you Prophet for nudging me to share with the class, otherwise I may have totally missed this Divine gift of love from God!

Written by Michelle Reuschling

Keys in this story: Gratitude, God's Prophet, God's Love (experienced His Light and Sound and peace) Cause and Effect (Sang HU sending love to God and He responded — she followed Prophet's inner nudge to share and received clarity), Growth in Consciousness, Soul (went to the second Heaven with Prophet), God's Grace (letting her go into Heavens)

Keys not yet studied: Prophet's Inner Presence (took her to the second Heaven)

The Protection of God's Love

God's Love and protection is real, but often it can be very subtle.
Those who have raised themselves up spiritually and invited Prophet
into their day will be able to better "hear" the guidance.

I love starting my day singing HU, a beautiful love song and ancient prayer of gratitude to God. This tunes me in spiritually and paves the way to whatever the day will bring. As I get in my car to do an errand I joyfully invite the inner Prophet to accompany me. I envision this as God's white Light shared through His Prophet surrounding me like a luminous shield of loving protection.

Driving home one day I approached a busy 'T' shaped intersection where I was going to turn left. Straight ahead the traffic approaching the intersection was coming down a mountain. Some cars would slow down approaching the intersection to turn right, and others would maintain their rate of speed as they continued straight through, passing by me as I waited to turn. Usually I would go all the way up to the end of the turn lane to make the left turn. This day I felt a nudge to linger back and even spiritually heard the words, "You are not in a hurry." I came to a stop about two car lengths before my turn. Suddenly a truck pulled out from the stopped traffic to my left and just froze in the middle of the intersection ahead of me. A car coming down the mountain road very fast was now on a collision course with the truck. The truck was in the lane of the oncoming car. The truck had pulled out not seeing the car coming down the hill, but when he did he panicked and stopped. As if in a movie scene the oncoming car quickly swerved left around the truck, then turned hard right between me and the truck, and amazingly straightened out into his normal lane of traffic! Between a fancy way of driving and me hanging back this head on collision was avoided. The whole incident seemed surreal it happened so fast.

In the moments after I realized the Divine Hand of God, working through His Prophet, was holding me closely. I wept tears of gratitude and relief as I thanked him for the nudge to hang back. I witnessed one of God's miracles of protection!

Another time I experienced Divine intervention I was driving along a scenic parkway enjoying the beautiful majestic views. I was leisurely following a small car that all of a sudden began to speed up ahead of me. This action sparked my awareness as a nudge by the Prophet (concentrated aspect of the Holy Spirit) to pay closer attention, and I was now more focused on what was in front of me instead of the scenic glances. I was about to witness Divine protection being with me once again! Suddenly the small car darted to the right into a scenic overlook and made a rapid U-turn right back onto the parkway in front of me! In a split-second I was able to stop and not hit it sideways. The driver of the car never saw me following behind. I felt like I was in a slow-motion bubble of the most serene loving Light of God surrounding me. The white light of protection I envision when I leave the house came alive! Taking a deep breath of gratitude, I marveled at how loved I am to have such awareness of just one of the gifts of how God expresses His Love for me. It has brought me such a gratifying sense of comfort and peace.

I know that preparing myself for the day by singing HU and inviting the safeguarding presence of God's Prophet into my day is a blessing and a gift of Grace. Through Prophet, God's miracles and events that we marvel about are delivered to all of us. We hear stories in the news, from our friends, or read about these events in books that are often referred to as miracles from God. These experiences seem hard to explain logically but have real impact in our lives. Yes, these miracles and wonders are happening every day, and I am so blessed to recognize them as gifts of God's Love and protection.

Written by Nancy Nelson

Keys in this story: HU, Gratitude, God's Prophet, Spiritual Protection, Cause and Effect (Nancy followed Prophet's nudge to stay back and avoided an accident) God's Love (loving light surrounding her), God's Grace, Receptive (followed guidance to stay back), Spiritual Protection

Keys not yet studied: Prophet's Inner Presence (gave nudge and then held and comforted her and put Light of God around her in second example), Personal Effort (asking Prophet to travel with her during the day) Connecting Spiritual Events (no accident and listening to Prophet)

God's Gentle White Light Transforms Me

Many times our initial experiences with the Light of God can be subtle. If we receive too much too fast it can put us out of balance. It takes time to acclimate to more and more intense experiences with the Light and Love of God. God and His Prophet know exactly what is appropriate for each individual.

I was a seeker. I traveled the world looking for a path home to God. I tried going to church with friends. I tried yoga and dance. I tried fasting and strict diets. I tried meditation retreats. None of these left me feeling any closer to God. Having seen nothing, having no lasting peace, and no lasting joy to speak of. During one of the first retreats I attended at Guidance for a Better Life many years ago, I received a vision of God's gentle white Light. In a moment this experience awakened something in me I did not even know was sleeping; a yearning to experience more of God's Love, and a desire to be able to communicate with the Divine.

Our teacher had instructed us to find a comfortable place to sit in the woods, and relax. We were told we might experience something new: see the beauty of the woods or an animal moving. But the key was to just relax. "Unplug" and just be. While I have loved hiking in nature since I was a little child, just relaxing in it was new to me. So I found a suitable rock, got comfortable, watched the wind blow the trees, and listened to the water in the creek flow by. I saw a chipmunk dart here and there. I just relaxed and enjoyed the woods. Then I saw a gentle white light appear like a cloud in front of me. My eyes were open, yet the light I was seeing was not physical light. As I tried to look closer at what it was, it disappeared; but a presence of peacefulness remained. What was it that I had seen? I felt lighter and freer and walked back into the class with a little more bounce in my step.

When we returned to class students started sharing their experiences. Del explained that Divine Spirit has many ways of expressing Itself to us, but one of the most direct ways is through the

Light of God. God had been communicating with me when I sat on that rock. Wow, was I blessed! I had finally found what I had been looking for.

Since then, especially at retreats but also at home using the tools Del taught me, the Light of God has revealed Itself to me. Each experience with God's Light has transformed me slightly — has left me with a little more peace, a little more confidence, a little more joy, a little more freedom. Sometimes I have asked myself "Why me?" I am an ordinary person, not a saint like I had read about in the Bible. I am a wife and a mom. I thought only special people or saints could have Heavenly visions, but I've learned that is not true. Because God loves all His children, He showers His blessings on us all. I consider myself to be extremely blessed to have a living teacher that can help me to not only have these experiences but to understand the message. He shows me how to integrate the peace, love, and freedom into my daily life. I am a living testimony that seeing God's Light changes us. It is the love I received in these experiences that changed me. Where I used to be fearful, now I trust. Where I used to have a kind of sour attitude toward life, now I am truly happy. The Light of God nurtured me and transformed me from the inside out.

The Guidance for a Better Life retreat center is on a beautiful piece of land, but even more than the physical beauty is the opportunity to be in the presence of a true Prophet of God. Here in a seemingly simple exercise of sitting in the woods, I saw the Light of God. There is something special about the opportunity to attend one of Del's classes. I have witnessed many people experience the Light of God during his retreats. Maybe Heaven will open a doorway for you to look through too.

God is still alive and wants to bless us. He is just as amazing as He was thousands of years ago, and His Holy Spirit still reveals Itself to us through many ways, one way is Light. I believe He wants to see all of us walk a little lighter, to see us all live with more peace, joy, and freedom. For us to receive His reassurance, that no matter who we are or where we are in our lives, He cares. He truly loves us.

Written by Molly Comfort

Keys in this story: Gratitude, God's Love (peacefulness remained), God's Prophet, Growth in Consciousness, Receptive (or would not have had her experience), God's Grace (to see His Light), Attitudes and Thoughts (was sour, now grateful and peaceful)

Communication With God

People through the ages have wrestled with the same questions, "Does God hear me and if so, what does His reply sound like?" The answer to the first question is yes, God hears you. Learning to recognize His reply is an art form, one that is very doable, and one Prophet Del Hall has been helping people gain fluency in for thirty years. Your ability to recognize the "Language of the Divine," to see all the ways in which God communicates with you daily, is one of the greatest attributes you can develop as Soul.

When do I get to talk to God?

When I was a child I had a question in my heart I never asked anyone. I wondered, "When do I get to talk to God?" I could not think of someone to ask this question. Who would know? Not my parents, friends, or even a priest. When I watched movies about the afterlife, I paid attention to see if they had any ideas about the matter, but I never saw anything that satisfied me.

I did not have anything I wanted to say; I wanted to listen to God. What would He tell me in that hoped-for meeting? Would He explain the why of everything, or was there something more, something deeper He would express? Though my mind wondered if only important people would be blessed with such a meeting, my heart always asked when, never if.

Still seeking an answer, I began attending retreats at Guidance for a Better Life in 1996. As soon as I arrived on the property, I felt like I had come home. When Del spoke about Spirit, I heard truth. I knew I had come to the right place.

What I did not realize until much later is that my question was already being answered. At that retreat I sang HU for the first time. Singing HU, expressing Soul's love to God, is communication. God hears every HU, every prayer, and answers in some way. When a beloved child tells God, "I love you," our loving Father does not sit silent. He answers, "I love you too," in countless ways. Learning to recognize and accept the love that returns time and again is one of the many joys of this path.

In time I began paying attention to my dreams, and most importantly, developing an inner relationship with Prophet. Through this relationship I can be in constant communication with God. The love I feel, a nudge to try something a little differently, a helpful dream, and awareness of how I can make my life even better, are all from God through His Prophet. His presence blesses me every day. Rather than one hoped-for meeting I found I could communicate with God daily, even every moment.

My mind had it wrong years ago. Every child of God is important and precious to God. He reaches out to us constantly, communicating in every possible way. The question is not are you important enough for God to talk to; the question is, are you listening?

Written by Jean Enzbrenner

Keys in this story: HU, God's Prophet, Soul, Gratitude, Growth of Consciousness

Keys not yet studied: Prayer, Prophet's Inner Presence

Door is Opened to Freedom

In a very real sense many people on Earth live in a prison. A prison of consciousness. It is here we are blinded to the divinity within us. It is here we are trapped by the illusion that there is nothing more. It is here we get so wrapped up with the non-stop distractions, that even if the prison door was open, some would not know to step through it. Fortunately, some do.

I was in my thirties and was experiencing an inner unrest. I did not know or understand at the time what it was, but there was something deep within me stirring. I did not know what this unrest was or how to resolve it. I was seeking something, but what? I had a beautiful family, friends, home, and wonderful comforts, but something was calling to me. One night the desperate feeling was so intense I called out in a prayer "I want to go home." It surprised me, I did not know what this meant, but it came from a deep place within me.

I received a brochure from Guidance for a Better Life in the mail a short time after that experience. After some consideration I decided to go, and it has changed my life in so many good ways. I am now blessed with a spiritual teacher who has given me spiritual tools and over time changed the unrest to peace within me. One of the tools given was the study of dreams.

I had a dream that seemed simple but defined me and my journey in life prior to going to the retreat center. In this dream I was in a clean, tidy, comfortable, and nicely decorated room. I looked around, and it became apparent that the room was a prison cell. The cell door was open, and on the other side were my spiritual teacher, the Prophet, and two other teachers. I was being given the opportunity to get out of the prison cell.

At the time I did not recognize I was living my life as if living in a prison cell. My life from all outward appearance was well, yet something inside me knew differently. The prison cell represented things that limited my freedom: fears, worries, vanity, attachments, negative attitudes, as well as unhealed experiences from past lives. I did not realize I was living in a prison cell, because it was comfortable and familiar.

In the dream I hesitated to leave the confinement of the cell. I seemed to be frozen in my old familiar ways. When the door started to close I made the decision to leave the confines of the cell and took full hold of my spiritual teacher. Through the years he has been teaching me and giving me spiritual tools to use to break free from the prison of human consciousness. The Prophet opened a doorway to a new way of living where I now experience love, joy, peace, and a freedom I have never known.

Written by Renée Dinwiddie

Keys in this story: Attitudes and Thoughts (now very good), God's Prophet, Spiritual Growth, God's Grace (given dream and sending Prophet to free Renee), Karma (from past life)

Keys not yet studied: Prayer, Peace of Mind and Heart (Renee now has love, joy and peace)

Greater Abundance Follows Past Life Healing

Whether we are conscious of them or not, the things from our past affect us in the present. We can attempt to "wall off" or ignore old areas we do not wish to look at, but they are still there. When we are ready to face old issues, Prophet can help us disentangle from the things that no longer serve us.

I had a dream I was in my house. It was a multi-storied bright, sunny, and open space. Suddenly I found myself in a different part of the house I did not remember being there, or I had not been in for a long while and had forgotten about. I was on a lower level, perhaps a first floor or basement, and it was a separate structure but was attached to my house and shared a common wall. I briefly caught a glimpse of this from the exterior and then was back inside. This attached section was old and in very bad shape.

When first walking around the large rooms it looked as if it might have potential. I thought to myself maybe I could fix it up and rent it out. Then I looked up and saw the ceilings — they were near collapsing. I noticed the floors — they were torn up and debris was everywhere. It looked as if no one had lived there for a while, with just a few remnants of former life there. It was so bad all I could think was how expensive it was going to be to fix all this. It would probably require a home equity loan, which I did not really want to do. It needed to be dealt with right away because it was a hazard. I was even afraid being in there because it was so unsafe. I was also concerned about the way it was attached to the nice, well-built home I lived in. I did not want this old section to cause it to collapse or become structurally damaged.

Then something very cool happened. I woke up while still in the dream and became conscious. This has only happened to me once or twice before that I can recall. At first I was relieved I was in a dream and not in any immediate danger. Then since I was not in my physical body and therefore not constrained by the body's physical limitations, I started trying things I may not have done otherwise, like putting my fists through the wall and jumping up high enough to go through the ceiling and punch into it. I was covered in dust and plasterboard but knowing it would not collapse on me physically gave me a sense of freedom and boldness to try such things. I realized this dilapidated structure was beyond repair and had to be demolished. I think this was my way of getting things started. I was very concerned when I awoke however, because houses sometimes represent one's state of consciousness when they show up in dreams. Prophet was trying to get my attention to help me, so I asked him for help in understanding the dream he blessed me with.

After a few contemplations and looking at it from different perspectives, he helped me see some pearls contained in the dream. I was excessively attached to something from the past, and it was negatively impacting this life. Perhaps this was not in an overt or easily noticeable way but in a fundamental (structural) way. This was symbolized by the section of house I not been in for a long time. The sunlit, multi-storied part of the home I usually lived in was positive, but this older attached section was bad off and potentially hazardous. The common wall between the older and newer sections suggested that not only was it something I had a hard time letting go of, there was also an attempt to keep it compartmentalized and isolated or unacknowledged. Even so, I was hurting my spiritual growth and limiting the freedom, joy, and abundance in my present life by closing my heart or trying to "wall off" this section.

This information was not totally new to me, as months prior to this Prophet had taken me back to a lifetime in the past that was probably the root of the issue. This spiritual travel experience was the beginning of a long healing process that continued with this dream. While it is true just one meeting with God's Prophet can dramatically change one's life for the better, something of this delicate and complex nature cannot be done all at once, not because he is unable to do it, but because it would have been too much for me to try and fix all at once. In Prophet's perfect, loving way, he was gently raising and expanding my awareness of the situation little by little, at a rate I could handle without being too much or putting me out of balance. All the while I was being held, loved, and protected in the Hand of God, which I was very aware of throughout.

What was significant about this dream was how clearly I saw the situation and understood. The dream spoke to me as Soul in my native language more directly and clearly than any words or mental dialogue could have conveyed while awake. What was also very significant was that I woke up in the dream, and with the boldness and confidence of Soul, I began to take an active part in taking down the old structure. It was a turning point in both understanding and accepting truth given to me by Prophet. I was ready to acknowledge it for what it was, let go of what I was holding onto, and move forward.

One morning while driving to work, shortly after this dream occurred, I saw a truck with the words "Precision Remodelers" written on the back. This awake dream caught my attention, and I knew it was a message for me. It reminded me of the house dream, and how I was concerned in the dream about how to get rid of the old rundown structure without damaging the nice part of the house. I could certainly use a "precision remodeler." I perceived a blessing and inner healing was taking place. Through this entire process that began months earlier with the initial spiritual travel experience, and even before then by conditioning and preparing me, Prophet's precision and expertise was safely helping me dismantle the wall in my heart and attachments to the past I had been holding, without doing damage. He has made it so the love and cherished memories from that time could flow forward into the present without any of the negative baggage, for that was being let go and replaced with Divine love.

I feel I am being remodeled and upgraded in that I can feel and appreciate love in new and deeper ways. I notice it in a more honest, loving relationship with Prophet, deeper trust, and more precise inner communication with him. I notice it in more genuine and intimate connections and exchanges with friends and family. I have also noticed more Soul to Soul interactions with others I meet throughout the day. I even notice it in a deeper savoring, wonder, and appreciation for nature and in those special little moments when I experience God's Love through the world around me. It is difficult to put into words, but it feels as if a shadow, one I did not even know had cast itself over my already blessed and abundant life, has been removed. I am beginning to see a richness, color, and depth of life and love I have not experienced before.

Prophet wants only the best for us and does not want us to settle for anything less than our true potential, and he knows what this is even if we do not. What was already a very nice house — a beautiful life filled with blessings upon blessings — is becoming even more beautiful, more joyful, more love-filled, and more abundant. It is sometimes hard to imagine, but there truly is always more. Anything is possible with Prophet, and with genuine love and rock-solid trust in him our growth, splendor, and potential to be a blessing to others has no limits.

Written by Lorraine Fortier

Keys in this story: God's Prophet, Spiritual Growth, Soul, Growth of Consciousness, Balance and Detachment (very attached to something from past), God's Love, Contemplation, Spiritual Protection (healing at correct rate), Karma, God's Grace (gave helpful dream and inner healing)

Keys not yet studied: Truth is Love, Prophet's Inner Presence

Healing Pink and Orange Light

*When you are blessed to know God's Love it builds the trust
needed to get through life's challenges. It gives us confidence that
even though sometimes very painful, our experiences are helping us to
grow in our ability to give and receive love. The greater the
challenge, the greater the opportunity — even though it might take
years to accept and understand the blessings of growth. Our trials are
not punishment from God — they are opportunities to grow closer. In
the following story the author prays for a dear friend going through a
very sad time and is witness to God's healing Light in response.*

I have been blessed with an amazing best friend since childhood.
When we were in elementary school we spent every possible
waking moment together. In middle school she moved about thirty
minutes away, and we begged our willing mothers to drive us back
and forth. Then in high school I moved several states away, and
during college we found ourselves on opposite ends of the country.
The periods of time between visits and distance between us might
have been extended, but it had no diminishing effect on our
friendship. Six months could pass without talking, and then with
one phone call it was like there had been no separation at all. Now
as adults the physical distance between us has become only a few
states, and we are able to see each other one or two times per year.

She has been there for me through many of my significant
moments: losing my mother at the age of sixteen, getting married,
and being blessed with three children. I have been there for her
through many of her significant moments: losing her beloved
childhood dog, her marriage, and her journey to motherhood. Since
we were kids we have both dreamed of becoming mothers. We
talked about different names and how many kids we hoped to have
one day.

She was blessed to conceive a baby girl in 2013 and was due to
deliver in June of 2014. We celebrated in the usual ways, and I
shared stories of my pregnancy, sleepless days with a newborn, and
how motherhood had brought about a deep love in me beyond my

wildest imagination. She was on the doorstep of her dream becoming a reality. It never occurred to me that something heartbreaking would change the course of our lives. Tragically during her delivery she lost her baby and suffered severe physical trauma to her own body. Feelings of shock, helplessness, and disbelief hit me harder than I can recall ever feeling in this lifetime. I was hundreds of miles away when I heard the news and could not bear the feeling that I had zero power or ability to ease the pain for my dear friend and her family. I could not even imagine what she was experiencing.

I wept, prayed, and sang HU for twenty-four hours straight after hearing the news. I prayed with everything in me to God to please lift even one ounce of the pain and suffering from her heart. Slowly God showed me I was not entirely powerless. With God anything is possible, and I am so grateful to know prayers are real, and that they provide the sacred opportunity to express our feelings directly to God. I am so grateful Prophet has given me the tools to express my compassion, and the deep trust to know that we are all in God's Hands. I do not know mentally why her life took this course, but I trust God that there was a reason it did.

The first day after hearing the news my prayers were answered, and I was blessed with a dream and a spiritual visit to my friend. In the dream her baby was alive and healthy and being cared for and nurtured by two loving Souls in Heaven. I was able to hold her and feel the warmth of her soft skin. It brought me peace to know that her daughter was being watched over and hope that maybe one day this Soul could try again to become her child. The mother and child love bond they share transcends their physical separation.

Prophet also blessed me with a very real visit with my friend. Her body had been through a very traumatic experience physically, and she was very weak and on bed rest. For a period of time she could not even ascend the stairs to her bedroom and had to sleep on her couch. I found myself as Soul sitting on the floor in her apartment and holding her hand while she lay on the couch. No words were spoken. The entire room was filled with a misty golden light, God's Love and Presence gently surrounding her and her family. Over her heart there was an intense pink light, which I believe to be God's healing Light — the pink color to me represented an emotional healing filled with strength, love, and hope. Over her womb there was an intense orange light, which I believe represented physical healing, and strength to aid in repairing the physical trauma. God's Light and Love surrounded her and held her safe and sound. It gently but intensely washed over her and through her physically, emotionally, and spiritually.

Words cannot fully convey the gift that this experience was and still is for me. In the year following her loss I am often taken back to this moment, and I know she is still being nurtured and cared for by our Heavenly Father. On the outer, I can support her with cards, phone calls, food, and honorary gifts in her daughter's name. Even more precious is the Divine opportunity to be able to pray to God to please, if it is His will, send strength, comfort, love, peace, healing, and even hope for a child in the future. God loves His children. And God loves when His children love one another.

My friend has again been blessed to conceive a child, this time a baby boy, due in October. He will learn all about his sister from those who love her. I am thankful to God for my lifelong friendship. I am thankful to God to know His Light is real and powerful. I am thankful to Prophet for showing me my friend being blessed with Divine light as it brought me peace and comfort. I am thankful to know that God's Light brought a profound healing to her, whether or not she is fully aware of its magnitude.

Written by Catherine Hughes

Keys in this story: God's Love (golden light), HU, God's Prophet, Soul, Gratitude, God's Grace (Inner Prophet taking her spiritually to visit her friend and to see God's healing Light)

Keys not yet studied: Prayer

Love the Lord With All Your Heart

The simple but profound truth is, you exist because God loves you. It is one thing to have someone tell you this — it is quite another to have a spiritual guide who can help you come to know this truth for yourself. Joy and abundance beyond measure are available when you personally experience God's Love.

"And he answering said, Thou shalt love the Lord thy God with all thy heart, and with all thy soul, and with all thy strength, and with all thy mind; and thy neighbor as thyself." Luke 10:27 KJV

My fervent prayer as a child and young adult was to truly know that God loves me and how to love God, not just in my mind. I wanted to come before God through love, not through fear and guilt that many churches promote. One of my very favorite passages in the Bible was about loving God with all your heart, mind, and Soul. This passage has been tucked away in my heart. It always was clear to me one of Jesus' key messages was that God, His Father, is love, how much we are loved, and the importance of loving others as ourselves. In everyday life I had a hard time loving myself and was harder on myself than others. Not being able to love myself it was difficult to accept God's Love, though it was always there for me. This sense of unworthiness dogged me much of my life.

In 1998 I was guided to Guidance for a Better Life. Over the years my spiritual teacher, who is a true Prophet of God, gradually guided me through every angle possible, a 360-degree view, to experience how much I am loved, and that I am worthy of God's Love. God loves us all, every one of us unconditionally. I learned that we are here on Earth to learn about giving and receiving love. I learned and began to experience the amazing inner joy of reaching out to others, instead of only thinking about myself.

A priceless experience was gifted to me a few years ago; one I treasure and hope to remember in my heart forever. It took place shortly after one of my friends, also a student of Prophet Del Hall, had shared a facilitation at a retreat that was full of love. There was a sense of expectant joy in the air as Del returned to the front of the room. Prophet suggested, "Let's come together, be really together for a moment. Let go, surrender with the inner Prophet's assistance." I/we merged into a gigantic white light ball which got brighter and brighter. I was aware of the particles of light, sparks of individuality within the greater light ball (God's Light). "In this moment you have everything you need," Prophet said. I felt my cares, everything, melt away. The more I surrendered, let go, the boundaries of various boxes that had contained my limited concept of God faded away, and my awareness of the limitlessness and expansiveness of the gigantic white light ball grew and grew.

"Just be." I experienced stillness, deep peace, and Divine love. I felt totally nourished in that moment of eternity and had everything I needed. As the love became more intense I accepted it, almost overpowering, and felt so much love for God. The flow back and forth between God's Heart and my heart intensified until it became a crescendo of golden waves of love crashing upon the shores of my heart. My heart was bursting with love for God. In that moment of eternity, I only wanted to love and praise God forever. In that moment as Soul I experienced my favorite Bible passage... "to love the Lord God with all my heart, mind, and Soul."

Written by Jan Reid

Keys in this story: God's Love, Growth of Consciousness, Receptive (surrendered more), God's Prophet, Soul, Peace of Mind and Heart, Gratitude, Contemplation (led by Prophet), Reverence

Keys not yet studied: Prayer, Prophet's Inner Presence

Prophet Brings a Gift of Peace

Every Soul is known and loved personally by God. We can each be given exactly what we need exactly when we need it. One of the greatest of God's gifts is peace, for with peace comes clarity; the clarity that allows us to hear those gentle whisperings from Spirit and the clarity to take the next step in life.

I was relaxing by the stream that flows down from the pond during a dream retreat at Guidance for a Better Life. I was enjoying quiet time with the inner Prophet and sharing the beauty of the surrounding paradise with him. The sun was warming my skin and the sky was clear and blue. The sights and sounds of nature were alive and delighting my ears and other senses.

We had been encouraged to allow Spirit to guide us to a special spot and then sit quietly while listening and remaining alert. Something that always has and always will amaze me is how Divine Spirit can be with, instruct, and bless every Soul individually as we participate together in the same retreat. We each have our own tailor-made syllabus with Prophet. He can be with us on the inner and outer and provide whatever experiences and blessings we need to learn, heal, and grow. Anything is possible with him. I had been going through some personal challenges that were ultimately very beneficial to me, but this did bring a few rough patches as I worked through the emotions brought to the surface. On this day, as always, he knew exactly what I needed.

As we sat together in silence my attention was drawn to the wind. It was dancing through the upper branches of the tall trees creating a very distinctive sound. It drew me upwards to it, filling me with joy as it caressed my face. I closed my eyes to listen and savor the beauty of the moment. I felt myself leaving my physical body and begin to travel into the inner spiritual worlds with Prophet. We traveled with the inner sound, following it up through the Heavens to the edge of a vast spiritual ocean. I heard a gentle rain begin to fall. In my inner vision I saw golden drops coming down from the ocean to the physical, showering the area where I sat. A deep peace came upon me and settled within. This gift of Divine love enveloped me and I relaxed into it. I remained in this Heavenly place for a while longer then slowly and naturally came back into my physical body continuing to feel the love, stillness, and peace inside. I felt lighter and so appreciated this precious gift I had just received.

It is such a simple word, peace. How much do you value it? Through life experience Spirit has shown me just how important inner peace is, and I value it much more now. This peace is necessary in order to have good communication with the Prophet, to have good discernment, and to be able to make good choices. It allows me to see more clearly and to recognize the Hand of God working in my life. It enables me to have a more positive and constructive attitude toward a situation. Peace is a key to living abundantly and really enjoying the gift of life.

Prophet knows me and he knows my heart. He knew just what I needed that day. What an incredible gift it is to be loved so perfectly. He knows you too and is with you right now, waiting to love you in his Divine way. Just ask for his help and let him into your heart. I promise your life will forever be changed for the better. May his peace be with you.

Written by Lorraine Fortier

Keys in this story: Soul, God's Prophet, God's Love (golden shower of God's Light), Peace of Mind and Heart, Discernment, Attitudes and Thoughts (positive and constructive), God's Grace (going into Heavens with Prophet and deep peace)

Keys not yet studied: Prophet's Inner Presence

Step Five: Spiritual Growth and Conditioning

This section is the final step in our "Keys to Spiritual Freedom Study Program." At this point we have covered a wide variety of topics. If by now you have studied and experimented using at least some of the Spiritual Keys, plus read and studied the stories of the "Keys in Action," and watched some of our videos, you may have already begun to have your own personal experiences with the Divine. If not, you may have grown in other preparatory ways such as: seeing more clearly your personal priorities and goals, feeling better about yourself, having more gratitude for what you do have, or by beginning to desire a closer relationship with God. That said, there is always more to learn and experience about God and God's Heavens, God's Prophet, and yourself as an eternal Divine being.

The following Keys will be introduced:

Spiritual Sharing or Silence

This Key gives guidance on when to share, or not share, your spiritual knowledge or experiences. This Spiritual Key involves the Key Discernment. Generally there are three primary concerns with sharing. 1. Someone unfamiliar with Prophet's teachings may try to or succeed in talking you out of your own knowingness or experience. 2.Your sharing might disrupt another individual's own belief or spiritual understandings causing them imbalance. 3.You may violate your own relationship with Prophet or another one of Prophet's students and no longer be trustworthy.

Whenever we share our spiritual teachings or our own experiences, it is important to do no harm, to ourselves or to another. If sharing would bless another and not become "showing off" (vanity) what we know about the Divine, perhaps share a little. **Think carefully if sharing something would benefit the other person** and not violate Prophet's trust or hurt yourself. Do not let your excitement to share cloud your discernment. It is best to be guided by Spirit when to share and what to share.

The above does not preclude sharing general information about the Prophet's teachings and general information about the retreats or books. Remember, your specific spiritual knowledge and experiences were given over time and under careful guidance. You have been prepared and personally blessed by the Divine to receive exactly what is appropriate for your own growth. **Sharing the same experiences or exercises with another less-conditioned individual may not be in their best interest.** More important than sharing is to give respect and freedom to others. We are not trying to convince or push our beliefs on anyone, that would be violating another's free will. If someone seems interested perhaps offer them one of Prophet's books, share the Articles of Faith posted online, or help them find his videos. Remember it is not your job to make someone understand or to be receptive.

Be discerning and selective with what and with whom you share. Giving someone a partial truth or too much truth that is not well understood can be more harmful to the recipient than sharing nothing at all. **If you have clear inner communication with Prophet it is best to ask for guidance on what the other person would most benefit from you sharing.**

At the retreat center, with Prophet's guidance, sharing of experiences is often very helpful to the one sharing and to the other students. Much personal and spiritual information is freely shared and discussed in class. Upon leaving the retreat much discernment should be exercised before sharing personal experiences or the experiences of others from the retreat. If those outside of the class wish to have more information, they too can come to the retreat center for themselves. This includes family.

Study Guidance: For you reading this book be cautious what you share with someone who has not read this book. I have attempted to guide you at the appropriate rate and introduced material in a certain order. You also have the benefit of the "Keys in Action" stories that illustrate the Keys more fully and demonstrate how well these spiritual principles and tools really do work if applied in daily life. **The first priority is to do no harm to another Soul.** A rapid change in a spiritual viewpoint can be disruptive, not a blessing. When appropriate, sharing with another hungry Soul can be a wonderful experience.

Give Respect and Freedom

It is important that we do not interfere into other persons' affairs without their permission. Doing so demonstrates a lack of respect and lack of love. It also takes away their freedom to handle their own affairs without interference. You can usually tell if someone is receptive to your help. If they are not receptive you are wasting your time making suggestions.

When we violate a person's freedom we open ourselves to losing our own freedom. When we violate a person's space by offering our advice or help without their permission it shows a lack of love and respect for that Soul. Love and respect another Soul enough to allow them the freedom and respect to handle their own affairs and work through their own problems without meddling.

With an understanding of the Key Cause and Effect and the Key Karma we see people's problems, challenges, and lessons are generally created by themselves. We certainly have compassion for other Souls, but we let them work through their own lessons. **We do not have the right to "butt in" and take over their life lessons. If asked, we can make suggestions that they themselves may decide to use. They too have the God-given free will to choose their own way.**

A subtle type of interference is trying to change someone's opinion or way of thinking. We do not have the right to push our beliefs on another. We do not pray that another person will change or see things the way we see things. **Trying to change another's state of consciousness, without their permission, is a violation of spiritual law and we will be held accountable.**

Give respect and freedom to yourself. If others do not show you respect and honor your boundaries, do not spend time around them. This Key is liken to the Golden Rule: Do unto others as you would have them do unto you.

A true Prophet of God will not interfere in another's business, personal affairs, or state of consciousness without permission. This is one reason why a student of Prophet's may want to invite the

Prophet to be with them daily. Students may request spiritual help, guidance, and experiences from Prophet daily. You may invite Prophet into contemplations and other spiritual exercises if you want his help and guidance. This also lets Prophet know you desire truth.

Study Guidance: Respect others enough to not give unsolicited advice. **Trying to change another's state of consciousness, without their permission, is a violation of spiritual law.**

Give Love First

If you seek more love in your life, then find a way to first give love. This Spiritual Key truly will bring more love into your life. It follows the principle to first draw close to God and then God will draw close to you. When one gives love, preferably without expectation or conditions, God's Grace will ensure love returns to the sender.

If love is given to a specific person, love may return from that person or it may not be returned. For God to ensure love is returned from a specific person would violate that individual's free will. **However, love will come into the seeker's life from somewhere, even if not returned directly.**

Also, the form of the love returned may differ than the love imagined or desired. Remaining flexible and open to the way the love is returned is important, but love will find a way to the one who first gave it, if the love was freely and joyfully given from the heart.

For example, a student of mine recently expressed she had desired more affection from her husband for many years, but was still waiting. She wanted more touching, kisses, and hugging throughout the day. After some mentoring it turned out that she was waiting for him to first show affection. Also, when she did do nice things for her husband she had an attitude of resentment. I suggested she ask me, the inner Prophet, each day for ways to demonstrate her love to her husband. She learned to first give love and began to really find joy in her heart when doing nice things for her husband. She truly began to joyfully demonstrate the love she had always had for her husband. Almost immediately her husband began finding ways to demonstrate the love he had always had for her, including the physical demonstrations of affection she had so desired.

Study Guidance: This principle truly works! God's Grace guarantees love will return in some way, shape, or form. For those of you desiring more love in your life, first find ways to give love. There are infinite ways to give love: do something nice for another, help someone move into a new home, take another person's shift at work, do repairs another cannot do, watch someone's pet, show extra respect, speak more kindly, pick up your mess in the kitchen, put away the food you got out of the refrigerator….. and on and on.

Richard Maybury's Practical Laws of Life

Richard J. Maybury is the author of the series of books called "Uncle Eric Books." His books are full of wisdom for children and adults alike. The following quote is Maybury's Two Laws of Life and is found in his book *Whatever Happened to Justice?*

1. Do all you have agreed to do, and

2. Do not encroach on other persons or their property.

These two laws would benefit any society that follows them. They have been included here because they are similar to the Key "Give Respect and Freedom." They remind us that our freedom stops where another's freedom begins. Love does not interfere in the lives of others without their permission. These two laws are spiritually sound, and spiritually mature Souls would follow them happily and naturally.

Prayer

As Soul you have free will to pray any time and in any way you wish. However, on our direct journey home to God, some general principles of how God and Prophet view prayer may be helpful, save you time and energy, and avoid creating negative karma.

Our primary prayer is HU, which is unencumbered by words. To find the perfect words to express yourself requires being somewhat mental, whereas singing HU is usually from the heart. It is a pure prayer because we send love without telling God what to do or asking for earthly material objects. Under Prophet's (a concentrated form of the Holy Spirit) care our needs are known and provided for without the need to ask repeatedly. Our prayer, HU, reflects our desire for the Heavenly treasures such as love, joy, peace, clarity, wisdom, humility, opportunities to serve, true freedom, etc. **When we HU and then listen, we show in our prayer we are mostly interested in hearing what God wants to tell us, rather than telling God what to do.**

When we HU, God sends some of the love we send to Him to other Souls in the form of specific blessings of His choosing. So every time we sing HU we are actually praying for other Souls, but letting God decide the specifics. Often God will send this extra blessing to those close to us or those we are concerned about, without our needing to ask. **It is okay to let God know before we sing HU, if it is His will, to please send some of this love to a particular person or troubled area etc.**

When we pray for specifics it is usually for others. For example, "God please help Sue with her XYZ problem, if it is in her best spiritual interest, and if it is Your will, thank you." **We do not assume we know what is best for another Soul or tell God what He must do!** But our prayer is always HEARD, and it does make a difference for the one we are praying for. God does like to hear we care enough for another Soul to take time to pray for them. We do not pray specifically for another Soul to change their opinion or their state of consciousness.

When we have a specific prayer for ourselves it is usually for things such as clarity, understanding of a situation, help to keep our heart open, strength to do what is right, asking what God wants us to do, etc. Generally we do not waste our time and focus praying to "win the lottery" etc.

Prayer has power and can also be used in ways that hurt people and add negative karma to the one praying. For example, a church group prays for someone to return to their church after that person chose to leave. The prayers may work and have the person return. All those involved in that prayer, which violated another's free will, pick up some very bad karma. It may be that Spirit led the person who left to the place Spirit had chosen for them. One of the most serious spiritual violations is to get between a Soul and their path to God.

Prayer should be a beautiful, personal, and sacred time to share what is in your heart with God, and to listen to Him. Your prayers are always heard, whether you recognize a response or not. Heartfelt prayers that are not rote or routine are favorably received. One heartfelt prayer touches God's Heart more than a long memorized list of many things or people. Really be "real" in your personal moment with God. Savor your time in prayer. **Do not always make it about asking for something; make it about spending quality time with your Maker.**

Study Guidance: Expressing gratitude to God is a form of prayer. Prayer is communication with God, a personal spiritual exchange, and is an **extreme privilege.** It should be a time of joy, not simply a check-in-the-box. Prayer should never be rote or routine. After praying it is best to **spend time listening to God.** In listening for God's response, we desire to trust God and surrender to His will rather than our own will.

Connecting Spiritual Events

Every day God is protecting, guiding, teaching, and often making life a little smoother for those under the care of His Prophet. Unnecessary obstacles in life are removed or mitigated by His Grace. **When one recognizes these everyday demonstrations of God's Love, a new and greater appreciation and trust in God's reality and Love grows.**

For example, you have a flat tire on your vehicle but at a very convenient time and place. Flat tires are going to happen to everyone, but having it at the best time and at a safe location is often by God's Grace. What if you were leaving home with your family to drive across the country in a couple days? It would be better to have to fix a defective and unsafe tire that goes flat while your car is parked in your driveway than while traveling. In this example you connect the timing of the flat with your family trip coming up in just a couple days and realize the blessing of the flat tire before your long trip. It's a sign of spiritual growth when you recognize the blessing of a situation rather than perceive it as a negative.

The following is an actual example of recognizing and connecting events where the Divine made life easier and safer. My son Del IV borrowed my twenty-five-year-old truck to get a load of mulch from the local lumber mill in Fishersville, Virginia. During the trip the belts on the engine that control the power steering and the water pump failed. However, the failure took place fifty yards before the turn into the business that does my truck and auto repair!

Kate, Del IV's wife, just happened to be in town in her car at the same time he was at the repair shop. It is very unusual for Del IV and Kate to be in town at the same time in different vehicles. He left the truck to be repaired and Kate brought him home.

But there is more to this story. The last time my truck was driven off the property was when my wife Lynne and I were coming home from the Richmond, Virginia airport. It was midnight, and we were very tired and just wanted to get home from our trip. I had a very strong feeling that my old truck might break down on the way home. I was so concerned about a truck problem I paid attention to every mile-marker along Highway 64. I wanted to be able to tell AAA our location by giving them the mile-marker closest to our location. I definitely felt the Divine got us home safe without any problems.

It turns out the truck did have a repair necessary and coming, but it happened fifty yards from the repair shop in the middle of the day, not at midnight on Highway 64. The Divine also had Kate in town to help Del IV get home without anyone having to drive down to town from the mountain to get him. The next day Del IV got the repaired truck and his mulch.

I believe these events were connected and orchestrated by the Divine as a gift of love. **If you pay attention you will learn to recognize and connect daily events where the Divine is protecting, guiding, teaching, or making life a little smoother, as a gift of love through His Grace.**

Events such as these remind us every day of God's Love and that He is aware of us and our lives. We learn through experiences that even the smallest things in our lives matter to Him. As we learn to recognize these kinds of blessings we may more fully appreciate our relationship with God and His Prophet! In time our appreciation grows into true love and reverence.

Study Guidance: Connecting spiritual events helps you to see Divine blessings more clearly, recognize cause and effect, God's protection and Love, and Prophet's constant presence. The Three-Part Prayer will help in recognizing and connecting spiritual events. **Once you begin to see the connections, it is difficult to not see them every day. Then you are even more certain of God's Love, guidance, protection, and of the presence and love of His Prophet.**

Step Five Keys in Action

River of Golden Love

Singing HU has many benefits for those that sing it. Ultimately though, it is not about us — it is a love song to God. It is a chance for us to give thanks for our blessings and express our love to God with no strings attached. God is a giver by nature, so it is not surprising to realize He sends this love right back, to us and to others, in countless ways.

Over the years I have come to appreciate HU more and more. It has many facets and layers to what it is, and what singing with a grateful, open heart can do. Learning about HU is like learning about God, it is never-ending and amazing. Singing HU is a pure way to send love to God. It helps tune one in to Divine Spirit and open one's heart to receive blessings of love, peace, joy, clarity, strength, healing, spiritual truth, and more. HU can raise one up to a higher spiritual view to be more receptive to Prophet's inner communication and teachings. It can also be a way of praying for others. It is not asking for anything specific or trying to direct God in anyway. Simply sing HU and send love to God with a gentle intent in your heart for others to be blessed, then surrender this prayer and let God take care of the rest. Our Father knows His children. He and His agent, the Prophet, know what people need and the best way to deliver the blessings.

We were gathered with Prophet on a beautiful winter morning to sing HU, a love song to God. I had a conscious intent in my heart for God to use the love sent in my HU song to bless other Souls in whatever way He knew best. I then surrendered the outcome. I maintained my focus on sending love to God. Then a scene came into my inner vision. I saw a river of gold and was drawn toward it. I stood alongside this beautiful flowing river for a while then began walking upstream. I could see HUs arriving at the source of the river. They appeared as containers of all types that were filled with love. Some looked like coins, others as blocks or shapes of different kinds. As the individual containers were poured into the river they were turned into liquid gold.

I then followed the river back downstream through a valley surrounded by mountains. In the distance where the sun met the horizon, I saw the river pouring over the edge and down into a swirling vortex. I had a knowing this golden river was a river of God's Love. It was being poured out from the Abode of God down to all the Heavens below. As God's Love initially went out, it was very intense and concentrated. I watched this from above and then experienced it from below as it came down into the lower Heavens. As it came into the lower material realms, below the fifth Heaven, it was toned down. And when God's Love came into the physical world it became even more subtle. It almost seemed the intensity of God's Love was being disguised in many ways so not to scare or startle anyone. It came as comfort to some, a smile to another, companionship to someone who was lonely, a warm meal to one who was hungry, a kind look, acceptance, and family. The delivery was so unobtrusive, gentle, or familiar that it was often not seen for what it was, a very personal gift of love from the Father to His beloved children. How beautiful it was to witness where our HUs go, and how amazing it was to be shown some of what God does with love sent to Him when we sing HU.

In reflecting on this experience I have gained a new perspective of the blessings in my own life. God's Love is infinite. It is sometimes soft and warm as in this experience, but it can also be more direct, intense, or seemingly disruptive. It may come as change in outer circumstances of life or through a life lesson that facilitates growth in some way. It may come by way of the Prophet showing truth about ourself or a situation, or by providing an inner experience that brings a higher view of life. I am very grateful for the gift of love that gives me the eyes to see and brings deeper appreciation for the ways God expresses His Love.

Written by Lorraine Fortier

Keys in this story: HU, God's Prophet, Gratitude, God's Love, HU (as a prayer for others), Balance and Detachment (surrendered and detached from the outcome of her prayer), God's Grace (to let her see God's Love from Its source going down to the lower worlds), Prayer

A Living Teacher

Singing HU tunes you in with Spirit. When sung properly it is a source of spiritual food for Soul by "raising you up" and "opening you up" to more directly experience the Kingdom of Heaven. The HU song is one of the greatest gifts God has given to Soul. Having a living teacher who can offer correction to help keep us on course is an even greater gift.

I earnestly tried on my own to know God in my life. I wanted to recognize His Presence and live a happy life. Into my early twenties I was an avid seeker. I tried different paths, meditation techniques, yoga, Sufi dancing — almost anything to quench the thirst I had inside for Spirit and for true peace. Yet all I found were dead-ends. An answer to a prayer led me to Del Hall and the Guidance for a Better Life retreat center. This is where I learned the importance of having a living teacher who fluently communicates with God and can teach me to recognize and understand my own communication with God.

It is a tremendous gift of love from God to have a living teacher and guide to show us the ways of the Divine. One reason I have found this to be invaluable is for the correction we can receive from him. I experienced the importance of this firsthand after having been a student of Del's for over twelve years.

I was using the tools and teachings Del had given me when I went through a time of hardship. I received an inner nudge from the Prophet to focus more on gratitude before singing HU to open my heart in appreciation. I followed his guidance and did this at home. Soon after, I attended a weeklong retreat at Guidance for a Better Life. Being a smaller, more intimate class, it was a chance to have more individual attention and focus more on the details of our journey.

HU is a beautiful love song to God, a sound vibration and prayer that can uplift us when we are afraid or need clarity. It is a cornerstone of the Prophet's teachings, and I love to sing it throughout my day. It acts as a tuning fork that brings one into alignment with the Holy Spirit, but that winter my pitch was off.

Instead of singing a pure HU, I was warbling. The effect was that I was not getting the spiritual nourishment nor upliftment that singing HU can bless us with. Even the best instrument needs to be tuned regularly, or it will be off.

In class Del pointed out that I needed to slow down and really sing love to God and to be precise, not only in the tone, pitch, and volume with which I sang HU but also in Its pronunciation. Without Del's seemingly minor correction, I would have gone on misusing this beautiful tool at home. I would not have had any lasting benefit in my daily life. I would have remained spiritually undernourished. This adjustment brought a real transformation in my quality time with the Divine, and as a result, my life began to transform.

Del once used an analogy of a ship crossing the ocean. A small error in direction would not affect a short journey, but for a longer journey a little misdirection means you end up on the wrong continent. There is a profound blessing in receiving correction from a living Prophet, precisely for this reason as we journey home to God. As a living student, we need a living teacher. One true blessing of having a relationship with the Prophet of our times is that he can give correction and guidance on the inner and on the outer as a teacher.

Proverbs says, the Lord corrects those He loves. As an agent for God the Prophet gives truth, love, and guidance as well as correction to his students. At times the correction is in the gentlest manner and at other times it is more direct. But when the truth is accepted by the student, myself included, and the changes implemented into our lives — we see the fruits of the Spirit. Life is better when following the guidance of the Divine. Correction and pruning is part of an abundant life and our growth as Soul. Having a living teacher is a gift I treasure to this day. His loving correction has truly helped me on my journey home to the Heart of God.

Written by Molly Comfort

Keys in this Story: Prayer, God's Prophet, Gratitude, HU, Soul, Receptive, God's Love (providing a living teacher)

Keys not yet studied: Proper Focus, Truth is Love, Spiritual Food

Brother's Passing

Losing a loved one is hard enough. It can be even more challenging when they take their own life. Too often people fall into feeling guilty at what could have been done to prevent it. This is a losing battle, one that will close your heart and pull you down. We must accept that they are ultimately responsible for their decisions — the good ones and the bad ones. We must also have faith that God does indeed still love them and that they will not be eternally damned. Ask yourself if this is your idea of something a loving God would do, punish you forever for one mistake? Eternity is a long, long time. Would you cut off your child forever, withdrawing all love for one lapse in judgment? Are those that take their own life still loved by God — absolutely. Are they still held responsible — absolutely. And what does that look like? Most likely a quick return into a new body to begin again, usually into a similar situation where they have another chance to face the challenges they struggled with before. Life is about growing into greater capacities of wisdom and love and it takes time. Time that a loving God graciously gives us.

I received a call from my mother who was frantically repeating over and over, "We lost him; we lost him." My eldest brother had died. He struggled most of his adult life with bipolar episodes. Numerous bi-polar episodes and other serious ups and downs took a toll on his marriage. After a divorce his life became more unstable, and his life seemed to be spiraling downwards. On his birthday we talked by phone; I was looking forward to having time with him in person at Thanksgiving. That time never came.

After starting a new job in another city he became extremely depressed and ended up at the mental health unit. On that fateful day my parents had gone to petition for his early release into their care, saying they could provide a safe environment for him. My dad had left the keys to the car by the phone, and when they were all napping, Dave got up and slipped out of the house. The car was his means to end his life.

My family was grief-stricken and my parents were full of guilt. I also wondered what I could have done differently, and I too started feeling guilt. In contemplation, connecting with the Prophet on the inner, I received very strong inner guidance not to allow my heart to fill with guilt. He assured me that anything I might have done would not have changed the outcome for Dave. I felt a release from guilty feelings shortly after my contemplation. Without the guilt I was more able to support and comfort my family.

Two weeks after Dave had passed I prepared for my early morning contemplation, singing HU and connecting with the Divine on the inner. Instantly I found myself at a favorite spot by the pond at the Guidance for a Better Life retreat center. Prophet was standing to my right, and my attention was drawn to the left by some movement. There was my brother Dave, looking like he had in his late twenties. He looked robust and healthy. I was very happy to see him. I introduced him to the Prophet but then realized Dave already knew the Prophet because he had brought Dave to me. My gratitude was immense to be with my brother once again.

My mother and father continued to suffer deeply with grief and guilt. I always thought my dad would live to be at least a hundred years old. He now seemed to age rapidly and was rather miserable and somewhat bitter. A month after his ninetieth birthday he had a stroke and died. I did not have the opportunity to say good-bye. Six months went by, and one evening as I sat down to HU at bedtime, suddenly there was my dad in my inner vision! He looked much younger, glowing with good health. It struck me how happy he looked and totally at peace. I do not recall him looking that happy or peaceful, ever.

I am very grateful to the Divine for giving me these precious experiences with my brother and my dad. Both experiences helped to heal my heart from my loss. And even though my brother ended his own life, breaking spiritual law, I know God still loves him and will care for him.

Written by Jan Reid

Keys in this story: Contemplation, God's Prophet, HU, Gratitude, God's Grace (by allowing Prophet to bring Dave and Dad to Jan) God's Love (healing Jan's heart), Cause and Effect (her brother's choices and actions in this life will have an impact on his next lifetime) — Keys not yet studied: Prophet's Inner Presence (released her from guilt)

God's Light Gives Peace to a Troubled Heart

Experiencing the Light of God can provide healing and comfort. Sadness, guilt, regrets, worry, and so on, can be washed away in Its presence. When bathed in the Light it also helps us to see clearly, including seeing ourselves and the actions that are holding us back. This combination of God's Love, truth, and action on our part, can lift us out of the darkest hole.

Back in 2001, I was going through a difficult time. I was facing a lot of change all at once and was feeling overwhelmed with sadness and a bit of fear for my future. I was twenty-eight years old and had recently bought my first home with my partner of eight years. I worked from home at this time. A few months before we bought our house together I had gotten into some legal trouble. I was waiting for my court date to find out whether I could keep my driver's license or not. This was causing me stress.

About eight months after we had bought our home, my partner and I broke up. This was largely due to my shortcomings, although in hindsight it was the best thing for both of us. We had gradually been growing apart but bought a home in the hopes it would make our relationship stronger. It didn't. Shortly after we broke up I lost my driver's license for six months. In a very short period of time I went from a new home where I had my office, to no home, and no place to work, and no driver's license. Not to mention the split with my partner. It was a difficult time in my life.

I moved out of the house into my younger brother's home and rented a room there. This was humbling to say the least, yet I needed this lesson. I always knew God was with me through this. Still I was sad and guilt ridden for my sense of failure. I had no spiritual tools but prayer, and it turns out, that is all I needed to get me through this time. I was not in any formal religion nor was I particularly "godly." However, I found out that even the "least of thy servants" can be comforted and shown God's Grace during times of need.

I was sleepless for the third night in a row, and as I laid in my rented room and bed crying — I prayed to God. I prayed for comfort and to be able to rest. Just then, I felt a warm blanket of blue light come over me. The light was in my inner vision, and it was very loving and peaceful. I fell asleep looking at this light and I woke up refreshed. The feeling of sadness and regret was replaced with hope and renewal. I took responsibility for my mistakes and took steps to rectify them.

I changed the way I lived my life, and soon after I found a spiritual path that was right for me. I really think this time of change, even though difficult, was the turning point in my life for the better. It showed me that God cared about me enough to comfort me, and now I wanted to do my part too.

Written by Tash Canine

Keys in this story: Prayer, God's Love (God sent Prophet to comfort Tash — blue light), Cause and Effect (how Tash was living life brought on her troubles), Growth of Consciousness, Discernment, Understanding Change

You Are Not Alone

You are loved and you are not alone. When you are blessed to actually experience these two truths, joy and abundance can more fully flourish in your life. An aspect of the Divine is always with you to provide love and guidance.

One of my earliest memories from this life is sitting in our playroom and the comfort that I received in these four words.... "you are not alone." I was about six at the time, and my parents were going through a divorce. I was blessed that both of my parents had given me a strong foundation that I was loved no matter what, yet I was still hurting inside and felt lonely. There was a sadness and uncertainty in our house that naturally came from the process of the divorce.

This particular afternoon I was watching the rain out the window and feeling very alone as I swung gently on our indoor swing. Suddenly I had the sense I was being comforted. No one was physically near me; I was physically alone, yet a presence was with me, and I heard and knew the truth in these words "You are not alone." I remember curling into that loving presence and feeling safe and secure in that love in a time when my outer structure felt unstable. I was safe in this presence. "It" knew my heart without me even having to speak. And "It" comforted me on such a deep level. I continued swinging, not wanting the presence to leave. Yet time moved on. I do not recall even thinking to ask someone what that presence was, I just knew it was a real experience. "It" loved me, and that "It" was speaking truth, that I was not alone, no matter what I faced in life.

It was not until many years later, when I was in my twenties and came to the Guidance for a Better Life retreat center, that I learned more about the presence I had felt as a child. One of the first truths I learned at the spiritual retreats was the same truth I had heard on the inner as a child, "You are not alone." God had sent us into this world with a guide to help us return Home, and to make the journey smoother. Over the years, this truth has become a foundation in my life. My teacher Del, the Prophet of our times, has taught me to recognize Divine communication and to see the presence of God's guidance in my daily life. God still speaks to His children. Just as it is promised in the Bible, our Heavenly Father has sent and blessed us with a Comforter who is always there, not only in our times of need, but in our times of joy as well. I am so grateful that this truth has become a living reality in my life. Prophet is this presence of Divine love that guides, nurtures, teaches and helps clear the way, so we don't have to wait until the end of this life to experience Heaven's gifts. He is a guide that can help us here and now to experience God's treasures of peace, contentment and most of all God's Love.

We truly are not alone. Listen for His guidance, it is there for each and every one of us during our journey here on Earth. Listen, and you too may hear God's Voice comforting and guiding you home to peace, to true security, and to love. Reminding you that you too are not alone.

Written by Molly Comfort

Keys in this story: God's Prophet (was with Molly when she was a child and comforted her in her time of need) God's Love, Peace of Mind and Heart (as a child)

Keys not yet studied: Truth is Love

Note: There is really only one "Prophet," but the spiritual authority works through various physical embodiments — i.e. different physical Prophets throughout history.

He Came to Us

One of the greatest benefits for students of the Prophet is his ability to meet with them inwardly, regardless of their physical location. His ability to teach inwardly within the spiritual realms and the physical waking state is cause for exponential growth. In a very real sense the student is never alone, and spiritual growth can carry on continuously.

On August 2, 2015 there was a HU sing on the mountain at Guidance for a Better Life in Virginia. I inwardly asked my spiritual guide, Prophet Del Hall, if I could join them from where I physically live in the Hudson Valley of New York State. My friend had asked me if I would be attending the HU Sing, and I relayed to her that I was going to joyfully sing from home. She asked if she could join me, and I was thrilled by her request; I value HU and for her to value HU too opened my heart.

An hour before the HU sing was to begin we walked along Arden Trail to a point my friend loves that overlooks the Hudson River. We came upon an incredible vista of West Point to the left with the Hudson Highlands in the distance, and the shoreline of Garrison to the right. It was a beautiful view and it was a perfect day: no humidity in the air, sunny with the sky speckled with puffs of cumulus clouds. After we found our own niches to sit in upon the rock, we looked out feeling especially grateful as we watched and heard a gaggle of geese take flight from the water to the sky. It was a beautiful sight, and I shared how my spiritual teacher Del likes geese and their sound, and how they mate for life. I said I could not help but know he was with us at that moment.

As we sat to take it all in, we noticed something floating out beyond on the water. I thought it looked like a package wrapped in a brown paper bag. My friend said it looked like a life preserver. It was too far to tell, but either way I recognized how being able to sing HU was a gift to me and my lifeline as well. I then read out loud from one of Prophet's books, "Nourished in the Light of God," and then we sang HU for twenty minutes with about ten minutes of silence afterward. As we sang, the sounds around us increased. The cicada in the tree to our left sang along with us. Loudly I heard a goose singing too, and I opened my eyes to view this one goose swimming close to us singing out its call as we sang out our prayer to God. In the distance, the gaggle of geese joined in. A train now passed by with the HU in its whistle, and the waves from boats that must have coasted by lapped upon the rocks, sounding like ocean waves. A gust of the perfect wind blew upon us. It was Heavenly.

As we sang, the Love of God was with us, and I experienced this: spiritually and inwardly the inner Prophet was on the water in a boat that looked similar to a canoe but very steady and sturdy. He paddled up to us and invited me in. I was able to step in without feeling off balance. We sat together enjoying the serene experience. Being in his presence immediately uplifted me and filled me with a love for God. As he paddled, we came upon the floating object on the water's surface. He encouraged me to reach over the side of the boat and grab it. I eagerly did. It was a package and was in fact wrapped in the paper of a brown bag! It was addressed to me, with my full name on it and with the word "Soul" in large letters. As I carefully opened it, savoring every moment of peeling the tape from the paper, I thought of my husband because that is how he opens his gifts — slowly and savoring the experience as the contents are revealed. When the package was loosened, a huge beam of light escaped right out, up, and from it. We were outside of God's beam of white, pure Light, and inside of it as well. My friend was there with us. She was on the rock singing HU and on the boat at the same time.

From this huge beam made of light and sound, a strand of light came out and went into my heart. I noticed Prophet had an individual beam coming from his heart, which went directly into mine. I was filled with such love that is really indescribable. I was enveloped into It. The magnificence of this beam of God's Light covered our original view and beyond, and the space it took up was above and beyond our vision. I was in the midst of this beam of light that went from the river to well into the sky and beyond, and with this, we were still, calm, and at peace yet full of such intense joy and happiness and complete love.

In the beam I knew the sacred Holy Book lay. I was encouraged to open the book randomly and read from it. There at home, I knew I was to do this too, and I saw my husband and two boys immersed in God's loving Light. Prophet and I stayed there, and I gratefully and willingly accepted the love that was being offered. The goose then made its call again bringing me back into my body, and the boom of the cannon from West Point made its point that we were in the protection of God's Love, inside of God's Heart, and in Its Light and Sound.

My friend expressed feeling at peace, calm and soothed. She said she would take it all with her and later on she let me know that she was still feeling it. I too have relived this experience every day since. Still sitting in the midst of love we saw what looked like a small white heart shaped piece of paper floating on the water coming toward us. My friend recognized this as a message that God surely loves her, and we were very thankful for the love that we felt and received, and for the gift of singing HU, a prayer and love song to God.

As we stood to leave, a beautiful yellow tiger butterfly floated gently by reminding us that God's Love is all around and could transform us if we allowed it to do so. I knew I wanted to take that with me and share it. Later as we walked and talked and enjoyed the many different viewpoints that single goose flew by us, calling out to us letting us know it was near, as I have surely come to know in the depths of my heart that He truly is.

Written by Moira Cervone

Keys in this story: HU, God's Prophet, Soul, God's Grace (Moira lifted up and experienced deep peace — also her friend), God's Love, Gratitude, Spiritual Sharing (invited friend to HU with her), Peace of Mind and Heart, Contemplation, Receptive, Prayer

Keys not yet studied: Prophet's Inner Presence, Personal Effort (took time to HU), Blending with God's Voice (inside and outside white light which is the Inner Prophet)

Prayers of Our Heart

God blesses us with the insights to live a life with less regret, but won't force us to follow the guidance. It's up to us to implement it and to do it in a timely manner. This story also shows how a loving God can provide another chance at a missed opportunity.

My father's health had been declining and within a short time period was failing rapidly. I had been in contact with him a few days prior, and during that time his lucidness and comprehension of the current date and time were off. Also, he was not being an easy patient to take care of for his wife, my stepmom. My father had been challenged through life with some mental instability and depression. From my view his day-to-day life was filled with fear and worry. His first marriage to my mother was not filled with much peace or love that I could see. I did see in his current marriage there was love and happiness, but due to his mental challenges those times were fleeting. Worry and fear were more constant companions, from my experience and observation. I feel true happiness and the experience of joy were never really known by him. I held a prayer in my heart from an early age that my father would have love in his life, and as I got older the prayer also included the wish for him to experience peace and joy.

I lived five hours away, so the phone was our primary line of communication. I had a nudge one night to call, but it was late and I was tired, so I decided to call the next day. I had been taught by my teacher, the Prophet, about the importance of following our nudges within the window of time we receive them because they are communication from the Divine. In this case I did not listen. When I called the next day and talked to my stepmom, I found out they had sedated him and were continuing to do so for his safety and comfort. He was now in hospice care, and I recognized I had most likely lost the opportunity to speak with him one last time. I wanted to tell him I loved him, and God loved him. I wanted to assure and comfort him about the transition of life he was going through, and tell him there was nothing to fear. In addition, I was holding a little guilt about the last conversation with him; I had not been as kind with him as I could have been and wanted to apologize.

I have been taught and know to be true, we are never alone; Prophet is always with us. After I got off the phone I immediately went to Prophet on the inner and apologized for not following my nudge to call the night before. I said a prayer of gratitude for his love and his care of my dad and stepmom as they were going through this challenge. I was singing HU, a love song to God, and immediately found myself spiritually in a room with my father who was resting comfortably in a bed and was fine. There were other Souls present, some I recognized as family members who had passed on and others I did not know, but their presence was comforting, and there was gentle light in the room.

My dad saw me and his face lit up, with me was Prophet, another spiritual teacher, and Jesus. He looked at me and said, "You know Jesus?" I said, "I do" and introduced Prophet and the other teacher to him. They greeted my dad and then left us to visit together. I had the opportunity to say the things I had wished to say and to hold his hand. After some time had passed it was time for me to go. I knew without a doubt my dad was being cared for and comforted, and we had our chance to say the things in our hearts. Even though his physical body was dying, he as Soul was alive and well. We were both gifted with the prayers in our hearts being answered. We both had one more opportunity to express love and caring to each other. What a huge gift to us both.

Within the week he passed on. Through the experience of my dad's passing, I will testify that the transition of leaving one's physical body when dying can be a comfortable and peaceful one. I was at a retreat at Guidance for a Better Life when my dad passed. The night before his passing, in contemplation, I saw my dad in a wheelchair being pushed by Prophet and the other spiritual teacher. My dad had a warm blue blanket wrapped around him. He waved and smiled, and I could feel he was at peace and happy. The color blue is a color Prophet uses as an indication of his presence. The color blue and the blanket indicated to me Prophet was caring for him during this transition.

The next morning a friend at the retreat shared she had a dream about a man in a wheelchair being wheeled onto a cruise ship, and she could hear his laughter. I knew that was my dad she saw, and he was being gifted with a joyful experience. You might wonder why she had that dream and not me. She is a dear friend, and Prophet gave her the dream to validate my experiences in case I had any seeds of doubt. The Prophet is with all of us. He hears the prayers of our heart, and my prayer for my dad was for him to experience peace and joy. Through my relationship with Prophet and in singing HU, I have been gifted with multiple blessings. From these inner experiences I know that we are loved, cared for, and the prayers of our hearts are answered in God's time. They are gifts of His Grace.

Written by Renée Dinwiddie

Keys in this story: Prayer (answered — to visit her dad, for dad to experience peace and joy), God's Prophet (gave Renee the nudge to call her dad), Receptive (NO, did not follow nudge), Gratitude, HU, God's Grace (Prophet took Renee to visit dad), God's Love (gentle light in room and dad being cared for and Renee having chance to say final words to dad), Soul, Contemplation

Keys not yet studied: Prophet's Inner Presence

A Prayer Answered

I have looked this testimony over many times while trying to create
the best introduction possible for you, the valued reader. It is a
touching story of the loss of a loved one, and the author's journey
through life afterwards. It contains wisdom on many aspects of the
journey of Soul while here in the physical. What though is the pearl? Is
it that "you are eternal," or maybe that "love transcends death," or
perhaps that "you will see your loved ones again?" Maybe it is that
"our prayers are heard." This testimony contains wisdom on all of the
above but to me the true pearl is this; you can, in full consciousness, be
taken into the higher Heavens if you have a teacher who is authorized
to do so. God's Prophet is a teacher and guide of this magnitude. There
is no limit to your growth and splendor as Soul if you have a teacher
who can help you connect directly with the Divine. I have been witness
to countless healings, miracles, and growth in consciousness through
the years from the Prophet helping people do just this. What is keeping
you from experiencing more joy and love? What is the prayer in your
heart? Are you looking for someone who can help you grow spiritually?
I know where many have found their answers.

Early one morning, when I was fifteen years old, my grandfather woke my brother and I up and sat us down on the sofa. My mother came into the room and she was crying. I was pretty sure she was going to tell us that my great-grandmother had died. We had never had someone close to us die before. Instead, my mother told us that our father had unexpectedly passed away. It was a devastating moment in my life. It hurt so much I closed down, withdrew, and put walls up around myself. For years I prayed to God, all I wanted was thirty seconds more with my father to tell him how much I loved him and to say goodbye.

I started searching for answers: Is there life after death? Where do we go when we die? Why are we here? Is there really a God? For many years I felt like my father was watching over my family and me, and that he was helping, protecting, and guiding me. I hoped this was true.

The death of my father affected all of my relationships. I always held something back, perhaps trying to protect myself from reliving that kind of pain again. Though I softened some as years passed, I was never really all in; not with my mother, brother, wife, children, or friends. With the birth of my children my heart did begin to open more, and the walls started to melt down.

Approximately twenty years after the death of my father, I had a very unexpected experience at Guidance for a Better Life. During a guided spiritual journey my spiritual teacher Del, the Prophet, took me into the inner worlds — the Heavens — in full consciousness. I left my physical body, and as Soul traveled with my teacher and visited my father. My father was healthy and younger. He sparkled and glowed and looked like he was bathed in a soft white light. He was filled with such an incredible love, more than I had ever experienced from him in the physical. I got to tell him how much I love him and missed him, which he already knew. We flew together in the Heavenly Worlds, and it was as if time did not exist. I will never forget this experience. When it was time to come back I really did not want to leave him. I did not want to lose him again. But one of the things I found upon returning consciously to my physical body was that my father and I have a love connection that will always be there. Before this experience I felt like I had a huge void or dark spot in my heart, now that was being replaced with love.

In one brief experience the pain I had buried down deep inside was healed. From that moment on, everything in my life changed for the better. This healing (which is one of many experiences I have had at Guidance for a Better Life) has affected my life in ways that have been so life altering and so positive that I do not have the words to express it in a few brief paragraphs. God's Divine Grace healed my heart and removed the walls around it, allowing me to give and receive more love in all areas of my life. I now enjoy more joy, true peace, abundance, and love than I could have ever imagined possible.

Written by Jason Levinson

Keys in this story: Prayer (to visit his father is answered), God's Prophet, Soul, God's Grace (traveling the Heavens to meet his father and healing Jason's pain), Gratitude

Keys not yet studied: Prophet's Inner Presence

Formal Childhood Prayers

*An important part of prayer is being able to "hear" the response.
God has equipped each and every one of us with the ability to
communicate directly with Him, but it takes practice. It is an art form.
As with all our retreats, students learn from both direct experience
and group discussions. One of the greatest realizations is that we are
heard. God truly reads the prayers of our hearts.*

In early childhood, at about the age of three, I was given a gift by my mother. She taught me to pray. I learned structured prayers to God, Jesus, Jesus' mother Mary, and to other Christian saints. My prayers were said at bedtime before sleep. Although I did not understand the meaning of the words of the prayers I was reciting, my young mind did not doubt they were heard in Heaven. As I grew more worldly, my prayers included petitions to God, Jesus Christ, and the Blessed Mother for them to watch over loved ones. Additionally, I was taught more sophisticated prayers to recite in church. Prayer had become increasingly compartmentalized, yet more urgently needed. Life was wrought with inconsistencies that my maturing mind began to wrestle with.

Questions about the behavior of the adults who were my examples were surfacing. Their behavior did not coincide with what was coming out of their mouths during prayer in church. My inner belief did not agree with many of the traditions and principles that were part of my religious education. Fundamental religious activities and concepts such as going to a priest to confess sins and going to hell if one died without doing so seemed preposterous. Even so, I continued to pray my nightly prayers, putting more focus on the words in hopes that by such intense effort; perhaps my prayers would more likely be heard.

As the years passed, I read many books and investigated many paths in search of some truth about God, myself, and life. One day I reached a place of despair that brought me collapsed to my knees, pleading to God to help me learn how to live. Within a year or so, a friend of a friend highly recommended a retreat at Guidance for a

Better Life. In my life I had never felt such welcoming love or been around folks who spoke about spiritual matters in a language that was so true for me. This was a prayer answered!

In time, I learned that prayer is so much more than petitions to my creator. Prayer involves listening with the ears and seeing with the eyes of Soul in order to follow the Divine's plan for my life. This plan, as it turns out, is so much better than my plan ever was. I learned the desires I held in my heart had manifested throughout my entire life, without me formally praying about them, were in fact prayers. The deeply held desires in my heart were heard loud and clear, and answered by God. He knows what is in our heart! God wants to bless us, even without formal prayers if it is in our best interest. To me, this ongoing journey of Soul that I am so privileged to be aware of is quite miraculous. I am so eternally grateful I received the gift of prayer.

Written by Bernadette Spitale

Keys in this story: Gratitude, Soul, Prayer, God's Grace (prayer answered), God's Love (felt through others at retreat)

Never Give Up on Love

Many marriages fail even when there is true love between the two Souls. For love to be of actual value it must be expressed and accepted, which becomes more and more difficult when our hearts are closed. When each partner is "right with God" and acts on His guidance, a marriage will truly flourish.

Having a beautiful life and enjoying it are two different things. Even a little lack of peace in one key area of our lives can create a wedge between us and true happiness. It can start to crowd out the joy and the love that is there by the Grace of God. My marriage produced three beautiful children in a wonderful home surrounded by family, friends, and loved ones, but issues between my wife and I always seemed to get in the way of a stable foundation. Despite the blessings and abundance God poured over our lives we were closer to getting a divorce than reaching our tenth anniversary. The love was there between us, but it never seemed to find its way. A wall of words; often harsh, bitter, and angry, expressed our growing frustration and unhappiness.

We tried counseling, worked on our communication, read books, listened to tapes, wrote down our goals together, but no lasting change came of it. We never could seem to clean the slate of the issues that plagued us. We had gone around and around in circles spinning our wheels until we were both worn out. It was affecting every area of our lives. A big part of this dream life was dying, and I felt helpless to do anything about it. In a place of resignation I arrived at Guidance for a Better Life in November for a weekend retreat. My heart was heavy. I was out of ideas, patience, and motivation. I was not happy with the results I was getting, and though I could not admit it at the time, I was very unhappy with myself. Something had to change.

There is a plus factor being in the physical presence of Del, my teacher, a true Prophet of God. Though communication extends beyond the physical, being there in person has its benefits. From the time I stepped onto the property I began to relax. In my experience, it is much harder to hear Spirit when we are uptight. We keep asking and keep praying with more volume and intensity and wonder why God does not answer us. Sometimes stepping back to take a deep breath and actually listen, with our ears and our heart, makes all the difference.

Within an hour of being on the property I was given an inner insight to a simple exercise to try when I went home. No words were spoken outwardly, but the Prophet, adept at reading hearts, spoke directly to mine. The suggestion? Bring a simple dry erase board to my wife and begin to write down all the issues in our marriage, and all those things she and I wished and prayed to be gone from our marriage; erasing each one, multiple times if necessary, until it was fully erased from our hearts and lives. Then on the other side of the board we were to fill it with those qualities we truly wanted to manifest, writing each one down as a foundation of our renewed covenant.

I felt hope well up in my heart for the first time in a while. If my wife was willing to try it there just might be a chance it could work. The retreat could have ended at this point and I would have been content, but my heart was still not conditioned to accept the healing I was being offered by the Divine. There were two more crucial components that were needed before I went home to share my gift. First, I was given the gift of remembrance. During an inner contemplation the Prophet took me back over every year of my marriage. With incredible clarity and detail, I was able to view my actions and regrets with kindness and understanding. Rising above the harsh emotional and critical viewpoint I was able to forgive myself, something that proved far harder than forgiving my wife.

The second gift was delivered when I sang HU together with the group. During the sacred love song to God, the space in my heart that was opened by forgiving myself was filled with such a deep peace that I committed never to let anything ever again steal it away. My heart was now ready. With my priorities put back in their proper order — God first, then my marriage — I felt confident all would work out for the best. When I arrived home my excitement to share this gift from God trumped any worries or concerns. I explained what I wanted to try and then wrote down a couple issues I was ready to let go of on the board. When I finally wrote down something I knew my wife would be thrilled to see gone, I watched her initial reluctance disappear. She then joined me in naming and then surrendering, one by one, the hurt and pain.

The results were stunning, greater than I could have hoped for. Every issue written down and erased seemed to lift almost immediately, like the Hands of God scooped it off our shoulders and out of our lives. These were things we had spent hours, weeks, and years "discussing" to no avail. Yet they seemed to melt away almost before we had written them on the board to erase them. For several hours that night, and for the next several days, we continued to write down these things slowly weeding them out of our lives. We had both prayed and tried and now, in God's timing and Grace, they were being removed.

Later in the week when we finally felt there was some room in our marriage and in our hearts again, we turned the board over for the second part of the exercise. We began adding the things we wanted to cultivate in our marriage: to help one another become the best we can be spiritually, to be a harbor of love, and to demonstrate our love and respect on a daily basis. It was as if the Hands of God were filling us up with these Divine qualities. Months later our relationship, rich and full with the fruit of the Spirit, is now also enjoyable, engaging, and fun. It is not only a better relationship; it is a transformed one.

God gave me a simple suggestion to follow through His Prophet, Del Hall. Following that advice in a timely manner has made all the difference in the world. It was the missing "peace" and the breakthrough we had been praying for. How grateful I am God heard and answered my prayer. The positive ripples from this simple gift will be felt for generations to come. This tool works in other areas of life, not just in relationships. Our ability to make conscious choices in our lives — to choose what we want to nurture and what we want to eliminate — is one of God's sublime gifts to us. Is there an area in your life you would like to welcome the Hand of God to transform?

Written by Chris Comfort

Keys in this story: God's Prophet, God's Grace (both Chris and his wife given a healing of their heart), God's Love, Prayer, Remembrance, Contemplation, HU, Receptive (first Chris then his wife), Peace of Mind and Heart, Discernment (better choices), Growth of Consciousness (both Chris and his wife), Gratitude

Keys not yet studied: Truth is Love, Proper Focus (in marriage and Chris's on putting God first), Personal Effort (Chris and his wife did their part to follow through on Prophet's suggestion)

Release from Defensiveness

We all have areas in our life that can rob us from experiencing peace and joy. However, we genuinely have the opportunity to transcend these areas that hold us back and experience more love and balance in our life, especially if we allow Prophet to help us.

You have probably known someone in your life that is defensive. Perhaps it is you who is weighed down with this character trait. As for me, I used defensiveness to cover up fear ever since my childhood. By the time I signed up for my first class at Guidance for a Better Life in 2006 my heart was pleading to be free from the destructive quality that affected my marriage, the parenting of my child, career choices, work relationships, school relationships, and friendships.

Early on in class we studied the role that passions of the mind like fear, anger, guilt, and worry play in blocking love from our heart, leaving us with limited ability to give and receive love. It was wonderful to finally find someone who taught the simple yet profound truth about what was keeping me from living in true peace and happiness. Naturally I wanted to have a greater capacity to give and receive love, but it would take some time to understand the mechanical defense mechanism I defaulted to whenever I began to feel fear. I recorded what was taught during class and brought my notes home with me to study and contemplate upon. My spiritual practices were important to me, so I reprioritized life around them.

I began to work in contemplation to find the source of fear that was the basis for my defensive personality. I was mercifully relieved to learn that errors in my early life could be corrected, and I could learn healthier ways to react under pressure. In prayer I asked God for help with self-discipline and spiritual maturity. Over time I learned to let go of useless and false concepts about myself and replace them with the accurate and useful truths that I learned at the retreat center and during contemplation.

My ability to learn and grow was enhanced when I focused upon my relationship with both the outer and inner aspect of Prophet. I prayed that his inner presence would be with me in every area of my life, and that I would be aware of it. I also prayed to listen better, to hear what was being communicated to me, and that I remember and follow his guidance along the way.

These days I seek to release destructive attitudes and allow the genuine kindness I feel toward other Souls transform my interactions with them. Because I have been blessed beyond measure to be both Prophet's student and to have a relationship with him, I am developing the awareness needed to become more conscious of my thoughts and behavior. Every so often I have an experience with an opportunity to react defensively that allows me to gauge the progress I am making toward more loving and tolerant interactions with others. Once in a while I may begin to experience a momentary flare-up of that old familiar feeling of the "fight or flight" response, but it never gets very far like it used to when it would overtake me.

Now I am able to silently sing HU and exercise conscious self-control, which allows me to stop and breathe in from the wellspring of love and protection offered by God. As Prophet's student I recognize these life experiences are spiritual growth opportunities that have been perfectly tailored for my personal lifetime syllabus, and that they are gifts of love to help me improve. The work is ongoing and the transformation of nearly everything about my inner being is altering my life in ways that words on paper cannot express.

The magnitude of having a direct representative of our Heavenly Father in the flesh among us during this time in history is indefinable. I am extremely grateful to have the opportunity to experience God's Love and care directly through His Prophet.

Written by Bernadette Spitale

Keys in this story: Prayer, HU, Contemplation, Growth of Consciousness, Attitudes and Thoughts, Soul, Gratitude, God's Prophet, God's Love, Remembrance, Discernment (developed "conscious self-control" over her emotional reactions)

Keys not yet studied: Truth is Love, Personal Effort, Prophet's Inner Presence, Proper Focus (reprioritized her spiritual life)

The Lord Spoke, Saying "I Love You"

To be successful on the path home to God you need to have remembrance of your experiences and blessings. Remembrance builds gratitude and appreciation in your heart, which makes you receptive to even more blessings. This can become an upward spiral drawing you closer to God, His Love, and His truth.

It was the middle of summer and the sky was a piercing blue above us as we sat nestled in the Blue Ridge Mountains of Virginia. A gentle breeze gave a slight reprieve from the hot and humid day which permeated the air.

This was a special day. As a student of the Prophet, I have been blessed to have many special and life-changing days, but this was to become a day that touched me deeply and has stayed with me giving reassurance and security. In class a fellow student had been sharing a story of how remembering and keeping alive her prior spiritual experiences had blessed her life. She had written many of them in her personal journals and had recently been appreciating, reviewing, and reliving some of the special times she had with God and His Prophet. She was keeping her blessings alive with remembrance and appreciation. Her talk naturally evolved into a discussion between fellow students. We shared about some of our own personal experiences with God over the years that had really touched and changed us, thanks to God's current Prophet Del Hall.

Gratitude was seeping out of every corner of our hearts as we recalled how much Prophet had not only taught us but helped transform our lives. We weren't expecting anything in return, just sharing our appreciation. It was almost as if we were speaking among ourselves about how he had blessed our lives, even though he sat quietly in the back of the room listening. When her talk and our sharing was finished he arose and went to take his place in his chair on the low stage in the front of the classroom. I could feel waves of peace, love, and appreciation spreading outward where he walked, like the fragrance of the sweetest rose permeating a room. I took in a deep breath. I felt anticipation for something, but for what I did not know.

Once seated, he spoke for God, as a true Prophet of God is ordained to do. "Come together with me. Come closer. Be with me. Just be together with me."

Remaining in our chairs we closed our eyes and listened. We followed our teacher Home to be with God. The Lord was calling us to be together with Him spiritually as Soul while we sat alive in physical bodies. We did not need to wait to know the Lord, through His current Prophet we could experience His Grace now. The following moments were full with the immense and immeasurable beauty of being present with the Presence of God. I lacked nothing nor did I want anything. This one moment was an eternity. All that mattered was loving God and being loved by God.

God speaks in many ways beyond words. On this quiet summer day He spoke in peace, fulfillment, quietude, gentleness, love, grace, absolute contentment, and more. With everything that I know of as me, and with all that I am, my heart poured out to the Lord, saying I love you too.

After what seemed like an eternity of just being and coming together inwardly with the Lord, Prophet arose and walked out of the classroom. Students slowly began to stir themselves and flow out of the classroom as well. The moment was over, but I was transformed. Being that close to the Presence of God brought such a security, and a clarity of God's Love for Soul that follows me into my daily life. I am so blessed. By the Grace of God I experienced His Presence hold me in loving embrace.

Relishing the blessing later that day with a good friend, I remember saying the amount of Divine love I experienced in those moments was enough to sustain me through eternity and transform my view of life to one of a lasting and true security in God's Love for Soul, for me. My friend wisely said, "if you remember it."

Written by Molly Comfort

Keys in this story: Remembrance, Soul (traveled Home to God), Gratitude, God's Prophet, Receptive, God's Grace (invitation to visit Heavenly Father), Spiritual Growth, God's Love

Guidance Finding a Child's Birthday Present

This is a great example of following the guidance of Spirit — of being able to recognize those gentle whisperings and having the trust to follow them. It is also a reminder there is nothing too "small" for Spirit to help us with.

It was the evening before the birthday party for my girlfriend's three-year-old son. I was arriving back in town after a long road trip, and I was on a mission to get this little guy a present. Ideally I wanted to find a Toys "R" Us, but I wasn't even sure there was one in my town. My car doesn't have GPS, so as I got to the outskirts of town I began to think of some other stores I did know of and headed toward that area.

As I proceeded, I found myself going a different way than I might normally go to those stores, and before I was even halfway there I felt a strong nudge to exit near a familiar shopping mall. Once I exited I felt another nudge to turn away from the shopping mall, heading in the opposite direction on a road I am pretty sure I had never driven. After about another half mile I rounded a bend, and there was a Toy's "R" Us I didn't even know existed in an area where I had never been.

I knew the Hand of God had guided me to this place, and specifically Prophet who I am blessed to have as my spiritual guide. This was beyond any coincidence, and I have grown familiar with the relaxed, gentle inner nudges Divine Spirit gives me throughout the day. I had already felt relaxed and "tuned in" all afternoon since I had enjoyed a particularly satisfying HU song that morning before I left on my trip. Singing HU every day and throughout the day helps me to stay in alignment with Spirit and "hear" God's Voice, which comes in so many different forms; in this case my own built-in GPS that guided me straight to where I needed to be.

My heart was already open to God's Love as I entered the store; such was my gratitude for the guidance I had just received. I browsed around for a while and eventually decided on a basketball hoop for toddlers that can be attached to a door or wall and used for indoor play. It was either between that or a freestanding one, of which there was only one left, and that one had a few more bells and whistles and was more for outdoor use. I felt good about the choice I had made, paid for it, and left the store. However, as I reached the parking lot I began to second-guess my decision, thinking about the freestanding hoop and how that might be better. My mind began weighing out the pros and cons until next thing I know I was headed back into the store to possibly exchange it. I went to the customer service desk still undecided about which toy to get but leaning toward an exchange.

As I reached the desk and began to speak to the employee about what I was thinking, a man and his wife approached and asked the same employee if a certain toy was in stock. The toy was a request from their son who had just sent them the specific brand and model number on their smartphone. To my amazement, it was the exact same freestanding basketball hoop I had just come back in to possibly purchase. Of all the toys in Toys "R" Us, this was the one they were seeking! The couple was pleasantly surprised when I was able to tell them their item was indeed in stock, and in fact, the only one left. I was even able to escort them to the section where it was, and sure enough it was exactly what they were looking for. They thanked me and left with their purchase.

To me this was an obvious confirmation my original instincts had been right. My mind had started to talk me out of what my heart already knew, but Divine Spirit intervened and gave me an "awake dream" (an out of the ordinary experience that got my attention) through the couple who were looking for the same toy. Not only did this help me with my choice, but the other family got served as well. They were able to find the right toy for their son, even receiving personal customer service in the process. It was clearly a win-win situation!

As if that wasn't enough, and as the saying goes, "Now for the rest of the story." Later on I was telling my girlfriend about my Toys "R" Us adventure, and she told me she and her son already had an outdoor freestanding basketball hoop. In fact, they had just taken it out of the garage the other day after a long winter and played in the early spring sunshine. She did not however, have one for indoors and said it would be perfect for inclement weather when he needed an outlet and couldn't play outside. So the indoor wall-unit was indeed the perfect gift! I did not know this at the time, but the one who guides me knows everything.

Some people speak of the grand miracles they may need to offer proof of God's existence, but to me the miracles are in the myriad everyday details of our lives that Spirit weaves itself into. To me that "weave" IS the miracle. God's Love was woven into every step I took that day, as it is every day. We are all inextricably linked and connected to that love if we only open our eyes to see it. God loves each of us personally, cares about what is important to us, and wants to bless us, from our greatest undertakings to the simplicity of finding a child's toy.

Written by Laurence Elder

Keys in this story: God's Prophet (guidance through nudges), HU, Gratitude, God's Love (all around even in the smallest details), Connecting Spiritual Events (recognized Hand of God throughout), Peace of Mind and Heart (he was relaxed and in tune which are forms of peace, allowing him to hear inner communication)

Keys not yet studied: Personal Effort, Spiritual Food, Consistency (HU daily), Proper Focus (on following Prophet's nudges and singing HU daily)

Love of God is All Around

God's Love is the food of Soul. It is all around us shining through into our daily lives in numerous ways. There is no lack of Divine love, it is simply a matter of learning to recognize it in all Its forms. Most fortunate are those who have been given the eyes to see this love.

One evening as I prepared for bed after a day at the Guidance for a Better Life retreat center, I knelt in prayer by my sleeping bag and asked to more clearly see the many ways in which God's Love pours into my life and to help me accept more of it. Sometime later I awoke in a dream and found that I was at my home a few hours drive away from the retreat center.

In this dream I was aware of my teacher standing next to me after he inwardly led me to my home. As I looked around I could clearly see that everything in my life is an expression of God's Love. I saw the smiles of my children and wife, the fruit trees in the yard and forest beyond, the furniture, house, and land; all these things are expressions of God's Love. As I looked around, seeing my usual surroundings in a new light, I perceived that all these everyday things of life sparkled with a golden light. Prophet, my teacher, walked with me and showed me that all my relationships and all the objects in life, from cars to couches, from food to fresh water, are all available to me by the Grace of God, and they are actual physical manifestations of the Light and Sound of God, the Love of God. I cannot say exactly how this information was conveyed to me, for I did not hear words spoken, but simply knew.

In this experience we even drove along my regular routes to the children's school and to my workshop and office. The way was paved with golden light. I could see there were no limits to the many forms of love, which are present in my life. I am constantly surrounded by God's Love: It is present in a fixed, static form that comprises buildings and items, it comes through other loved ones in my life, and there is also a dynamic, flowing love, which constantly pours forth into my heart, through the Prophet, from the very Heart of God.

So take a moment to look around your own life, and with Divine help and inspiration, see it all in a new light. There is no need to seek the Love of God, for you have this already in the measure you can accept today. With gratitude for the life we have today, let us draw nearer to God and find a more abundant life tomorrow, as God responds to our invitations and draws nearer to us.

Written by Timothy Donley

Keys in this story: God's Prophet, God's Love, Gratitude, God's Grace, Prayer, Growth of Consciousness, Peace of Mind and Heart

Keys not yet studied: Living Without Doubt, Proper Focus

Family Reunion in Heaven

A family prays to send love and comfort to a loved one who has just passed away. They all three were blessed to witness her arrival in Heaven. The following testimony is one perspective of the joyous reunion.

Aunt Mildred was one of those delightful ladies who was always cheerful and a pleasure to talk with. I admired her strength and her attitude to be happy and enjoy life. Her husband and sister, who was my grandmother, passed away several years ago. Because her health was failing she stayed in an assisted living facility. She recently had gotten the flu and was very ill.

It was a Sunday afternoon when my sister-in-law called to tell us that Aunt Mildred had passed. My husband and our two children sat together and sang HU, asking the Prophet to bless her during this time of transition. As I sang HU and was in contemplation I saw a beautiful field of green grass with rolling hills beyond. In the distance I saw a beautiful white city with tall white spires. In the field, family and friends who were already in Heaven gathered with joy and excitement to welcome Aunt Mildred.

As she walked towards the group her smile was huge and her eyes were bright with joy and wonder. As she came close to her deceased husband Chet, he stood still for a moment. He looked as though he had a lump in his throat; so overcome with emotion he could not move or speak. Then he took a step towards her, and she paused for a moment, tilted her head a bit as she looked at him sweetly, and then they embraced tightly, as though they would never let each other go. Grandma stood beside them in anticipation to welcome her sister. They embraced and then Aunt Mildred smiled broadly as she looked up to see the next person to welcome her. Grandma turned to me with eyes very bright and loving, and as I hugged her I must have said, "I love you Grandma," for she said to me, "I love you too dear" in her sweet loving voice. Those were the last words we had said to each other just before she had died several years earlier. It was as though we picked up right where we had left off!

One by one all my family members in Heaven came over to see me, and I got to hug each one. Grandpa shook my hand vigorously, just like he did when I was a little girl. He was laughing and his eyes sparkled with merriment. My dad, who had died twenty-five years earlier, looked young and healthy as he smiled at me, taking in how I had grown up since we were last together. As I hugged my other grandpa he slipped a black olive into my hand. I was delighted to experience that again, since I had forgotten he would do that for my brother and me at family dinners. I noticed he looked much younger and appeared very healthy and vigorous. I realized that when we were all together on Earth, my family seldom hugged each other. Here in Heaven everyone was joyously embracing. Perhaps here they were freed from hang-ups and had learned something about expressing love. In Heaven there is much more to experience than playing harps in fluffy white clouds!

I prayed for Prophet to bless the gathering, and he appeared on the inner. Everyone turned to look at him, and they gasped in awe.

Being in his presence was a huge blessing, and they knew this was very special. After the inner Prophet left no one spoke a word for a while, for they were so awed by being in his presence.

Later I introduced my husband and children to their relatives they had not met in this lifetime. It was such a joyous, happy occasion, and it was beautiful to see Aunt Mildred with her loved ones again, and to see her healthy and happy. And then there was even another blessing, as our cat Tigger, who had died a few years earlier walked by. The whole experience was blessings upon blessings! Thank you Prophet for making this possible. It was a joy and a comfort for me to see them all happy and well and to know Aunt Mildred was okay and was welcomed into a new life.

Written by Diane Kempf

Keys in this story: Prayer, HU, God's Prophet, Contemplation, God's Grace (Delivered by Inner Prophet, who took her into Heaven to see Aunt Mildred's welcoming), Gratitude

Keys not yet studied: Prophet's Inner Presence

Step Six: Spiritual Keys Study Guide

After completing Step One through Step Five I **once again suggest** reflecting upon how you are digesting the first five steps. If you have struggled or feel you have the "Spiritual Indigestion" I described earlier, perhaps take a break from moving forward for a while. There is no rush! Remember, at my retreats where I personally mentor each student, I take a minimum of two years to introduce the first five steps. I suggest continuing to sing HU daily to strengthen yourself spiritually. This will help you be better able to accept God's teachings and continue to grow without causing the mind to reject the truth and new spiritual concepts you are learning. Remember, you will get so much more out of this book by going at the pace that is right for YOU.

When you choose to continue, whether now or later, know that some of these Step Six Keys have already been introduced in the earlier Steps when reading the stories I shared, but will now be covered in greater detail.

When you have completed your study of the Step Six Keys, you will have been exposed to all the Keys shared in this book. I teach so much more about God and His ways in person at my retreats, but I have shared with you here all the Keys I have formally written down to date. You now have a wealth of spiritual wisdom that can take a lifetime to integrate and digest. To help you more fully see how the Spiritual Keys work so well together, and in many cases **must work together**, I have added twenty-five additional stories written by my students. I picked a variety of stories to best illustrate the Keys as a living ball of wisdom. God's Keys given to His Prophet have the power to open the gates to Heaven. I pray you have ALREADY been blessed, but there is always more.

The following Keys will be introduced:

Five Common Blocks to Spiritual Growth

The five common blocks that dramatically slow or block growth are:

1. Lack of consistency.
2. Not willing to make sufficient effort yourself.
3. Resisting the help on the inner and outer offered by Prophet.
4. Not including inner Prophet (Holy Spirit) in everything.
5. Complacency of the necessary requirements for spiritual growth.

These five categories of pitfalls lead to no growth or unnecessarily slow growth. **Not staying spiritually nourished is the start of most problems** for spiritual students and contributes to all five common blocks.

I recommend doing a contemplation to ask Prophet for insights on this topic for you personally. This contemplation, or series of contemplations, will reveal your most serious block, or potential block, to growth. With this information you can make a course correction, and it is YOUR responsibility to do so. Nearly everyone has at least one primary block or weak area, and most have several. Even so, few recognize when they have fallen into one of these five ruts, and many resist Prophet when he points them out.

The first common block to growth is a lack of consistency! Imagine how ineffective and even damaging binge eating, drinking, or exercising can be to individuals. Staying spiritually nourished is the primary area where consistency is vital. Steady growth generally yields better results over the long run than stop, start, stop, start growth. It is dangerous to one's path when they allow themselves to become undernourished spiritually, even for short periods of time! Possible consequences include poor decision-making and vulnerability to the negative side, Satan. When undernourished one is less likely to understand lessons or be receptive to corrections by Prophet and then fall behind.

The second block to a reasonable rate of growth is not being willing to help oneself, not being willing to work for insights, clarity, and spiritual nutrition. One can pray for clarity and understandings of these teachings, but then must read and study scripture, pay attention to dreams and awake dreams, recognize the Prophet's blessings daily, and **make the effort to go deeper with their experiences.** Those at the retreat center also help themselves by writing letters to Prophet and testimonies that have lasting value, contributing at retreats, and looking for opportunities to serve in other ways. You also help yourself immeasurably by doing all the above with Prophet.

The third block to growth is resisting help and guidance from Prophet. This may be due to not truly understanding the significance of God's Prophet, seeing mostly the man side of Prophet, or a person's stubbornness or vanity. Rarely does a spiritual student believe Prophet when this resistance problem is discussed. A classic example of resistance, the opposite of receptive, is when Prophet says something and the person shakes their head "NO" even before really considering the information shared. When one resists help from Prophet they are actually resisting God's LOVE and BLESSINGS.

The fourth block to real spiritual growth is NOT doing everything with the inner Prophet. This is mainly the challenge for advanced students. Without being led by the Holy Spirit throughout the day, one never REALLY lives this path of love. The goal is to be in tune with the Holy Spirit (Prophet) in every area of life. **Advanced students have the opportunity to bring the Light, Love and blessings of God to others when they do everything with the inner Prophet.** To not do so is a terrible lost opportunity to be used by Prophet to bless others and to serve as a coworker for God. Advanced students who still write letters to Prophet, read scripture, prepare facilitations for retreats, teach others, and try to understand their dreams by themselves, are not really living this path. One must be in tune with the inner Prophet to truly be a coworker for God.

The fifth block to growth is complacency. It is very insidious in that it "sneaks up" on the person. Either a student does not do spiritual exercises consistently, or the exercises are done rote or without bringing in the Prophet. One should remember that contemplations are a sacred moment together with the Divine and an opportunity to draw nigh to God. Another form of complacency is one's attitude toward the teachings of God and access to the Guidance for a Better Life retreat center. Over time one may begin to act as if these teachings are available to everyone and that this opportunity is guaranteed to remain available. They do not have remembrance that it is only by God's Grace they have this access and opportunity. Being too familiar with a Prophet of God leads to a dangerous form of complacency that is difficult or even impossible to overcome. <u>Advanced students are usually more susceptible to complacency than beginners</u>. Sometimes complacency sets in when one's life becomes very abundant and good after a few years of Prophet's mentorship and guidance. Then, sadly, the motivation for further growth is reduced and the student's growth plateaus or reverses.

The above common blocks to growth can slow one's progress or even completely block progress. Some advanced students begin to plateau or even slide backwards spiritually due to the above blocks. Others may grow slowly but never attain their full spiritual potential in this lifetime. What a shame that would be!

Study Guidance: God offers the **opportunity** through His chosen Prophet for tremendous spiritual growth, but there is **no guarantee** of success. Many of the success factors however, are within our control. **Being proactive** is a necessity in nearly every aspect of one's spiritual journey if they desire to be successful. **A passive or lazy person who does not learn to become proactive and internally motivated will not succeed.**

Proper Focus

To achieve success in most any endeavor in life requires good and proper focus. To grow spiritually to higher and higher states of consciousness also requires not just focus, but **proper focus**. One can have great ability to concentrate their focus, but if that focus is not applied to the appropriate and necessary topic then it is NOT proper focus and therefore has little value.

I have taught for many years that without **"Proper focus, proper practice, and prolonged determination"** one cannot achieve their true potential spiritually. Many of the Spiritual Keys and other teachings I share need to be **practiced, and put into practice,** to develop useful and meaningful proficiency. If the **"practice"** is done sloppily or done incorrectly, then one is often worse off than having no practice at all. It would be like an athlete practicing swinging a baseball bat totally wrong. They would develop incorrect muscle memory, thereby decreasing their hitting ability. In this example, improper practice actually harms their ability more than NO practice. I keep a watchful eye on my students at Guidance for a Better Life retreat center to catch improper practice or lack of practice. This is especially important when it comes to singing HU. Most of the amazing spiritual benefits of this love song to God are lost through **improper practice or lack of practice**.

To grow spiritually involves a gradual growth of one's consciousness. The mind tends to resist change, yet change is necessary for growth. To reach, experience, and understand a higher view of life spiritually, plus learn to actually live this higher and wider view, takes time. There is nothing quick about integrating spiritual truths into daily life. Therefore the concept of **prolonged determination becomes important.** Right motivation over many years is required for high levels of success.

Study Guidance: One of the most important areas of focus is in developing trust and love for Prophet. Prophet is the Master Key for profound spiritual growth. Prophet's teachings, if integrated into daily life, bring abundance to your daily life and a closer and loving relationship with the Heavenly Father.

Truth is Love

Truth by itself often is of little operational value. For truths to be useful and helpful in our daily life, or the life of another, the understanding of more than the raw truth is necessary. Without clarity of truth, some truths can be misapplied and actually lead one in the wrong direction or to incorrect conclusions. **Having clarity of truth implies having a depth and breadth of understanding.**

Prophet can provide clarity when one does follow-through and goes deeper on topics read or discussed. Doing contemplations, reading scripture, studying Keys, and writing letters to Prophet can all add clarity if Prophet is included. **Clarity must be EARNED through personal effort and asking for and accepting assistance of Prophet. When Prophet brings clarity by correcting a person's misunderstanding or false self image with a truth, it should be taken as a gift of love.** Illusions can become a wedge between you and spiritual growth.

To share a raw truth without providing clarity, and an understanding of how it applies to the receiver's life, is not a gift of love. Sharing advanced truths of God when led by vanity can harm another and retard your own growth. To share a truth of God when the other person is not receptive is often a violation of spiritual law and that person's free will. To share to the point of making another out of balance is not an act of love. Be cautious when sharing multiple truths. Taken together, in total, several true statements can sometimes lead to a falsehood. Sometimes it is better to not share a truth, but instead remain silent. We wish to do no harm. It may not be necessary and kind. If it is true and necessary and kind, combined, then perhaps share. Again, check in with Prophet.

To be used by Prophet to help another Soul become receptive to God's Love, is often more important than the specific truths shared. This is best accomplished by being consciously aware of Prophet everywhere you go and by becoming a walking example of the Path of Love.

Soul has what I call a "Truth Detector." God built into Soul the ability to know truth, even when the mind is not convinced.

Remember, Soul can accept truth and adapt to change faster and more comfortably than most minds. As Soul becomes nourished and more active in our lives, this ability to recognize truth when it is heard or read improves. **This valuable gift from God must be protected to remain properly calibrated.** If I hear someone share an untruth or misinformation during my retreats, even if unintentional, I quickly provide a correction. If I do not, then others may assume what they heard is truth, and letting that happen can damage truth detectors or students' trust in themselves. Having confidence in one's truth detector is vital.

The following story is an example of truth being a gift of love. Imagine you are going into an important meeting with two friends. On this day your breath is very bad and may negatively impact the outcome of the meeting. One friend does not want to hurt your feelings, so they say nothing about your bad breath. The other friend tells you your breath stinks in time to use a breath mint to correct the problem. Which person is a better friend? I believe the one who gave you truth in time to make a correction also gave you love, and is your better friend.

Study Guidance: God is sometimes called Truth and Love. Generally, any truth that Prophet provides to one of his physical students, however uncomfortable it might be, should be received as a gift of love. Prophet would not give that truth at that time if not guided to do so by the Heavenly Father. A sincere desire for TRUTH is required for spiritual growth. There are absolute spiritual truths, like the truth in the law of gravity. Sharing truths on any topic with another **is not always a gift of love**, even if they are receptive.

Spiritual Food

Our physical body consumes food, providing itself with nourishment to promote growth and good health. A lack of sufficient nourishment can cause serious health problems and mental impairment, including poor judgment. Soul must consume spiritual "food." Without sufficient spiritual "food" Soul has little influence in our daily life. **The potential benefit of Soul's clarity, wisdom, higher point of view, intelligence, ability to give and receive love, peace, and so much more are only possible when Soul is well-nourished.** So how do we feed Soul a proper diet of nutrition, "food?"

We already know singing HU potentially brings spiritual nourishment to us, especially to our real selves, Soul. If we sing HU every day it brings us our "daily spiritual bread." When Soul is "well fed" we grow spiritually stronger. This enables Soul's special attributes to contribute positively to our daily life. But how exactly does singing HU bring this nourishment?

Singing HU can make you more receptive to experiencing God's Light and Sound, whether perceived or not. **This Light and Sound, the Holy Spirit, is what primarily provides spiritual nourishment.** Singing HU with love, and not in a rote way, usually makes us receptive to receiving more of God's essence, His Light and Sound. This is the "food" we need and should seek daily, even throughout the whole day.

Prophet literally becomes God's Light and Sound when he accepts the profound Spiritual Authority given from God at the time when he officially becomes His Prophet! So when we sing HU we most likely receive nourishment, but when we are in the inner or outer presence of Prophet, we ARE in the presence of God's Light and Sound. If receptive we WILL receive spiritual nourishment. Recognizing and including Prophet while singing HU is a wonderful way to stay nourished while also improving one's relationship with Prophet.

Making the "Three-Part Prayer" a way of life both nourishes and improves one's relationship with Prophet. It consists of: 1.

Recognize and reflect upon something you are grateful for today. (Gift from God given through His Prophet) 2. Ask Prophet for a dream or any experience that will help your relationship with Prophet grow. 3. Tell Prophet you will be receptive. (Meaning you will be watchful and receptive for the answer to this prayer) You may start doing this spiritual exercise at night before falling asleep. Over time and with a little effort this "Three-Part Prayer" should naturally evolve to being done throughout the entire day. Doing so will greatly improve one's relationship with Prophet **while also gaining quality nourishment consistently.**

Reading and studying scripture, including my books, with the inner Prophet is a spiritual exercise that nourishes. Watching Prophet's videos nourishes. Listening to his audio books or podcasts nourishes. Thinking of and caring for other Souls nourishes. Spiritual coworking and being a servant of God nourishes. Living in the moment nourishes. Taking relaxing walks with the inner Prophet nourishes. For students at the retreat center writing letters and testimonies with Prophet nourishes. Spending time at God's Temples of Learning and the Abode of God with Prophet nourishes. Remembering and being grateful for our sacred experiences and blessings nourishes.

Besides staying well-nourished spiritually, **do not needlessly deplete your nourishment.** Having negative thoughts, guilt, worry, a poor view of self, anger, and being around negative people or environments can rapidly deplete your spiritual energy.

As you grow spiritually Prophet can use you as a coworker, a servant of God, to bless others. This is the most rewarding activity of Soul, but **Soul must be well fed** and listen closely to Prophet. Prophet knows God's will for other Souls, so you are only a **coworker** if acting in accord with guidance from Prophet. As a coworker you are used to bless others **in the way God wishes them to be blessed**, and God's way is best for that Soul.

Study Guidance: Consistently receiving your spiritual food, daily spiritual bread, is both the foundation and a continuous necessity for the extraordinary spiritual growth Prophet offers. This is not possible to achieve in a passive manner, personal effort is required. Prophet is actually training Souls to become servants of God, the most rewarding activity of Soul, and this is impossible to accomplish without both your daily spiritual bread and a trusting and loving relationship with God's Prophet.

Consistency

Imagine how ineffective and even damaging binge eating, drinking, or exercising can be to individuals. **Staying spiritually nourished is the primary area where consistency is vital.** Steady growth is usually more effective than stop, start, stop, start growth. It is dangerous to one's path when they allow themselves to become undernourished spiritually, even for short periods of time! Possible consequences include poor decision-making and vulnerability to the negative side, Satan. When undernourished one is less likely to understand lessons by Prophet and then fall behind. **Lack of consistency is the first common block to spiritual growth.**

Another important attribute for success in any serious endeavor is self-discipline. When one works toward being consistent in staying spiritually nourished, that **effort can improve self-discipline.** Consistency and self-discipline are two important attributes for spiritual success or for nearly any other type of success. Acquiring the attributes of consistency and self-discipline are important in most areas of life. They will often positively spread into other areas of one's life. Not being consistent is one of the Five Common Blocks to Spiritual Growth.

Study Guidance: Consistency in diet choices, physical exercise, self-control, reading scripture, staying spiritually nourished, doing everything with the inner Prophet, and integrating the Spiritual Keys into daily life produces real results and helps us maintain upward spiritual momentum.

Living in God's Time

Living and spending most of your time in the moment is a worthy goal. Much of life's stress and strain is caused by thinking about what may happen in the future, whether that is the next hour, day, month, year, or even years ahead. **Few problems exist right now!** Right now you are probably clothed, fed, sheltered, and safe. It is difficult to enjoy life when we are living in the future or past. God gives us life one precious moment at a time. Spending most of one's time in the moment reduces stress. Thomas Jefferson said, "How much pain have cost us the evils which have never happened."

As coworkers with God and Prophet we desire to be guided by the Light and Sound of God, the Holy Ghost, in everything we do. **To be in communication with God requires being in the present moment.** When our attention is entangled in the past or in the future, we usually are NOT being led by Spirit. **God is in the moment**. If guided by Prophet one can review the past and plan for the future without being entangled, or out of the moment.

Another aspect of living in God's time is enjoying where you are in your consciousness now. As a spiritual student enjoy the level of consciousness you have now, there will be time in the future to enjoy a new level of consciousness.

Living in the moment can sometimes prevent procrastination. Do it NOW. Surrendering our agenda and wanting to do God's will helps us in being patient enough to live in the moment. We do not give up our future desires, goals, and dreams, but we trust in God's timing. Taking a "long view" on your spiritual path reduces stress and helps you relax. Know and trust that God and Prophet will guide you at the perfect rate of growth, and that they both want you to achieve your goals in life.

Time and space as we think of it is only a lower-world phenomenon. At the Soul plane and above, time as we know it does not exist. Therefore, Soul always lives in the moment. When we travel "back in time" we are actually traveling to a current state of existence. It only seems to be traveling back in time based upon the physical plane as a reference.

Study Guidance: Our goal is to be guided daily by the Holy Spirit, and that requires living in the moment. Most of our stresses and worries are found in a potential future, while most regrets and guilt are from the past. Living in the moment, in God's time, greatly reduces many stresses of life.

Chrysalis to Freedom

Real freedom from the human consciousness, the consciousness that limits our spiritual growth and quality of life, is available when we truly and consistently operate as Soul. The human consciousness is like a prison, with old destructive habits and knee-jerk reactions. Going from a strictly human perspective of life to that of Soul's view is a substantial change. **It is a major transformation, much like the transformation a caterpillar goes through while within a chrysalis and then breaking out as a beautiful moth or butterfly.**

Operating daily as Soul is one of our primary goals on this spiritual path; yet, it is much easier to talk about than actually accomplish. Sure, by now, after years of study with Prophet one has often experienced themselves as Soul. Many times Prophet uplifts his students above the Soul plane during retreats. Many times individuals are given the opportunity to experience themselves as Soul and to perceive others as Soul. However, maintaining Soul's high view once leaving a retreat takes proper focus, proper practice, and prolonged determination on the individual's part.

To consistently operate as Soul, rather than from only the mental state, requires self-discipline. That means controlling the negative passions of the mind and the lower emotional states. Taking charge of one's emotional state requires strength, determination, and discipline. One gains the necessary strength by staying CONSISTENTLY spiritually nourished and recognizing and being in Prophet's inner presence daily. We already know singing HU provides nourishment that strengthens Soul. However, even HU cannot provide the "high-octane" nourishment necessary to have the spiritual strength to break through the "glass ceiling" to the Soul plane.

Living in the presence of Prophet provides the necessary "high-octane" nourishment to break through the barrier, or "glass ceiling," between the Etheric plane (fourth Heaven) and Soul plane (fifth Heaven). Prophet's inner presence nourishes while the loving and sacred relationship with Prophet strengthens Soul enough to gain freedom. The disciple must provide the necessary effort, discipline, determination, consistency, receptiveness, and motivation.

Study Guidance: God's Love and Truth has a transformative effect on one's life. It can transport you from the narrow human state to the boundless one of Soul, a state of true freedom.

Prophet's Inner Presence

The inner Prophet is ALWAYS with his students whether recognized or not. The inner Prophet IS a concentrated form of the Light and Sound of God, known by many as the Holy Spirit. My students have seen the Holy Spirit as a beam of light during many retreats. This beam of light and sound IS the inner Prophet that is always near you. Recognizing and focusing upon his presence can be of tremendous importance and benefit.

There is no barrier, special spiritual exercise, or secret password for advanced students to be able to recognize the inner Prophet if their love of Prophet is strong. One simply decides to! Just do it! Prophet is already with you; you know his outer look and his inner look — just decide to recognize his presence.

To be directly within his presence, God's Light and Sound, just ask Prophet. Though Prophet is very close, he will not violate your free will by placing himself, in the form of a beam of light directly over and around you without you asking. The benefits of Prophet's presence close by are great. But when the beam of light, the inner Prophet, is directly over and around a Soul all things are possible. **You are now in a concentrated and endless source of love, joy, peace, strength, wisdom, protection, clarity, and stability.**

Advanced disciples of Prophet should strive to walk through life in his Presence at all times. This is how one brings the "Light of the World" with them to other Souls. When within his light a disciple becomes a true coworker with God through His Prophet. Then wherever they go others can be blessed. To not ask to be surrounded in God's Light and Love through Prophet is an opportunity lost for both you and everyone you come close to all day.

To prepare for the above, view Prophet in your spiritual eye before singing HU. Take his hands if offered and look into his eyes. Spend quality time this way and let the experience evolve without trying to direct it, keep it from being rote. Then during your spiritual practice each day picture Prophet in a similar way until it becomes a way of life. Sometimes you may perceive his physical form, spiritual light, a flash of blue light, peace and comfort, warmth, or his love for you.

Study Guidance: The inner Prophet is always with you, but you must ask to be enveloped within the Light and Love of God that he is. Asking ensures you are giving permission because Prophet will not violate your free will. One should never take this most sacred opportunity for granted or be cavalier about it.

Blending With God's Voice

Prophet IS an aspect of God's Voice. As coworkers (servants of God through Prophet) we desire his input in all things. Prophet may blend his consciousness with a spiritual student, but primarily with Soul, not the lower human consciousness. This often begins to happen when the person **is being used to bless another Soul and needs direction.** They may be guided to just listen or given the perfect words to share. They also may become more perceptive to the other Soul's receptiveness or lack thereof.

These special moments when Prophet allows the blending of his consciousness are not done on a regular time schedule or consistently. **They are special and sacred gifts not to be taken lightly.** Spirit may often give guidance through nudges, but these are <u>not</u> examples of blending.

When a person desires CLARITY while studying scripture, writing letters to Prophet, writing testimonies, or studying Prophet's class discourses or books, ask for Prophet's help. If one is sincere and spiritually nourished then Prophet may blend his consciousness with them. This can be of great benefit to any serious student of the ways of God.

Once a disciple becomes established and initiated into the true God Worlds above the Soul plane, a more permanent type of blending may develop. A disciple is more than just a student of God's ways. A disciple not only studies, but does their best to integrate the teachings into all areas of daily life. A true disciple actually learns to integrate their life around the teachings!

Study Guidance: When one is allowed to blend with Prophet's consciousness, one can more clearly see how and in the precise way God wants to bless another. This is very important in being a servant of God and in doing His will.

Living Without Doubt

To have a reasonable chance of successfully manifesting one's spiritual potential in this physical life, **one must always know, assume, and claim their divinity.** Soul IS a child of God and therefore as His child, IS a divine being. Any hesitation in accepting this most important and fundamental truth may be spiritually fatal.

Soul is eternal and lives forever. God lives, He is real, and knows you personally. He created the real eternal you, Soul. As Soul your growth and potential have no limits.

Soul is created by God with love. **You exist because God loves you.** No matter what you do, you are still Soul, still divine, and always loved by God, your Heavenly Father. Never doubt this truth, never waver!

Study Guidance: Your true eternal self is Soul, created by God with love. Soul is created out of God's Voice, the Holy Spirit, more specifically, God's Light and Sound. Never doubt that as a child of God you, as Soul, are divine.

Personal Effort
(or Opportunity Lost)

Most all those who have been students for many years at Guidance for a Better Life have the potential to reach high states of consciousness. They each have the necessary "raw material," good enough karma, the learning environment, and qualified teachers available to obtain permanent entry into the Kingdom of Heaven in this lifetime. Each has proven to be able to receive intense amounts of God's Love, has experienced themselves as Soul, has traveled the Heavens with Prophet, been ordained by God Himself, gone back in time, learned of past lives, and studied scripture with the Living Word.

Although high potential exists for all these Souls, some will not actually do what is necessary to achieve permanent results. Most humans, including many Guidance for a Better Life students, are destined for failure in achieving the very high initiations in the worlds of God. They simply refuse to make the required and **sufficient personal effort** over a prolonged period of time for success. Some will not succeed in this lifetime. Such is the state of the human consciousness. For Prophet it is like watching a very capable swimmer slip beneath the surface and needlessly drown because they refuse to make the required effort to stay afloat. Not making sufficient personal effort is one of the Five Common Blocks to Spiritual Growth.

Over the course of instruction I make it very clear the responsibilities of Prophet in one's growth and the responsibilities of my students. **The primary responsibility for students is to stay spiritually nourished.** When Jesus talked about "daily bread" he was referring to daily spiritual nourishment, not physical bread. As an example of this in the Bible, when Jesus was tempted by the Negative Being during his forty day fast to turn stones into bread, Jesus said, "It is written, Man shall not live by bread alone, but by every word that proceedeth out of the mouth of God." Matthew 4:4 KJV The Word of God IS spiritual nourishment. Once an individual begins looking at this understanding of "daily bread," it is found all throughout scripture.

Study Guidance: It is by the Grace of God one is allowed to find, recognize, and be taught by the current Prophet of the times. To not make every reasonable effort to lay hold of and maximize one's potential in this "gift life" could result in a sacred opportunity lost. Sufficient personal effort and accepting help from Prophet is required over a prolonged period of time. The transformative spiritual growth, true freedom, and abundance being offered to you is worth your effort. You are responsible for making the most of this golden opportunity. Make this Key "Opportunity Found."

Step Six Keys in Action

A Sky Full of Love

*God uses His Light as a major way to deliver blessings to Soul.
The light may come to us in the dream state, during prayer, or
contemplation, while spiritually traveling, or in the following
example, in the waking state. The more we are blessed to experience
the Light of God, the more conditioned we become to accepting the
blessings contained within the light. One of which is comforting us
through lifting sadness from our heart.*

"The heavens declare the glory of God; and the firmament sheweth
his handiwork." Psalm 19:1 KJV

I was driving the fifty-minute commute to my new job. As I did
each morning, I sang HU the entire way into the city. Not an innate
morning person, I appreciated the peaceful time to express my love
directly to God. It was a time of great change in my life. It was one
of those transitional periods where a relationship, job, and living
arrangements all had recently ended. Everything was wide open,
new, and uncertain. It was an amazing opportunity to put more of
my trust and focus from the changing temporal world and onto the
solid foundation of the Divine.

My experiences at Guidance for a Better Life had blessed me with
seeing the Light of God many times. At the retreat center in the
presence of my spiritual teacher, Del Hall, I experienced this light
many times — flashes of pink, bursts of blues and orange, beams of
white and gold. As my spiritual strength and endurance developed
under his guidance, so did the length, clarity, and intensity of the
light I experienced.

The common thread at this time was my experiences with the
Light of God all occurred at Guidance for a Better Life in the
presence of Del. Though I spent several weekends a year there, most
of the year was lived off the mountain away from the retreat center,
and that life was surely in need of the Light of God! It is not possible
for the Prophet to be with each of us physically everywhere, but
spiritually we can be aware of his presence throughout our day and
in doing so, invest in our relationship with God through His living

Prophet, whom He always blesses us with here on Earth.

So that morning as I drove into the city I experienced a mixture of sadness and hope, wondering about my place in God's great creation. Where am I heading? I wondered. What is God's plan for me, and for my life? The morning sky was slowly transitioning from dark to light — a metaphor for my life the two years I had been coming to the retreat center. The sun was just waking, the colors of the day beginning to stir.

Suddenly the sky filled with the purest blue light. It was not an everyday, afternoon blue sky. It was startling. It stretched like blue fire from one end of the horizon to the other end. It surrounded me in a bubble of grace and warmth. I had seen the sky fill with supernatural blue light once before on a farm — years before I started coming to the retreat center. That was also during a time of great transition. It tugged at my heart then as it did now, but I had not been conditioned to accept the amount of love present in the light. It had opened my heart and soothed me, but I did not recognize the holy Presence of God and the unconditional love that was there for me.

Fortunately the road I was on was a highway, a straight road with few cars at this time and no traffic lights. I continued to HU. The sky again filled with blue. I recognized this as the Prophet's presence. Though not limited to it, the color blue is often the spiritual calling card of the Prophet of the times. As the sky filled I felt my heart fill with God's Love. Yes, I was going through changes in my life, and maybe a few hardships, but I was not abandoned. I felt my sadness lift, replaced by a certainty that I would not take a single step alone. The Prophet, visible or not, would accompany me every step of the way, both at retreats and off the mountain.

From the beginning Del, the Prophet, has inspired me to take the love and light I experienced every time I set foot on the property and bring it with me into my daily life. Singing HU and appreciating the hand of the Divine that touches my life on a daily basis has helped me draw nigh to God and deepen my awareness of that sacred, unbreakable connection. There is stability and love in my life now that I did not even dream of then.

That day God declared His Heavenly Love for me. The sky full of spiritual light was a Divine gift that brought profound healing. Fears and doubts fell away, replaced by confidence that I could experience Prophet in all areas of my life and not just when I was at class. To walk in the Love of God is immensely personal and a direct reflection of one's relationship with the Divine. My relationship with Prophet has grown over the last twenty years. It has enhanced all my other relationships and delivered me to the very Abode of my Creator.

How grateful I am God never abandons His children. He provides healing, clarity, protection, and a Prophet here in the physical to teach us, guide us, and walk with us all the way back to the Heart of God. Thank you Del, for guiding me on this sacred journey.

Written by Chris Comfort

Keys in this story: HU, God's Prophet, Spiritual Strength, God's Love, Prophet's Inner Presence, Connecting Spiritual Events (noticed God's Light in sky and how he was feeling), Gratitude, Spiritual Protection, Living Without Doubt (confidence God never abandons), Receptive, God's Grace (healing of fear and doubts, experience of the Light)

I Saw Neale Again

When your time here in the physical world comes to an end you will carry on in the other worlds of God — it is not "lights out" forever. Believing in life after death is one thing. It is quite another to know this truth from personal experience.

For several years I had been attending retreats at Guidance for a Better Life and was blessed with my own experiences of Heaven. I had experienced this many times and knew Heaven was real and that loved ones were truly in a better place after they died. I knew they would be okay, and they were still loved by God. This all became even more real to me in April 2005. It was then a high school friend of mine was in a severe car accident while driving home from work. He was alive but in shock when first responders arrived on the scene. He was taken to a local trauma hospital where he was pronounced dead.

When my dad told me Neale had died, I was in shock and disbelief, even as I saw the tears in my dad's eyes. As details of Neale's accident and medevac flight came out, it became more real and slowly sunk in. I was very upset and disturbed by it all. I felt a strong urge that I needed to see my teacher at Guidance for a Better Life. Fortunately that same weekend there was a spiritual retreat scheduled.

I attended the weekend retreat, and on the last day of class, just hours before leaving, we did a spiritual exercise as a group. While singing HU, I saw Neale walk into the room with my teacher Del. Neale gave me a big hug, and I knew that he was okay. He looked happier and more alive than he ever did on Earth. I got to see firsthand that after a loved one translates to the other side, whether they believe in God or not, they spiritually live on. This experience has brought me so much peace in the years since Neale's passing. I know without a doubt there is indeed a place for all Souls in God's mansion.

Written by Michelle K. Reuschling

Keys in this story: HU, God's Grace (to see Neale again), Living Without Doubt, Peace of Mind and Heart, Gratitude, Soul (she experienced the truth that Soul lives on after the physical body dies — Soul is eternal), God's Grace (delivered by Inner Prophet — brought Neale to Michelle)

Spared by a Hair

*Keep your heart and mind open to the little things in life that seem
to slow you up or change your plans in one way or another. Instead of
becoming frustrated and letting them close your heart, consider
perhaps they may be a blessing of protection, and be grateful.*

One morning as I was going about my normal routine getting
ready for work my hair dryer stopped working. It had on rare
occasions in the past done the same thing, but it did not happen very
often. Usually I would not have time to wait for it to start working
again, so I would just skip that step in my routine and continue on.
On this particular day I heard the voice of the inner Prophet say very
clearly this was meant to delay me by a few minutes. I had the
conscious thought; "This is one of those times that a two-minute
delay saves you from getting into a car accident." I trusted
completely this was the case whether I ever received outer
confirmation or not.

I had been softly aware of Prophet's presence throughout the
morning, but after my hair dryer stopped working, and I heard his
inner voice, I slowed down and very deliberately asked Prophet to
come with me to work that day. It was a good reminder that
consciously asking to be in Prophet's presence is better than just
knowing he is always with me. I stood in my bathroom and hit the
test and reset buttons on my hair dryer for about a minute. My
husband came into the bathroom, and I told him my hair dryer had
stopped working, but I was not going to get frustrated or rush
because I knew it was Divine protection. On that particular day I was
leaving early to pick up my sister who had asked for a ride to work.
The extra stop meant I really needed to stay on schedule to make
sure I made it to work on time, but the Divine communication
overrode everything I was "supposed to do."

After a minute or two the hair dryer resumed working, and I
completed my routine. I picked up my sister a few minutes late, and
we headed down the highway to the neighboring town where we
both work. About fifteen minutes into the drive I noticed traffic was

slowing down and starting to merge into the right lane. Up ahead was a multi-car accident. Fortunately it did not look like anyone was seriously hurt, but it was definitely not the way they had intended to start their day. There were three cars that had rear-ended one another and then a few yards back another four cars in their own wreck, most likely as a result of the first wreck.

The accident had literally happened just a few minutes before we came upon it. There were no emergency vehicles on-site yet. One woman was sitting in her car dialing her phone. One man was gingerly climbing out of his car and looking back at the scene. Another woman was holding her face and slowly shaking her head, as her air bag had deployed. The car engines were still smoking. I looked at my sister and told her what had happened while I was getting ready for work. We both knew without a doubt we were protected by Prophet.

When I arrived home that evening I shared with my husband what had transpired. He said he had prayed for extra Divine protection for me that morning as I drove away. He had heard me say I felt my hair dryer was slowing me down on purpose and wanted to pray for protection.

Later that evening I shared the story with my father, Del Hall, God's Prophet of the times. We live on the same property, and he shared with me he had consciously given me a double-dose of protection that morning when I drove by on my way to work. When he hears a family member drive by on the way to town he often places a bubble of God's Light, as Divine protection, around them and their vehicle. On that particular day he had felt drawn to make it a double-dose. He had not known consciously that my sister was going to be riding in the car with me, but it partially explains the double-dose of protection he bestowed upon his two daughters.

If I had not seen the car accident as outer confirmation I still trusted I was being delayed for some Divine reason. God's timing and God's plan are always at work. I am grateful for the eyes to see and the heart to know.

Written by Catherine Hughes

Keys in this story: Prophet's Inner Presence, Spiritual Protection, Living Without Doubt, Receptive, Gratitude, Discernment (that being delayed was for protection), Contemplation (inner dialogue with Prophet before work), Living in God's Time, Peace of Mind and Heart, Proper Focus (trusted the Divine over her schedule), Prayer (husband prayed for her)

The Flute of Heaven

My father has led many a seeker on journeys into the Heavenly realms during both waking and sleeping states to experience the Holy Spirit — the Sound and Light of God. These travels help shed light on your true nature as a spiritual being and pull back the curtain on the Heavenly Kingdom.

When I was a young boy my parents played traditional Japanese flute music each night to help me fall asleep. The gentle melodies seemed to be the only thing that could coax me into rest. The soothing compositions brought a peace that was largely absent during my waking hours. I looked forward each night to the familiar sounds. I am so grateful they played this beautiful music, but nothing could compare to the music of the Heavenly flute I heard in a dream, years later.

This dream was given to me seven years ago. I awoke in full consciousness to find myself in a region of pure light. As far as the eye could see was vibrant, pulsating, yellow light emanating from a central figure. Closer to the figure the light became ever more pure, whiter and whiter, finer and finer. The light itself seemed dynamic and alive. In the middle of this light-filled universe sat Del Hall, my spiritual guide, a true Prophet of God. He played a traditional wooden flute.

His music filled this world, the most beautiful sound I have ever heard! As he played, I did not know if a minute had passed, or a day, or a month, or a year. I could not tell distance either: Del sat in the center of this beautiful world, but was he three feet away, or three miles? There was no way to tell, for there was no matter in this realm. It was only the pure Light and Sound of Heaven. As he played, the music brought peace that far surpassed anything I had experienced before. This peace entered me and filled me, and it lives in my heart to this day. It is a gift that keeps on giving. Simply placing my attention on this dream brings back the serenity of this beautiful music. This is the peace that surpasses all understanding spoken of in the Bible. Upon waking, I was overcome and gave thanks for this incredible experience.

This was more than a dream. It was a journey into Heaven. The fifth Heaven, where only purity and goodness and light exist. There was no time, no near or far, no shadow, no high or low. There was only the Source, and the Light and Sound of God. In the Bible, Saint Paul said he knew a man who was caught up to the third Heaven (Second Corinthians 12:2). This means that there is at least a first Heaven, a second, and a third. This dream took place in the fifth Heaven, where there is no matter, only spiritual light and sound. There is no evil, only goodness and light. As a Prophet of God, Del Hall is able to take his students into the Heavens in full consciousness. To the fifth Heaven and beyond.

This dream motivated me to continue my spiritual path without hesitation. It showed me that Del was no ordinary preacher or spiritual teacher. Something I had already known in my heart, but this left no doubt. He is the modern Prophet of God, able to share the Light and Sound of God. Following his teachings and guidance had led to this experience, and the understanding of it.

Many have heard references to the Light of God. Few have heard of the Sound, the Heavenly white music. Yet scattered references to it exist in the various world scriptures. Having experienced it, I can tell you it is unlike anything else. It is more than "music." It is the Voice of God, and it carries all the qualities of God's Love, Mercy, peace, joy, and more! It can be experienced by man today. When guided by Prophet this sound, this beautiful Sound of God can carry Soul back to Its eternal Home.

Written by David Hughes

Keys in this story: God's Love (a gift to perceive His Light and Sound), God's Grace (by His Grace to journey into the Heavens), Personal Effort and Proper Focus (this experience motivated David to continue his Spiritual path), Growth of Consciousness, Prophet's Inner Presence, Soul (only as Soul can you travel into the Heavens), Gratitude

Reassurance Just When I Needed It

One of the greatest blessings is when we receive clarity on a major decision we are trying to make. Spirit can use anything in our life to help deliver this clarity to us. It can also give us the courage to follow our heart and act on the guidance we receive.

It was a difficult decision to move on after twenty-two years in a relationship. For quite some time I had been on the fence about my decision, and the indecision was wearing me out, along with the relationship itself. I did not have the energy and courage to follow through. The inner and outer guidance I was getting indicated it was time, or past time, to make the decision and move on. That got my attention, but distractions seemed to keep popping up to delay my taking action.

I decided it would be important for me to attend the Step Four weekend spiritual retreat at Guidance for a Better Life. Prophet provided very helpful clarity and input that weekend, thank you! Nearing the Virginia border on my drive back to Asheville, North Carolina, I thought I heard an alarm clock going off. I closed the car windows and the sound stopped. Well, a few minutes later this whole scenario repeated itself. Again, I closed the windows and the sound stopped. I tried to reach around in the car for where my alarm clock might be, but I could not find it. Normally my travel alarm clock would eventually stop beeping and stop for good. I knew it wasn't the alarm clock because the sequence continued most all the way back to Asheville, and it seemed like a sign.

When I crossed over into Tennessee there was a huge sign saying, "Change is coming. Experience history in August." I had strong inner guidance it would be important to begin getting my things in order. When I got home I had some serious talks with my significant other, although I did not yet have the courage to tell him I wanted to leave. I prayed for assistance from Prophet to find my inner strength and courage.

In June I was again at the retreat center and developing inner strength and courage was one of the areas we focused on during the eight-day retreat. Around that time a movie had come out called "We Bought a Zoo," and one of the pearls shared at the retreat was how the main character only needed twenty seconds of courage to take an important action, which he did, and it changed his life. During the last evening of the retreat our area of Virginia experienced a unique storm, a derecho. We stood outside watching the sky as it sounded like a freight train roaring up the side of the mountain, although the trees did not seem to be moving. The sky was spectacular and looked like a July 4th celebration. During this amazing storm I felt strength in the presence of the Prophet and found a depth of inner strength and courage I had not known before. I was finally at peace. I knew what I needed to do as Soul. It felt like the Divine had done most of the heavy lifting to give me the strength and courage to follow my heart, now I had to do my part!

When I returned home to North Carolina I continued to receive a lot of support and guidance on the outer and inner. A friend suggested I write a letter to my significant other to say what I would want to say, without giving it to him. This would help me focus on what I would want to say in person. I found the suggestion very helpful. In my heart I knew this suggestion, that came through my friend, was from the inner Prophet. As Soul I was getting a deep inner call to make this change, and if I did not heed it I felt I would start dying inside. It was important to me to make this change with love, rather than getting into blame and anger.

The following week while I was at work, I saw a U-Haul truck go by with a huge picture of an Indian woman on the side of it. I ran outside and saw the name of Sacajawea written on the side. This was an awake dream to me because I have a close affinity with that name. During the next few days I researched prices for a U-Haul truck rental to move to Virginia. By the end of the week I had the inner knowingness that it was time. Holding the hand of the inner Prophet, I took a deep breath and received the first twenty seconds of courage, and then the next, and the next. I had a long talk and interaction with my significant other. I was able to share with him what I really wanted to convey from a place of love. He and I talked and talked, and cried together. That night was really tough, and I slept restlessly.

As I headed to work the next morning I had doubts as to whether I was making the right decision. I started singing HU, a love song to God, and asked for assistance from Prophet. Rounding the corner into the parking lot at work, lo and behold there was a U-Haul truck sitting smack dab in front of my office. And in big letters on the side it said "VIRGINIA." It was the perfect reassurance I needed at that moment! God's timing is always perfect, impeccable. Thank you dear God and Prophet for your reassurance, comfort, love, and guidance. I appreciate and love you.

Written by Jan Reid

Keys in this story: Prophet's Inner Presence, God's Prophet (at retreat center retreats), Spiritual Strength, God's Grace (answered prayer and gave Jan extra strength and courage), Soul, HU, Prayer, Connecting Spiritual Events, Receptive

Prophet's Love During My Mom's Translation

This is a truly beautiful story of the author's mother and family being prepared for her to leave this world for the next. It was done with so much comfort, love, and tenderness that reading it will strengthen your faith in and love of God.

My mother attended a retreat at Guidance for a Better Life in 2001. One of her favorite experiences that both she and I remembered vividly took place when the class walked up the hill to meet with Del and Lynne to go for a hike. As we reached the top of the hill she put her hands out slightly in front of her, palms up, and looked at me strangely. "It's not raining is it?" she asked, as if she knew something unique was happening but wanted verification. I said, "No it's not, why?" She went on to explain that she was seeing and feeling a golden shower of light raining down upon us. Her description of the experience was breathtaking.

March 16, 2016 my mom went into the emergency room with sharp stomach pains. The doctors kept her for a few days for an obstructed bowel and did what they needed to do to address the problem. When her symptoms subsided they sent her home. The following week she was back in the hospital for the same problem again. On March 30 the doctors performed exploratory surgery to see if they could find the cause. It turned out my mother had stage four cancer throughout her lower abdomen and into her colon. The doctors gave her six months to two years to live depending on how aggressive her treatments were, but over the next few weeks her health progressively worsened.

A few days after her surgery, while taking a nap, she sat up in bed slightly startled and asked who was in the corner of the room. I did not see anyone. Then she said, "Oh, that's my grandmother," and she smiled and settled back down in bed. My mother believed strongly in an afterlife and had many experiences during her life to support her beliefs. We talked for a little while about her having seen her grandmother and also about similar experiences she had had like that before. My mother still had a good sense of humor and joked that while it was great to see her grandmother again she really did not like the message seeing her brought.

Over the course of the next several weeks we felt God's Love and blessings in so many wonderful ways. Some of the blessings came through the love and care my mother received from the doctors, nurses, staff, family, and friends. My mom was extremely grateful! There were many days and nights she would talk or mumble in her sleep. One night she started talking about a beautiful bridge and then peacefully drifted back off again.

During a spiritual contemplation on Saturday April 2 I was with Prophet. During this inner experience I was filled with an incredible white light, and then I was wrapped in a beautiful blue light. When I see and experience blue light I am reminded Prophet is always with me. Shortly after this I saw my mother bathed in a golden light. I have come to know gold light brings love, blessings, and gifts directly from God.

Early the next week I had the following spiritual experience in the hospital room with my mom. I found myself on a beautiful arching bridge over a clear blue river. The bridge was very peaceful and serene, and on it there were beautiful flowering baskets hanging. I was with my mother and Prophet. I held one of my mom's hands and Del, the Prophet, held the other. We helped her walk across the bridge and down into a grassy area that looked like a park. It felt like springtime, and there were beautiful flowers and trees all around. This was the type of place my mother loved. We were greeted by my great grandmother, one of my mom's favorite people. My mom loved her grandmother very much and would speak and tell fond stories of her often. When my mom was a child her father was drafted into World War II. Her mother went to work to help support the family. As a result, my mom spent a great deal of time with her grandmother who helped to raise her.

When I saw my great-grandmother in the park she looked younger, healthier, and much more energetic than she did in her final years. After seeing my great-grandmother I noticed there were about a dozen other people present in the park to greet my mom, including her parents. Del and I let go of her hands as she was welcomed into the group of her family and friends. I recognized some of the Souls there because they were people I had known myself. I recognized others from pictures because they were deceased individuals, family, and friends I had never had the opportunity to meet. After a short period of time my mother came back to Prophet and me, and we walked back over the bridge. Afterwards I found myself back in the hospital room. I had similar experiences several times over the next week, sometimes in spiritual contemplations, sometimes in dreams, and sometimes just sitting in the room as my mother slept. Each time we crossed the bridge and went to the park she seemed a little more relaxed.

Many times I was aware that Prophet Del Hall was spiritually sitting quietly with us in the hospital room. Sometimes I felt the entire room being bathed in the golden Light of God. As Prophet's presence and love enveloped the room, it brought me an incredible feeling of peace, which helped me through the long days and nights of this trying and challenging time. Sometimes I felt his presence as a blue blanket of peace and comfort, while at other times, as his arm lovingly placed around my shoulder.

My mom was an incredible example of grace and peace throughout her experience in the hospital. She had a great attitude, a light humor, and an inner peace with which she faced each hard decision. During those three weeks in the hospital we talked, sat quietly, laughed, cried, and got her affairs in order. We were given the most incredible gift of being able to tell each other how deeply we loved one another, and how much our lives had been blessed by our relationship and the love we shared. Being given this time and experience with her was a precious blessing from God, even more so because I did not have the opportunity to do this with my father, who passed away suddenly when I was fifteen years old.

On Saturday April 9 the doctors notified us that the extreme pain my mother was in was due to additional complications in her lower intestine. Attempting to remedy the situation would require that they remove her lower intestine and bowel. After speaking with her doctors it appeared further intervention would not really affect the underlying cause of the problem, and it would significantly decrease the quality of life she had remaining. After hours of quietly considering her options, she consulted with us and decided she would rather be placed in hospice care. It is my sense that part of the inner peace she had with her decision was due to the fact Prophet was sharing experiences of the inner Heavenly Worlds with her. On Sunday April 10 at noon she was moved to a hospice care facility. By 4:00 pm that same day she peacefully passed into the Heavenly Worlds. She was conscious and coherent right up to the end and had the beautiful gift of her family being by her side.

In her last few minutes her breathing became very labored. I held one hand and my wife held her other, while others from the family stood close by and touched or supported her in whatever way they could. With incredible love and compassion my brother told her that it was okay to go. My wife and I sang HU quietly and focused internally on Prophet. I watched as my mom appeared to look past us to where I knew Prophet was now standing with an outstretched hand. I put my hand on her heart and closed my eyes. I took several deep breaths as if to prepare for what I felt was coming next. We were once again on the beautiful bridge; I held my mother's left hand and Del held her right hand. We started to cross the bridge, yet I knew this time I would not walk with her down into the park. Crying, with a strange mix of sadness and happiness, I let her hand slowly slide out of mine as she walked across the bridge and continued on with Del. They walked down into the park and were once again greeted by her friends and family. I watched from the bridge. After a few moments, the people around her dispersed, disappearing in a similar way that the ball players did in some of the scenes from the movie "Field of Dreams." She stood alone with Prophet in the park. She put her hands out before her, and I saw a beautiful golden shower rain down upon them. Then she glanced back towards me and smiled as if to say how much she loved me, thank you, and everything was alright now. Soon after, I found myself back in the hospice room holding her hand, yet she was no longer there.

Since that time I have been taken in several dreams to visit her, and I look forward to having more. She seems to be more settled and comfortable now. She looks much younger, more beautiful, and healthier than she has in thirty years. By the Grace of God, I was allowed to witness as Prophet comforted our family and helped my mother cross over from this world to the next.

It is incredible to see and experience Prophet's hand in my daily life and to know that as Soul we are eternal and do not die. What a gift it is to know that we, God's children, are truly loved so much that He sends His Prophet to walk us back home to God and help us through every aspect of our lives. Thank you for the love, peace, support, and comfort with which you have blessed my life.

Written by Jason Levinson

Keys in this story: God's Love, Prophet's Inner Presence, Contemplation, Living Without Doubt, Living in God's Time, Prayer, Karma (mom's was good), Receptive (mom receptive to Prophet's help), Gratitude, Soul, HU, God's Grace (extra time for the family to say goodbye and several trips across bridge to relax mom), Attitudes and Thoughts (mom's was good)

HU — An Ancient Name of God

When you express your love and gratitude to God by singing HU, it is received; you are most certainly heard. Deeper realizations and insights on the profound blessing of HU will continue to grow every year for those who sing it.

Each spring the students of Guidance for a Better Life and their families come together for a Spring Clean-up Weekend to help prepare the retreat center for the coming year. On the surface it looks like work, but really it is sheer joy. Traditionally the weekend includes a bountiful potluck dinner Saturday evening and a family HU Sing Sunday morning.

This year we gathered in the Beach House on Sunday morning as in years past. My view from where I was seated at the back of the room allowed me to see all the families together and the excitement and smiles of the children. I love hearing their beautiful voices, and it is a treat having them join us. Prophet Del Hall began by reviewing and explaining that HU is both a love song to God and an ancient name for God, and when we sing it we are essentially calling His name. He reminded us to be fully present in the moment when singing HU, to put love into how we sing, paying attention to how we form the word and enunciate the sound, and to do our best to sing in a pleasant, natural tone that blends harmoniously with others. In this way we demonstrate love and reverence to God.

Prophet then did something I will never forget to emphasize the profound sacredness of singing HU. He did a kind of role-play, acting out what it might be like as God hears us calling to Him by singing His name. In a light-hearted but purposeful way, he turned away from us and pretended to be God busy at whatever He might be doing. When God hears someone singing His name and calling to Him he turns to them and asks, "Yes my child, what can I do for you?" Prophet turned and looked directly at us as he said these words, but he was no longer play-acting; it was real. Physically I was in the last row of a room full of people when he did this, but my inner experience was as if I was the only one in the room. I was up very close to him, face to face, and God was looking right at me through the eyes of Prophet. In His Eyes was eternity. An endless well of Divine love poured out, seared through me, knew me, and melted my heart. Love poured out of me back to Him. In an instant I was nurtured, loved, comforted, reassured, strengthened, and personally recognized by Almighty God, my Heavenly Father. My heart was so full, and I felt more tender and softened as I sang this beautiful love song and ancient name of God, carefully forming and savoring every precious HU I sang to Him.

This experience has sweetened and renewed every HU since. I remember how it felt to be held in that gaze of Divine love. I re-experience how that love tenderized my heart and brought forth an even greater love and appreciation to express back. Singing HU was an incredibly beautiful prayer before this, and now it is even more beautiful, more personal, and more sacred. I feel closer to my

Heavenly Father, and though I know He hears every HU, every prayer, somehow this experience has made this knowing exist at an even deeper level and be even more real. Prophet taught me about HU over twenty years ago. In the time since he has revealed some of its profound blessings and has given layer upon layer of experiences, understanding, and insights, and yet there is still more to learn, as I experienced here.

What happened this day also shows that, as a Prophet of God, Del can be teaching in a room full of people and be working with each one of his students individually on a very personal level. It gives one a glimpse into the Divine nature of Prophet and one of his many aspects, the Voice of God. He also provides a perfectly clear channel for God to reach out to us. What I experienced is really what Prophet's mission is all about: to take down walls and remove barriers between God and His children, to strengthen our communication and love connection with God, and to bring us closer together with our Father in Heaven.

Written by Lorraine Fortier

Keys in this story: HU, God's Prophet, Living Without Doubt, Living in God's Time, Receptive, God's Love, Peace of Mind and Heart, Growth of Consciousness, Reverence, Prayer

Opportunity of a Lifetime

Many are content to squabble for scraps of God's Love and teachings. Others are soaring free from the bounds of Earth to the very Abode of God Himself to receive the ultimate spiritual nourishment. There is no judgment here — it is what it is. In God's perfect plan, and at the perfect time, everyone will eventually wake up and begin to yearn for more. They will begin craving to know more of God's truths and ways and look for a guide to lead them Home. If your good fortune has brought you to the Prophet — step through the door before it closes.

In the fall of 2008 I moved to Virginia from Michigan. I moved to Virginia because I wanted to be closer to the Guidance for a Better Life retreat center. It is here I experienced God's Love and now realize that It has always been with me. I learned about my Divine nature as Soul. I learned about the sacred prayer, HU, and spiritual truths that have begun to slowly set me free from passions of the mind like anger and fear. Most important it was here I met Del, my spiritual guide, which has changed the course of my life.

I had recently been accepted to graduate school, but going there would mean I would not be as free to attend spiritual retreats at Guidance for a Better Life. I had a dream, given to me by God, which helped me make the decision to move by showing me what was in my heart. In the dream I was asleep and was invited down to the retreat center, but I took a detour and by the time I got there Del was gone. I was very upset I had missed him. When I woke up I had a knowingness that gradually turned into a conviction that I needed to move closer. I did not want to miss out on the teachings or being with Del. There are windows of opportunity in life and this was mine. Del is now the Prophet of our times, which means he can show the way home to the very Heart of God. It is a privilege to know him and be in his presence. I thank God I was woken up spiritually allowing me to become a student and build a relationship with His Prophet.

In time I was blessed to be invited to and attend my first Reunion (An advanced, eight-day retreat held at Guidance for a Better Life retreat center each summer). It is a special week to focus on God and His Divine teachings of Light and Love. I was given an experience during the retreat that I will never forget. The line from "Amazing Grace," "I once was lost, but now I am found," means more to me now than ever. I was taken in full consciousness by the Prophet to the twelfth Heaven. This is sometimes called the Abode of God. I knelt in the sand on the edge of the ocean. I was told I could look up to see an aspect of God. Golden light, which was actually God loving me directly, blazed as I looked out across the dazzling water. Just then an eagle soared overhead. It swooped down and snagged a fish from the water. The majestic bird launched back in the air with the fish clutched in its talons. Then I became the eagle biting and tearing at the fish with excitement! Oh the joy to be able to fly! I felt the strength of the eagle and the freedom to be able to glide through the sky. At God's Ocean there is the absolute best spiritual nourishment to be found and consumed. God's Love nourished me like a fresh fish nourishing an eagle. I felt like a spiritual eagle soaring!

Before I met Prophet I was in some ways like that fish, one of many Souls swimming in unison through life. Then Prophet came and gave me the opportunity to follow God's ways and taught me the eternal teachings of God. I was absorbed into the body of the Holy Spirit and made new by the Grace of God. Once I experienced Divine love and myself as Soul there was no way I could go back to the old ways of life and be content. The fish is also a symbol of spiritual nourishment, which I found at the retreat center. I was craving spiritual food, and I still need it to thrive. It is as necessary as breathing.

As the eagle I was allowed to experience some of the attributes God gives Soul: joy, strength, and freedom! We each have these and more God-given qualities, but swimming in our regular schools of life we are not often taught about the truth of Soul. I thank Prophet for allowing me to become his spiritual student in this lifetime. I have learned what no earthly school could ever teach. I have been to Heaven! I have experienced God's Love and His Light and Sound! I know I am Soul and so are my loved ones and friends! I also know

God loves you just as dearly. Are you like an eagle, just waiting to stretch your wings?

Written by Carmen Snodgrass

Keys in this story: God's Love, HU, Soul, Truth is Love, Proper Focus (on first seeking the Kingdom of Heaven), Peace of Mind and Heart, Spiritual Food, God's Grace (taken to the twelfth Heaven and made new), Gratitude, God's Prophet, Prophet's Inner Presence, Discernment (dream helped confirm what was in her heart, and helped her make the decision that was right for her)

Prayer for a Friend Answered

This is a touching story of witnessing a prayer for a friend being answered. The true pearl though is that we are heard. One of the greatest gifts we, as Soul, have been given is inner communication with God. The catch is, a lot a folks are not aware of or do not know how to develop it. One of the most important skills taught during our retreats is how to listen to, trust, and respond to this inner communication. This is part of teaching a man to fish versus handing him a fish.

Last year I had a friend who had a house fire. Although they did not lose much physically it was very hard on them emotionally and financially. They had to live in a small two-room hotel room (that is a small bedroom and a living/kitchen area) for over six months until all of the repairs were made to their house. This means two adults, two kids, a dog, and a cat in that two-room space for six months. This was a very stressful situation for the whole family, and I was concerned for them. Before bed one night I said a prayer. I prayed to God that during this time they would find peace and love. I also asked the Divine for a dream to let me know they were doing okay.

That night I had a dream about my friend that gave me much comfort and gratitude. I saw my friend and his family sitting on the bed in their small hotel room watching television. I was looking at them from the back of the room, so they had their backs to me. They were all leaning in on one another, and I could sense they were smiling. It looked like they were very happy together. We were not the only ones in the room though. There was a bright figure embracing them all. This bright figure was the Prophet sitting with them and embracing them all in his love and light. It was a moving experience to see this first hand. I am so grateful I was allowed to be there and to know they were truly doing okay. I thanked the Prophet for taking me on this journey. It is so wonderful to know I can talk to God, be heard, and be answered.

Then a couple of weeks after the dream I felt as though I needed to do something more for him. I had a nudge to give some money to him that had been given to me. I found out that our office was raising donations for his family, but I wanted him to know this money had a special meaning to me. I had a fifty-dollar bill that had been given to me from Del, someone I respect very much. I wanted to pay it forward. I waited until I could talk to him alone. I explained where the money had come from, and that it meant a lot to me to be able to pass the money and the love that was with it on to him. As I handed it to him I said a quiet prayer for this to truly help him in some way. I believe he could feel the love that was passed to him.

That night I again prayed that it would help him in whatever way was needed. Then, a couple of days later, he came to me with a big smile and explained they had bought a couple of air mattresses with the fifty-dollar gift for the kids to sleep on. He said that it was the first night since the fire they had slept through the night. It made me feel so grateful I was able to help by listening to the Divine on the inner, and that I acted on what I was given. I am so thankful I was able to be a conduit to pass along some of God's Love to him and his family. Since I started attending spiritual retreats I have learned to listen to my nudges and see the truth in my dreams. This has truly brought more peace and love into my life.

Written by Anthony Allred

Keys in this story: Prayer, Soul, Gratitude, Prophet's Inner Presence, Attitudes and Thoughts (Anthony's was beautiful and loving), Receptive (family was receptive to Prophet's presence), Cause and Effect (Anthony's prayer had an effect on family), God's Love (passed to family whether recognized or not)

God's Promise Fulfilled Lifetimes Later

Earth is never without a true Prophet of God to help show us the way home. Once you connect with the Prophet you will never again walk alone. The name, face, and scope of their individual missions may change, but at his core, the Prophet is the same eternal presence. What a comfort to know that even with the passing of lifetimes we will not be forgotten.

I was sitting on the soft sand, smoothing it and playing with it with my small hands. I was about two or three years old in another lifetime long ago. The people of our group were busying about doing their chores, some were chatting with each other. A few were watching the leader of our group talking with another man who had just arrived.

I began to watch this man intently as he was standing on a small hill talking to our leader. There was something very special about him as light seemed to emanate from him. He had a staff in his right hand, a long grayish white beard, and his white cloak was gently flowing in the breeze. The hood of his cloak covered the top of his head to keep off the hot sun. I watched in awe, for he exuded love, and his eyes were bright with love. He caught my eyes looking at him in awe and recognition. Somehow I knew he was God's Prophet, though I did not have the words for it. I had seen those eyes before, and I knew that he loved me. He walked towards me and put his hand out to me as he came up to me. I put my small hand in his, and I knew he was making a promise to me. As he walked on he put his hand gently on my head, and I could feel love flowing from him into me. I was transfixed and continued to watch him as he and our leader were sitting in the shade under a tent awning talking with each other. Somehow I knew that one day he would find me again.

It is now, in this lifetime, and you are in front of me holding out both of your hands to me. I put my hands in yours. The love in your eyes bore into mine, as I realize they are the same eyes I saw as a small child lifetimes ago. You have found me, though you have always been with me. You are God's Prophet; I know it with all of my being. You are the one that Jesus asked God to send, when he asked God to send us a Comforter after he was gone.

But God's Prophet is so much more than a Comforter. He has shown me the way to God, and he has shown me I am loved and that I am a Divine child of God. The Prophet is my teacher, my protector, my healer, my redeemer, and so much more. He is with me always and will always be with me. Having an inner relationship with God's Prophet makes life so abundant and a joy to live.

God's Prophet is here for you too, dear reader. He is here for all of God's children, for God loves each and every one of us, no matter what. Let him into your heart, listen to his loving guidance, and know that you are loved.

Written by Diane Kempf

Keys in this story: Soul (traveled into the past), God's Love, God's Prophet, Living Without Doubt, Connecting Spiritual Events, Karma (good), Remembrance, Spiritual Growth (over lifetimes), Gratitude, Proper Focus (on Prophet over lifetimes), Receptive (to Divine revelation to recognize Prophet in past life)

Taking Care of Business

When facing challenges in life we can handle them better if we surrender to the guidance and flow of Spirit. Prophet can lead us through anything. This doesn't mean we don't make the effort to prepare and plan; we still need to do our part. The greatest of which is being receptive to Divine guidance.

During some of the early years in which I attended retreats at Guidance for a Better Life my teacher mentioned enjoying the song "Takin' Care of Business" by Bachman-Turner Overdrive, and we even listened to it during some of our breaks. Although I remembered this song from when I was a teenager, it took on a whole new dimension in light of the spiritual training I was receiving. Not only is it fun, upbeat, and motivating, it also reminds me of how we are here to "take care of business" spiritually — to wake up to our true Divine nature, nurture our personal connection with God, and help others to discover their divinity. Over time this song has become part of my personal "awake dream" language. When I hear it, it opens my heart, reminds me of my spiritual priorities, and of my cherished relationship with my teacher Prophet Del Hall.

In the past year I have been blessed with a huge door opening in my life; after decades of being a freelance professional musician I am now teaching music at a college. It is both fun and exciting, yet extremely challenging. I find myself way out of my comfort zone much of the time, dancing on the precipice where preparation meets surrender. I have pondered on the fact, that some of the things I have been doing professionally for so many years are much more challenging to teach than I thought they might be.

Recently I sat in my car about fifteen minutes before my afternoon songwriting class began asking Prophet for help. Although I think I was doing a satisfactory and functional job delivering the material, there was a flow, or a "sweet spot" I just had not found yet. I was following a rigid outline and nervous to depart from it. I knew my students had way more potential than had been brought out and so much more to share, if they just felt a little more comfortable opening up. I knew there was more. I also knew there was nothing I could do to make that happen; I had to surrender. I sang HU for several minutes, helping me relax, let go of my mind chatter, and focused inwardly on spiritual guidance.

As I entered the classroom I felt a strong nudge from Prophet to put on the song "Takin' Care of Business." The guidance was just to put the song on, without introducing it or saying a word. After it was done playing, I began a discussion with the class. It turned out the song was a perfect segue into the outline I had already planned for the day. Instead of sticking to the outline however, I allowed the discussion to unfold in a much more spontaneous way. One by one the students shared on a deeper level than I had ever heard before, and I was talking less and listening more. I felt I was more in the role of a "facilitator," which is something I have witnessed and aspired to from observing my teachers Del and Del IV facilitate their retreats.

I am grateful for being given the experience of being a facilitator that day. By surrendering my personal agenda and going "off-script," I was actually more in alignment with God's script and in the flow of Spirit. And the prayer that was in my heart was answered; more important than covering my exact lesson plan that day was my desire that the students and I share an experience of openness and connection. The points in my outline that were important still got covered, but in a more seamless and inspired way than I could have ever planned or thought of on my own. God loves each of us and wants to help us take care of the everyday business of our lives, whatever that may be. Thank you Prophet for always knowing the best ways to help me "take care of business!"

Written by Laurence Elder

Keys in this story: God's Prophet, Personal Effort, Receptive (surrendered his agenda), Prayer, Proper Focus (on priorities), Contemplation, HU, Connecting Spiritual Events (Laurence talking with Prophet and the excellent class results that were in his heart), Balance and Detachment (detached from his strict agenda), Gratitude, Living in God's Time (he was in the present moment so he could listen to and be guided by Prophet as a coworker)

I Am Not Alone — The First Time I Experienced God's Light

God is a living God. As uplifting as scripture can be it seems a shame to think God only spoke to His children in the past. I am confident God is alive and well. He still loves us and communicates with us in this day and age. One of the many ways the Divine can communicate to us is with spiritual light. The following is a beautiful story about seeing the Light of God for the first time. What a blessing!

In 1995 I was living in California, but was working here in Virginia for a one-year temporary job-assignment. I was in a searching and seeking phase of my life — though not sure what I was looking for. It was an unsettled time, lots of change in several areas of my life. I had no real direction or rooting in anything or anywhere it seemed. I saw a small advertisement in a local magazine for Guidance for a Better Life. I was immediately interested and called and spoke to Del on the phone. I can remember our conversation like it was yesterday. We talked about various things and the types of classes he was teaching, but it was something in his voice that spoke to me on a deeper level. I knew I wanted to go no matter what the next class was. Back then the school offered a mix of wilderness skills and spiritual retreats, and it turned out the next class was a tracking class. Driving up to the school alone and taking this class was a whole new experience for me, as I had never done anything like this before, but I was excited to go. I was open to learn and to whatever adventure was in store. I enjoyed the class and found I had a natural ability to see the tracks in the dirt during our practice sessions.

While there I was more relaxed and at peace than I could ever recall. At the time I was afraid of the dark and being in the woods at night, but not as much here. I felt safe and protected and knew I was in good hands. I slept like a baby. One night after class was over and everyone had gone to bed, I stood on the grassy hill overlooking the pond. I was soaking in the beauty of the clear sky and the brilliant stars, appreciating the calmness and grateful for the courage I had to

313

stand there "alone" in the dark and still be at peace.

I became aware of a bright white light over my right shoulder just out of my peripheral vision. It surprised me, but it was a gentle presence that did not scare me. I turned quickly to see it, but when I looked it was gone. I eventually settled down and went back to looking out over the pond, enjoying the peacefulness, and saw the white light once again. This time I turned slowly hoping to see more of the light and what it was; but as I turned around enough to look directly, it was gone again. This happened again, but this time I did not turn at all and used wide-angle vision we were taught in class to observe and be aware of the light without looking directly at it. It was comforting, gentle, and non-intrusive yet it seemed to hold so much more. I was not sure what it was, but I liked it and I knew I was not alone.

The next day I mentioned my experience to Del, and he helped me understand that what I was seeing was the Light of God. Divine Spirit can come in many forms and one is light. Later I would learn this presence is always with me whether I see it or not. Out of great love for me though, it chose to introduce Itself in a way that would not scare me. It was, as I learned in later spiritual retreats, offering to have an inner personal relationship and help guide me spiritually. In time, by nurturing this relationship, by singing HU, and being grateful for its blessings, this relationship has grown in trust and a true love connection has developed.

Almost twenty years later, as I sit writing this story in the same spot on the grassy hillside looking out at the pond, I am filled with appreciation, love, and awe at how every aspect of my life has been transformed because of this very real, very present, and very personal relationship with Divine Spirit. In the past twenty years I've gone through zigs and zags, and ups and downs in life, had relationship changes, career and finance changes, and relocations of homes, but the one constant has been this ever-growing love connection. It is the solid foundation upon which my life rests and is a source of peace, stability, comfort, joy, and happiness even on some of the more difficult days. I am truly never alone. What a magnificent discovery and journey this has been and continues to be.

Written by Lorraine Fortier

Keys in this story: Gratitude, Prophet's Inner Presence, HU, Growth in Consciousness, Contemplation (Lorraine at peace overlooking the pond was a form of contemplation), Receptive (because she was at peace and felt safe), God's Love (peace, feeling safe, experiencing His Light through Prophet) Living in God's Time (for those few special moments), Living Without Doubt (Lorraine knew the presence was good)

God's Guidance Brings Peace

One of the many blessings of having Prophet as your spiritual guide is learning more about yourself. Once you have clarity on why you do what you do, you can make a conscious choice to change if you desire.

I am Soul; I am not my physical body. My physical body though, has type one diabetes. This requires a certain amount of daily attention in order to stay in the body God has blessed me with! One of the effects of diabetes is that eventually your body does not recognize the signs of low blood sugar which, if left untreated, can be life threatening. I have learned through attending spiritual retreats at Guidance for a Better Life how to recognize and trust God's guidance throughout my day. God and God's Prophet arranged a series of events, which helped me manage diabetes and brought peace to me I didn't even know I was missing.

One day I drove to work with extremely low blood sugar, and I didn't recognize my sugar was low. I only began to recognize the problem when I arrived at work and tried to park my car. I was having difficulty parking and began to realize my sugar was very low. I believe God protected me and other drivers that morning by

315

guiding me to work safely instead of possibly having an accident while driving with low blood sugar. This experience made me really nervous and gave me the motivation I needed to do something about it. It just so happened I had a doctor's appointment the next week. Interestingly, the six months prior to this, I had to keep cancelling my doctors' appointments due to work conflicts. I see this as a blessing from God: aligning the perfect timing for this appointment to coincide with this experience so that I would be more receptive to what the doctor told me.

At the appointment the doctor said, "You have a fear that your sugar will go too low so you keep your sugar high, this is common for type one diabetics." I felt Prophet speaking to me through the physician that day. I hadn't realized I had this fear, but it was true. I had a fear of having my blood sugar drop so low that I would go unconscious. Also, and more importantly, I do not want to hurt anyone else if I were to drive and have an accident because my blood sugar dropped. During this appointment I was set up with a blood sugar monitor which checks my sugar every five minutes and sends the readings to a device that I carry. It alarms if my blood sugar begins to drop, giving me a warning so I can correct it before getting to a dangerous level. Since I have been using this device, it has increased my peace and reduced my fear. Even though this fear was not an all-consuming, have me by my throat kind of fear, it was stealing some of my daily peace. It was just lurking there almost undetectable, always on, in the background of my life, but nonetheless robbing some of my peace. At my core I am peaceful, but this Divine healing has given me back my daily peace.

During a retreat at Guidance for a Better Life just prior to the visit to the doctor, I had an experience with Prophet where I saw God's orange Light traveling through my veins. I've learned that no matter what the color of God's Light, it can heal you. I know I was receiving a healing related to diabetes during this experience. Now, this does not mean I think I will be cured, but that I have gotten protection and healings from some of the physical side effects of the disease. Being guided to the doctor that day when I was very receptive to his advice and using a blood sugar monitor was a way this healing and protection have manifested. By having less fear about dropping to dangerous levels, I can keep my blood sugar in a better range, which in turn will help me stay physically healthy and not have some of the long-term side effects of high blood sugar. Thank you Prophet for your daily guidance and bringing peace to me I didn't know I was missing.

Written by Emily Allred

Keys in this story: Soul, God's Prophet, Spiritual Protection, Truth is Love, God's Love (God's orange Light benefits her health), Receptive (Emily was more receptive to the doctor because she knew the Divine set this all up for her), Connecting Spiritual Events (cancelling doctor's appointment until her low blood sugar event), God's Grace (healing by reducing her fear and increasing her peace)

Orange Light on a Past Life

Any desire for healing or spiritual growth that does not take past lives into consideration is building on a partial foundation. You are at this moment the sum of all your experiences from all your lifetimes. Thus, a true spiritual healing needs to have a broader scope than a single lifetime — it must go to the root.

In many lifetimes we are not aware of the Prophet. He is always with us whether we realize it or not. In some lifetimes we may meet the Prophet of the time in his physical presence. Those encounters always affect us even if we do not realize it at the time. In other lifetimes we may be consciously aware of him. In the real "gift lifetimes" he is our teacher, and we can nurture a relationship with both the physical and the inner spiritual part of him.

During a recent contemplation at a retreat at Guidance for a Better Life, I found myself in an orange-lit world. Del, a true Prophet of God, was inviting us to meet with the Prophet from the time period over two thousand years ago, as we were then. During this contemplation I was aware of the Prophet from those old times. I saw his robe and part of his face. Mostly I was aware of his Holy presence. Because I was also being bathed in spiritual orange light I knew this could be a past life experience. That meant the Prophet had taken me to the second Heaven where memory patterns and histories from our past lifetimes are stored. Since the orange light was visible, this particular lifetime with the former Prophet may be significant for me.

There is another aspect of the orange light. It is associated sometimes with physical healing. Present physical ailments may be the result of past life choices or experiences, though not always. Del has stated there really is no need to know of a past life unless it can help us live a better life now. Soul lives in the present. Through many years of being in the physical presence of the current Prophet and through our ongoing inner relationship, I have received blessings of physical and emotional healings. This experience with a very special Prophet of that time and being bathed in orange light let me know it was a significant lifetime for me. I felt I received a healing I needed to live this life more fully. I am grateful for this lifetime, being guided by that former Prophet, by the current Prophet, and having a relationship of love and trust with both.

During another retreat, Prophet led us in a discussion that went deeper than we had before regarding healings, which all of us had been blessed to experience so many times. An analogy of tuning a guitar was used. A guitar can be tuned, but if there is a kink anywhere in a guitar string, the guitar can never really be tuned quite correctly or for very long until the kink is taken out or the string replaced. Each fret on the neck of the guitar represents a past life in this example. The Causal plane, where there is often orange light, may have a memory pattern or a karmic record. If the guitar string is kinked at a certain fret, a past life, it can affect all future lives in a negative way. A kink could represent a significant hurt, sorrow, sadness, misunderstanding, or even a physical injury that is the root of a current illness or pain. Though we may receive many healings, until we receive and accept the healing from the root of the issue from the old lifetime, it will be difficult to rise up to a higher viewpoint consistently and permanently. In other words, God through His Prophet can heal issues from our past, today!

Lifetime after lifetime can occur with little or insignificant change to enslaving patterns, such as fear, guilt, lack of confidence, and ignorance, among others, before Soul has the opportunity to consciously meet the Prophet and develop a relationship. A greater freedom, which may be manifested as more joy, peace, making good choices in life, clarity, better health, and more, comes at God's timing as the Prophet works at the right pace for each Soul to untangle an "old kink in a guitar string."

Written by Martha Stinson

Keys in this story: God's Prophet, Prophet's Inner Presence, Soul (Living in God's Time), Receptive (to former and current Prophet, and accepting healings), Contemplation, God's Grace (taken back in time and physical and emotional healings), Gratitude

Journeys to the Fifth Heaven

It is not quite as simple as "Heaven" and "Earth." There are multiple levels to Heaven within the vast worlds of God. Whether known as planes, realms, spheres, mansions, or one of many other names, these are real places. The Prophet is trained and authorized to bring his students on spiritual journeys into the various Heavens to gain in wisdom and understanding; and how exciting it is.

It was mid-March in the mountains when I attended a retreat held in a cozy log cabin. The trees were still bare, for it wasn't quite spring yet, but we students were beginning to unfold and grow like new spring leaves. We were just beginning to come into the realization of ourselves as Soul, and that we could be free from our cumbersome bodies to explore God's Worlds, guided and taken by God's Prophet.

One evening, as Del guided us in contemplation, I saw the Prophet in front of me and I took his offered hand. Together we slowly traveled up into the Heavens to the Astral plane, then to the Causal plane, to the Mental plane, and then to the Etheric plane, pausing along the way to meet other Prophets of old residing and teaching on those planes. When we reached the beginning of the fifth Heaven, the Soul plane, two former Prophets greeted us. They each came next to me, one on either side, and with current Prophet they brought me up into an amazing world of beautiful yellow light. As I looked around all was filled with the light. I felt so free, and so peaceful, since I was unencumbered by my physical body and the distractions of my mind. It was still and quiet while I took in the beauty of the yellow light all around me. I looked at Prophet; so excited and grateful to be there. I was also grateful for the two former Prophets who helped me get there and those on the other planes who had appeared and welcomed me on each plane of the journey. This experience showed the possibilities of me, as pure Soul, with Prophet. I wondered; if the Prophet of God could take me to a beautiful yellow world of light, what else is out there? My excitement grew to continue on this amazing journey to explore God's Worlds!

A year later, I again had another opportunity to visit this beautiful world. When the experience began, I saw Prophet in my inner vision and heard a high-pitched sound. The high-pitched sound became the sound vibration HU, and Prophet and I traveled up a column of this sound that appeared to be light flowing in gentle waves. Higher and higher we went, until we burst out of the lower worlds and into the Soul plane, the fifth Heaven. Again there was the feeling of peace, freedom, and stillness as I looked all around me. This time I looked below me, and I saw the beautiful purple light of the Etheric plane, the fourth Heaven below. It looked like a swirling galaxy of the most beautiful purple light I could ever imagine. I was awestruck as Prophet and I floated there, looking down on the beautiful purple world below us.

My excitement continues to grow as I continue on this amazing journey, to learn about God's Heavenly Worlds of Light and Love, but also importantly, I have learned about myself as Soul. I have learned to accept God's Love and to pass it on to others in many ways; and what a joy and a blessing it is to do so. Thank you Prophet for these exciting steps on my journey as Soul. I am grateful and excited as I look forward to the next step with you, for there is always more.

Written by Diane Kempf

Keys in this story: Soul, God's Prophet, Prophet's Inner Presence, Contemplation, HU, Gratitude, Spiritual Growth (always more), God's Love, God's Grace (to travel the Heavens), Proper Focus (these experiences as Soul motivated Diane to focus on her spiritual path), Remembrance (this experience was given many years ago)

At Peace During Surgery

In life there will always be situations that provide an opportunity to buy into worry or stress. Fortunately, the inner Prophet is always with us, and we can choose to focus on his ever-present presence instead. This loving relationship blesses us, and others, in countless ways.

At age sixty-three I once again needed hernia repair surgery, the third attempt in four years to repair a recurring ventral hernia. This procedure involved a more extensive abdominal wall reconstruction. The surgery could take up to four and a half hours, followed by a four to seven day stay in the hospital before I could go home. The first two hernia repairs were simpler outpatient procedures. This surgery was different in still another more important way. This time I knew more deeply that God's Prophet would be with me every step of the way. This greater awareness of his inner presence blessed me in many ways.

Going into the surgery I felt love, comfort, peace, and reassurance on a deep level. I have been a student at Guidance for a Better Life for over twenty years, where my spiritual teacher is Del Hall, God's chosen Prophet. My relationship with Prophet has grown over time. While he is my teacher in his physical body, there is much more to Prophet than the physical. His physical aspect could loosely be described as only the tip of an iceberg. The other, inner part of our relationship, unseen from the outside, is very real and far greater than what is readily apparent. This invisible bond of love has grown, deepened, and strengthened over time. I rely on this bond more and more as it evolves and grows. It is through this love connection that Prophet blessed me before, during, and after the surgery.

Over time Prophet has helped me open my heart to love and gratitude for God's blessings. Prophet is the Divine channel who brings these blessings and a more abundant life. My growing love for Prophet is in itself the greatest blessing. He comforted me throughout this time. The week before the surgery I surrendered the outcome many times, and repeatedly surrendered worries as they popped up. I sang HU, a powerful love song to God, and asked Prophet to be with me throughout all that was to come. My wife Diane also loves and trusts Prophet and did the same. We planned for the coming disruption in our daily routines with peaceful calm and trust. At 5:30 the morning of the surgery I dropped Diane off at the entrance to the hospital. I parked the car and walked back to meet her. But during that walk I was not alone, for I was accompanied spiritually by Prophet. I felt a warm, comforting sense of even deeper peace come over me. I felt the love and prayers of loved ones. I moved in a palpable cocoon of God's Love and protection, with a clear awareness of Prophet's inner presence. I savored each step of the way. I paused for a moment to give thanks, deeply grateful for each moment, not alone, but in the security of God's Love through Prophet's presence. To knowingly walk anywhere spiritually with Prophet is a special blessing.

Diane and I checked in and eventually moved along to a waiting area. Prophet's comforting inner presence was constantly with us. I sensed worry and stress in other surgical patients and their loved ones. I prayed they also receive a measure of peace and reassurance as they waited. We next progressed to a more private prep room where our children Sam and Michelle joined us. Their loving presence and support brought still another measure of comfort. The inner Prophet stayed with me spiritually as I was wheeled to the operating room, got on the table, was hooked up to various monitors and an IV, and went under general anesthesia. He was there during the surgery and when I first woke up afterwards. I was given the good news that the procedure went smoothly and quickly, lasting only two and a half hours of the possible four and a half. There were none of the possible complications from the previous surgeries. The blessings and good news kept coming.

I was eventually moved from post-operative recovery to my hospital room, where I was greeted by the loving smiles of my wife Diane and daughter Michelle. A close friend of ours who works at the hospital stopped by to check on me. God's Love came in many forms through many channels. The post-surgical fog was still clearing when Prophet Del Hall and his wife Lynne arrived unexpectedly, actually physically walking into my hospital room. This was a wonderful surprise. I felt so much love from their smiles and voices. It was amazing! Prophet kept his tone light as he joked that they were "Just in the neighborhood," but he also said he woke up that morning with the intention of visiting. Prophet stood at the foot of my bed and asked questions about the surgery.

At the same time and without drawing attention to it, he took hold of my toes as he continued to talk with me. As the distributor of God's Love, Prophet can heal with a touch. His visit and touch were great blessings. When I thanked him, he said it was a pleasure and reminded me the healing came from God, only through him. With simple yet profound certainty he told me he loved me. His words went deep into my heart, remaining there still. I was blessed on levels beyond a physical healing, but don't know the specifics. I do know the physical healing can increase my lifespan and quality of life. Most importantly, these can provide more opportunity to grow spiritually and have a deeper, more loving relationship with Prophet in this lifetime.

My physical recovery continued to move ahead at a good pace after Prophet's visit. I was able to walk a little that afternoon a few hours later. I switched from heavy pain killers to Tylenol after a couple days, and was released to go home the morning of the fourth day.

I was blessed in many ways throughout this whole process. Prophet led me to good doctors and caring nurses. I felt the love and prayers of family and friends. I have enjoyed a recovery to normal activities well ahead of the original schedule. But the greatest blessing, overarching all others, was awareness of Prophet's constant presence. His physical visit to the hospital reinforced his close inner presence, which had comforted me throughout the whole process of surgery.

The inner Prophet is always with me spiritually. He will always love me. He knows me better than I know myself. Through God's Grace Prophet blesses me in ways I may never know. He is the living embodiment of God's Love sent to bless all Souls.

Written by Irv Kempf

Keys in this story: Prophet's Inner Presence, God's Love (Irv is now more Receptive), Proper Focus, HU, Prayer, Spiritual Protection, Gratitude, God's Grace, God's Prophet, Growth of Consciousness (more love, trust, and recognition of Prophet's Inner Presence and of Prophet's love)

How My Life Has Been Transformed

Your potential for spiritual growth is beyond what you can humanly comprehend. Fortunately God knows and loves you enough to always have a Prophet here on Earth to help you turn your dormant potential into a dynamic actuality. He can also ultimately help show you the way home to God.

When I was growing up I was taught that dreams were just the brain processing the day while I was asleep. I was also taught that God does not really "talk" to us anymore. When I was told He stopped talking two thousand years ago I was very disappointed. Occasionally in the last two thousand years it seemed God would talk to a saint, but it was implied that saints were some kind of special people and God only talked to them, not us. The spiritual path seemed to be about making sure you followed all the rules, if you could keep them straight, and you did not mess up. Even then you were not sure exactly what that got you. We believed, or wondered, if God was there, but there was no teaching on or discussion of real communication or love.

That all began to change for me in the early 1990's when two of my friends met Del Hall, who is now God's true Prophet. He had talked to my friends for a long time about God, HU, dreams, true Prophets, different Heavens, and more. When my friends came home they excitedly shared much of what they had learned with me. One thing that really stuck out to me then was the idea that dreams are actually real experiences in God's Heavens, or planes, while our bodies are asleep, not just random brain activity. It was also explained that true Prophets of God can meet with us and work with us in dreams. Something about all that struck a chord in me, and I believed it and hoped it could happen to me too.

Soon after that I had a dream in which I met Del and his wife Lynne just after they had finished teaching a spiritual class. At this point I had never met Del or Lynne physically, nor had I ever even seen a picture of them or been to any kind of spiritual class or retreat yet. In the dream the students were milling around afterwards, and I was alone talking with Del and Lynne. Del recommended a book, whose title I did not remember when I awoke. Then the dream ended.

I woke up astonished, immediately realizing I had just experienced what my friends had shared about. I knew it was real, and I could not believe it had happened to me. I had just met Del in a dream! I never looked at dreams the same again. Now that I knew they were real, I started trying to understand what I was being shown in them. I have had thousands of dreams since in which God's Prophet has given me help, guidance, and answers to questions and problems in all areas of my life. I have come to see dreams as an ever-present source of Divine guidance in my life to make my life better and to help me learn and grow. They have become a part of the fabric of my life and my family's life. In the most special of these dreams I have felt God's profound Love for me in Its purity, coming through His Prophet, touching me deeply and leaving a lasting impression. Through these dreams, with the blessings and insights they contain, God is demonstrating His Love for me. He is taking an active and personal interest in my life and is communicating with me. Wow.

That one original dream was the turning point of my life, and my life since has been completely transformed. From that moment on I became the seeker. I now knew there was something more to life that was real and incredible, and I was hungry to find out what it was. Little did I know how amazing it would be. If what Del had told my friends about dreams had been true, then the rest of what he told them must be true too. I started attending spiritual retreats at Guidance for a Better Life a few years after that original dream. Under Prophet's very careful guidance I was given experiences with the Divine and helped to understand them and apply them to my life. Through these experiences I was given the chance to know for myself that God is real, and I am never alone no matter how it seems.

There is a huge difference between knowing and believing — it changes everything. When I was ready Prophet took me home to God in full consciousness via spiritual travel to experience God's Love. Prophet took me again and again until I could fully accept that

God truly loved me. And then, it finally sank in and I accepted the truth. GOD LOVES ME!

On my knees before God the Father, in that profound and loving presence, I knew for sure I was loved by God no matter what. There was great peace and fulfillment in that love. God loves me and will always love me, no matter what. That is the truth. It is impossible to fully explain God's Love, or Its impact when it is accepted. It is pure, unconditional, and unchangeable. It will never end or diminish. Nothing will ever replace it or can substitute for it. There is true security and peace beyond all description within God's Love. It gives life, joy, hope, meaning, and purpose. It can change what nothing else seems to be able to change. It transforms, heals, blesses, uplifts, and gives freedom. There is very simply nothing like it.

Prophet also showed me my own Divine nature. I am Soul, an eternal being with a God-given, Divine nature, "So God created man in his own image." Genesis 1:27 KJV He gave me the experience of myself as that eternal spiritual being God created, and in that experience I knew that I go on no matter what. Death is not the end nor one hundred thousand deaths; whether physical, mental, emotional, or social. That changes a lot. Many fears just drop away. I can also see that same divinity in everyone else now. You are Soul too.

Prophet has also shown me what was in my heart. He carefully pulled aside the layers of human desires, shortcomings, fears, and insecurities I had picked up over lifetimes. I could then see a great love I have for God, and a deep desire I have to be a refined instrument for God so that others may be blessed. That is the fulfillment of my existence. In serving God and being a blessing to others I have found myself, who I really am. What a gift. I have not lost anything, and in fact, I have gained everything. There is great peace in knowing with certainty what is truly in your heart.

The key to all of this has been the Prophet in both his inner and outer form, but mostly his inner form. Even before I knew who or what he was, he was working with me, guiding me, and blessing me and my path. He has been showing me the way home to God and giving me the experiences, including dreams, I needed to grow. He has been protecting me, especially from myself, so I could stay on the path as I desire to in my heart. He has been teaching me what my experiences mean, about the Divine principles I need to know to live a balanced and abundant life, and also about what I could aspire to spiritually. He has also healed me of many of the burdens I was carrying from this life and others, so I could walk more freely and with more joy through life. And very importantly, he has given me great comfort when I truly needed it in the face of my fears, mistakes, and apparent setbacks. God, through His Prophet, has made real a life I never knew could be possible: to know God my true Father, to know His Love, to hear His Voice daily in my heart and know it, to know His constant Presence through the comforting presence of His Prophet, to have purpose, and to live a life of being an instrument of God's Love and truth to others. I am blessed beyond all comprehension.

With Prophet a life like this is possible for you too. Thank you God for sending your Prophet to find me. Thank you Prophet for taking me home to God. Thank you also to my two friends who helped me get started in this lifetime.

Written by Bobby Clickner

Keys in this story: God's Prophet, HU, God's Love, Truth is Love, God's Grace (going home to God), Spiritual Growth, Growth in Consciousness, Prophet's Inner Presence, Gratitude, Living Without Doubt, Soul, Spiritual Protection, Spiritual Sharing or Silence (the spiritual truths shared with Bobby blessed him greatly, and brought him to Prophet. What if they had not shared?)

Dreams can be a source of Divine guidance. You can learn to remember and understand your dreams. In the Bible "an angel of the lord came, in a dream" is stated several times. Usually the part "in a dream" is forgotten. My book "The Pearl of Dream Study" is very complete and easy to understand.

The Most Important Relationship

Separation from God is pain. This pain manifests in countless ways, but more often than not people do not make the connection to the source of it, which is being separated from God and their own Divine qualities as a child of God. They just feel something in life is off... or that they are missing something. They are, and it's the most important relationship one can ever have.

I could tell you I was in a sleep-like state before I came to Guidance for a Better Life, but I have come to know that was not really true. Although I have been awakened to the reality of God, I wasn't asleep because I was aware enough to listen and follow the nudges that got me to the retreat center. Comparatively speaking I was not "truly alive" before I met Del Hall, but I would not have used those words until recently. My life has always been basically great. So what spurred me on to search for this teacher? It wasn't a need I was conscious of. As far as I was concerned, I already had a relationship with God. Maybe you feel that way too. This is not to suggest that you don't. It's just to say there is so much more, and it can be so much sweeter.

This is my testimony to a relationship that continues to bring out the best in me; a relationship with the Prophet of our times. It inspires me to be pure and true; to do everything I can to show reverence and love for God and the beloved Souls that come across my sphere of influence. My family, spouse, friends, grocery store clerks, and business clients are some of the beneficiaries of God's Grace in my life. Investing in this path and establishing this relationship has made positive ripples that have reverberated into more than just my life, but the lives of those around me. That is what makes it so beautiful.

After a few classes at Guidance for a Better Life, what seemed like a really great life, now had something deeply missing. I could not forget the words of my teacher Del. He had something I knew I needed, and I had to come back for more. Before long I could not go back to my weekend parties. I could not be satisfied with the many material comforts I had surrounded myself with to ease the pain of separation from God. What seemed like enough of a relationship with God now seemed shallow. How had I not noticed this before? Simply put, I was not meant to see what I lacked until it was shown to me. Del removed the curtain of illusion and showed me truth. The clarity I gained on what was missing in my life came just from being in His Presence.

There are countless true stories I could share of the absolute miracles I have been privileged to witness and have experienced for myself. Rather than share one of my most precious memories with you, I would like to give you a taste of the various aspects of the Prophet I have experienced over the years, and how they have changed my life for the better.

If you have ever been the recipient of an anonymous gift, you know how wonderful that can be. However, knowing who to thank is even sweeter. It allows you the opportunity to get to know the giver. This is how it was for me as I woke up to the realization that God always has a Prophet in the flesh to guide and uplift Souls on the inner and on the outer. In other words, it is possible to meet with the Prophet of our times in his physical body here on Earth. In addition, it is possible to interact with his inner presence, which can be felt and communicated with in everyday life.

He can give us day and night time dreams to guide us. He can link us up with the Light and Sound of God "the highway to Heaven" and escort us back to the Heart of God in this lifetime. He can comfort us in times of need and share in our joy. We are protected from harm, unless we open ourselves to harm through disregard of Divine guidance. He can teach us, help us grow by becoming more comfortable with positive change, heal us in ways that nothing else can, take us back to past lives, show us our eternal nature, redeem us, set the future, act as a physical representative of God, and even more.

I learned the spiritual authority that comes through the Prophet does not originate within the personality of the man, although we may like the personality. What comes through is very ancient. I found out through experience I have known this ancient Presence in other lifetimes. It has had many faces, but the message has remained similar. God's truth has not changed: "God loves you. You exist because of this love. You are Soul, which is eternal and your true home is in the Heart of God. There is but one way to go home, and that is with the current Prophet of God."

I recognized this truth when I first heard it. Perhaps because it was not the first time it was shared with me. I know it has taken me many lifetimes to gain enough experience and good karma to recognize that God's Prophet truly is, Del Hall. If this resonates with you, please know we have been given the gift of an aspect of God that is with us all of the time. We are never alone, and one day we will make it back to the highest Heaven with this guide. It is not a free ride. You will have to make the effort to take the steps. Nobody can walk this path for you, but for the sincere of heart, I can say that when in weakness, I have been carried. It is achievable with proper practice, proper focus, prolonged determination, and a relationship with the current Prophet of the times. His hand is out to you. Will you take it?

Written by Tash Canine

Keys in this story: God's Prophet, God's Love, Gratitude, Reverence, Truth is Love, Growth of Consciousness, Soul, Prophet's Inner Presence, Proper Focus, Living Without Doubt, Personal Effort

For God So Loves the World

There is always a Prophet of God on Earth to lead Souls home to God. If you are fortunate enough to find and accept God's Prophet he will never leave you. Through all time and over many incarnations he will be there lovingly guiding, protecting, and teaching you the ways of God.

As I walked along the beach, I felt the warmth of the sun on my face and the ocean breeze softly caress my skin. It was a beautiful warm day on a lush tropical island long, long ago. I watched the ocean water gently lap at my feet as I walked in the sand at the water's edge. Then I noticed that all had become quiet, still, and peaceful, almost like the world had paused for a moment. I looked up and saw him walking towards me. His eyes were bright and filled with love. He looked at me with such intensity that I gasped when I realized he was the Prophet. I paused and watched him with awe as he walked by, radiating love to me. I knew I was blessed to be in his presence. He was God's chosen Prophet of that time in history, and the one through whom God's Light and Love flowed.

Meanwhile, my physical body sat in a warm cabin on a cool early spring day at Guidance for a Better Life. Prophet Del Hall led a small group of students in contemplation to this time period long ago on this island to experience a past life. Only God's chosen Prophet can do this. In that experience I was blessed to see God's Prophet of that time.

At another class during contemplation, Prophet took us to yet another past lifetime to have an experience with another one of God's Prophets. I was a young teenage boy living with a large group of people in a hot sandy desert. Life was harsh and difficult as we traveled from one place to another, finding little food and water along the way. I herded our goats to a rocky place that had some dry grasses for the goats to eat. I looked among the rocks for one of the goats that had strayed away from the others. That is where I saw him, God's Prophet of that time, Melchizedek, petting the lost goat! I watched the goat stand still while it soaked in Prophet's love. Life was so difficult in that life, and it seemed the idea of love, at least for me, was totally foreign. As I watched, Prophet beckoned me over. He showed me how to lovingly pet the goat, gentled by his touch. The goat softly bleated as it enjoyed the loving attention. This may have been my first lesson in how to give and receive love in that lifetime. Prophet demonstrated this in a way I could understand. This was an important step for me to grow and perhaps have a more fulfilling life. He knew exactly what I needed in that lifetime.

During yet another class, Prophet Del Hall led us in contemplation to experience three other past lives where we had known the Prophet of the time. In one lifetime I was a young boy about twelve years old in ancient Greece. It was early morning on a summer day as I walked across a stone courtyard. A group of about twenty boys gathered for instruction from the great Prophet of that time. I met with the group and sat down in the courtyard with the other boys. The stones still felt cool from the night before, though the day promised to be hot as the sun peeked over the building nearby. Prophet walked up to our group with his eyes sparkling and his face lit up with joy to see us. As he spoke he regarded us individually in such a way that I knew he loved each one of us as unique beautiful Souls. Two of the other boys excelled in the teachings, yet Prophet patiently spoke so every one of us could understand.

The scene changed as today's Prophet took us to experience another lifetime about 2,000 years ago where we knew the Prophet of that time. Here, I sat with a small group of people around a campfire. As the fire crackled and sparks flew up into the air, the Prophet of that time, Saint Paul, spoke with us as we made plans to spread the word of Jesus. It seemed to be a dangerous mission, as many people back then were against us and the teachings of Jesus, but I trusted God would protect us and help us to do His will.

Again the scene changed to a time shortly before Saint Paul's. The Prophet of that time stood on a hill with a crowd gathered around him. I stood there as I looked up at him, completely transfixed in awe. It was Jesus! As he spoke to the crowd with love in his voice and wisdom in his words, I knew in my heart that he was not only God's Prophet, but he was truly God's Son. He radiated a presence that was breathtaking as God's Love flowed through him to the surrounding crowd and beyond.

Prophet Del Hall teaches that God always has a chosen Prophet on Earth. The same Light and Love of God flows through all God's Prophets, though each may have a different face and personality, since God chooses the perfect Prophet for each time period. These past life experiences showed me more deeply that this is true. I experienced some of the past Prophets of several different time periods. I truly was blessed to have been in their presence.

God's Prophet is here for all Souls. He is the one who can lead you home to God. It is an amazing gift of God's Grace to know His Prophet, even if you never meet him in the physical. If you wish to develop your inner relationship with Prophet you may ask him to teach you and guide you in dreams and contemplations. Blessings and abundance will follow, for your relationship with Prophet is the key to everything truly good in your life. This includes love, peace, joy, contentment, clarity, being able to recognize and "hear" God's guidance, and being used to be a blessing to others. Prophet is already always with you and has always loved you. For God so loves the world that He always has a Prophet to lead His children to Him.

Written by Diane Kempf

Keys in this story: God's Prophet, God's Love, Contemplation, Give Love First (with the goat), Soul, Growth of Consciousness, Living Without Doubt, Truth is Love, Prophet's Inner Presence, Remembrance, Understanding Change, Gratitude, Connecting Spiritual Events (over a long time in history), Spiritual Protection

Jesus Helped Me Accept Prophet's Love

Many people struggle with the idea that God always has a living Prophet on Earth to teach His ways and truths. Yet, it is the truth. Jesus himself prayed to his Father to send another Comforter. This means mankind will never be alone, and it is not a betrayal of Jesus to follow the current living Prophet — if you are fortunate enough to find him.

In the late 1990's I had developed a renewed interest in the teachings of Jesus. During this time I also sat down and read the whole Book of Revelation. I felt a strong reverence for Jesus in my heart and a desire to be right with him, but I was also battling with fear of not following Jesus and the true way into the Kingdom of Heaven, if I followed the spiritual teachings Del Hall had shared with me at Guidance for a Better Life. I had taken a few classes with Del and been greatly blessed by the Divine love and the Light of God I had experienced in his presence and when sitting outside on the retreat center property. At the time I did not know that in the years to come Del would be ordained by God to be His chosen Prophet of the times. I did know I had experienced an incredible love that stretched my heart wide open and left me feeling more at peace when I attended classes with him. I had not, however, resolved the issue of whether following the guidance of a spiritual teacher other than Jesus would be betraying the Son of God.

I was blessed in the summer of 1999 to be able to spend a couple days sitting outside in contemplation on the school property after a spiritual retreat had ended. During this time alone, within the spiritual presence of the Prophet at that time in history, the fear of what would happen if I did not follow Jesus as my Lord and Savior was brought fully to my attention. As a result of looking at this and confronting this fear, a beautiful thing happened, I felt this trust within me that everything would be fine if I followed the teachings of God that Del had shared with me. This helped me to not make a decision based on fear, but rather, follow my heart and make a choice based on love. When I later shared my experiences while sitting out in the woods with Del, his response to me was very reassuring. He helped me see that the teachings of God he was sharing with me, and developing a relationship with God's current Prophet, did in no way go against or separate me from Jesus. As I later came to learn, what Del was teaching us were, in fact, the same eternal teachings and path of love Jesus taught two thousand years ago. It was a true gift from God that came through Del, the blessing of knowing I was not in any way turning my back on Jesus by having love for the current Prophet of the times and following his guidance.

That same summer I was given additional reassurance I was making a good choice by going to Guidance for a Better Life retreat center. This time it came through a dream in which I was riding on a crowded passenger train, as a newscast through the train's sound system delivered messages about all sorts of horrendous, disturbing world events. I then distinctly felt Jesus' presence with me and heard a voice I knew to be his say, "Don't worry about Armageddon and the great plague, follow your heart and stay on the path of love." The sound of his voice was so calming and instantly brought peace into my heart. I then remembered how Del had taught me to keep my heart open and follow the inner guidance within it, and how he had often referred to the teachings of God he shares with his students as the "Path of Love." I experienced deep love for everything Del had taught me and knew Jesus had purposely chosen words I would identify with Del. I felt the desire to return to Virginia soon, so I could go up to another retreat. The sounds of the scary newscast faded away, and now I saw beautiful mountains outside of the train window and was blessed with real peace in my heart.

I awoke from this dream knowing Jesus did not want me to worry about the future, and he was helping me to let go of fear related to anything I had read in the Book of Revelation and the fear of thinking I was not following him. Whatever the future might bring, I would be fine if I listened to my heart and followed the inner guidance of the current Prophet. I would not be turning my back on Jesus and condemned to a life in hell by following the Prophet of the times. I knew Jesus wanted me to know the teachings of God's Love Del had shared with me and other students, and that they hold within them the key to living an abundant life. This is a life that is not burdened by fear of what the future may bring or fear of being disconnected from Jesus in any way.

I am so glad I made a choice based on love, not fear, and chose to return to Virginia and attend more classes with Del. I have been blessed, as a result of this choice, with more awareness of my true nature as Soul, an eternal being who is always loved by God and His Prophet. I have been blessed to know my spiritual teacher of past decades is now God's chosen Prophet, the one who has been ordained by God to deliver His message to the world and to help His children to draw nigh to God. This choice has also helped me to love and appreciate Jesus more than ever. Biblical scripture has unfolded into deeper layers of meaning to me now that I am able to read it with the help of Prophet's inner and outer guidance.

One never needs to stop loving a Prophet of the past in order to build a relationship with and accept the love of the current Prophet of today. Jesus still visits me in dreams and his love is still with me. I have been truly blessed by God sending Jesus to me in a dream to reassure me I am not turning my back on His Son. Jesus himself asked the Father to send a Comforter. The current Prophet of God IS that Comforter and so much more, sent by the Father, so I am actually following Jesus' and the Father's wish by following God's current Prophet.

Written by Roland Vonder Muhll

Keys in this story: Reverence, God's Love, Soul, God's Prophet, Truth is Love, Living Without Doubt, Proper Focus, Peace of Mind and Heart, Spiritual Strength (Roland is stronger now from his experience), Receptive (more receptive to Del now), Attitudes and Thoughts (Roland has a better attitude for being teachable), Chrysalis to Freedom, Contemplation, Prophet's Inner Presence

Handprint in the Sand

God's Love comes through in many ways, and there are clues to it everywhere in our daily life. One of the goals our retreat center has always had, has been to help folks recognize the Hand of God in their life, regardless of the specific retreat they may be attending.

In my late teens and early twenties, I was searching, searching for a sense of purpose and a life that had meaning. Eventually, an answer to a prayer for a teacher led me to Del Hall at Guidance for a Better Life. In 2001, I began taking his awareness and survival classes. I loved them. There was something special about leaving phones, televisions, and modern conveniences behind for a weekend or a week and staying in the mountains. Our wilderness stay included amenities: running spring water, comfortable straw padded shelters, delicious meals, and a refreshing pond to take a swim.

In these early survival classes, Del was teaching us to be aware, to perceive, and recognize the many wonders in life of which we had been largely unaware. Midway through one awareness class, my eyes had begun to open to the world around me. The jagged break of a blade of grass or lightly trampled leaves on the forest floor showed evidence of a deer, scratch marks on a tree showed a black bear, and gnaw marks on a bone showed evidence of a mouse or chipmunk. We practiced following animal prints in a muddy field and on the sand bank near the pond. He taught us to see the tiny piles of dirt, which pushed up to the side of the animal track, indicating the animal's direction of movement.

Many of these involved looking with the sense of sight, but we also used our other senses. Scratching the bark off of a tree branch, he showed us two identical looking trees actually had distinctly different smells — one a delightful wintergreen scent and another a rather putrid scent. We also tasted and cooked a variety of delicious edible plants. These experiences helped broaden my view. There was so much more around me that I had never even noticed! It was a blessing to have a teacher who could point out these tiny details that brought a wonder to living on Earth.

338

Del gave us the opportunity to practice using another sense to "see" as well, the sense of touch. He set up a sandbox and pressed homemade plaster animal prints that he had gathered over the years: a wolf, deer, and mountain lion. By pressing these into the sand, he left indentations of the paw and hoof prints. Blindfolded, it was difficult to feel at first, but after a few tries I began to feel with my fingertips how the sand went down into a little valley where the animal's pawprint was. I could "see" without my eyes!

After a break, Del smoothed the surface of the sand and pressed his own handprints in it. He wanted us to see if we could find his handprints while we were still blindfolded, using our intuitive senses. I recall kneeling before the sand box and almost instinctively placing my hands in his prints, like my hands were being guided to his by an unseen magnet.

I was not consciously aware of this being a "spiritual exercise" so to speak, but as my hands rested in his handprint, I experienced God's Love. It settled over me like a warm and comforting blanket of light. At once soothing and calming, it also quenched a deep thirst. Eventually I let go and gave the bandana to the next student to be blindfolded. Walking away for a moment of quiet, I didn't have a logical explanation for what had just happened. I had experienced God's Love in a handprint and still felt it stirring within my heart. A flame that had been smoldering for a long time had just been sparked and ignited. Love. God's Love had touched me.

After composing myself, I stood back and observed the other students. They each responded to Del's handprint in a unique way. Some seemed likewise touched, pausing to accept the gift hidden in the sand. Others could not seem to find his prints without looking. God's Love will not encroach on another, nor force Its way. It takes receptivity on our part to recognize and accept love when it is offered in countless ways throughout our day.

A few years later, I again attended this awareness class and Del shared with some of his recurrent students he had put "something extra" into that handprint in those early classes — Love. Part of a Prophet of God's anointing involves his ability to share God's Love with others. This can be done in countless ways, on the inner during prayer or contemplation, through a glance, or a seemingly simple class experience in the woods. This confirmed what I already knew in my heart, there was something special about my teacher and his retreat center. I experienced Divine love here and was given tools to experience and recognize it at home too. This was, and continues to be, life-changing!

Del no longer offers these survival classes, but I recall them fondly. They were stepping stones along my, and many other students', spiritual journeys to awaken us to "the more" in life. While Del was pointing out the many ordinary things around us we were unaware of, and now had the skills and tools to recognize, he was also showing there is more to life spiritually. These survival skills classes were a way he could introduce students to spiritual survival skills and tools as well.

He described animal tracking as reading the wood's morning paper and seeing the current events of wildlife. Simultaneously, he was teaching us to "track" and recognize God's communication with us and God's Love for us. He was teaching us to see those fine "dirt piles" that showed God's Hand at work in our lives: guiding, protecting, or showing us a better way.

Clues to God's Love are all around us, we just need the eyes to see. Here in a seemingly simple experience in the mountains of Virginia, I experienced God's Love directly through a handprint. This, among many other experiences, confirmed what I knew in my heart — I had found what I had been searching for.

Written by Molly Comfort

Keys in this story: God's Love, Receptive, Prayer, Growth in Consciousness, Gratitude, Connecting Spiritual Events, Contemplation, Prophet's Inner Presence

Wild Edible and Golden Light

One of the most popular and fun outdoor skills courses we used to offer was the "Wild Edible Plant Weekend." Folks really loved the transformation from looking out at a sea of green to actually seeing individual plants and learning how to identify and use them. It is amazing how many things are right before our eyes that we do not see until someone shows us how to truly look.

About eighteen years ago I attended a "Wild Edible Plant Weekend" at the Nature Awareness School, now called Guidance for a Better Life. It was my second class on the mountain. During the weekend class Del took us on a walk to identify some of the specific plants we were learning about in class. The group of us came to a patch of plantain. Del was describing how much he loved this plant and how many uses it had medicinally. You could just feel the love he had for this little plant in his voice as he spoke about its benefits. He then picked a few leaves to show us some of the details. The leaves were a shiny dark green with parallel veins found on the underside. As he was holding them in his hands I began to see a golden glow of light start at his hands and ascend up to his arms! I watched in awe! I wondered if I was seeing things — I blinked and rubbed my eyes. Nothing had changed except the golden light began to glow brighter and brighter! I looked around and noticed that no one else was seeing what I was singularly honored to see.

I filed this experience away but did not forget how it had touched my heart. I continued to process, on my own, what the experience really meant. I knew what I saw was real and it had really happened. This was at a time in my life that I was hungry to learn more about the Divine and the Love of God. I had read in scripture that God has love for all of us and for all living things.

The next class I attended I spoke to Del of my experience with the golden light. He very simply said maybe it was God's Love coming through him. Since I was the only one that saw the golden light I felt very grateful to have been given such a personal gift. I believe the gift was personal because I have always had a special love of plants, flowers, and trees. It was years later I would also learn more about Del's spiritual connection with the Divine, and the real reason I was so blessed that day. This was my first understanding many years ago of the Love of God being expressed in golden light.

Written by Nancy Nelson

Keys in this story: God's Love, Receptive, Gratitude, Growth of Consciousness, Remembrance

It's All About the Relationship

As Soul — an eternal spiritual being, you have one life. You do however, live many physical lifetimes. Reincarnating over and over again you gain in wisdom, understanding, and in your ability to give and receive love. Having the opportunity to be taught by the Prophet of the times is one of the greatest blessings of any physical incarnation.

The greatest blessing of my life is my relationship with the Prophet of God. Our relationship began many years prior to attending my first class at Guidance for a Better Life in 1997 and meeting my spiritual teacher, Del Hall. I spent much of the first twenty years of my life lost and troubled and the next ten slowly waking up and finding focus and direction. I sought peace and balance through music, meditation, therapy, intense exercise, and other spiritual retreats. There were individuals who helped me along the way; other spiritual teachers, mentors, and friends filled with love and wisdom, and I was doing the best that I could, but there was still something missing — I did not yet have a guide who could take me all the way home to God. Even still, I had a strong calling to be closer to God, to grow spiritually, and to move from the "narrow human state to the boundless one of Soul," which was a yearning I became more clear of when this quote was shared with me in my first weeklong spiritual retreat with Del.

Later, years after I had established my connection with Prophet, I looked back at my youth and realized God had been there all along, even before I was aware of Him, watching over me, and keeping me out of harm's way despite my ignorant choices. I somehow managed to emerge unscathed from life-threatening circumstances, avoid incarceration, a serious drug habit, or the many other pitfalls that might have prevented me from fulfilling my spiritual calling; His Love and protection were there.

Running daily was one of the tools I discovered early on, it helped me start to turn things around and channel my energy in a positive direction. Many years later when I began attending Del's retreats, I was given a dream in which Divine Spirit explained to me that I came into this life with an energetic imbalance, and running daily was a way to correct that imbalance. I recognize this now as a gift from the Prophet, who gave me the nudge to start running before I became his student in the physical. He also brought me an understanding of the truth about it in a dream when I was ready.

One day while in my mid-twenties I was out on a run, and my heart was full of pain. I was distraught and stressed out, about what I don't even remember anymore. I cried out to God and asked for help. Deep inside I somehow knew He heard me and was listening. I remember my plea to this day — I asked Him to simply hold me. An amazing thing happened — I felt a deep peace fill me; I knew He loved me, and I was actually being held. In hindsight, once again the Hand of God through the Prophet was there for me, even before I consciously knew of him.

When at the age of thirty-one I began taking retreats at Guidance for a Better Life, I discovered God had an individual "syllabus" for me. Over time the Love and truth of God would be revealed to me in a very personal way I could integrate into my life and accept deeply in my heart. I began to have my own personal experiences with the Divine. Prophet taught me that I am Soul, a Divine spark of God, and that God truly and deeply loves me. I also learned I am so much more than my physical body. I learned this by traveling as Soul with Prophet in the splendorous inner worlds of Spirit and having real experiences with God's Light and Sound that were necessary for my spiritual unfoldment. Seeing and experiencing the Hand of God that had been there all along reinforced on a deeper level that I am never alone.

I became an intern at the retreat center in 2001 and spent nearly four months living on the property, and many more pages turned in my syllabus. Lessons came in all shapes and sizes. Seemingly simple tasks such as mowing grass, washing a pickup truck, and sweeping a dirt floor became focused studies in efficiency, effectiveness, and economy of motion, but even more than that, the importance of serving with an open heart. One day as I swept the inside of a shelter before a class, my teacher Del took the broom from me and finished the job. I watched as he meticulously and lovingly arranged the circle of straw around the fire pit and observed the clean and precise line that was formed between the straw and dirt area. I realized my work was inferior in comparison and vowed to do better next time, but I still hadn't gotten the bigger lesson. As students began to arrive, several commented on the fire pit and how beautiful it looked. One tried to thank me, but I explained that I couldn't take the credit. He told me he really felt the love that had been put into it, and I never forgot that. I was shown that any act done with love, no matter how small, is important in the eyes of God and makes a difference! When our primary focus is to carry the love of God in our heart as we go through our daily walk, people really feel this and are affected by it! This is a topic that is still discussed in our classes, which continues to evolve and pay dividends in my life.

Little by little I was learning how to give and receive more love, and in the process of doing that I was also being shown what parts of myself were in my way. The lessons were not always easy. On the contrary, I was stubborn, and even though as Soul I wanted and had asked for this, I came into this life with certain blind spots, weaknesses, and attachments, which Prophet continually pointed out; sometimes very gently, and other times with great intensity. Always with love, and always with the perfect delivery.

There is only one individual who has the ability to know me that intimately, and that is the Prophet of God. He knows us better than we know ourselves. Prophet wakes us up and teaches us on the outer and the inner. He will use whatever means is available, including other individuals, to achieve this. Long before I knew the Prophet personally in this life, he was working through others to help prepare me, and I now recognize his Divine hand in all those encounters.

Del emphasized the importance of this relationship and continually pointed me to the Prophet of the times, even before he was Prophet. When I felt I had hit some kind of wall with my growth, he pointed out that my inner communication with the Prophet was lacking. I began to work very hard on this relationship; after all, any worthwhile relationship requires work and nurturing. Over time as this love connection grew and blossomed, I experienced a peace, freedom, and joy beyond anything I had previously imagined possible. I learned a truer and deeper meaning of surrender. I could relax and turn over my personal agenda to Prophet, knowing and trusting that following God's will and His plan for me would be better than I could have ever planned in my limited mind. I learned to trust God's timing over my own. I became less self-centered as my innate desire, as Soul, to serve and be used to be a blessing to others was ignited.

There always has been and always will be one individual at any given time, with the designation of Prophet on planet Earth, to show individuals their true eternal nature and lead them home to the Heart of God. It is an unbroken chain throughout history. This is a great comfort for me knowing there is always a way home to God, and someone here to shine the light. When Del became the Prophet, I already understood this. I had developed a deep trust and love for the former Prophet on the inner, but I also loved and trusted Del as my teacher on the outer, so when the role of Prophet went to him, the transition was seamless and made perfect sense. My relationship with the Prophet is sacred and immeasurable, and something that will ultimately transcend my physical lifetime. Unlike my possessions, money, status, and other earthly attachments, my relationship with Prophet is something I can actually take with me into future lifetimes, along with other divine attributes and spiritual growth. It is an investment in my "spiritual bank account," that will pay dividends for eternity.

As I settle into mid-life and approach the "Big Five-O," I look back at this lifetime and realize I am truly a different person than the whippersnapper who set foot on the retreat property for the first time nearly twenty years ago. I was extremely self-centered and totally blind to it. I was rigid and set in my ways. I was led largely by my ego, fed by a deep insecurity, which is now healing at the core as I recognize my true eternal nature and accept more and more of God's Love. Long-standing commitment issues are starting to melt away. I have received countless blessings, healings, and lessons that continue to nourish me. I was taught the HU, a sacred love song to God, that has become as integral a part of my life as breathing. I have some of the most beautiful Souls on the planet to call my spiritual family. I have love in my life and a new and blossoming career. And I have gratitude! As my teacher has been telling me for many years, gratitude is the secret to love.

To "take the long view" is to know that as Soul, my true eternal self, I have one life but have had many incarnations and physical "earth suits." I feel blessed to be aware this is indeed a pivotal lifetime. All have the opportunity to "draw nigh" to God, as is spoken of in the Bible. God is real, God loves all of us, and He is reaching out His Hand. A relationship with God through His chosen Prophet is available here and now to any of His children who genuinely desire it, and my relationship with His Prophet is the key to unlimited spiritual unfoldment and abundance.

Written by Laurence Elder

Keys in this story: God's Love, Proper Focus, Receptive, Personal Effort, Consistency (Laurence runs every day to keep his energy in balance), Truth is Love, Soul, Living Without Doubt, God's Prophet, Growth of Consciousness, HU, Gratitude, Remembrance, Understanding Change, Spiritual Strength, Living in God's Time, Prayer (to be held), Connecting Spiritual Events (Prophet using others to help him, and recognized Prophet's protection as a child)

The True Prophet of God

Learning to listen to your heart and know truth when you find it is so very critical. If you are not fully confident in your ability to recognize truth it will be nearly impossible to lay hold of the most amazing truth that can bless your life, and the lives of those around you, in almost limitless ways. God always has a Prophet in the "role of Son" here in the physical to show us the way home to our Father.

I was born into a Christian home and was brought up in the nurture and admonition of the Lord. I accepted Jesus as my Lord and Savior at age nine and was baptized by my father, who was a Baptist minister. During my college years, I rededicated my life to Christ, prayed the sinners' prayer, and meant it with all my heart. Jesus truly became Lord of my life. With Jesus in my heart I grew in faith throughout my adult years, attending church regularly, singing in the choir, and teaching Bible classes in Sunday School for seven years. Jesus became more than Lord and Savior, He became my true friend. My life was not always easy, but I had an anchor. Looking back now I see clearly how well He was preparing me for what was to come.

I studied about biblical experiences like the miracles of Jesus, Saul of Tarsus being struck blind and converted by the Light and Voice of God, and John's amazing visions that disclose God's ultimate plan of redemption in the Book of Revelation. But never in all my years of attending church, did I ever personally experience what I am about to share with you. God led me to Guidance for a Better Life seventeen years ago and Del Hall became my spiritual teacher who knows and loves Jesus as the Son of God. I knew in my heart that when Del spoke, God was speaking to me through him. Over the years of attending spiritual retreats with Del and other students, this truth has been affirmed and confirmed beyond any shadow of doubt that Del is the true Prophet of God. Many times I have heard and felt Jesus vouching for Him and encouraging me to listen and learn from him. I have learned so much more about myself, about Jesus, and about God in these seventeen years than I ever learned in church.

I am not disparaging the church by any means. My church experiences were exactly what they needed to be, and I am eternally grateful for them. But since then Del has been teaching me so much more: learning God's eternal teachings and ways to tune in and more clearly communicate with Him, experiencing Divine love firsthand, recognizing and appreciating how God guides and teaches us through His Prophets with nudges and so-called "coincidences" that are really the Hand of God, and through dreams as we sleep, and awake dreams during the day. These are all gifts from God, a part of the "Language of the Divine." As I am becoming more fluent in this Divine language, my life is changing in amazing ways.

I used to struggle with finances and relationships due to self-indulgence and self-centeredness that I could not even see in myself. God, through Del, has opened my eyes to the truth about myself and healed me, and he healed my marriage in profound ways that have resulted in a life of joy, peace, plenty, and love. This is the abundant life Jesus spoke of, and it keeps getting better and better!

My prayer life too has been supercharged! One of the most important things Prophet has taught me is the HU, the perfect prayer. I begin by sitting comfortably with my eyes closed and thinking of something I am grateful for. It could be anything, my wife, a beloved pet, the smell of a cup of coffee. That gratitude brings an inner smile to my heart and opens me up to accept God's communication. God speaks to us through an open heart. Then I sing HU, an ancient name for God as a pure prayer, a love song to God, not asking for anything. Singing HU and then listening in silence afterward within that quiet tranquility, has become the mainstay of my life. Why? Because it raises me up to a higher viewpoint and tunes me in to God's communication that gives Divine guidance to help me make better decisions in my daily life, and gives amazing spiritual growth experiences that can truly be described as "biblical" in proportion. Singing HU is a way of drawing nigh to God, and God responds as promised, drawing nigh to us (James 4:8).

Here is the amazing experience that I was given on February 9, 2013. At a Guidance for a Better Life retreat, after singing HU, a love song to God, I sat with my eyes closed, quiet, calm, peaceful, and relaxed. Prophet Del Hall, who has been teaching me in my physical life, appeared in front of me in my spiritual vision. He was standing in a wide, intense beam of golden and white light. His hands were outstretched toward me. I looked with reverence and awe into his eyes where I recognized an ancient, Divine presence. I felt waves of Divine love wash into me as I reached up and held his hands tightly in mine. He lifted me up into the beam of light, into himself, and I heard the rushing of a mighty wind. I could see that, as Soul, I too was a glowing ball of God's Light within him! We flew together, swinging from side to side, zigging and zagging in harmony with each other. I felt joy and peace that words cannot convey. It was Divine elation, comfort, and protection, and I felt more loved and more enlivened than I have ever felt before! This experience was absolutely real. I experienced the Holy Spirit of God, the Comforter as Jesus prayed His Father would send (John 14:16), which filled the disciples of Jesus at Pentecost. I knew I was in the presence of the true Prophet of God, the embodiment of the Holy Spirit, who can teach us in the physical as well as go with us on the inner wherever we are, guiding and teaching us, reminding us of the things Jesus taught, and taking us ever further, just as Jesus promised (John 14:26). I continue to re-live this experience with reverence and awe, knowing the Holy Spirit, embodied as the true Prophet of God, is always with me throughout the challenges and the twists and turns of life. He continues to teach me inwardly as well as in the outer physical world. From this experience I know that no matter what happens, I am loved, comforted, and protected. Thank you Prophet! Thank you Jesus for leading me to him!

For my Christian friends who are reading this, I must include a word of encouragement to trust and rely on the Holy Spirit, the true Prophet, to help you dig deeper into spiritual truths. Ask Jesus to reveal to you the Divine truth. Is it really possible the Comforter, the Holy Spirit, is now in these end times incarnated on Earth, as the true Prophet, teaching and preparing us for when Jesus returns? In the book of Revelation, John foretells the emergence of the false prophet, who will deceive and point Souls to the "beast", the antichrist whom many will follow to their doom. Would not the Heavenly Father send a true Prophet to counter the false prophet, or would God leave His beloved children alone as prey to the compelling deception of a well-liked world spiritual leader, who will vouch for a popular and well-liked world political leader, the antichrist? Remember the popular song from the mid-1990s that asked, "What if God was one of us?"

The Bible warns against false prophets and the antichrist, and John recorded God's warning against adding to or taking away from the scriptures (Revelation 22:18). So often this verse and others are dogmatically distorted to the point of putting up walls, which keep us from seeking the true meaning of the scriptures. In our fear of God's wrath, we use labels like "cult" and "heresy" to dismiss what is actually God's higher truth. Isn't this exactly what the Pharisees did with Jesus? I have witnessed these walls coming down. Guidance for a Better Life is not a cult in the sense of distorting truth. Quite the opposite, these are the pure teachings of the Holy Spirit, unpolluted by the limitations of the human mind. These teachings have taken nothing away from my Christianity, rather they have deepened my love for Jesus, for the Heavenly Father, and for God's true Prophet, the Comforter, the Holy Spirit, and opened up the true meaning of the Holy Scriptures.

Read this book with an open heart. Ask the Lord whether He vouches for the truth of these sacred personal experiences. Recognize the Hand of God in your own life daily and give thanks for it! Sing HU and be receptive to God's outpouring of love and guidance. Over time, you may begin to sense a calling to come meet us at one of the events at Guidance for a Better Life retreat center, or continue study through books and online offerings. There is so much more to experience and learn when you are ready.

Written by Paul Harvey Sandman

Keys in this story: Living Without Doubt, God's Prophet, God's Love, Gratitude, Prayer, HU, Growth of Consciousness, Prophet's Inner Presence, Receptive, Soul, Spiritual Protection, Truth is Love, Reverence, Discernment (better decisions), God's Grace (healings)

Dearest Prophet

You opened your home and your heart to me
You opened doors for me I never knew existed
My eyes opened to truth
and my heart to God's Love

You've shown me there is more to me than just the role I was
playing in this or any other lifetime
You've shown me how to live in balance and harmony
by walking it with you

You've corrected many of my missteps
And turned misunderstandings into revelation
You encouraged me
to be more than who I was
and be who I am... Soul

You've re-introduced me to old friends, to family
and to the key to life — my relationship with the Divine
For that I am so grateful

You've shown me incredible patience and devotion
When others would have given up on me
You would not let go

You let me crawl when I needed to humble myself before God
and hugged me when I needed comfort
and encouragement

You gazed into my eyes and saw past my masks
and allowed me to see through your eyes

The view atop the mountain
has transformed me
I am different in so many ways

You have re-lit a fire in me
Smoldering for ages
The courage to follow my heart
To put God first
in all areas of my life
has made everything sweeter

Role Model, Teacher, Protector, Guide
An ever-present inspiration
Slowly building a foundation
So I could stand tall beside you
Never on my own and
Never alone

There is always more
There always will be
But the peace I feel
And the Truth that has touched my heart
has made the climb so well worth it —
a thousand times over

How can I ever thank you enough
Beloved Prophet.

Written by Chris Comfort

A More Advanced View of the Spiritual Keys

You now have some basic understanding of many Spiritual Keys and have read stories of my students applying the Keys in their daily lives. Hopefully you have begun to see the value a living teacher can provide to you and have put some of the foundational Keys such as: HU, Gratitude, Attitudes and Thoughts, and Discernment into practice. I call them "Foundational Keys" because they are essential to the effective operation of all other Keys. I now want to go back to the definition of the Keys again.

Keys seem extremely simple. Students sometimes feel they already understand and use certain Spiritual Keys. Often this is not true. It is best to be humble and respectful regarding ALL Keys. They are ALL very powerful spiritual tools and truths that can greatly benefit one's life! ***They all have deeper meanings and use than the simple English words used to describe them. The deeper use and meanings are gained through study, contemplation, life experiences, and discourses from Prophet.***

Individual Keys do not stand alone and independent of other Keys. Part of the secret of each Key is how it relates to, affects, or impacts other individual and groups of Keys.

I have included the following writing, "Spiritual Keys — Introduction to the Non-linear and Dynamic View" with the hope it inspires you to look deeper at these Spiritual Keys. This letter was first written to me by one of my advanced students. I then suggested the author address it to my other students to benefit them. She is sharing with them information consolidated from my retreat discourses, experiences gained through dreams I gave her, and months of inner teaching and instruction I provided her spiritually on the inner (Not physically, but as Soul I spiritually visited her, as Soul, and taught her). It offers an amazing insight into how the Keys interrelate, and how your personal growth also impacts the overall effectiveness of individual Keys. It might be best to read this several times.

Spiritual Keys — Introduction to the Non-Linear and Dynamic View

I was drawn back to the discourse Prophet brought us during my Reunion 2019 facilitation on non-linearity in the operation of the Spiritual Keys. This topic originated from a dream Prophet gave me during the Step Four, "Prophet Shares Spiritual Keys" retreat that year I shared with you all. In this dream, I was with Prophet in a very tall building in which he and Lynne lived. I was sleeping over, and as I was getting ready for bed he called me into a room and began showing me different things. One of these things was a model of some kind that was constructed of interlocking pieces and hinged parts that allowed it to expand and contract in a sphere. I somehow knew he was showing me a dynamic version of the Spiritual Keys. This version was not a single "fixed" sphere model as he originally described the interconnections of the Keys to us. In his hands, this new model became alive, and it moved in all sorts of ways as he moved his hands in a fluid-like way. He asked me if I remembered the name of it, but all I could remember was it began with the letter "p." He said it was something very popular and well-known a long time ago. That is where the dream ended. I was fascinated by his discourse that followed during my sharing and tried to take in as much as I could of what he said, but there was a whole lot in what he gave us. I have been digesting it ever since, gently continuing to think about it, but not quite ready to write it down and try to work with it to go further, until just recently. I will do my best to capture what he shared with us, and hopefully this will be of value to you.

Prophet's Discourse

Dear Prophet: In your discourse, you explained to us the significance and meaning behind what you were showing me in the dream. You talked about the eternal and infinite nature of God's Word embodied in the Keys, and how it is both changeless and changing, and non-linear. There is a changeless aspect to the truth within the Keys and how they relate and connect to each other. This is like a baseline or steady state that first needs to be captured and understood like Paul and Lisa did in their talks. This baseline has no variables in it though and is modeled by a single fixed sphere, where the sphere is made up of interlocking Keys that share interrelationships, each Key like a puzzle piece of a 3-D spherical puzzle.

Then there is the dynamic. The changing and non-linear nature of these same eternal truths as was shown in the dream. The model you showed me included those variables that influence us and our state of consciousness in daily life. This model had infinite, ever-changing combinations depending on the context of the situation and the influence the variables have on us personally, and results in an infinite number of possible spheres, expanding and contracting as you demonstrated to me in the dream. It is a more accurate and real model of how things actually work and is complex and fluid. I had a thought about this, perhaps the expansion is when the variables influence our consciousness in a positive and uplifting way, and the sphere contracts when the impact is in a downward or negative direction.

In my dream, you held this model in your hands and moved it around. In this I see you, the Living Word made flesh, and your role in the dynamic, in that you choose what and how much you want to show us at any given time of the Word. The Word of God and His teachings are eternal, but at any given moment in history a particular Prophet on the outer is only showing mankind a certain level of the teachings, and this is ever-changing over time, according to what God says we are ready to comprehend and understand. I can see this as I study scripture from the Old Testament to the New Testament, and now today; you are bringing us even higher truths with more clarity, breadth, and depth of the same eternal teachings Jesus and the Prophets of Old shared during their times on Earth. This will continue in the future, infinitely so, if God wills it. Mankind as a whole is only ready for a certain level of the eternal teachings, but as individuals this is also true for us depending on the amount of effort we make and what God knows to be our own measure. This relates to the non-linear nature of the Keys, that is, our personal variable and what we bring to the equation in any given moment.

Our personal variable has a significant and non-linear impact on how operational and effective the Keys become in our life, meaning it carries greater weight than other parts of the equation. In this equation, say for a particular Key like "Receptivity," the personal variable is multiplied, not additive, with the other components of the equation (such as level of trust and love for Prophet, remembrance of the quality of the teacher, gratitude for the opportunity to be a student, experiences of reverence at the Abode of God, past life/baseline we came into this life with etc.). This means if variables influencing our state of consciousness take this personal variable to zero, the whole thing goes to zero — that is non-linearity! Changes in the positive or negative direction in our personal variable have a greater overall impact on the output or result. While the truth in any particular Key (and its potential to help us have a more abundant life) may be changeless from moment to moment, our own personal state of consciousness from moment to moment changes and can increase or decrease the overall net effectiveness of that Key in our life, and this in turn impacts the relationships and interconnections that Key has to all the other Keys. So from moment to moment the operationalization and practical application of the unified sphere of Spiritual Keys/eternal teachings in our life looks very different, and it changes in an infinite number of combinations depending on circumstances and our own state of consciousness.

Our "personal variable" though is really a set of variables or sub-components that impact or contribute to the overall effectiveness equation of a Key. Things like: What kind of relationship do we have with you, Prophet? How receptive are we — in what areas are we more receptive or less? How trusting are we in you — do we trust in some cases but have a harder time coming to the same degree of trust in others? Do we know ourselves well enough to be aware of what it is that causes us to be more or less trusting or receptive to you? What are we doing about it? Are we sufficiently and consistently spiritually nourished — is it still fresh or have we let our daily bread go stale? How free are we from the passions of the mind? How are these passions influencing us on a given day, or moment to moment even — are they relatively under control and pushed over in our hearts or is there one we still struggle with and need to be extra vigilant? Go deeper, which passion is more likely to bite us under what circumstances, possibly making our use of the Keys to help us in a challenging situation less effective, or worse, fail because of this one personal variable? Have we eaten and slept properly or are have we let ourselves get out of balance physically, mentally or emotionally? These personal variables and other external factors like work, family, finances, societal stability etc. have a significant impact on how operational the Keys may be for us in any given moment. The possible combinations are ever-changing and infinite in both the way we see them due to our personal component we bring to the equation, as well as the ever-higher truths you choose to show a particular Soul at any given time. This is what I have been digesting since Reunion... it was quite a bite for me, but I feel you teaching me on the inner even if it is complicated to properly express in words.

As I reflected on this further during the writing process, I began to see how our personal variables also impact our focus from day to day, moment to moment, and something new has come to light. There is a dynamic aspect to my focus and to the whole phrase "practice, focus, and prolonged determination." Focus is very dynamic, and it does change for the better or not so good depending on how well we are operationalizing the Keys at a given moment in time (the "practice"). Being aware of the many personal variables we do have control over that influence this can greatly increase our success in maintaining proper focus over time. This will not only help with having prolonged determination but resilience as well. Resilience is perhaps just as important as prolonged determination; how well and how quickly we bounce back after getting off track is very important to having the spiritual stamina to climb God's Mountain with you. Doing our part then needs to include understanding what each of these personal variables looks like for us and how they are affecting our ability to integrate and put the Keys into practice. I found it is not so helpful to be asking simple questions like, "Am I receptive to Prophet?" or "Do I trust Prophet?" because it is not likely or accurately going to be a yes or no answer. Instead I began to ask, "Where am I not..." or "Under what circumstances am I not..." The real value is digging deep enough with you to help me to find those areas or situations where there is a partial yes or qualified yes, and figure out with your help — why. I think this could be a game-changer in my ability to fully operationalize the incredible gift contained within the Spiritual Keys you brought to us, rather than being mediocre to moderately successful at realizing their true potential. Perhaps it is only the dormant potential within the Spiritual Keys we see in the static, baseline/steady state model of the sphere, but the true life-giving, life-changing value and road to permanence (permanently being established in and becoming one with the Light and Sound of God, the Holy Spirit) comes when that potential is unleashed, and we not partially but fully operationalize them, which I think is what you may have been showing me in the dream.

In re-reading the handout Paul Nelson gave us during his Reunion talk on his study of the Keys and what they teach about "practice, focus, and prolonged determination," I saw how my focus, the noun version of the word, carries a certain priority and degree of importance because it is the "central point of attraction, attention, or activity." It conveys a choice (conscious or not) to give all or a majority of all of my attention to something, otherwise my focus is scattered. Whatever my focus is on also involves a significant investment of other resources like my attention, time, and energy towards a given thing, goal, interest, or desire.

The Key of Economy teaches us to be wise investors of our God-given resources; so taking this to heart, I want what it is I am focusing on not only to be a conscious choice, but also a decision that aligns with my overarching goal to seek the Kingdom of God and live His ways righteously. The same applies to my subordinate goals like the kind of person I want to be, the kind of life I want to live, and things I want to accomplish or pursue in this lifetime. "Practice" involves studying and gaining deeper understanding of the Keys and other scripture and truly laying hold of what I've learned; but "practice" also refers to putting this understanding and clarity into practice — applying it in daily life. Through both types of practice, my focus is becoming sharper, and I am becoming more disciplined in maintaining focus on what I choose. I am also quicker to detect and more effectively able to course correct when I find my focus and other precious resources are on something that is not aligned with my long-term goals. My relationship with you Prophet is the Key to being able to do this. It is only doable because of our sound, reliable and ever-improving inner communication, and my absolute trust and deep love for you. You help me in so many other ways as well, but I need to do my part. Self-discipline, knowing myself and my vulnerabilities, and having right motivation are important components for my success.

In continuing to study the Keys with all this in mind, I have gained some insights into how my personal variables are limiting my ability to fully realize and apply the Keys in my life, and I will continue with you on this. Ultimately, making use of the Keys you brought to us will, among other very positive benefits, ensure my focus stays where I want it to stay — on being a servant of God, on our mission to share the eternal teachings with the world, and on being your devoted and dependable disciple.

With Love to My Guidance for a Better Life Family,

Lorraine Fortier

Traveling the Heavens

I hope by now you, as a distance-study student, have become comfortable with at least some of the foundational Spiritual Keys. Even my retreat center students are still learning to actually use the wisdom contained within the Keys in daily life. Most do not fully utilize all the Keys, but one can keep working toward that goal. Most do however live the foundational Keys such as: HU, Gratitude, Discernment, Spiritual Food, Receptive, Contemplation, God's Prophet, Three-Part Prayer, Balance and Detachment, Economy, Prayer, and Truth is Love. Even using a few Keys can add abundance to one's life, but the more the better. By now you may also recognize how well they work together, continue to look for this as you read on.

The sacred experiences shared in this section, "Traveling the Heavens," are only possible when Soul has been spiritually nourished consistently over time. This goes back to the very first Step where I introduced Soul and the HU. If Soul receives Its daily spiritual bread, the same daily bread Jesus talked about, it is strengthened and becomes more active in one's life. Now it can travel with Prophet throughout God's Heavenly Worlds. Those early Keys are now of extreme value for the continued spiritual growth that can only be accomplished by direct experiences found in the Heavens. Now the great love, trust, and receptiveness developed over time in God's Prophet allows his students to relax and enjoy the most beautiful and Holy experiences a child of God can ever dream of having.

To give you an idea of the sacred and grand adventure that awaits the persistent seeker of God's ways and truth, I share thirty-five additional testimonies documenting the experiences my advanced students have been given. These are just a sampling of the profound opportunities the world is totally unaware of even being possible. The years of integrating the Spiritual Keys, the Keys to Heaven, into their lives under the ever-watchful Prophet now become a reality of extreme value; beyond what any student could have ever thought possible when they were first introduced to **seemingly simple** spiritual concepts. Now they more fully understand why God's chosen Prophet is truly the Master Key. They now know the very long separation from their Father, since the time of the Fall from Heaven, is over and they are being welcomed HOME once again. They are welcomed because they have grown more spiritually mature, responsible, and wise, and now think of others with love, not just their selfish selves of long ago. And, importantly, they have accepted and opened their hearts to the one God sent to bring them HOME to Him.

Over time and with sufficient effort a knowing, trusting, and loving relationship with the Heavenly Father is possible with the help of His Prophet. I know of no earthly religion that believes this to be true, but I promise you it is absolutely true. God sends His Prophets to take mankind up His Mountain, higher and higher, where no clergy or organized religion can take you. Only those Souls who truly want God more than a religion or man's approval will have the courage to follow the one who knows the way HOME, the home where God created you — Soul.

The following stories, written by my students, are examples of traveling the Heavens of God. They are being shared to show you what is truly spiritually possible. This is done after proper preparation has occurred, usually over several years. When the student is ready to travel with the Prophet safely into the vast spiritual worlds of God their growth in understanding and experience accelerates. In these higher worlds called spiritual planes, mansions, or Heavens, the student is shown God's teachings and truth directly. By teaching through spiritual travel, certain spiritual understandings, concepts, and even the truest meaning of scripture is attainable. Over time students develop a rare view of life, of God and God's Love for them, of the representatives of God, and even of themselves as Soul. There is no better way to know God's teachings than to experience them for yourself. The testimonies in this section cover three important areas: traveling to God's Temples of Learning, traveling to the Abode of God on the twelfth Heaven, and the opportunity to be ordained by God Himself.

The Keys are still the solid foundation for further spiritual growth, but so much more beyond the amazing Keys themselves has been given to my students over the years. The stories in this next section may be beyond your interest or comfort level. They show what is truly possible with a loving and trusting relationship with God's chosen Prophet. If you have enjoyed and been receptive to the earlier parts of this book, then perhaps continue. If you have struggled to accept and try some of the Keys so far, then I suggest stop reading this book for now, take a break, and maybe come back at a later time to read the final sections.

For two reasons I do not list the Keys in the last thirty-five stories of this book. First, by the time you get this far in my book you should be able to find the Keys that are part of the story. Second, the last thirty-five stories cover topics that may seem impossible, so reading them with an open heart is important. Trying to find the Keys is somewhat of a mental exercise, and in doing so you might miss the message and potential benefit of these special stories of sacred experiences. Finding the Spiritual Keys in these thirty-five stories is not as important as being receptive and open while reading them.

God's Temples of Learning

In this first section of "Traveling the Heavens," students are guided by the Prophet and travel spiritually, as Soul, to God's Temples of Learning. Each plane or Heaven below the twelfth has at least one temple. The primary teacher at each temple is a former Prophet of God who served on Earth during a particular time in history. God personally chooses these extraordinary teachers. These are Holy places where nothing but God's living truth can exist. The Light of God, the Holy Spirit, is extremely concentrated in each temple and comes directly from the Source. One only gets to experience these sacred inner spiritual temples of learning as Soul, not in a physical body. They also must be invited and escorted by God's Prophet. Spending time at one of these special and sacred places is a stunning opportunity for spiritual growth and often has a profoundly positive impact on Souls. I have shared stories of fifteen different experiences for you to explore what is possible.

The Lord's Temple

Within the spiritual realms exist temples filled with the Light and Love of God. They are every bit, if not more, real than places you may visit here in the physical. They are "God's churches" where Soul may be taken to experience God's pure truth, unadulterated by man. In the following story the author experiences one of the core truths taught at the retreat center. You are more than your physical self — you are Soul, a beautiful child of God.

One weekend last fall I was attending a three-day spiritual retreat at Guidance for a Better Life in the mountains of Virginia. The air was crisp and cool as the day rolled into evening. Outside the golden, orange, and red tree leaves danced in the wind. I felt sweet anticipation as my teacher Del, a true Prophet of God, began to lead us in a contemplation. While he spoke initially, all was now quiet in the room, as each of us journeyed inward.

The Prophet stands beside me in my inner vision. As Soul we approach the edge of a pond, and I begin to see what is really before me. A temple arises out of the water. It is eternal; there is no end to this immense and beautiful temple which forms. It is not like any building here in the physical. This building is alive, containing living truth, living water, and living love. It is a temple made out of love. God's Love.

Following inner prompting, I knew to look at my heart. I see myself as I truly am, without any shell. I see Soul. I, like you, am a very bright and beautiful light. This light is so bright it is almost blinding. As I look at myself and then again look up at God's Temple of Learning, I recognize I am made of the same substance I see before me — Love.

With a grateful heart, I approach this temple by grace. I could not come here alone; it is only with the Prophet of God that one can enter these Holy Temples on the inner and only with a grateful and loving heart. At the entrance stands the temple guardian welcoming me and everyone in our group with so much love. I feel incredibly blessed and come to tears of joy at this sacred opportunity.

As I walk inside this living temple the beauty is beyond words. To say I am standing on love may seem impossible, but I am. Everything is emanating bright light. Del IV's masterpieces of art surround the room. Some of his art adorns the classrooms at the physical Guidance for a Better Life retreat center. Yet unlike his paintings on Earth, these ones are actually alive, pulsating with the Light and Sound of God. Colors swirling and blending and dancing on the walls — art at its finest. Words cannot give true credit to their beauty. In the center of the room I see a beam of light and sound, which flows forth onto the floor.

I step inside and am given the opportunity to see this beam from a new direction, a new perspective. I look downwards. It is like a flower with a concentrated treasure of the most brilliant blue in the center. Life flows up and outward from this core. Like flowing water, the energy and love flowing forth emerge from this center. I am brought to tears of gratitude as this light flows into and through me. The blessing of being able to consciously travel here with Prophet, and to then have my own personal, intimate experience with this beam of love is one that continues to touch my heart today. God is alive and showers His blessings upon us. By grace, I was given the eyes to see.

I become aware again of Prophet, who has been beside me on this entire journey. Now he and I begin to dance, a dance of Soul. I experience freedom and joy with a depth that comes from being this close to the Divine. Slowly the experience comes to a close. I am escorted out of the temple and express gratitude to Prophet. With awareness I return to my physical body. When I open my eyes in the classroom, I see the world differently. As Soul our true nature is to see the beauty and magnificence of God's creation with awe, wonder, and gratitude. As the art in the temple was alive and uplifting, so too are we. We are beautiful Souls with a majesty that only God can create. It has just been hidden and disguised beneath our skin. You are more than just your physical body.

There is more to me than my body. I am Soul! I am beautiful! Years ago these were just words to me. But after years of personal experiences with the Divine, thanks to my teacher Del, now I see the divinity within me. It has been revealed by the Grace of God. Would you like to see clearer and witness the truth of who you really are?

Would you like to travel to one of God's Temples of Learning? Perhaps the Prophet can guide you too. Perhaps he can help you see who you truly are — a beautiful Soul.

Written by Molly Comfort

Escorted to the Heavens

It is hard for some to understand or accept that they too can travel into the Heavens as Saint Paul described in 2 Corinthians 12:2. It seems impossible or even blasphemous to consider. I can assure you — it is not. Each one of us is Soul, a Divine child of God that exists because God loves us; we too are worthy of making the journey. To do so we need a teacher who knows the way.

In the Bible Saint Paul says he knew a man that was caught up to the third Heaven. He also mentions that he did not know if it was in the body or out of the body... but he was caught up to paradise and heard inexpressible things. If you continue reading it sounds like he was actually sharing his own personal experience.

Did you ever think about the magnitude of that statement? While alive he was taken to visit Heaven. But who took him, how did he get there, and can we go? If he mentioned a third Heaven that implies there is a first and second Heaven. What if there are many more than three Heavens? What if you or I could be escorted to them to develop our relationship with God and experience just how much He loves us?

Over many years I have personally been taken by the Prophet on journeys into Heaven to experience some of the wonderful and inexpressible things Saint Paul suggests exist. At a retreat many years ago I was among a small group of students who sat with Prophet as he led us in a HU sing. As we sang this love song and ancient name for God, I became aware of a white beam of spiritual light that encompassed the room and all within it. This beam of light emanated from far above us, farther up than I could see with my physical eyes.

As we continued to sing HU, I had an incredible feeling of being raised up into the light. This was indescribable! As I settled in, I felt as if we were in a spiritual elevator of sorts. We would rise up, and then for brief periods of time we would pause; this appeared to help us acclimate to our new surroundings. I had no idea where we were going or what to expect, but I had an open heart, a deep trust in the Prophet, and a wonderful child-like excitement. Sometimes as we were moving up the planes of existence, or Heavens, I would catch a glimpse of color and or hear a faint Heavenly sound. From many more trips through the planes, I have seen and experienced that there are certain colors and sounds associated with each Heaven. Here are the major colors and sounds associated with the various planes of Heaven I have experienced; Physical plane Green-Thunder, Astral plane (first Heaven) Pink-Roar of the Sea, Causal plane (second Heaven) Orange-Tinkling Bells, Mental plane (third Heaven) Blue-Running Water, Etheric plane (fourth Heaven) Purple-Buzzing of Bees, Soul plane (fifth Heaven) Bright Yellow-Single Note of a Flute. From the sixth Heaven up to the twelfth Heaven the primary color changes from a lighter and lighter yellow to a brighter and brighter white. Some of the sounds are Wind, Humming Sound, Violins, Woodwinds, and HU.

Only a direct representative of God has the authority, the capability, the wisdom, and the discernment to escort Souls up the planes and to do so safely. As it is phrased in the Bible, we traveled "in spirit," meaning as Soul, our true self. We left our physical bodies behind and were taken to these beautiful Heavens. Our physical bodies were always protected until our safe return. As we rose up through the planes I felt lighter and lighter, less restricted, freer, more peaceful, and truly alive. As we passed through each plane it felt as if another restrictive layer of clothing had been shed. As each of these layers fell away I saw myself brighter, purer, and more beautiful. There were times when we would pause on a particular plane and Del would introduce us to a great spiritual being, guide, or temple guardian whose form radiated with a brilliant Heavenly light. During some of these journeys we were invited into a magnificent spiritual temple for personalized experiences of some kind. These temples were made of and emanated an incredibly beautiful Heavenly light and sound.

Each of these experiences with the light and sound changed me in some unexplained way and helped to prepare and condition me for another step on my spiritual journey. These visits, interactions, and experiences also blessed me with many insights, lessons, teachings, and practical information on how to live a more abundant and more joyful physical life here and now. Those first journeys were similar to being a tourist passing through a new city, but with each experience I have been able to remember and more fully incorporate the gifts, teachings, and love I have received. Over the years, through these and similar experiences, I have been blessed with witnessing how much God loves each of us, and how much He wants to bless all His children. These blessings are not just reserved for the saints of the Bible but also for you and me. Whether it was for Saint Paul two thousand years ago or us now, there are opportunities to be consciously escorted to Heaven with a Prophet of God, and to experience God's vast and incredible Love.

Written by Jason Levinson

The Precious Moment of Now

God's Light and Love flows spiritually through the Prophet into the world. It has always been this way — for all time. God never leaves us without someone authorized to pass on His Light. The names, faces, and scope of their individual missions change with the passing of the centuries, but at their core, God's eternal Light and Love continue to flow. Learning to become present in this presence is key to living an abundant life — here and now.

It was late summer in 2006, and I was attending a spiritual retreat at Guidance for a Better Life. Del was about to take us on a journey into the inner worlds of Spirit. As a Prophet of God he is authorized and uniquely qualified to help Souls discover their true nature and learn about the nature of the Divine. He does this, in part, by providing opportunities to have direct personal experiences with the Holy Spirit, the Light and Sound of God. One quality I have come to appreciate and value is that of the present moment, because Soul lives in the present and because God gives us life one precious moment at a time. This is something Prophet has taught me through experiences such as this one.

He began with a prayer that we would feel and know God's Love for us in some way. I was relaxed and looking forward to whatever was in store, grateful for this opportunity to continue to grow spiritually, something that is very important to me. We sang HU, a love song to God. It was totally dark with no physical light, but I could see a brightening as we sang. With my physical eyes opened or closed I saw the room was getting lighter, and I could see the other students and the room around us.

I became aware of a beam or column of white light coming into the center of the room. It grew very bright. Del asked us to look down at our feet and take note of what we saw. Spiritually, my legs were out-stretched in front of me. I looked at them and noticed an old crude splint on my right leg and only a stump in place of my foot. It reminded me of a medical contraption one might see used in the 1800's or an earlier era such as this. The light intensified to a brilliant white, which became concentrated like a laser beam and zapped my right leg. The splint and stump were gone, and I was no longer crippled or constrained by them. The splinted leg and stump symbolized some sort of impediment, passion of the mind, faulty thinking, or negative attitude I held that was holding me back spiritually. I trusted that since I was not shown specifically what it meant then it did not matter. Whatever it was had been removed by the Grace of God's Light, and I was grateful for it.

I spiritually rose up and went with Prophet. I no longer saw myself in physical body form, but as a ball of light, Soul, just as my Father in Heaven had created me long ago. I felt boundless and free! We flew and went into a kind of warp speed where I could see stars and light passing by incredibly fast. A burst of light came from the center of where we were traveling, then all became calm and still. I felt a sense of deep peace, love, and total trust. There was no time, no thought. I was immersed in the present moment and experienced an awesome now-ness for what seemed an eternity.

We began to sing HU once again as a group, and Prophet and I continued our journey. He brought me to one of the inner spiritual temples. Once inside, we went directly to the beam of light that was flowing into the center of the temple. I noticed it was the same beam that had entered the physical room we were in when we started, and it was the same light that had healed me. As above so below. Prophet walked over to It and stepped inside. When he did so, he became the beam of light. What I witnessed was that spiritually the Prophet was the beam, the light itself. He then brought me into It with him. Even though we were in our Soul bodies as light, I could see his eyes as if we were in the physical. I looked deep into them and saw an expansive nothingness and everything in them. Now was all that existed. I felt a joyful peace and contentment just being in this eternal moment with him.

Still inside the beam of light, I became aware of a shower of golden light raining down upon me. It was a strong windy kind of rain that cleansed me inside and out. I felt it scouring the spiritual dirt and impurities away, and the wind blew me dry. I saw an image that looked like Niagara Falls, and I jumped into it becoming immersed in the Holy Spirit and Its waters of life. It was beautiful, both cleansing and strengthening. It felt like a continuation of what had occurred earlier, nurturing the healing and replacing what had been removed with something positive. I continued looking into the Prophet's deep, endless, loving eyes at peace and totally in the moment. I felt so many things at once: peace, safety, security, perfection, stillness, love, and appreciation.

Over time, with Prophet's continued help, I have assimilated and integrated realizations, truth, and wisdom from sacred experiences like this one into my life. I spend a lot less time walking around in a daze of thoughts and emotions, thinking of past mistakes or worrying about the future. I am more at peace. When truly present, not merely physically there, I can listen better and be more sensitive to the needs of others. I am able to slow down and savor things in life like a beautiful sunrise, watching my kitty wake from sleep, enjoying a peaceful drive into work, or finding satisfaction in doing my best at whatever task or daily chore I am doing. Life is just sweeter. I have found the splendor of living is best experienced in the moment and learning to be more fully present with the inner presence of Prophet does truly lead one to a life more abundant.

Written by Lorraine Fortier

Journey to Tibet

If this beautifully written piece does not excite and inspire you with grand possibilities, then I do not know what will. The experience was one that helped cleanse and condition the author rather than teaching the higher ways of God.

Fresh snow danced across the huge stone steps leading up to the doorway of an ancient Tibetan monastery. The jagged peaks of the Himalayan Mountains towered around us silhouetted by the fading evening light. Slowly, the temple door opened.

My body was thousands of miles away sitting peacefully in Virginia. Our spiritual journey was being guided by Del Hall. After singing HU, a love song to God, my consciousness had shifted naturally away from my body much like in a dream, to the distant Tibetan evening. Del's whole class waited excitedly on the stone steps. This is a very real place; our spiritual journey had brought us here in full consciousness.

An ancient monk clothed in white reverently greeted Del by the immense wooden doorway. They spoke for a moment and observed our group of newcomers. As the door opened it revealed a massive rotunda bursting with light. The light filled my being with hope, reverence, and love. This was no ordinary light. It was the Light of God. As the light shone upon our group I felt it purify, uplift, and nourish me spiritually. Clearly this was no ordinary temple. It was a true Temple of God, ordained and sustained by Him directly, unspoiled by the hand of man, and accessible to man only under the guidance of a true Prophet of God.

Del and the white-robed monk led us into the temple. Our small group paused just inside the door, absorbing the scene with awe. Workers in the temple moved purposefully about the rotunda busy in the responsibilities of this sacred sanctuary. The light seemed to come from everywhere at once, filling every corner and leaving no shadows. I watched the white-robed monk ascend a beautifully curved staircase, his hand upon an ornate golden banister.

He observed our group steadily. Slowly his gaze met mine, and he spoke a single word: "Love." The energy in his voice entered my heart like an arrow! The single word spoke more than many volumes of literature, more than any eloquent speech. It was more than a syllable, more than a word. A mountain of wisdom and meaning surged behind it. It reached deep within me, speaking to the innermost part of my being, Soul, the true self.

The power of his message still reverberating within me, a gentle hand touched my arm. A worker from the temple led me to a hidden staircase descending into the foundation of the temple. He motioned me forward, and I walked carefully down the stairs. Before me hung a narrow rope bridge leading to a stone platform. In the middle of the platform a small fire burned, and on the other side of the fire was the white-robed monk himself, sitting hooded and cross-legged. Behind him stood two full bookshelves holding ancient texts from forgotten kingdoms.

I crossed the bridge eagerly, but with a slow and measured pace. I sat across the fire from him, and his deep gray eyes met mine. Immeasurable love and peace emanated from him. Not a word was spoken, but I found myself drawn into his eyes, like an invisible force pulling me into another world. I traveled into his eyes as Soul. Everything changed; eternity seemed to exist in a moment. The temple guardian's endless eyes became my entire universe. Love was everywhere, but not love as I had known it before, it was a love that transcended emotion, time, religion, everything. I had truly experienced God's Love. In the days following this experience I was able to share it with the class. Others had similar experiences, personalized for their own spiritual growth. Del guided me in understanding these sacred events. He told me that this teacher had used a single word, such as "Love," to teach others before. Since the class the word he spoke has unfolded into hundreds of different nuances and applications.

Del explained that the basement seemed to represent the "cave of fire," a spiritual rite of passage that all seekers must go through on their journey home to God. This is a period of great trial and tribulation. This proved to be an accurate interpretation, for the next several years were a period of intense honesty and self-discovery. This was not always easy! But it led to a state of greater peace, freedom, and stability. Somewhat, one might say, like crossing the narrow rope bridge in the temple onto the solid stone platform.

Although I had previously taken a wilderness skills class, this experience took place during my first spiritual retreat. In the ten years that have followed, it became clear that this was only the tip of the iceberg.

Written by David Hughes

My Key to God's Blessings

God's Light plays an integral part in purifying the seeker so that he may be able to accept more of God's Love and teachings. The Light of God removes barriers to lasting growth such as fear, vanity, anger, and unworthiness. Again the seeker was taken to a temple for the purpose of his growth, not so much the higher ways of God. Once the barriers are gone (or at least lessened — it's a process) God's truths and blessings are easier to accept and integrate into the seeker's life. At this point one starts operating more as their true self, Soul, and life becomes an even greater joy to live.

I have been a student at Guidance for a Better Life for over twenty years, with a desire for a more abundant life. I seek an ever-closer relationship with God, with a life filled with more love, peace, joy, and meaning. I seek to give more love to others as a husband, father, friend, and teacher. I seek to live life from the higher perspective as Soul, which was created to do these things. These are some of the aspects of the abundant life God would like all His children to enjoy.

But there are stumbling blocks to receiving these blessings that only the presence and help from the Prophet can remove. There are limits to what I can do on my own. Along the way I have been shown that I've carried limiting burdens of fear, anger, and worry all my life. They were so familiar to me they were hard to give up, even though they are a heavy load to shoulder. Over the years God's loving Grace, given through His Prophet Del Hall, has steadily freed me of more and more roadblocks to an abundant life. Only after these burdens began to lift, and I enjoyed the resulting sense of lightness and freedom, did I begin to grasp the magnitude and necessity of Prophet's help. Only the Prophet is authorized by God to take us into the Heavens. This cleansing continues and there is more room in my heart to receive the abundance of God's blessings. What follows is one of many healing experiences in the Light and Sound of God Prophet has brought to me.

At a recent spiritual retreat at Guidance for a Better Life, we sang HU, a love song to God. The group was led by Del Hall, God's

Prophet. In my heart was a prayer to draw nigh, closer to God. With my physical ears I could hear both the beautiful HU and the words of Prophet. He offered us the opportunity to surrender our fear, anger, and worries. The love in his voice, Prophet's voice, touched me deeply. That love opened my heart to consciously receive more of God's blessings. My attention shifted to my spiritual eyes and ears (see glossary). My inner vision was flooded with softly swirling, warm blue light, which coalesced into the face of the Prophet, Del Hall. I was drawn to his eyes, which conveyed a deep measure of God's Love that words cannot do justice. I felt Prophet's joy as he offered the priceless gift of accepting my fear, anger, and worry. I gratefully surrendered these to him, happily giving them over. I felt a heavy burden lift, more than I knew I carried, bringing on a state of deep relaxation, peace, and comfort. With this new feeling of lightness came an awareness of moving through God's Heavens.

Prophet had still more blessings in store for me. He took me through regions of purple and then golden white light. We arrived at one of God's Temples in the inner worlds. The temple itself was made of golden white light. Prophet gave my hand over to the guardian of this temple, who then led me into a beam of white light. Once inside the beam I found myself standing in a living cascade of God's Love, a pulsating waterfall of light. I cupped my hands together and drank double handfuls. The Prophet encouraged me to drink even more deeply of God's Light and Sound. I tilted my head back and gulped all that I could. God's Light and Sound washed through me, at once cleansing and nourishing and healing me from head to toe, both inside and out. At the same time I sensed an expansion of my heart, giving and receiving more of God's Love. From another perspective I saw that at the same time I was cradled in the arms of the Prophet. I was rocked gently back and forth. I was at once loved, cherished, protected, and secure. I could feel the power of God's Love in Prophet's arms.

Who would want to leave those arms? I certainly did not. I only did so reluctantly when called back to my physical body. As I returned I was given still more gifts, blessings to take with me. I was given the certainty that I am always held in Prophet's arms, where I am loved, protected, nurtured, and cherished. Another gift is that the inner Prophet takes me back to relive the experience, which continues to sustain me. A still further gift is that I have more love in my heart for Prophet.

Prophet has God's authority to safely carry us into the Heavens while we live in our physical bodies. There we are immersed in God's Light and Sound. As Soul we directly and purely experience the blessings of God's Love. With Prophet's help the blessings of our Heavenly experiences are integrated into our daily lives. With his help we operate in our daily lives more as Soul, manifesting the best of what we were created to be. With his help I personally am a better husband, father, friend, and teacher. I do enjoy a bigger heart with a greater capacity to give and receive love. I am closer to God. I am blessed with an abundant life. The Prophet loves, protects, and guides me each step of the way.

Written by Irv Kempf

Heaven on Earth

We live in this world but are not of it. We are so much more than our physical bodies; we are Soul, made from the Holy Spirit — the Light and Sound of God. Experiencing this true reality is a special blessing and opportunity available for Prophet's disciples.

I stood on the steps of God's Temple with Prophet as the other Souls in our group arrived. We had been invited here to visit this sacred temple, and its guardian met us at the doorway. We traveled here in our Soul bodies, our true inner selves, safely escorted by Prophet. This was a rare opportunity we had been given to have individualized learning experiences that would nourish, cleanse, fortify us, and aid us in our spiritual growth.

Prophet, the temple guardian, and I walked inside and without a word being exchanged went directly to the beam of God's Light and Sound in the center of the room. I could hear crackling and popping sounds of the dynamic life-giving energy of the beam; Its sound was loud in my ears. It did not appear as a solid beam of light as I had seen before but as large white shimmering sheets of light that had texture. We went into It, and the three of us stood inside this beam of Light and Sound of God in our Soul bodies, which were also made of this same light and sound. Inside there was stillness and timelessness. The only word that could describe what I felt was "complete." I was complete. In this beam there was nothing I lacked. As Soul everything I could ever want or need was right there.

Just then, I became aware of being both inside the beam in the temple and also sitting in my chair back in the classroom. A long shaft of white light from the beam connected me in my Soul body inside the temple with me in my physical body that sat in the chair, the light coming straight into my heart. It felt as if a solid connection of God's Light and Love was made between these two aspects of me. I felt something was being downloaded through this light and was integrating into my physical being. There came a sense of continuity, oneness, and sameness between the part of me still in Heaven, the part of me on Earth, and the light that connected us. A shower of golden light then cleansed and nourished me. I asked for whatever might be holding me back in life to be let go. I cupped my hands and drank of this golden "water of love" as it poured over me and bathed me. I was so filled with love and appreciation for these gifts from Prophet that I spiritually danced in joy.

Soul as created by God is complete, but we are not always conscious of it down here in the physical. Often we search for things outside of us to make us feel whole, secure, or good enough. We forget our true nature, which is one reason God sends His Prophets. Prophet Del Hall helped me remember who I really am, Soul. I have been his student for a long time. It has been a continuing process, during which he has lovingly helped me recognize and manifest my own Divine qualities as Soul and come to know the real me. Through many experiences such as this one, he has helped the dormant qualities of Soul become activated. Prophet's inner form is the Light and Sound of God, the Holy Spirit, the Presence of the Divine.

Experiencing myself as light and sound, Soul, in the beam at the temple was wonderful, but it was not that alone which brought about the feeling of completeness. It was being inside of Prophet's inner form as the Light and Sound of God (the beam) that made it so; with him and in him I lack nothing.

The completeness I experienced inside the beam, feeling I had everything I could ever want or need, does not mean I now shun earthly comforts and pleasures or no longer welcome the blessings of family, friends, or material wealth. It just means I do not need those things to make me feel whole. It is so freeing to know I do not need material things for self-esteem or self-worth, nor do I need others to make me feel good about myself, looking to them to fill something I feel is lacking in me. I am free to express and accept love more purely, appreciating my loved ones and those I interact with for who they are and the joy they bring to my life with no strings attached.

These gifts from Prophet have added so much abundance, fulfillment, freedom, and sweetness to my life! I nurture them by staying spiritually close to him and by being present in his presence throughout the day. Living life in his presence is very much like living inside the beam of light and sound. It is the relationship with Prophet that brings the glories of Heaven into everyday reality while one is still living on this Earth.

Written by Lorraine Fortier

Gifts of Freedom

"How much pain they have cost us, the evils which have never happened." Thomas Jefferson

One Saturday evening at a three-day spiritual retreat, we sang a long HU gently tapering off as Del said, "Thank you." The HU and discussion throughout the day had blessed all of us, but there was still more. We were invited to visit one of God's Temples in the inner worlds. Del, the Prophet, began guiding us, both inwardly and outwardly. I took Prophet's hands on the inner, turned as he did, and we were at one of God's Temples of Learning.

We walked up the steps onto the temple porch where I fell to my knees in reverence to be at a Temple of God. I have visited these temples many times and recognize more now, what a privilege it is to be there. Inside, the temple guardian greeted us and spoke about spiritual liberation. He said that it does not happen overnight but over time and by degrees. Every HU, every moment listening to the Divine, can bring a degree of spiritual freedom. Over time, seemingly small things add up and may lead to a life-changing realization. It seems the single event changed everything, and it did, but not without all the small moments that came before it. It is like years of freezing and thawing slowly expanding a crack until a rock suddenly breaks free and falls from the cliff. It seems to happen in a moment, but was years in the making.

Leaving the temple guardian, the Prophet led me to the heart of the temple where a book lay open on a pedestal. This book is the Living Word of God, always fresh and perfect for the seeker in that moment. I read in golden script, "Live joyously," and then, as Prophet urged me, I turned the page and read, "for I am with you." I have often hesitated to embrace life fearing all that could go wrong, all the mistakes I could make. These words reminded me that I am never alone; Prophet is with me and loves me. Even if things appear to go wrong, all the love, support, and help I could ever need are right there. Prophet's presence frees me to live with joy.

I turned and hugged Prophet. He became the beam of the Light and Sound of God, and I was within It. The light shimmered and flowed around me and through me. I leaned my head back and drank the light, watching it clean out any impurity I no longer needed. This precision healing cleans out negative things like fear or worry, I no longer need, but leaves what is needed to learn from and grow. I asked for it to wash away any resistance to truth. I drank more, and the light broke black crust off my heart and washed it off me. I stayed as long as I could, wanting to be as clean as possible.

The only way to freedom is through accepting truth. Sometimes it seems that facing the truth would be uncomfortable or something I do not want to know. Resisting truth however, is what causes pain and discomfort, not the truth itself. Hidden in the dark, a fear grows until it seems enormous, impossible to solve. Often, simply admitting the truth to the Prophet and myself evaporates the problem. Only by accepting truth do I begin to see a solution.

I returned to my body full of love and blessings to bring greater freedom into my life. The experience was beautiful, but unless I remember it and integrate what I learned into my life, nothing will change. Freedom comes when I do my part. I received precious gifts, but they can only bring freedom if I remember them in my everyday life. That is my privilege and responsibility, and that too, is a gift from God.

Written by Jean Enzbrenner

Divine Wisdom Written Upon an Ink-less Page

This wonderfully written account of journeying spiritually to a temple within the Heavenly realms contains many pearls of wisdom. Among them, God has given us free will to follow our heart and sculpt a life that brings love and beauty into the world. Through His Prophet, God is there at every step of the way to guide and comfort us. Ultimately though we must walk the path for ourselves — this includes living our life.

One evening during a retreat at Guidance for a Better Life, after singing HU for some time, I was taken on an inner spiritual journey to a temple where my prayers and questions were answered in a most unexpected way. Although my physical eyes were closed as my body sat in the mountains of Virginia, I became aware that inwardly, I was being welcomed into a Temple of God, a place where Divine wisdom was available in vast quantities. A former Prophet of God welcomed me to this temple. I knew that I had come there by invitation, and my journey was made possible by the Prophet, and the Grace of God.

In this temple, I was aware of deep maroon tapestries on the walls and rich curtains, which separated areas for private prayer and contemplation from a main hall, a great rotunda. As I looked around the rotunda, I could not miss the golden book enshrined in a great beam of white and golden light passing through the center of the room. The book seemed almost alive, glowing with the Love and wisdom of God. I had experienced other temples before, and to me this temple felt much the same as others, which I had been privileged to experience.

These different temples, though guarded by different spiritual teachers and built in different styles, all had one thing in common — the living, flowing Love and wisdom of God. Unlike the houses of worship found in the cities and hamlets of humanity on Earth, which reflect different views of what we think God might wish to teach, these inner temples are filled with the living waters of God's Love and wisdom, actively flowing direct from their Source, unfiltered by human bias, shortcomings, and cultural distinctions.

At this time, in this particular temple, I noticed the floors and walls, which seemed to be a polished white marble. I moved across this great floor to the book, and reached into the beam glowing with light, and humming with Divine Sound. As I made contact with the book, which really seemed to be an aspect of this beam of light and love itself, I found myself drawn into what seemed to be a higher truth, greater and more beautiful than my perception of the great temple itself. Surrounded by love and deep peace beyond understanding, I was aware I was not separate from this love and peace, but actually a part of it. Accepting more of my identity as a true child of God, I became more aware that what I experienced is actually a part of my true nature, not simply as a man, but as Soul.

After some time, perhaps a minute or two that seemed to stretch out across a beautiful eternity, I gently came back into the main part of the temple. Then, just as gently, my consciousness shifted away from this inner experience and back into the physical and the retreat center in Virginia. As I opened my eyes I brought back not only the deep peace and love of this experience, but also an actual page number to look up in a physical book of scripture. Excited to see what other wisdom might await me in this book, I opened to the page I was given on the inner, and found one of the very few pages in the entire book, which are completely blank!

In prayer as I sought to better understand this experience and incorporate it into my life, I saw that the blank white page rhymed with the polished white marble of the temple floor and walls. As I discussed the experience with my teacher Del, he helped me realize this was actually a very direct answer to a prayer I often had at that time in my life. I had been asking for God to show me what He wants me to do in life, and what my next steps should be on my journey in service to the Divine. It became clear that the choice is actually mine, as it always has been. God has given us free will to live life on our own terms, and use our gifts as we see fit. Divine suggestions and guidance are available, but our course in life is mainly up to us. Free will is ours to use as we choose, and it is up to us to actively choose our destiny to be in harmony with the Divine. As we boldly begin to create the life we wish to live, the Light of God helps us see the best choices more clearly.

It is the enslaved nature of the human consciousness that wishes to be told what to do. It takes the strength and courage of Soul to set a course into the unknown, seeking help from God every step of the way. The meek shall inherit the Earth, but the bold and courageous, guided by Prophet, will inherit the Kingdom of Heaven. And so it was that God wrote an answer to my prayer and questions upon a page with no ink, presented to me in a sacred temple where fresh wisdom flows out like the cool, refreshing waters of a spring. When next you pray, why not ask God to have the Prophet bring you too to such a place? There is room for you, and there is a Prophet who is ready to take you for a visit. What would you like to do?

Written by Timothy Donley

Studying at a Temple of God

Not only can Prophet lead his students through guided spiritual experiences while in the physical, he can meet with them in the inner dream worlds. There is a great benefit to having a teacher who can help you experience God's Love in both the inner and outer states.

After attending a few retreats at Guidance for a Better Life with Prophet Del Hall he started coming to me in dreams. Over time I started to notice a trend to these nighttime adventures. In most of the dreams he was teaching and leading discussions with a group of Souls, some of whom I recognized as fellow students and friends from the retreat center. As my interest in the spiritual teachings grew,

Prophet responded by guiding me in the dream worlds to complement his outer teachings. There is great benefit to having a teacher who can teach on both the inner and outer states because there are limitations to having a teacher only on the outer. Sometimes I wake from a dream with a brief image or knowingness that I spent some time with Prophet. Other times I recall vivid details of the teachings and consciously retain a valuable lesson upon awakening. Each experience is another step on this grand journey.

The Prophet is qualified to teach us in both the dream and awakened states. In the physical, we often gather for classes at the Guidance for a Better Life retreat center. In the dream state Prophet can safely lead us to the Heavenly Worlds and continue teaching. My dreams evolved to where he guided me to visit spiritual college campuses that are actually God's Temples of Learning. I was very fortunate to be invited to these holy sanctuaries.

In one such dream I attended a class in a small house where Prophet was teaching me and several other students. The decor was not fancy, with white walls and wooden benches, seemingly to not detract from the primary purpose of my visit to this sacred place. The atmosphere was very welcoming and loving. His teaching continued for what seemed like several days, even though it all happened in one night of dreaming. One day we walked outside the house as a group onto a beautiful college-like campus that was more glorious than anything I have ever seen on Earth. Perfectly manicured lawns were interlaced with walking paths and lovely landscaped gardens. The building architecture was spectacular, and the structures seemed to glow with a soft golden light. Prophet led us to a large stone building that rose into the sky, which reminded me of a grand clock tower. He invited us inside where we gathered in a quiet room, and he explained to us how his presence is able to nourish and sustain Souls with Divine love. God's Love is Soul's life-source, without it Soul would not exist.

Despite having this dream several years ago, I still vividly recall the images and feel Prophet's presence and love from this experience. What appeared as a college campus in the dream was actually one of God's Heavenly Temples where God's Light is concentrated. Souls are taken to these holy places by the Prophet to study and learn God's ways and experience God's Love. While this dream was certainly a wonderful adventure, the real pearl is being in Prophet's presence and experiencing God's Love. Thank you Prophet for guiding me on this grand journey.

Written by Chris Hibshman

Temple Music Room

Prophet can see our future and thus knows what we will need before we do. As a gift of love Prophet can prepare us to be ready for what's coming, even if we do not understand it at the time. Often with the benefit of hindsight we realize how our experiences have been perfect tailor-made gifts of love.

In the Old Testament of the Bible there are stories of how the Lord greatly blessed the Israelites with miracles upon miracles, yet they had the tendency to forget rather quickly about all the ways they had been blessed. I realized that in the past I have behaved quite similarly, having spiritual amnesia about the ways I have been so greatly blessed and then not trusting fully. My behavior and level of trust has changed in the past year and a half, and I am reminded how important it is to remember and savor the blessings and special experiences that are gifts of God's Grace.

Recently I have gone back to take a look at my early experiences written in journals from when I first started to take classes at Guidance for a Better Life. I am blown away by the amazing experiences I was blessed with from my very first class in April 1998. Spiritual truth and teachings have been woven throughout these classes from day one. At my second class in May 1998 I continued to be blessed. One of the skills we had been taught was to experience wide-angle vision. Rather than focusing on a particular spot, with wide-angle vision you use a softer wide gaze, which can totally change your perspective and view. It is similar to the shifting of perspective when looking at a 3-D piece of art.

Late one evening I felt drawn down by the retreat center's pond, and I practiced the art of wide-angle vision. To my amazement, as my vision shifted I saw a stunningly brilliant pure white church or temple. It was such a beautiful, peaceful scene. Then my mind kicked in and tried to make sense of it, and the scene faded. The next day in class my memories were triggered during the sharing session. I realized how blessed I was through God's Grace to see one of God's many Temples on the inner spiritual planes. Since I tend to not be a visual person, this was an extra gift from God. Over the years since, I have had many opportunities to visit this temple and other temples when taken by Prophet Del Hall. These experiences have always bathed me in God's Light and Love, and I have benefited from these spiritual showers with deep peace, love, clarity, joy, healings, and knowingness.

Recently I had a special experience in this temple that was tailor-made for me. At a weekend retreat as a group we sang HU, a precious love song to God, for about twenty minutes. In the quiet time after the HU I experienced God's white Light pouring into my spiritual eye and heart, along with a deep quietude, peace, and love. I found myself in this special Temple of God and saw a book of Holy Scripture with God's Light shining upon it. Shortly afterwards I found myself in a large room in the temple that was lit up with white light and golden light around the edges. Golden light generally signifies God's Love. In the middle of the room was a large grand piano!

Later, in class, I shared with Prophet and the other students that recently my employer had given me keys to her church, so I could go play the piano and sing on my lunch hour. I love to play piano and sing, and also find it brings balance in my life. When I shared my experience in the temple, it was pointed out and emphasized that God loves me so much that He gave me this special gift that was perfect for me. Del said I had now been given keys to God's Temple and can go there any time I choose to remember and re-experience this.

God knew there would soon come a time in my life when this would be extra important and a huge blessing. This past month my job has changed significantly, temporarily, and I have been working long hours at several offices out of town and have been unable to go to the local church to play piano at lunch. However, I am able to go with Prophet to God's Temple of Learning at any time, day or night, and experience a shower of God's Love and Light while I am playing the piano and singing praises of joy to our living God.

Written by Jan Reid

The Golden Book

The following is an amazing testimony to the magnitude of the spiritual worlds of God, and it contains a very applicable piece of wisdom for our daily lives; do whatever you are doing for the love of it, for it is the never ending list of "small things" done with an open heart that sculpt a life of gratitude.

White marble steps ascended before me. As Soul, I stood at the steps to one of God's Temples of Learning in the Heavens. The temple guardian, a former Prophet of God, stood at the entrance welcoming us. I thanked him for the opportunity to enter and learn more about the ways of God. His gracious smile welcomed me upward, and I excitedly climbed the steps, the warm glow of golden light radiating through the doorway behind him. As we stepped through the door, my eyes adjusted to the brilliancy of the Light.

Prophet Del Hall had led us here in contemplation while our bodies sat in Virginia. All of God's true Prophets work together, and now Del, the current Prophet, was giving me the opportunity to learn God's ways and truth with this former Prophet.

We stood in an expansive circular room with a tall, domed ceiling. Its white walls seemed to both absorb and reflect the source of the light in the center of the room. A beam of light and sound entered through the ceiling, cascading down to the floor sustaining, nurturing, and giving life to this spiritual temple and all within it. In the center of the beam of light and sound (Holy Spirit), I saw a golden book resting on a simple pedestal. This living book, with wisdom and love directly from God, is a tremendous blessing to have the opportunity to see and touch. During other journeys to God's Temples with Prophet, I have experienced Its words transform and take a life of their own, as if they are written specifically for the reader at that moment in their journey.

Now this opportunity was given to me again. The guardian escorted me to the beam containing the golden book. Instinctively and gratefully, I knelt before it, relishing in the Presence of God's Light and Sound. I experienced a soothing, gentle sound come in like a whispering wind. God's Voice is not always a booming thunder as often portrayed in the movies, but can be soft as a gentle whisper. Then I looked and saw words appear in the golden book, "Listen for me always. Always listen." It was as if I heard, and then saw the instructions Soul had innately known. The pure Light and Sound of God continued to flow through me. Weights I had been carrying were lifted almost imperceptibly. A stillness existed in the sound that was vibrating around me. I somehow heard both sound and quiet, yet words could not describe it, and I wanted to continue listening forever. As God's Light continued to shine over and through me, I felt nurtured, uplifted, and restored.

I then had the opportunity to walk with the guardian, who was the primary teacher in this temple. One of God's many Temples, it is unique in Its shape and layout, but contains the same primary source of nourishment and life, the beam of God's Light and Sound. Down hallways, I have seen and entered rooms for learning. I have seen another area with a rectangular pool with healing waters, and an inner courtyard surrounded by gardens with benches for quiet reflection. On another spiritual journey, I have been led to a healing room. As we were walking around the spiritual temple this time, he shared "Remember to do what you love and to do what you do with love." He demonstrated this very thing as he was teaching me, through his humble and loving demeanor. He was teaching for the love of God's teachings, with love.

Months later this experience is still bearing fruit in my day-to-day life. Today, as I began my day in prayer, I was reminded of this wisdom. Do what I do today with love. Today it involves teaching my children at home, something I am so grateful our country gives us the freedom to do. It involves story time and snacks, dishes and laundry, gardening and planting a few seeds. It involves taking our eldest to an orthodontist appointment with this wisdom in my heart. These are not chores, rather an opportunity to demonstrate my love for God by caring for those I love with a grateful heart. What a gift! This life is lived all the while listening for the Voice of God, asking is there a better way to do this? Is there a need God sees that I can help fulfill? There are countless golden opportunities to demonstrate love by how I live, remembering to listen for His guiding Voice always.

Written by Molly Comfort

Dream With Past Life Records

It is true that you only live one life, but not in the sense that most people have been taught. You are Soul, an eternal spiritual being. You do not "have" a soul, you are Soul. You are one Soul, the same Soul, for all eternity. However, Soul lives many different physical lifetimes. Each serves as a unique opportunity to grow in wisdom and love.

During a morning contemplation I asked the Prophet for some insight about a relationship in my life. Afterwards I went about my day. Just before bed I thought about the things and people in my life that I am very grateful for. Then I drifted off to sleep.

I joined Prophet in a dream. We walked through a beautiful garden courtyard, entered a set of glass doors, and walked down a hallway into a very plain and simple room. After we sat and talked for a little while some people came in to visit with me. Most of the people I knew from the past, some of them were very good friends. A few of them I had not seen in years and others looked familiar, but I could not recall from where. This caught my attention and raised some questions. Where was I and what was going on? Was it my birthday or had I died?

Prophet brought me back from my thoughts. He directed my attention from the people in the room to a nearby wall, which had a very beautiful and unusual wallpaper on it. It was made up of hundreds or thousands of tiny photos, images, or scenes. At a glance this made up a bigger picture. I was surprised when I noticed that the larger picture was an image of me. As a visual reference for the reader, a few weeks after this dream I came across an image made in a very similar way called a "Photo Mosaic." The image in my dream appeared to be alive and fluid. Though the majority of the images were unfamiliar, as I looked more closely I saw that a few of them were from significant periods in my present life.

Prophet explained to me that this giant collage was a record of many of my past lives. Hundreds and thousands of little images and scenes from hundreds and thousands of years. As he talked he slowly walked down the hall, I followed. He turned, stopped, and faced the wall. There I noticed a small image that for some reason brought a smile to my face. In this picture there was an eighth century Chinese warrior who was riding a beautiful gray horse across rolling green hills. I knew it was me from a long time ago. I remembered that day, my horse, and that particular valley. In the picture next to it I saw myself walking in the hot desert during the time period when various pyramids were being built.

As I looked around I saw many other scenes, and though the person I saw in them did not look the way I do now, I clearly knew that each had been me. The settings or surroundings I saw myself in varied widely. At times I had been in ancient forests or on white sandy beaches, inside castles, or next to primitive huts. And in other pictures I was in what appeared to be long forgotten cities or among civilizations that no longer existed.

Prophet chuckled, and I looked over to see what he was looking at. "Here I am," he said pointing to a person in one of the scenes. "What were you doing?" I asked. He said, "Watching you, cheering you on!" He smiled. As he did he gazed into my eyes, and I felt an incredible wave of love wash through me. I remembered this ancient love from many other lives deep in my heart. He showed me many such lifetimes, picture after picture where he, the Prophet, was watching over me, guiding me, and indeed cheering me on. In most of the lifetimes I had not been aware of the Prophet's presence, though in some of them I was blessed to be aware of and to have a conscious relationship with him.

When I looked back at the pictures again, many of the images were moving and playing out a scene from a specific time. Prophet took his hand and touched one of the pictures. As he did it zoomed forward, and the picture became life sized and alive. We walked inside this living scene. For that moment, while I was in the scene, I had no recall of being in the hallway looking at pictures or of sleeping in my warm bed. I was fully immersed in the experience of that life. I could see, smell, feel, and experience every detail of that time period as clearly as if I was living in it in the present moment. When I had remembered that life, the lesson, and the love, we stepped back out into the hallway with a smooth, flawless transition. I looked at many different images. Prophet offered to take me, and we went back into any of the lives I was drawn to or had questions about. This trip back through my personal ancient history was incredible and "off the chart" amazing!

I came back with a new sense of peace and appreciation for the lives we live and how our relationships with others span across eons from one time period to the next. Though our bodies may change in appearance, the relationships and/or strong bonds of love we form continue on with us from one life to another. I saw many people I knew then and could identify as the same Soul now, even though they looked different physically. In some of the lives I was a white person, in some a black person, in some Chinese, in some male and in some female. The color, sex, or nationality I had been seemed trivial and irrelevant in the big picture. The variations and combinations of race, gender, and nationality are endless but each life is specifically designed to help us experience and learn from a new perspective.

I saw that in different lifetimes I would reincarnate with many of the same Souls. Sometimes we had good relationships and sometimes we rubbed each other like coarse sandpaper, but each life had a common thread, which was to teach us all how to give and receive love. Sometimes we were friends, sometimes not, sometimes work associates, other times warriors in combat, the list was endless; farm workers, family members, children or parents, husbands or wives. I thank Prophet for this incredible gift. It provided me with a much clearer understanding of how we are connected, and it helped me to have a greater love and appreciation for all the unique Souls and relationships I am blessed by God to have in my life. Through this dream gift, Prophet also allowed me to see how each person and each life encouraged growth in many different areas. I awoke back in my warm bed.

Later I learned Prophet had taken me to the second Heaven to a Temple of Learning. There I found the images of many of my former lifetimes. I had been invited into this particular temple by both Prophet and the guardian of the temple and keeper of these records.

The way Prophet can show us our past lives is as varied and individual as each person. I have seen some of my past lives as files in a file cabinet, been shown them in dreams, in contemplations, in the beam of light at a temple, and had glimpses or flashes of them in the course of a normal day. One of the main reasons to be shown past lives is to help us live a better, more fulfilling, joyful, and abundant life this time. Another reason is to help us realize that we are Soul, an eternal spark of God and that the real us does not die when our current bodies wear out. A third, and perhaps the most important reason, is to help us know that each Soul, whether consciously aware of it or not has had a long and personal relationship with God and His Prophets through many lifetimes. When we come to the point in our lifetimes that we are able to consciously recognize God's Love for us and then our love for God, we and our lives become greatly blessed.

From this dream and other experiences, I have realized past lives are as real as any day in this present life. We have good days and tough days, but we each do the best we can. Each day, like each life, we live, love, grow, and learn a little more. It takes thousands of days in many lifetimes to experience and learn to become spiritually mature and about all the wonderful things God has in store for us. We exist because God loves us. The lives in which we grow the most are the ones in which we are blessed to have a conscious relationship with and learn from a true Prophet of God. Our potential rate of growth in these lifetimes is exponential. With the Prophet's help, guidance, and love we can see the world and God more clearly as it truly is and come to know our Heavenly Father more intimately. This provides a life that is abundant beyond imagination.

Whether we are aware of it or not, God and His Prophet are always with us, seen or unseen, guiding, loving, nudging, rooting for and cheering us on during our journey home to our Heavenly Father.

Written by Jason Levinson

As Soul I Remembered the Sound

Our journey through the Heavenly Worlds, our experiences with the Light and Love of God, and our spiritual growth will continue on forever. In a very real sense, there is no "finish line." Most of us however, can point to an experience or a time in this life when Soul was stirred. A time when we knew without a doubt there was more.

It was one of my early visits to Guidance for a Better Life for a spiritual retreat. I did not know what to expect, but God knew what I needed and led me to that retreat. I am so grateful for the Divine guidance.

I first heard it as the weekend began. We were sitting in the field as a group singing HU with the Prophet. It was the beautiful sound of a flute. I have always loved that sweet angelic music, but this specific sound was so much more. It was not the physical sound of any instrument I had ever heard. It was a beautiful and distinct spiritual sound flowing through everything. I was drawn to follow this flute-like sound as if I remembered it from long ago. As Soul, I recognized that sound was coming from God and was not a physical sound. It filled me with love. I was comforted and at peace with a sense of being more complete than ever before. As my physical body sat in the field, I was free to spiritually soar with Prophet. In what seemed like an instant we were in a place where I unknowingly longed to be and experienced a freedom like no other. Later I learned the flute-like sound is found on the fifth Heaven. As Soul I was familiar with this place.

The next day we were blessed with an offer to be taken spiritually to one of God's Temples. These temples are located in the Heavens. I accepted the opportunity and was led by the Prophet to a beautiful Heavenly space unlike anything I had a reference for in the physical world. It immediately felt so much more real than anything I knew in my everyday life with a heightened level of crispness and clarity. As I stepped forward I heard that now familiar spiritual sound of the flute, and it was again so beautiful and full of God's Love. It carried me in comfort and peace. Looking up, my vision was filled with light emanating from what I could only describe as something looking like a castle. I went inside with Prophet showing me the way.

We stepped into a large rotunda, and I saw a huge beam of amazing, pure-white light flowing down into the temple. This active, sparkling beam of God's Light felt alive and nourishing as it illuminated the room and beyond. I recognized on some level that this was a very significant experience. I walked forward and put my hand up toward the beam as I looked to Prophet to see if I had permission for this sacred act. With his affirmation, I put my outstretched hand forward and just let the light glide over my hand. There was so much in that light. It is God's Light and Love, which I felt as peace, strength, love, comfort, and so much more. There were no words spoken, but this experience has had a lasting impact on me. I have had many more experiences over the years with God's Light and Sound, but in this life real change started with that intense and loving moment.

As Soul, I longed to reconnect with the Light and Sound of God. I wanted to let it flow through me as a child of God. The experiences that weekend gave me a reference. It started my foundation in this life to really know there is so much more. There is more than just this physical world. Visits to Heavens are possible. God truly loves us unconditionally. I could feel His Love in my experiences. There was so much more of God's blessings I was not yet ready to accept, but they are there for me as I continue to grow stronger on my spiritual journey. I am thankful for these experiences, and the continued inner and outer guidance of the Prophet.

Written by Michelle Hibshman

Changed by Visit to the Freedom Temple

You are so much more than your temporal earthly body. You are an immortal spiritual being created out of the Light and Love of God. You are essentially a piece of the Holy Spirit individualized by lifetimes of experience. You have freedom, spiritual power, and a capacity to give and receive love beyond your wildest imagination. You need only find the one who can help awaken you to your true self.

Having a relationship with the Prophet has changed my perspective on life. While Earth is a beautiful place to live, I have seen places where the Light of God is brighter, the Love of God seems to flow more freely, and Soul does not need a physical body to move about. In these other worlds, or Heavens, there are sacred temples where Soul can go to learn of God's Love and wisdom. Each temple has a primary teacher. These teachers of God's ways and truth were once God's chosen Prophet here on Earth during their incarnations. Interestingly, my visits to these temples have been made while my physical body sat peacefully in Virginia.

In September I was at the Guidance for a Better Life retreat center. We sang HU softly, and I began to think of things I was grateful for. Del explained the temple guardian had invited us to spiritually visit this Temple of Learning. Like in all of God's Temples, the guardian is also the primary teacher. I was taken there by Prophet in what seemed like an instant. Prophet and I stood outside. The temple was tall and cylindrical with a domed roof. It was beautiful to behold and built with the finest craftsmanship. The material it was made of glowed from within like it was made of light. I had never seen anything like this.

I entered the threshold and saw others were also gathered there to listen to the guardian speak. To paraphrase, he said that the way to liberation is through love in service. Give all the love that you can, and in doing so you will be granted riches beyond what you can imagine. By riches he was referring to spiritual wealth. These are the treasures that truly bless and can be kept beyond the grave. Treasures like love, peace, and wisdom. This really rang true to me. To become a conduit of God's Love is not to be a martyr. As quickly as love is given to another God replenishes it.

After he had finished speaking I turned to see the Holy Book across the room. It appeared as an open book floating over a pedestal, which was also made of the same fine material as the temple. A beam of reflective light cascaded down over the Living Word of God, this special Holy Book of living scripture. This light was part of what made the temple. It was alive and moved with purpose. This was unlike any light I was used to seeing on Earth. It was the Light of God! I stood before this sacred Holy Book. Prophet held my hand. Our hands became a beautiful cup that looked like crystal but was made of light. We dipped the cup into the pages of the Holy Book, which had become a pool of light. I drank the light. Prophet and I stepped into the beam of God's Light, and I breathed in deeply. I experienced Divine love while standing in the beam! I had everything I needed in that moment, and I felt complete. I so much wanted to bring this love back to my daily life and to other Souls who also thirst for God.

I became aware of love pouring into places in and around me. These were invisible places, as if my very atoms were getting larger and able to hold more light. I kept breathing in this light. Prophet was inches from me now. He was made of light also. Part of him melted into me. Then we came apart. Still holding my hand, he left the beam first then turned to help me. I stepped out slowly. My first step out was so grand! This moment was a special one. I was different. I saw myself as Soul, my true self. I was made of light, and I was wearing a garment that flowed around me. I did not walk. I floated. A part of me deep inside was stirred in such a way that I began to cry tears of joy.

This experience is one of many incredible spiritual journeys I have made with the Prophet. This particular experience continues to bless and teach me as I relive and contemplate on the many layers of meaning it holds. I thank you Prophet for taking me to the temple. Remembrance of this experience brings me strength. It sharpens my focus, warms me with appreciation, and reminds me of the Love of God that is present in my life.

Written by Carmen Snodgrass

Loved Just the Way I Am

*You will never be loved by God any more than you are loved right
at this very moment in time. You can however, grow in your ability to
recognize and accept His Love in ever greater amounts. More will
always be there for you as you become ready.*

I was blessed with an opportunity to visit one of God's Temples.
Following the cadence Prophet Del Hall set, I began to walk twenty-
two steps from the beach area by the pond where our class had
gathered in our Soul bodies. He counted "1, 2, 3..." aloud. After
walking the twenty-two steps with him, I looked out and saw ripples
of color on the surface of the pond and perceived the temple. I saw
steps made of white-light and its guardian greeted us at the door.
Upon entering I saw detail in the dome's interior I had not noticed
during previous visits. There were stained glass windows and ornate
wood carvings. A rainbow of colors outlined the wood carvings.
There is always more in the Heavens of God.

I walked into this sacred place with Prophet who was guiding me
on this inner spiritual journey, and went to the beam of God's Light
and Sound in the center of a great rotunda. We walked into it. I was
instantly brought up the beam toward the ceiling. Looking down the
beam to the floor below I could see the area brightly lit, but where I
was there was no light that I could perceive, just sound. The sound
grew louder in my ears, and I felt as if I was absorbed by and
disappeared into It, but my awareness of being an individual Soul
was still the same. This was the first time I experienced the beam
like this, through the aspect of sound alone. I had been praying to
have more clear and precise inner communication with the Divine,
and specifically, with the inner aspect of God's Prophet. I wondered
if this could be a way of calibrating or tuning my spiritual hearing. I
was experiencing the sound aspect of the beam when Prophet
brought my awareness to the light. At first I could not see it so I
imagined it. I perceived light showering down upon me and through
me. I was being blessed with a spiritual shower of God's Light. It
cleansed me of any "road dirt" I may have picked up living in the

physical world, anything that could be a block to giving or receiving love. This prepared me for blessings to come. Soon after, Prophet mentioned the light changing color, and I could see bright golden light showering down upon me, this was love direct from God. I drank of it spiritually, again and again, letting it wash over and through me.

We sang HU and came back into our bodies. I felt lighter and could still hear the sound in my ears, but it was a little different than the sound I heard before inside the beam. Soul is an individualized piece of the Holy Spirit, the Light and Sound of God. Was this my own sound without the Heavenly sound of the beam I heard before? I think maybe it was, and it was beautiful. Prophet said, "Just be." I felt calm, still, and peaceful. I was so in the moment, not one thought was in my mind. He said in several different ways that God loves me. He will never love me more than He does in this moment. As a child of God He loves me, and always has loved me — just the way I am. I am worthy of His Love. Then he spoke these words but in first person, as the Voice of God. He said it again, knowing this was something I needed to hear. "I love you, just the way you are." In the place I was in, with my heart as wide open as it was, these words sank in deeper than ever. I knew at a level not experienced before this, that I am indeed loved by God and His Prophet. I do not need to do anything special for this love. I am lovable just as I was created.

This filled voids in me I barely knew existed, but I could feel them filling. It soothed me, reassured me, and brought more confidence, stability, and security with this knowingness. I accepted the truth and love in those precious spoken words, and this has changed my life and healed past lives. I thank God for the miracle of His Love.

Written by Lorraine Fortier

The Abode of God

I considered not including this section of "Traveling the Heavens" in my book. The stories of visiting the primary Abode of God are so sacred and so beyond the consciousness of mankind that I questioned even covering this topic. However, I believe God wants His children to know He loves them, and He is reachable and at least partly knowable. One of the primary roles of His Prophets is to bring us closer to our Maker. So, I have included fifteen different experiences of my students at the Abode of God.

There are so many blessings from even one visit, but the main purpose of each visit is primarily to KNOW God loves each of us. In these stories God Himself expresses His Love directly to those Souls so fortunate to travel to this special Heaven. The Souls who have persevered years of training and testing are now among those whom the Prophet guides HOME to God. There is so much of God's Love, Mercy, and Grace in the twelfth Heaven that it is poetically called the Ocean of Love and Mercy, and it appears as such to Souls brought there by Prophet.

After absorbing the magnitude of what you have just read, ask yourself, what in your heart of hearts are your spiritual desires and goals? Is your loyalty to a certain path or teaching (however good), to approval of others including family and friends, or to God? This is perhaps the most important personal decision one can ever make. My focus, loyalty, and my free will is to serve God, our Heavenly Father, above all else. Once again I say, **"Over time and with sufficient effort a knowing, trusting, and loving relationship with the Heavenly Father is possible with the help of His Prophet."**

My True Home

Even after traveling into the Heavens, visiting God's Temples, and experiencing the Light and Sound of God, nothing can compare to seeing the Face of God Himself. It is beyond imagination, beyond description, beyond "belief." It is beyond the limited power of words to describe.

God's realm is sometimes referred to as the Ocean of Love and Mercy. It is like a vast ocean where time and space cease to exist and are replaced entirely by God's Love. But it's not the love we think of when we often hear the word. It is beyond emotion, beyond religion, beyond the mind, beyond anything one can experience in our world. It is love with the power to purify, to renew, to create, and to destroy.

When I first arrived at the Ocean of Love and Mercy, I found myself kneeling on a golden sandy shore. The Prophet of our times had brought me here. My physical body was sitting peacefully in Virginia, but here at God's Ocean I knelt as Soul. Beside me, kneeling in reverence toward the Heavenly Father, was the Prophet himself. Whoever serves in the role of Prophet during any point in history — Jesus during his time, Isaiah during his time, and all the others — is the one ordained by God to bring Souls home to Him for that point in history. This is part of what Jesus meant when he said, "I am the way, the truth, and the life: no man cometh unto the Father, but by me." John 14:6 KJV It is only through the living Prophet that one can be taken to our Heavenly Home and see God, face to face.

Back when I was a young kid so many years ago I had made a solemn statement to myself: "I want to go home." I didn't know what I meant back then — but now I did. This was my true home. God's Ocean, the birthplace of Soul.

Kneeling with my head down, I observed with awe the golden sand of the shore and touched it with my fingertips. Gentle waves broke upon its surface, gracefully gliding up and down the beach. Softly we sang HU, the beautiful love song to God. Now, unlike when I had first learned the HU, I was able to sing it as a true love song to God. My relationship with Prophet had opened my heart to

God's Love and expanded my ability to both give and receive love. Now when I sing HU, it is filled with real love and gratitude to my creator, the Heavenly Father.

Prophet then asked me to raise my head and behold an aspect of the Lord, my God. One can never see all of God, so He appears in the forms which we can understand and accept. There are infinite aspects to God, and the true form is beyond description, beyond comprehension. He appears in the way which He knows will bless us.

As I raised my head I was surprised by what I saw. Hovering above the waves of the Ocean was an enormous hand-carved wooden flute. With Prophet guiding me I went to it and touched it, trying to memorize every detail. I examined the finger holes, the mouthpiece, the stunning craftsmanship, the beautiful grain of the wood. I noticed the mouthpiece, and that end of the flute, was made entirely of God. The middle of the flute was a blending area, both God and Prophet. And the far end, where the music emerged, was made entirely of Prophet.

Prophet guided me to go inside the flute. I entered it, and within it streamed Heavenly white music, the Sound of God. It was like a waterfall without water, or a great wind with no wind. There was only the Music, the Sound of God.

The Music poured over me, around me, and through me. It penetrated me, and I became part of the music itself. I was still me, but I was vibrating in harmony with the rhythm of God's Music. It was incredible.

After a few moments of this incredible experience, Prophet guided me to see yet another aspect of God. The vibration of the music still ringing within me, I looked out once more over the golden waters of God's Ocean.

And then I saw Him.

He appeared as a human figure, but enormous and made entirely of living, flowing ocean water. He was muscular and strong, with curling hair and a mighty beard. His white robe flowed around His body majestically, and His Eyes displayed a love beyond what any mortal heart could ever hold. The love flowed out of Him, personal yet impersonal, strong yet gentle, immense and never ending.

As He approached, Prophet gently guided me into God's Heart. White light surrounded us. All was utterly still and peaceful, yet at the same time active and alive. Within God's Heart was the most peace I have ever experienced. It was the most intense love I'd ever felt, and yet there was peace so great that it held me in perfect balance. The longing, the aching, the hunger that had pained me so many years ago — it was gone. Everything I'd ever need was here, now. I was home, really home, at last. Home in God's Heart.

Gently, slowly, the Face of God appeared to me within this tranquil sanctuary. His Eyes were filled with the strong, gentle, indescribable love that only He possesses. His body slowly formed beneath Him, swirling with every color imaginable. He knew me.

He reached out with His right Hand and gently touched my shoulder as if to say, "It's okay, welcome home." His touch penetrated deep within me with vibrations unimaginably high and intense. The feeling of His touch reached to my very heart, changing something inside of me forever. I would not be the same after this moment. His touch uplifted me, transformed me, changed me from the inside. I was changed forever, by His touch. His touch still lives in my heart to this day.

Written by David Hughes

God Touched My Heart

*You are loved by God, and one of His desires is for you to know
and live in this love daily. With the Prophet as your guide you can
spiritually travel into the Heavens and experience this love from an
aspect of the Divine for yourself — before the end of this physical life.
Many who have been blessed to experience God's Love directly have
one thing in common — they desire for you to experience it as well.*

It was while I was deep in contemplation that I was blessed with
an amazing experience of God's Love. It was given to me after
singing HU, an ancient name for God, for a good length of time. As
I sat with my physical eyes closed, my attention on the inner reality
within me, I was aware of my spiritual teacher whom I know as the
Prophet, right beside me. He guided the real eternal me, Soul, higher
and higher through world upon world of God's creation, the house
of many mansions Jesus spoke of two thousand years ago. Prophet
took me all the way home to the Abode of God Himself. I can best
describe it as an expanse of God's Love and Mercy, one so vast it
was like a boundless ocean.

To be allowed to consciously return to my true home where God
created me as Soul was a profound gift in and of itself. Yet God
always has more love to give, for amid the ocean waves of God's
Love, there appeared the Lord Himself in a form I could relate to,
one more personal than the boundless Ocean. The Lord placed His
Hand on my heart and held it there. His eternal Love poured into me,
and I knew beyond any shadow of a doubt that God truly loves me,
and has always loved me. Without conditions and without judgments
He loves me. It is a love that has no beginning and no end. During
that moment I knew His Love is eternal and that it is personal, for
God knows me and loves me just as much as any other part of His
creation, and He loves me just as I am. I did not earn this gift, but I
was blessed to be able to receive it by the Grace of the Lord.

In the years since this Divine blessing of blessings there have
been many times when I have not felt as loved as I did during that
moment in eternity. Love is more than a feeling though, for when I

408

remember this blessing of standing before God as He touched me, I know that whether or not I feel loved, God loves me, and that all is well as I walk in His Love. This gift of God touching my heart, for which I thank the Prophet, the one whom God has ordained to take Soul home to Him, is a blessing that was not given to me just for my own benefit, or to be hoarded selfishly like a prized possession.

This gift of Divine love has blessed me with a greater capacity to give and receive love. It has helped to liberate me from selfish desires, to think more of the needs of others, and to truly hear and know in my heart what God, through His Prophet, is asking me to do. I also know that the love was given to me so I can testify to this: God is real and God loves you.

Written by Roland Vonder Muhll

A Personal Embrace from God

It is one thing to believe that God loves you. It is quite another to be escorted by Prophet to the source of all and experience God's Love for Soul firsthand.

In special prayer time reserved for God and myself, I experienced something that is somewhat hard to put into words. I received blessings of love, reassurance, and comfort of lifetimes, and the experience is deeply engraved in my heart. It both transformed and reassured me.

Savoring the opportunity to express the love I have for God by singing HU, my love song to Him, I was taken, as Soul, to His Abode. I found myself on my knees on a white sandy shore of a vast and sparkling Ocean. This Ocean was alive with love! Prophet has taken me spiritually to this magnificent Ocean before during contemplation, and each time has been very different for me. This is

God's Home, the Ocean of Love and Mercy, and I was privileged to be there again. The love emanating from God caressed and penetrated every atom in my being. I looked up to see an illuminated figure of the brightest, but gentlest, golden light with open arms reaching out to me! In awe and humbleness, I did not hesitate to extend my arms to the loving reaching arms of God!

I was immediately drawn into an intense loving embrace from God Himself! ME! The love from this embrace was so pure and deep, I cried as many emotions poured through me, among them were love, gratitude, and joy. I mouthed the words "Thank You," expressing my gratitude with everything in my being. I felt God's Love for me as I sent even more love back to my Creator. This love exchange was so intense; I can only describe it as a penetrating knowingness of God's Love for me that fulfilled everything my heart has ever desired. In that moment IT was ALL! I know my Father recognized me, and I could have stayed in His tender embrace for eternity!

After a time basking in His Love, I sensed an illuminating blue light on the screen of my inner vision. I knew this to be a calling card for God's chosen Prophet, Del. A very familiar love, similar to what I had just experienced, was palpable. I thanked him for escorting me to the Abode of God, where I could experience my true home and fullness of my Heavenly Father's Love for me.

I was enjoying the peace filled quiet time after singing HU, when I was further blessed to see where the extra love in my HUs sung to God were being distributed! In my inner vision I could see our beautiful blue earthly abode being drenched with golden waves of what I perceived as Divine liquid love! The planet was surrounded in the golden Light of God's infinite Love. God took the love in my HUs, expressions of my enduring love for Him, and magnified them to an unfathomable and profound degree, then distributed them as blessings from our loving Heavenly Father.

The HU for me this day was a gift I will treasure for all time. I am so blessed to have known how deep, personal, and sincere God's Love is for me, and how He wants everyone to know the glory and agelessness of His eternal Love for us all.

Written by Nancy Nelson

Drawing Nigh Unto God

God has no shortage of love for His children. There is however, only so much love we can receive at any given time. The more we do our part to raise up, draw nigh, and stay spiritually nourished the more of God's Love we can accept and then be privileged to pass on to others. One of the best ways to do this is by singing HU.

Gratitude filled my heart as I sat on a couch in the great room in the home of my spiritual teacher, Prophet Del Hall, singing HU with a small group of students. It was just before bed when Prophet invited us to sing HU, a love song to God. HU is a pure way to express love and give thanks for the many blessings in our lives. HU has been an incredible blessing in my life for nearly fourteen years, and over this time my love and appreciation for the HU continues to grow. It is an integral part of my day and in making God a reality in my life. When I first began singing HU I would often cry because my heart was beginning to open to the beauty and abundance of God's Love in my life.

Ever since I was a young child I knew I loved God, but I'm not sure I really knew how to express my love for God, until I sang HU. I would say my prayers at night, and this allowed me to share my love while also providing me with a sense of comfort, but there was such a difference in my experience of expressing and receiving love with my Heavenly Father when I sang HU. Perhaps, it is because HU is a pure prayer in that it is not asking or telling God what to do. Or maybe it is because HU opens my heart and uplifts me to a higher view of life where I am better able to recognize and receive God's blessings. Many of these blessings have often been gifts of peace, love, healing, joy, comfort, and clarity. I have learned these Divine gifts are an expression of God's Love for me. Singing HU is also drawing nigh unto God and when we draw nigh unto God, He draws nigh unto us.

So on this night as I sang HU in Prophet's home, I focused on expressing my love and gratitude to God. Although my physical body resided on the couch, spiritually I was kneeling. On the inner spiritual planes God's Love and Light filled Prophet's great room and then opened up into the vast ocean of God's Love and Mercy. I continued kneeling in reverence on the shore at God's Ocean with my hands outstretched in the living water. In this beautiful and sacred time nothing else mattered except expressing the love and thanks within my heart by singing this precious love song to my Heavenly Father.

In the quiet time that followed the HU sing, I looked into the eyes of the inner Prophet and graciously accepted his hands as he led me into the vast ocean water. It is only through Prophet, my sacred relationship with him, and the bond of love we share that it is possible for me to reach God's Heavenly Abode. God's Hand rose up from this great ocean, lovingly holding Prophet and me, lifting us up and bringing us closer for me to experience this aspect of God. God's Hand drew us closer to Him eventually welcoming me to rest my cheek against His. An indescribable love and beauty overwhelmed my being. I was cheek to cheek for a moment in eternity with my Heavenly Father. In this moment I realized God truly knows my heart, my dreams, my prayers, my strengths, and my weaknesses. God knows me and He loves me just as I am. This sacred experience was and is very tender and endearing to me.

Later I was drawn to look up the definition for the word "endearing" and it reads, "making dear or more beloved." In reflecting upon this sacred experience, it was not that God loved me more than before, for His Love is unconditional, it was that I was able to experience more of the love God has for me. It was a greater acceptance of God's Love that has always been available for me. I ask myself, "What do I do with God's amazing Love?" And the answer that resounds within my heart is, "Share it and pass it on."

Written by Shanna Canine

In Our Father's Eyes

*This is an amazing testimony on visiting the Abode of God.
Traveling spiritually in full consciousness to the source of all — to
the Home of Our Father. Guided there by the Prophet to receive
healing, revelation, comfort, and a profound insight — we are
each loved unconditionally by God. Being able to accept this
love changes everything.*

Do you know we are welcome in Heaven? Do you know God loves you no matter what you are facing in life? Out of the many, many blessings that being a student of Del's has given me, this following experience stands out as one that gave me an understanding that God's Love for us truly has no conditions. Knowing this has given me a peace that has changed how I walk through life.

Some years ago, I was going through a time where I was struggling with jealousy and envy. I was not comfortable in my own skin, and thought if I was more like someone else or had what they had in their lives, then I would be happy. While logically I knew that this was unhealthy, I could not seem to shake it. In my eyes, I was not deserving of love.

During a weeklong spiritual retreat at Guidance for a Better Life Del led us in singing HU. After some time, I became aware I was in front of a huge ocean made entirely of God's Love. Instinctively, I knelt. I was not alone, Prophet was next to me holding my hand. Beside me were Souls as far as I could see. Each one of us was made of glowing, shimmering light. Each one of us was beautiful. We were each kneeling along this beach in love and reverence to our Heavenly Father. As I looked out over the wide expanse, I saw pure white light reflecting in the distant water. The light came closer to me, and I saw a form appear sitting in a gigantic chair. The Heavenly Father was seated before us. I could see and feel our love going out to Him with each HU and then returning back to us in a beautiful rhythm.

413

As I was kneeling before this immense ocean of God's Love, I was experiencing such a deep, deep peace. I have never experienced this much peace in my life. I needed nothing and I lacked nothing. Peace filled every fiber of my being. Tears streamed down my face as I accepted the love that was being offered to me. Then, our Heavenly Father arose and came towards me across the water. With such a gentleness He lifted my head and kissed my forehead. "I love you and I am glad you are here." His Eyes filled the sky, immense and loving. His Love continued to pour into me, filling every part of me.

I knew then, as I do now, that He loves me without conditions. He has the same love for you, no matter what you are struggling with inside or going through in life. Our Father truly loves us unconditionally and accepting this love truly changes us.

For days, and now years later, I close my eyes and return to this living experience of God's Love. Seeing the love in my Heavenly Father's eyes, face to face, gave me a confidence in His Love for me that is unshakable. Thank you Prophet for guiding me home to Heaven to meet our Father, face to face.

Written by Molly Comfort

"My Peace I Leave With You"

There is a deep, eternal peace available for you. Not world peace or the kind of peace from a joyful day of relaxing, but rather — a lasting peace of the heart. The peace that comes with seeing clearly, truly knowing the ways of God, and accepting His Love. With this peace, Soul comes into harmony with itself and the Divine, and man can rise above the trials and tribulations of life in the physical. This peace is your birthright as Soul and only needs to be awakened by drawing nigh to God and God's Prophet.

The Lord said to me, "My peace I leave with you," during a recent experience I had at Guidance for a Better Life. I had also read in the Bible that Jesus once said this to his disciples. So I asked myself: What did that really mean? I do not presume to know completely, but I can tell you there is a peace, which surpasses all understanding — something else I had read in the Bible. I know this because Prophet took me to the twelfth Heaven where I experienced these things myself. Peace was there and more.

It was a Sunday morning during one of the smaller retreats held during the winter. Del invited us to join him in singing HU. As we sang I noticed his presence as the inner guide with me. Each HU became a wave of light and sound we "surfed" in Soul bodies. With each wave Prophet and I drew closer to a beach. Throughout this experience I heard various sounds. First the sound of wind, then a high pitched humming sound, which gave way to something like that of the sound of a whirlpool. We were on the returning sound wave; part of the Light and Sound of God that Soul must be linked with in order to go home to God.

We arrived at what appeared to be a beach of a great ocean. I felt a humble submission take over my whole being. I had to kneel. The Prophet knelt with me for a moment and then grasped my hand to lift me up. As I looked out from where we were an expansive horizon of blinding bright light was all I could see. Emanating from this vista was a peace that is beyond anything I had ever felt. I was shown that some of God's peace was being distributed throughout the worlds during our HU song. I could see the HU truly is a prayer that blesses many Souls I may never know.

The peace I experienced that morning is still with me today. Accepting the hand of the current Prophet of God leads to peace, security, and more. My ever-growing awareness and love for the Divine allows me to access this gift of God. It lives in my heart. I wondered if Jesus said those words so many years ago as an invitation to accept him and have this deep peace. I have come to realize our Heavenly Father loves us very much. He always has a living Prophet to guide us home and distribute His blessings. He has given us a Comforter today. We do not have to wait until we leave the physical world to experience this. I am so grateful.

Written by Tash Canine

A Hunger Fulfilled

Many go through life seeking something they cannot quite put their finger on — they just feel like there has to be something more to it all. Often when one comes to know what is truly in their heart they also find out what the "more" is.

God's Love for Soul infuses our very nature and is part of who we are as His beloved children — to love and be loved. Loving God back with all my heart and all I am brings fulfillment to what I only knew earlier in my life as a longing deep within; the root or reason for I did not know. It was a longing for "something more" I could only chase after in vain through outer means. When I met Prophet he began to teach me about the nature of God and of my true nature as Soul. Over time I learned this longing was for something the outer material world could never satisfy. Everything in the physical is temporary, and though I was not aware of it at the time, what I longed for was something more lasting that would always be. I began to value and be nourished by eternal truth and the inner spiritual world he helped me experience. I came to recognize a loving personal relationship with God and His Prophet was the "more" I sought.

After twenty-five beautiful, life-enriching years as Prophet Del Hall's student I was given an experience that revealed still more about this longing within. I was seated in class with other spiritual students as we sang HU. My single-minded focus was to send love and give thanks to God through singing this love song. I thought of my Heavenly Father and how I love His Ways and His Word. I thought of how much I love His Son and how grateful I am that He continues to send us His Prophets throughout eternity to teach us in the physical. I have come to know I am spiritually lost without God's Prophet showing the way home to Him. Even with the best of intentions there are just too many pitfalls and traps along the way, and we are blind without a guide who is wise to them. Simply being in Prophet's presence on the inner, or like this day physically being with him, is a privilege and a blessing I have come to appreciate and cherish. This did not happen overnight though, it developed naturally through the years, and gradually a sacred loving relationship emerged. It is because of my relationship with Prophet my dearest dream as Soul became possible.

I sang HUUUUUU. My eyes closed, I journeyed inward with Prophet through the Heavens and the many spiritual planes to a place where God Himself resided. Too infinite to experience the Allness of the Divine, I was shown an aspect of this Great Being seated in a chair and was drawn to Him. On my knees before God, I swam in indescribable bliss. I was so happy being at the feet of the Almighty singing love and praise to Him. Doing so satisfied an innate desire so core to my being as if programmed into my DNA. The world would have you think being humble before God and giving praise and glory to Him is a lowly act, but I found it brought rest, satisfied my deepest hunger, and was a cause for rejoice. I felt more alive and more me than ever!

I turned and looked behind, over my left shoulder, and saw my lower self's earthly desire that used to negatively influence and control my life; then I turned back to the Lord God saying, "I want this more." My vision was filled with an all-encompassing brilliant white light. I saw Prophet's strong arm reach out to me — he had been there the whole time. He gently took my hand and walked me into the welcoming Light of God. It felt like I was coming home to where I was first created, from the source of love itself — God's Heart. And in this homecoming I had the sense a new chapter in my journey had begun. A quiet solidness filled me, one that comes from knowing who you really are and being confident in what is most important to you. As I came back into my physical body following this experience, I felt a stronger love and commitment to God than before and a deeper desire than ever to serve Him.

I think back to how my journey began in this lifetime with a gnawing desire for something more I did not think had anything to do with God or spiritual matters. I just thought I was the restless type with a wild hair, never happy with things as they were. But I know differently now. If you have an indescribable longing for something more in life or an ache in your heart for love, it may be the call of Soul. God's Prophet is here and can help you understand this Divine language and find answers.

Written by Lorraine Fortier

God Cherishes His Children

God loves and cherishes His children. This love lacks nothing. It contains everything we need to live a life of love, joy, and true purpose. It is God's Love for us that also gives us the Prophet, a way for Soul to find Its way home to Its Heavenly Father.

On a warm summer evening in late June about fifty of us were gathered for a weeklong retreat at Guidance for a Better Life taught by Prophet Del Hall. A soft breeze flowed into the room through the open windows. The sounds of birdsongs drifted in as the birds began to settle down for the evening. Prophet led us in a beautiful soft HU, lovingly sung to God. As we sang I felt the real me, Soul, lifted higher and higher as Prophet brought us closer and closer to God's Home. Before long, I found myself on my knees beside Prophet on the sand at the edge of a beautiful calm ocean. The "water" seemed alive as it gently flowed and lapped at my forehead that touched the sand. It was a loving energy welcoming us to God's Home.

I looked up from the sand to see an aspect of God, a brilliant pulsing white light with huge brilliant light rays that radiated out in all directions. It seemed to consist of a tremendous amount of energy. As I knelt in reverence and awe, God's huge Hand came toward us with His palm opened upwards. I felt welcomed and sensed we were invited to sit in it. In God's Hand we were immersed in golden light that radiated from it like a warm presence. I felt peace, comfort, protection, and love. And I felt something even more that touched me deeply; I felt cherished. God brought His Hand closer to His Face, where I felt even more loved and cherished as He gazed intently at me. God's beautiful loving Face was huge and surrounded by golden love that radiated out of Him. There was so much love in His Eyes for me! God brought His Hand to His chest and placed Prophet and me in His Heart. In God's Heart I felt even more peace, comfort, protection, and love. And I felt "home." It was a feeling of being home greater than I have felt anywhere on Earth. As God's child, where else would I truly be home but in my Father's Heart?

It seemed like only a moment we were in God's Heart, yet that moment was so rich it seemed like an eternity. Then God placed Prophet and me lovingly back on the sand at the water's edge. I looked up at God's beautiful loving Face while love poured from Him to me in intense waves. The love had everything I needed in it. I was so filled with love it seemed I couldn't hold another drop of it, yet somehow, I was able to receive more and more. Thank you Father, I love You! What a joy it was to tell God I love Him, directly to Him, face to face! Wow!

Afterwards on the beach I reached my hand out to hold Prophet's hand in love and gratitude for bringing me here to my true loving Father. Later, Prophet gently brought our true selves, Soul, back to our seats in the school building. The evening had turned into night, quiet and very peaceful. This experience touched me more deeply than I can express. It helped me to truly know God not only loves me, but He cherishes me! I am a child of God, loved and cherished by my Father!

But why did I get this experience? I am just an ordinary person. I am a wife and mother with an ordinary full-time job. We are not living 2000 years ago in biblical times, yet an ordinary person like me was blessed to see God. I feel I was blessed with this experience, so I could tell you about God's Love for you, dear reader. I wish you could truly know deep in your heart how much your Heavenly Father loves you and cherishes you, as He loves and cherishes each and every one of His children.

Written by Diane Kempf

"I Love You"

It is one thing to be told, "God loves you." It is quite another if you are blessed to actually experience God's Love for yourself. The following testimony takes it even further with the author being told from an aspect of God Himself that she was loved. To truly know deep down that God loves you is a rock to build your life on.

If you could travel to visit God and could hear God tell you directly "I love you," would it change you? It changed me when I was blessed with this sacred experience. One of the primary missions of the Prophet of God is to take you home to the Abode of God. While I was singing HU, a love song to God, during a retreat at Guidance for a Better Life, Prophet took me to an expansive and magnificent ocean where I was blessed to witness an aspect of God.

Prophet and I were standing on the beach at the water's edge when I saw an enormous sphere of electric light over the ocean. I knew with every fiber of my being that I was witnessing an aspect of God; It was alive, active, and full of love. It was so magnificent, and yet this was only a fraction of what God is. I was continuing to sing HU when I realized I was singing directly to God. I was being allowed, by the Divine, to express my deep love and reverence to God. Then something sacred and fortifying happened; I heard very loudly and clearly, with my physical ears, the words "I love you." At first I thought someone around me was talking, but I realized no one was. God was speaking directly to me. Wow! Being blessed with this experience has given me a security in life that no money or other material item could ever compare to. This experience has fortified me, and I return to this moment often to relive it.

Thank you Prophet for taking me to this glorious ocean where I was blessed to hear God tell me "I love you." People have always told me that God loves me but hearing and experiencing it for myself made me understand the truth in this statement. God truly does love me. Really knowing this has forever changed me.

Written by Emily Allred

I Held Her in Heaven

We all, as Soul, live many many lifetimes. During our earthly incarnations we develop love connections with other Souls, and often we are blessed to reincarnate with the same Souls to continue our journey together. The following is a beautiful story of a mother-to-be meeting her future daughter in the inner spiritual worlds.

I have a daughter who is nearly two and a half years old. My pregnancy with her almost seems like a dream now. I can recall snippets, but mostly I remember the wondering and the waiting. A lot of that goes on in nine months. "What will she be like? Will we get along?" As first-time parents my husband and I really had no clue what to expect. While much of this time is fading from memory there is one experience I had while pregnant I will never forget. It has forever changed the way I see my daughter, and the way I view our family. Prophet allowed me to meet and hold my daughter, before she was born, in Heaven.

I was five months pregnant while at a retreat at Guidance for a Better Life. This is one of my favorite places to be. As a group we sang HU and focused on sending our love and gratitude to God. In the quietude after singing HU I left my body spiritually, as Soul, and Prophet took me to Heaven, our true home. Each journey to this sacred place has been different. Each visit has helped me, degree by degree, to understand the tremendous love God has for me personally and for all of His creation.

This time, I knelt with Prophet at the edge of God's Ocean. It was night and the water was calm. It was a gift of love from God to see it this way because there is a special beauty to me about the physical ocean at nighttime. I could feel the presence of God's Love and peace all around me and in me. I savored being in the moment experiencing the quiet stillness, like being held in a loving embrace.

Just being allowed to be here was a most incredible thing, and yet Prophet gave me another personal and sacred blessing. I looked out across the water to see a beautiful being of light emerge from the velvety depths of God's Ocean. This being was in a female form. As the being came closer I saw she was carrying something, and to my surprise it was the Soul that would be my future daughter, Camille. The beautiful being stood in front of me holding this precious Soul in her arms, as one would cradle a cherished baby. Camille was made of God's Light and Sound. The way she moved in this being's arms was the same as in my womb, as though bursting to get out, a literal bundle of joy.

The being of light silently handed Camille to me with care, and I was allowed to hold her for a moment. It did not feel like my daughter and I were meeting for the first time. It was more a reunion of two Souls happy to see each other once again. I loved her and she loved me. How incredible to know the Soul being born into my family was indeed a Soul I had known and loved before. I was speechless. To be here in Heaven was amazing in itself, but I was also being reunited with a Soul that was to be my future daughter. Now I was even more excited and could not wait for her to be born. I could not wait for the moment when she, Soul, would animate her physical body; the moment when she would take her first breath of life in this world, and I could kiss her sweet face.

Then I gave her back to the being of light who returned into God's Ocean. I was filled with wonder and appreciation that God allowed us to meet in this sacred place. Soul, being eternal, is ageless, yet I was allowed to meet her in the form she would be taking in her new physical embodiment, that of my daughter. In this way I could hold her as I was so longing to do. This was a stunning gift from God.

Being allowed to meet my daughter before she was born into this life taught me more about the remarkable love God has for each Soul. I learned that Soul is a child of God whose true home is in Heaven. Our sons and daughters are not randomly selected, but are given to us with purpose by God's loving design. It does not matter if we are born into a family or adopted. Our families are part of a love story that started before this lifetime and will continue into future lives. In His timing God will reconnect us with our loved ones again.

I am so grateful Camille joined our family, and I can love her again. She is such a delight! I look forward to the day when I can share with her the story of how I held her in Heaven.

Written by Carmen Snodgrass

Before the Source of All

When you recognize the Love of God is in every aspect of your life, the little things and even the minor annoyances look different. To actually be taken on a spiritual journey to the source of God's Love puts things in perspective even more. It can inspire one to be a point of light for others so they too may return home.

As a student of Del Hall, the God-ordained Prophet of our times, I have been shown how to recognize the many blessings in my life, to listen to Spirit in the stillness of my heart, and to recognize who I really am — Soul, a spiritual being loved immeasurably and unconditionally by God. These truths are keys to a more abundant life God makes available to us through the teachings of His Prophet. There is no disconnect between God's Love for us, whether it be at the top of the spiritual mountain or in our daily lives. Knowing this is comforting; experiencing it is truly special.

It was the summer of 2014. I was at our annual retreat known to students at Guidance for a Better Life as "Reunion." During the retreat we were spiritually taken by Prophet to our physical homes. I was shown the amazing amount of love there. Everything in my home and around it was a gift from God. God's Love was there in my family, all our interactions, and in the laughter and the love we shared. It was also in things I saw as the minor annoyances of daily life such as the messy piles of children's clothes on the floor. The piles meant there were plenty of clothes for the kids, many of which were hand-me-down gifts from a dear friend. There was a working washing machine and dryer to clean them and three beautiful children to wear the clothes. There were also many subtler gifts; I did not realize how much they touched my heart, such as the amazing view of the sunset I often admired from my porch at the end of the day. All was by God's Love and Grace. It was amazing to witness.

As I was spiritually standing in my home, I was then shown the source of this love. I was taken by Prophet to the Abode of God, taken before the source of all! Here, from everywhere and from everything, came love. It too was God's Love, the same love I experienced in my home, but on a scale that was unimaginable. It was like being so close to the sun you could not see anything that was not the sun. All of creation originated here. I was humbled and in awe. As I knelt before the Almighty I felt my capacity to love stretched beyond my comprehension. I actively received more and more, finding my innate way to gratefully accept God's Love. Prophet's spiritual presence kneeling beside me was also humbling. His teachings, guidance, and love brought me to the source of all, yet here he too knelt in reverence. His love for me as Soul, and his devotion to God inspires me daily. Appreciation overwhelmed me. I cannot put into words the gratitude I felt at that moment.

As my consciousness returned to my physical body at the retreat center, I had a nudge to open a specific book. I opened to a page of scripture that described the Voice of God traveling out from Heaven like a wave, carrying all life with it and then returning back to the Source, bringing with It those Souls ready to serve God. The paragraph resonated perfectly with my experience! As I read this, still basking in the jaw-dropping wonder of my experience, I spiritually heard another layer of insight, as if spoken directly to my heart: "And now we are sent out again, not in ignorance, but in knowingness; not in darkness, but as points of light; not in forgetfulness, but to remind other Souls; no longer lost in the wilderness, but to help others find you again." The words emphasized to me that as a student at Guidance for a Better Life I have received so much, experiencing the glories of God many times over — love, blessings, insights, healings, clarity, and peace. My cup truly runneth over! Now the opportunity has come to give back in a greater measure and to share my gratitude and appreciation for God's teachings.

This experience helped me to more consciously recognize the Love of the Heavenly Father that flows in my life. There is something special about recognizing the love in one's life and its source. Whether it is through a child, a spouse, a pet, or a beautiful sunset — love is love. It blesses us from On High. As I look now at the view in my home I still see heavenly love.

With Prophet we have the ability to return to the Source. Yet God's Love is not reserved solely for the Heavenly realms. It is everywhere throughout our lives. Prophet can help us recognize the love that sits like unopened presents under the Christmas tree. It may be disguised as a messy pile of clothes, a sink full of dirty dishes, or toys strewn across the living room floor, but God's Love is there. Del has helped me to see the love and abundance throughout my life. Recognizing it on a daily basis and expressing my appreciation and gratitude for it has only made it multiply. The Prophet is here now to help those who are ready to follow the calling of their heart and witness God's Love for themselves, here and now.

Written by Chris Comfort

The Throne of God

As beautiful as this Earth is, it is but a pale shadow of the inner Heavenly Worlds. Those fortunate to be taken there spiritually by Prophet know this well. Even so, it is in this physical world where we live and love and serve. Cherish your time here.

In the winter of 2012 I was blessed to kneel before the mighty Throne of God. While I was singing HU, the Prophet of our times Del Hall, raised me spiritually from my body to the heights of Heaven. I perceived it as an ocean, where the rhythmic waves were not composed of water but of endless Love and Grace. Prophet led me, swimming through the shining waves. Light came from all directions, below the water and above, filling me with gentle peace and joy. As we swam farther from the shore the light grew whiter and more bright.

We crossed into a realm beyond description. The light around us flowed together to create a room, with walls and all within it made of the same pure, dancing light. There were others in the room, all kneeling down in reverence to the Lord. I knelt as well, with joy, so grateful to have reached this sacred place. Beneath my knees there lay a carpet made of light leading to the Throne of God Himself. My eyes moved along this path until they came to rest upon His shining Throne.

And there appeared the figure of the Lord. I know what my eyes could see was but a fraction of His true, eternal self. With Eyes so filled with Love, He gazed out from His Throne and spoke a single sound. At first it seemed to be the faintest whisper. Yet from His lips came forth such Love and Power, in all directions, that I'm sure it reached the boundaries of creation. The loving power of His Voice rushed through me like a mighty wind. It stripped away impurity and left the real me: my true, eternal self. As His Voice kept moving through me, two words came to mind: duty and responsibility.

As the vision faded, the song of HU resumed within me. Slowly my eyes opened, and I could see this world for the shadow that it is, a quickly fading flame beneath the greater worlds above. Yet in this world lay the duty and responsibility. These tasks are not a burden, but a joy and blessing to fulfill. With each day comes the chance to make this blessing a reality. To live each moment kneeling, in my inner heart of hearts, before the Throne of God. To live as Soul, the real me, my true eternal self, and follow Prophet's guidance throughout my daily life. To do this is a privilege. It makes my life a joy to live and fills it with abundance.

God always has a living Prophet here on Earth to help us, to raise us into Heaven and guide our daily lives. Seek truth with a pure heart, and you will find the Prophet of our times. He is the Living Word, the link between the Throne of God and man.

Written by David Hughes

A Visit Home

All must go through the Son to get to the Father; this is the way it has always been. In John 14:26 Jesus states quite clearly, "I am the way, the truth, and the life: no man cometh unto the Father, but by me." In the following testimony of spiritually traveling into the Heavens to meet God, it's about as literal as it gets. The Prophet, in the "role of Son of God," though not literally, is the way home to God.

At a spiritual retreat I was graced with the following experience in which I was taken back to my true home to be with my Heavenly Father. One evening a group of students sat with Prophet and we sang HU. The sound was so sweet. Sitting with Prophet in itself is a huge gift as it blesses all in his presence. I gratefully sang expressing the love I have for my Heavenly Father. Shortly after closing my eyes, I found myself face to face with Prophet on the inner and experienced the deep love I have for him, and he has for me. When escorted by a true representative of God, as Soul we are able to travel throughout the Heavens and can even be taken to the Ocean of Love and Mercy, the Abode of God. On this day, it was to this magnificent place that we were invited.

There are many levels of insight to go through to truly understand something, but to know it deeply, beyond a shadow of doubt, comes only through experience. To consciously experience the Light and Sound of God in any form is a gift of grace and to be taken to this Ocean, before God, our Heavenly Father is a gift, the magnitude of which cannot be expressed in words. As if on an elevator, we traveled up through the spiritual planes on God's beam of Light and Sound and arrived upon a magnificent beach. As we arrived I dropped to my knees and wept, as I was overcome with a feeling of sacredness, gratitude, and joy. Our true self is Soul, a Divine spark of God, and our true home is in this amazing Ocean of God's Love and Mercy.

Both Prophet and I were on the beach at the water's edge, heads bowed. Before us there was an incredibly vast, sparkling, beautiful ocean as far as my spiritual eye could see. It was breathtaking, with a crystal clear blue sky, a gentle caressing breeze, and living water. The waves gently rolled in as if to greet us, and then the ocean stilled completely. Toward the horizon the water's surface began to shimmer and bubble, and out of the ocean arose a brilliant light truly brighter than the light of ten thousand suns; though this description doesn't really do justice to what I witnessed as this is not a light that can be compared to anything in the physical world. Within the light was the Great Heavenly Father. There are no words glorious enough to explain what I was allowed to experience. At that instant, to my core, I felt completely enveloped and saturated through and through with God's Divine Love, Mercy, and peace.

Shortly after I felt a shift, and though I still experienced God in all His Glory and magnificence, He now manifested Himself in a way that was much more personal. In awe, I stood at the water's edge and once again felt the soothing waves as they gently rolled in upon me. I felt my heartbeat quicken as I was invited into the living water, into the ocean, by God Himself. I was slowly and lovingly drawn forward by a wave of love returning back to Its source in the center of everything, back to God. He gently scooped me up in His loving Hands and then into an all-encompassing, welcoming embrace. I was held by my Heavenly Father, reminding me of a long forgotten memory deep in my core. To this day I can still see, experience, and relive that moment and know some part of me is still graced to be present there with Him. At home again in my Father's arms I felt secure, nurtured, nourished, loved, joyous, and complete. He then raised me up and kissed me on the forehead. I was allowed to gaze deeply into His Eyes as He looked into mine. It was at that moment I was once again overcome with emotion, for I truly knew how much I am loved! I cannot over emphasize the significance, the feeling that it brought, and the profound realization that it was and is. To truly know God loves me is a gift of grace beyond measure.

The next thing I remembered I was back on the beach next to Prophet, I was weeping on my knees with a true joy like never before. Not only did I know how much I am loved by God, but also how much I love God and His Prophet. I wish I could bottle what Prophet and God gave me that day and share it with you, actually share it with everyone. For if everyone knew how much they are loved, truly loved by God, it would change everything!

My hope and prayer is that this testimony will inspire you to do whatever it takes to seek out a Divine relationship for yourself. To reach out to Prophet, whether through reading scripture, or singing HU at home in private contemplation. There is nothing separating you from this relationship, for he is already with you, deep in your own heart. All you have to do is ask with a sincere desire as it says in John 16:24 KJV, "Hitherto have ye asked nothing in my name: ask, and ye shall receive, that your joy may be full." God truly does love each one of us, as we are all His children.

Written by Jason Levinson

The Return to Heaven

God sent Souls to Earth from the Heavenly Worlds to grow in their ability to give and receive love and learn about giving back to life through service to others. We have not been sent on this journey alone. The Prophet, in the role of Son of God, has been right there with us the whole time and is ultimately the way home. The following is an incredible account from someone who experienced this round-trip journey during a contemplation.

Cool, crisp October air brushed the side of my left arm. Beyond the water of the pond, orange-gold and yellow leaves reached up into the clear blue sky like steeples crowning nature's church. The timeless beauty of the mountains nearly took my breath away. Gradually I closed my eyes. A song of HU began and grew, and I began to sing along. An amazing group of Souls, who devote their lives and hearts to God, filled the mountains with their sacred song.

We sang the purest song we could, asking nothing in return. My heart opened to the Love of God. It poured in like a waterfall. Had it been there all along?

While my outer eyes were closed, my inner vision opened wide. Somewhat like a dream, colors danced before my eyes. As we continued singing HU a form appeared in front of me. God's Prophet was before me, and he took me on a journey I would not soon forget. He took me to the golden shores of Heaven. Gentle waves were lapping on an endless sandy beach. Golden light, abundant joy, and boundless creativity filled the air with utter bliss. Splashing in the water made me feel just like a child again. What joy! What peace! What wonder here!

Suddenly and violently, everything began to shake. A mighty rumble filled the world with words I could not understand. Words like thunder — loud and low. The floor of Heaven cracked and split! Below, a dark and dismal pit. A new sensation — gravity — pulled me into the abyss, but I was not alone. Scores of Souls were screaming, tumbling deep into the lightless hole. Deeper, deeper, down and down, it seemed the fall would never end. Yet I felt another presence too, one serene, calm, and benign. The Son of God was holding me, protecting me within his arms. At first I screamed and pulled and clawed, a vain attempt to climb back up. Regardless of my struggle, I just kept falling down. So then I begged, I cried, and prayed. "Please take me home! Please take me home!" But still to no avail. The Mighty One who carried me just seemed to smile in response.

At last when all my hope was lost, I rested in the mighty arms of Prophet. I relaxed into his loving hold and felt his love surround me; the arms of strength, the arms of peace, the arms of everlasting love. I found I needed nothing else, even in this endless pit. No longer did I struggle, no longer did I beg — for everything I'd ever need was here, and now, with him. I rested in his strength and leaned into Prophet's chest. His heart opened and enveloped me. Within it was a door. A door of light. I entered it and then to my surprise, I was once again upon the sands of Heaven's ocean shore. Familiar breaking waves of gold and sand beneath my feet — and then I knew without a doubt I'd never really left.

But somehow I was different now. I was not here to splash and play, self-serving in God's Love. Having once lost this realm of bliss, on my return I loved it all the more. No longer did I feel it was a place to serve my selfish needs. Heaven is a place to give, to serve with all you have. On bended knee I lowered down onto the golden ocean shore and thanked the Lord, the God Most High, for the journey I'd been on.

I'd learned a lot from my round-trip within Prophet's arms. You don't find God by searching, scrambling, trying to climb to Him. You don't find God by begging, pleading, praying to get home. You find God when you love His Prophet, love His Son, with all your heart, with all your mind, and with all you are. And when you return home to God, you may find you've never left. But don't expect to be the same as you were before the trip, for the journey will have taught you much; much more than words can say.

God always has a Prophet here on Earth to lead us home. The Prophet now is Del Hall, and he lives in Virginia. He's reaching out his hand to you — will you take hold? Will you accept?

Written by David Hughes

It's a Gift to Thank God

What if you could know with complete certainty that God is real and have an opportunity to thank Him at His eternal Home for the gift of life? Thanks to Prophet Del Hall, some fortunate Souls have been blessed with such a gift.

During a weeklong spiritual retreat we began a long contemplation. Prophet led us in singing the names of many of the great Souls who have served as the Prophet of the times in the past. These are Souls who have been ordained by God and given the sacred responsibility of leading Soul home to Him. We sang the names as a beautiful form of prayer, and my heart filled with gratitude and appreciation for how the Prophet has always been with us, in one form or another, over the course of history. After a while, I knew we had arrived at the Abode of God.

The Presence of God was very real, more real than anything on this Earth, although I cannot describe exactly what God looked like. There is no need to, for the love that came out of God and enveloped me was real enough. This is the eternal love that God always has for His children, a love that never fails, a love that you can trust with complete certainty is always there for you and me, and all of His creation. I heard the voice of the Prophet tell us that we now had an opportunity to write, in our heart, a thank you note to God. As I knelt upon what appeared to be a beach, one composed of light and sound at the edge of the vast ocean of God's Love, I began to express my gratitude for what God has blessed me with. I thanked the Lord for the gift of Him creating me as Soul, an eternal being made of God's Light and Sound. It is such a privilege simply to exist. I also thanked God for the stunning gift of Him having given us a Prophet who leads Soul home to God.

I then became more aware of the Prophet kneeling upon the shores of this vast ocean beside me; he was filled with love and reverence for his Creator. The love and appreciation I felt for Prophet, the one who had taken me and other beautiful Souls home to God, was a deep love, deeper than feelings alone can express. It was a beautiful true love for the one who has been a constant companion, guide, teacher, healer, and liberator of Soul throughout the ages. In this moment with him, in the Presence of the Lord, I knew that my love for him is the key to our enduring relationship, one that has existed throughout the ages. It is a relationship that leads to a true love relationship with God.

Once you begin to express gratitude to God for His blessings, how do you ever stop? Each expression of gratitude led me to recognize another blessing and yet another blessing. Nevertheless, there came a point when I knew it was time to stop writing with the hands of Soul, and I reached out to give my note to the giant Hand of God. The Lord graciously accepted my expression of gratitude as He took the note with His Hand and reverentially placed it within His Heart. I know from this experience that God truly appreciates it when we express our gratitude to Him for the gifts He has given us over eternity. To know God appreciates me for who I am and has a personal love for me within His Heart is a true blessing. It is one that can uplift me on days when I do not feel as loved as I did during that precious moment in front of Him. Perhaps the greatest gift from this journey home to God is that it allowed me to recognize everything in life is a gift from God.

When my consciousness eventually returned to my physical self here on Earth, I was amazed by what we had been given. It was a gift I know would not have been possible without God having created a Prophet, ordained by Him, to take us home to His eternal Abode. I was filled with deep peace that night and went to sleep conscious of the real me, Soul, still being at the Ocean of God's Love. It is a truly peaceful place in which to rest, far from the worries and concerns of daily life and the restlessness of the mind. As profound as the blessing we were given that summer evening was, the blessings have continued.

Every day God continues to pour out His blessings into my life, like a river flowing out of a boundless ocean that never runs out of water. The blessings include the one of being able to wake up every morning, knowing that another day awaits me with new opportunities to give and receive love. The path that day may lead to some unexpected places, or some obstacles that are not easy to go through, but I have learned to trust it will all work out in my best spiritual interests. This is because we have been blessed with the perfect guide, the Prophet, to help us navigate our way and lead us to an abundant life of love, peace, joy, the clarity of Soul, and all blessings God has to give us.

Written by Roland Vonder Muhll

\

Ordained by God

This third section of "Traveling the Heavens" shares examples of my students being ordained by God Himself at His primary Abode. All God's chosen Prophets throughout history have been ordained by God, but in a very different way than in the following stories. Most of my serious students have had experiences similar to these five stories you are about to read. I shared just five stories but believe that is enough for you to know what is possible with Prophet and sufficient effort. Each Soul received to their measure. I did not feel it best to share the writer's names in this final section. These experiences of Soul are far too sacred to casually share with the world. These Souls are now spiritual teachers in training and are used to guide and bless those who wish to learn God's ways and truth. They are now the sacred and trusted inner circle of God's Prophet, and their duties are not taken lightly. They carry the inner Prophet with them, bringing Light to all who are receptive.

Ordained by God Testimony One

On several sacred occasions during Reunions at Guidance for a Better Life, we were ordained by God. To say we were blessed with a rare and special gift is an understatement. It is a privilege beyond description. Like many of the blessings and experiences God has bestowed upon us at the retreats, we were lovingly and methodically conditioned for this during the preceding years by His Prophet, Del Hall, so when the time came we could accept the immense love behind the gift and remain in balance. He also ensured we had a certain degree of spiritual maturity to handle this responsibility and a certain amount of experience and understanding of the eternal teachings in this lifetime to know what we were signing up to do.

One of these special experiences occurred while attending our Reunion in July 2007. Prophet had taken us on an inner spiritual travel to the Abode of God, something in itself a rare and glorious blessing. I was standing next to Prophet at the edge of a great ocean of God's Love. He asked us to extend our right arm at a 45-degree angle and point our index finger. We all have free will and God would never force this gift on any Soul. He asked us to answer individually in our hearts, if we would like to be ordained to serve God at whatever level was right for us. I affirmed that, "Yes, absolutely I wanted to be ordained." God's Finger came out and down toward me and touched mine. White hot energy, God's Holy Spirit, ran through my fingers, down my arm, and then through my body. I kept my finger out as long as I could. My breathing was very deep and heavy as wave upon wave of Divine love came into me and ran through me. I wanted to stay connected and did not want to let go. I breathed in everything I could of this experience and felt it changing me inside. Eventually I had accepted all I could handle and had to let go. Del IV, Del Hall's son, was sitting next to me during this and gently put his hand on my shoulder. It was reassuring and helped support me in receiving what was being delivered through the awesome rawness of this Divine love direct from God Himself. Prophet helped us understand the magnitude of what occurred, at least as much as we were capable of grasping at the time. We were ordained as Soul, not our physical embodiment and thus, this gift will carry forward with us beyond this lifetime. We were now authorized by God to serve at whatever level we could, to share the eternal teachings we have been taught, and help Souls find the Prophet of our times and the Source. He helped us see how in this Divine gift of love, God was also putting future events in order, predetermining and predestining those we would be led to teach or bless in some way, perhaps arranging circumstances for us to meet certain people or providing experiences that would help prepare us and those Souls with which we would someday interact. It would act as a time release gift that would release its endowments to us over time providing all we need to serve in whatever way we are called to be instruments of God. We were fundamentally changed by this forever. We were now Agents for God, no matter where we are, no matter where we go after this lifetime, for eternity. Wow!

The second time I was ordained occurred during the 2010 Reunion. Prophet once again having taken us on an inner spiritual adventure, provided us the special opportunity to visit the Abode of God. We were blessed with amazing experiences of being held in God's Hand and taken into His Heart, allowed to witness the miraculous power contained in a single drop of water in God's Ocean of Love, and come to know a few aspects of the infinite reality of God. At one point during all this I was sitting at the water's edge with Prophet and was looking into the water. When told, I looked up with my arm outstretched and pointed my finger. I saw another aspect of God, His endless, expansive Eyes looking at me, surrounded by a swirling mass of white, curly hair. His finger was outstretched toward me. I knew what a huge blessing this was and had appreciation for the rarity of this gift because of the first ordaining experience three years earlier. I gazed into His Eyes as our fingers touched and the connection made. I was eager to receive this gift and wanted to accept all I could, so I asked Prophet to help me accept all I could handle (all he knew I could handle). God then said, "If you have the courage, accept even more." I continued to hold my eyes fixed on His. He looked deeply into me, and I knew I was being personally recognized by God. This was not by random chance that I was receiving this gift. He intended it for me and the other Souls chosen to be ordained this time. He said, "Okay that's enough."

Once again, I found it hard to let this connection go and continued looking into His Eyes. I was drawn into them. My chest was heaving as I breathed in and out deeply as if I was doing a really intense workout, but I didn't feel I was overdoing it. It felt like I had been properly trained and prepared for this, and I was. Afterwards, I stood on the beach with Prophet and felt pumped with life, energy, enthusiasm, appreciation, and Love. I hugged him, and we walked to a spot on the beach that was shaded by palm trees and had nice rocks to sit on. We shared a toast to celebrate this special occasion with ocean water (actually God's Light) in crystal clear goblets he had for us. We sat and looked out over the ocean at a brilliant starburst of light, and I knew what I was seeing was yet another of the many, many ways to experience God. I wanted for nothing and could have stayed there forever!

In June of 2013, the group of us attending Reunion were ordained again. A prayer I had at the start of this Reunion as I surrendered and yielded the week to Prophet, was to be stretched spiritually and for my heart to be expanded with a greater capacity to love. Prophet took us to the Abode of God. When we arrived I was on my knees and my head bowed. Knowing what a privilege it was to be there made it even sweeter as I savored this precious opportunity. We began to sing Sugmad (one of the ancient and Holy names of God) and ended by saying, "I accept your Love!" What a beautiful song this was, it opened my heart. When asked to look up, extend our right arm, and point our index finger, I did so with conviction and zeal. I saw a brilliant-white shower of light and sound, energy — Love coming toward me. Whatever was coming I wanted to accept it with all I am. I accepted all I could then still more. God said, "Accept even more, as much as you can." So I asked to accept all that Prophet knew I could handle and then asked for more once again. What came seemed to come in distinct waves. It was like each request to accept more was responded to by God by another intense wave of love. It was indescribable. I was so full of Light and Sound, God's Love. Then He said, "Go be with Prophet." I looked into Prophet's eyes, such deep love exchanged between us. I thanked him for bringing me there. I began to feel a sharp sensation in my chest area that spread to my neck and down my right side (right side is symbolic to me of the inner and spiritual, left being the outer, material or physical). I knew this was not a negative thing, and I had no fear or worry. I only felt trust that it was a good thing whatever was happening. I attributed this to what had just occurred in my Soul body on the inner. The massive amount of Divine love of God was working Its way into all my bodies on all the planes, now appearing as some physical discomfort. I had the sense I was being stretched, and my heart was expanding as this occurred. It was an answer to my prayer! Prophet put his hand on my heart to sooth the intensity of the feeling. It did not just go away though, it felt as if it was being digested and becoming part of me on all levels.

That night, I dreamed I had gotten a new job with a higher security clearance and authorization. A formal announcement was made and printed on a yellow flier that was sent around. I was given new access to special rooms where special satellite data was brought down to the ground. There were three particularly special satellites brought together there that were usually not. In the dream I was getting familiarized with my new position, office, and people I would be working with, and my responsibilities. I saw this dream as acknowledging the ordination and helping me integrate this new role by making it operational in my daily life, much like learning a new job.

In reflecting back on these sacred experiences, I now see how the three ordinations that occurred in 2007, 2010, and 2013 were a process. They gave us an opportunity to accept as much of the gift as we could at that time, then allowed for a period of a few years afterwards to acclimate to the Divine love we received, and integrate the reality of what occurred into our awareness. It also gave us time to practice putting it into operation by stepping up to our calling and stepping out in our mission, in increasingly open and public ways. Part of acclimating was also gaining a deeper realization that I was not only born to answer God's calling but created to answer it. I became more aware of how deep and ancient this desire to serve God is in me. It has been there since I was created eons ago, when I was set apart for this purpose. It is encoded in the very beingness of who I am, and it brings indescribable peace, happiness, and contentment being able to fulfill this yearning in my heart.

I did not casually accept what was being offered on these three occasions, however; it continues to be a joyous opportunity and a sacred privilege to serve God through His Prophet that carries with it certain responsibilities. These responsibilities include: keeping myself nourished and in tune with Prophet, so he can advise and guide me to what is best for each individual I am led to; putting that Soul's best spiritual interests first; helping them find the Prophet and the eternal teachings by supporting and guiding them as needed; and very importantly, doing no harm.

Accepting this gift also meant I was committing to serve God and His cause. Specifically this includes Prophet's mission to remove any barriers or walls between God and His children so they know they are loved, and it is possible to have a personal relationship with God their Father. It also meant I would help uphold and defend God's Spiritual Laws, keep the eternal teachings alive and pure, share them with others, and help them find the Living Prophet of our times, so they too may find their way home to the Heart of God. This has been a dream come true and fulfills an everlasting desire to love and serve the Lord God. Thank you God and Prophet for allowing me to be me and for allowing this joy-filled, sacred privilege to be so.

Ordained by God Testimony Two

The experiences I share of almost inexplicable gifts from God are far beyond what I can depict in a relatively short testimony. They are living gifts from a Living God that are timeless. It is also important to note what is written here is not the totality of any aspect of the Divine I have perceived. In June of 2007, 2010, and 2013 I was taken to the primary Abode of God as Soul by Prophet via spiritual travel and ordained by God. The first one came in 2007. Lifetimes worth of wisdom and blessings were imparted in what was called a weeklong retreat. These are a few of the highlights I recall.

It was the beginning of summer, but the weather was quite chilly on the mountain throughout the week. During this retreat we went into contemplation led by the Prophet Del Hall. He guided us in spiritual travel through many Heavens. As we passed through each Heaven we stopped at various Temples of God. We were allowed to interact with past Prophets and thank them for their service and sacrifice on our behalf. These were teachers many of us have had in past lives. My love for them was still very much alive and theirs for me. Some of the students, including myself, were shown significant snippets of past lifetimes with these beautiful Souls. Some of the experiences were discussed during the retreat and further insights gained as Del helped debrief what happened. Our whole class ended up in a vast expanse of peace, light, and love much greater than those we had passed through to get to this destination. It seemed as though we were being lifted up on a spiritual elevator by Del.

As I looked out, my perception was drawn to many Souls humbly paying reverence to an aspect of their Heavenly Father. Each of us was able to sing HU while being very close to an aspect of God. Some were face to face, while others lay in God's Hand. Still others rested peacefully in this presence never leaving their knees. It was unique for each of us. I recall being given a garment of white light here, as the Prophet helped me accept this gift and wear it confidently. It was the armor of God and so much more. What is contained in such a gift I ask myself sometimes. Security, protection, strength, and love are some of the qualities of this gift. They have helped me get where I am today and continue to help me grow. There is so much to this one gift I could write a whole book on it.

At home in the very Heart of God, I was ordained. On my knees, I reached out my right hand as if reaching for life itself. I trembled in awe and anticipation of the greatness that beheld my vision. A flow of radiant heat, in the form of an energetic impulse went into my being. I perceived my right finger being touched by God. I knew this was a major blessing, but still scarcely recognized the significance. The latter two ordainments allowed me to grasp what had occurred more deeply, and as I grow, my reverence for this experience grows. As I put on the garment given to me by God, I gained some of the spiritual strength needed to accept my first ordination; the ability to live in accord with Divine obedience, discernment, loyalty, and truth. It takes conditioning to be able to accept such a blessing. I have come to know that access to these gifts does require living in agreement with the ways of God. The Prophet continues to show me these ways and help me stay attuned to them. It is an active way of life, where one stays spiritually nourished and awake, by remembering and going back to reflect on what was experienced.

I received my second and third ordainment's similarly in 2010 and 2013. I remember looking up the definition of ordination at that time. "Conferring holy orders on someone" was one definition. Another that seemed to stick with me was "Being put in order." My life was put in order by God, and I was given the most humble authority for God to speak through me via the testimonies I share. I have the sacred honor to share my gifts with you. They help remind me of my Divine birthright. I live in this world, but am not of it. I am not just a body with a Soul. I am Soul that is eternal and does not perish with the flesh. The same is true for you dear reader.

You too can develop a relationship with the Divine through the Prophet of our times. Be inspired that it is not as simple as Heaven and hell. There are many Heavens, each one appropriate to the Souls inhabiting them. Take comfort that we are not obliged to learn everything there is to learn in one lifetime. We are given many lifetimes to absorb and integrate the lessons of living. Many opportunities to learn and grow under the tutelage of trained Prophets. What I say to you is true. It is real. As real as the times I was taken by the Prophet to the Heavenly Father. As real as it was when I knelt before the Great One and put out my right index finger as His touched mine; as real as the immense stability contained in those moments of eternity. As real as it was then, it is now. I have shared a mere fraction of some of the gifts of God with you. There is always more.

Ordained by God Testimony Three

As a little girl growing up I went to Sunday school where I especially loved to sing the song, "Jesus Loves Me." I sang it in my little girl voice, "Jesus loves me this I know, for the Bible tells me so..."

I knew God loved me for the Bible said so, but God and Jesus seemed so far away. As I grew older, like a small seed inside me, a yearning for God began to grow. It sprouted and grew, and I was about fourteen or fifteen years old when I knew and voiced the prayer in my heart. I was alone in our basement listening to the Neil Diamond song, "Brother Love's Traveling Salvation Show." When Neil said, "Take your hand and put it out to the man up there; that's what he is there for," I looked up, I reached my hand up as high as I could reach, and I looked up to Him. I couldn't see Him, I couldn't sense Him, I couldn't touch Him, but I knew He was out there. I so wanted God to take my hand as I reached up to Him. With tears streaming down my face, I begged to God as I sang along, "Take my hand dear Lord, walk with me this day, in my heart I know, I will never stray..."

I grew up and had forgotten about this experience, though I still had a deep yearning inside of me. I began going to Guidance for a Better Life where Del taught us how to listen to God's communication to us. He taught us to sing HU, a love song to God. Singing HU is a beautiful way to express our love to God, and it helps us listen to Him better. One day Del led us in contemplation where he, as Prophet, took us to God's Ocean of Love. It was an immense ocean of love that went on forever. I found myself kneeling in reverence on the soft sand at the water's edge with Prophet beside me.

It was very peaceful as tiny waves lapped at the sand. I looked up and saw God looking at me with an immense amount of love in His Eyes. I saw His Hand reaching out to me. I stretched up my hand towards God's with all of my being. I so wanted to touch Him. As God gently touched my finger, brilliant white light that felt like love, flowed through my hand, down my arm, and filled my whole being.

More and more light and love flowed into me as I took in all I could. After it stopped, I was still kneeling on the sand, but I was changed forever. God had reached down, touched my hand, and filled me with His Love, transforming me in a way words cannot describe. I was now different, I would say "more," than I was just moments before. I looked up and saw Prophet smiling beside me, looking at me with such joy and happiness. He had spent many years preparing and conditioning me for this moment, to be ordained by the Heavenly Father. I was so grateful to him for bringing me to God's Ocean, making this amazing experience possible.

After this experience I remembered my deep prayer and reaching up to God many years ago. My prayer was answered in a way that was so much more than I could have imagined. In those moments before God, not only did He fill me with His Love and transform me, but He ordained me. All of us blessed Souls brought to the Abode of God by His Prophet that day, to stand before God, were ordained to be a co-worker of God. We were ordained to pass on God's Love that flows through God's Prophet to us, and then as God wills it, to bless others. It was made possible by Prophet. Only a true Prophet of God can take you safely into the inner spiritual worlds and to the Abode of God Himself. Prophet is the way; Prophet is the only way to go home to God. As Jesus said, "I am the way, the truth, and the life: no man cometh unto the Father, but by me." John 14:6 KJV God's current Prophet is the way for Souls today. God loves us so much that He always has a living Prophet on Earth to lead us to Him. Through my love and trust for Prophet he took my hand, and he brought me face to face with God. Wow.

Ordained by God Testimony Four

God reached down and touched me. My hand, outstretched as high as I could reach, as His immense Hand reached down to touch me. By the Grace of God I was given this experience. Here is my story.

We had been silent for some time, singing HU and journeying inward following the prompting and guidance of our teacher, Prophet Del Hall. We were safely traveling the vast inner worlds with a God-ordained Prophet at our sides. At each Heaven, we rested briefly thanking the guardians and teachers present, before continuing on to the Abode of God at the twelfth Heaven. I had traveled here by Divine grace and the guidance of my teacher before. Much like a mountain climber needs conditioning to become acclimated to the altitude before traveling further up the mountain, we had received conditioning as well. Each brief rest in the Heavens allowed us to acclimate to the intensity of the love which was present.

Now we were here. Peace is too small of a word to describe the vast stillness and peacefulness that permeated every atom of Heaven. There were no disruptions here. No distractions. An ocean full of God's Love stretched out as far as I could see. I knelt before my Creator's creation, my heart singing in praise. Then Del called us to stand before the Ocean while looking down. When we looked up, we would see an aspect of God. Words in the physical world can only capture so much of Heaven, much like a photograph can only capture so much of a moment. This moment in Heaven had life. A vibrancy. A fullness. A splendor.

Moments later, I saw an ocean well up out of the Ocean. It had a human like form which I perceived as flowing water, but It was actually light. We were instructed to raise our right hand and point our finger upward. At this point we could give permission for our finger to be filled with Divine love. God will not violate free will, and giving permission was essential. I gave complete permission. The form of God I saw was faceless, yet His immense Hand reached down to touch me. As His Love came into the tip of my finger, my finger felt as if it was burning with intensity, yet simultaneously His touch was gentle and soothing. Eventually, Del instructed us to put our hands down.

Then we were given the opportunity to touch our own hearts. I could feel my heartbeat respond to the Divine love which flowed through my finger. Next Del suggested we touch our third eye upon the middle of our forehead. I felt ripples of love vibrate throughout my body from just one touch of the Divine love that God had placed in my finger. Then Del encouraged us to look into our finger, and I saw God's Eyes, loving, pure, and familiar.

After several moments of silence, Del suggested we kneel to touch the Ocean. With a gentle touch of my finger, a tidal wave of God's Love grew across the Ocean joining and rippling with the other waves my fellow students sent. This wave looked like music dancing across the vast expanse, each touch of God's Love joining others in a crescendo.

Del spoke sharing that we had been ordained in the highest order — the Melchizedek Order. I knelt in appreciation, turning to and leaning onto Prophet on the inner who had led me to the twelfth Heaven and stood beside me as I stood before God. His presence calmed and comforted and fortified me. God's Love is glorious and wondrous, but also has an intensity and power when it is direct.

Like Michelangelo's masterpiece, of God reaching down to touch Adam, took many years to come to its full magnificence, this experience has taken many years to more fully manifest in my daily life. It is ongoing, and always will be, this painting has no end. In the physical, Michelangelo's painting faded over time, so too our memories can fade and need remembrance to be kept alive. I am so grateful God reached down to touch me. Daily, I pray for His Love to continue to flow through me in whatever manner He wills.

Ordained by God Testimony Five

One of the greatest joys for Soul is being allowed to pass on God's Love to another of God's children. It can come through in many ways, and we may each participate to our measure. Those who have been ordained by God are blessed with being able to pass on even greater amounts of God's Love.

In June of 2013, while at the weeklong retreat known fondly and accurately as "Reunion" at Guidance for a Better Life, God invited us, including me, to be ordained. Reunion is so filled with an abundance of love, joy, clarity, potential for growth, and friendship that it is more like a lifetime than a week. We began the first day with a joyous HU, a grateful love song to God, yielding the week to the Divine and declaring ourselves to be vehicles for the Divine. From the moment of this first HU, I felt we were welcomed into the Holy Abode of God.

During the week Del Hall, beloved Prophet, led us on an invitation from God to gather and travel spiritually to the primary Abode of God. We sang love right to God, through a HU song. I experienced myself with Prophet, lying face down on the sand of a vast sparkling and alive beach like no physical beach. Prophet led us to speak aloud these words, which came from my heart: "God loves me. He really does love me. He has always loved me. He will always love me. I am worthy of God's Love." We are worthy of His Love because He created us. He desires for us to experience His Love.

On this beach of God's Light and Sound, my heart was opened more to receive His Love directly, and to give love. I was invited to stand up, with my head down, my right arm held out with my index finger pointing up. I heard through the Voice of God we were being invited to be ordained by Him, and that it was necessary to accept His Love now, if we wanted, or we would not be ordained. I cannot have God's Love flow through me if I do not accept His Love. The love is always available, but accepting more of God's Love is an ongoing process for me. We signaled our hearts' intent by saying out loud, "I accept your love God!" I silently repeated this again and again as I perceived the Presence of the Lord and His Love above me.

With the intent of God, and my intent in accord with His, I was ordained. I knew by God's Grace, Mercy, intent, will, and action something had passed on to me through what would seem to be my outreached index finger of my right hand. At that moment I was open and receptive enough, through years of conditioning from Prophet, to accept this gift from God Itself. I fell back to the sand on the beach where Prophet was checking on me, and each of us, to make sure we were okay and in balance. I welcomed him and was comforted by his familiar presence and love. We sang a soft song to our Heavenly Father in a slow cadence of love and gratitude. I felt I could sing that song forever.

Being ordained by God for me was not seemingly dramatic like a bolt of lightning, and yet in every moment thereafter it became apparent I was changed. Initially after the experience I felt there was a large open core inside me, and my legs felt weightless. Breathing in, I could feel God's Love more. It was nourishing and freeing and gave me the ability to love God more, though my love for Him did not come close to His for me. Even after the week when I was home, concerns and worries continued to fall away. Love filled the larger open space inside me, and it felt like my body was hanging over the openness like a big shirt on a hanger. Daily experiences wove together and lit up as communication from the Divine. I saw more of God's blessings in all of life. However, being ordained was not about any sensations, though there were side effects of accepting more of God's Love and being touched by His Light and Sound. The extent of the intent of being ordained that I am aware of is, if I continue to team with the Prophet, I am more able to be a part of God's distribution of His Love and Light, when I continue to be receptive to God's will. Sharing blessings is truly the greatest reward of life.

I was ordained because of God's greatness, not my own. It was by His Grace, not anything I earned, though I have shown interest in the teachings of my spiritual teacher, Del the Prophet, for many years and developed a relationship of love and trust with him. One does not have to earn God's Love, however, individual effort does count. Prophet Del Hall has stated perhaps the most important passage in the Bible is, "Draw nigh to God, and He will draw nigh to you." James 4:8 KJV It was through God's Mercy that I, as my real self — Soul, was ordained. This manifests in seemingly small ways: a smile, listening, being aware that each person I interact with every day is also a spark of God, and doing everyday tasks in God's name.

Recently Prophet invited the public to the school, a rare opportunity to be in the presence of God's ordained Prophet, who is the Light Giver, to receive teachings and sing HU. Del spoke before we began the love song to God. After we sang HU we sat in silence. There was then time to share individual experiences. Many expressed receiving a personal form of God's Love, though the intent of the HU song was to send love, not get anything in return. Del said he hoped those new to the HU song would feel free to share it so others could experience sending love to God, and begin to receive God's Love more consciously. In fact, he said, he was ordaining by authority from God, everyone there to be able to share the HU, the love song to God, with others. It was quiet, perhaps not dramatic to everyone, but it was real for those who chose to accept this one aspect of an ordination. God so wants to bless His children. As His children we, as Soul, whether consciousness of it or not, have the same desire to bless others with the Divine blessings we have received. One of the greatest blessings and joys of Soul is to share God's Love with others.

Wow, You Are Still Reading

If you have made it this far and are excited at your new view of life and the possibilities it may bring, congratulations! If you are still feeling in balance and over any spiritual indigestion, so much the better. Not everyone is ready to accept this magnificent and expansive view of life in its entirety, and that is okay, God loves everyone and He will assure that their time will come for another opportunity, in this life or a future life.

Our Father always has a Prophet to guide His children to this higher understanding of life. When the time is right every child of God will have the opportunity to meet His current Prophet. When that **"opportunity of lifetimes"** does come, whether with this Prophet, or a future Prophet, one's spiritual growth often takes a giant leap forward, if they are receptive to him. A leap only available with God's personally chosen, trained, authorized, and spiritually empowered Prophet. God empowers His Prophets with the same love for Soul that His only Begotten Son has always had for us. God empowers His Prophets with the authority to share His Light and Love, to redeem, to heal, to bless, to comfort, to raise up, to protect, to share peace and strength, to provide guidance, and to travel the Heavens: just as He did for His Only Son. His Son works daily and directly with, and supports all true Prophets of His Father. There is no separation between the two, both are dedicated to serving the will of the Father. **One never is asked, nor is there ever a good reason, to stop loving former Prophets. We ALL serve the Father faithfully, with great love and compassion for His children, and the deepest desire for them to also KNOW the Love of Heavenly Father as we do.**

Soul lives forever, so in God's time there is no rush, but once you catch and lay hold of the possibilities, why go back and close the door this book opened for you?

Thank you for reading my book, watching our videos, and allowing me to share what I can at this time in history. There is coming a time when the Father's Son and I will share more fully, but the world is not yet ready. The views, teachings, and the window into Heaven you now know are the foundation for the future I allude to above and below. You have now been somewhat prepared, if that is even possible, for the profound blessings the Father is preparing for the children He Loves so deeply. YOU are one of those He loves, even cherishes.

"The days of any religion or path coming between me and my children are coming to an end" saith the Lord. December 29, 2013

Glossary

Awake Dreams — God can reach out to you in a nighttime dream while you sleep or even during the day when fully awake. When this happens during the waking state it is called an "Awake Dream." Both types of dreams can guide, protect, comfort, teach, and bless you. Awake dreams are also known as signs, coincidences, or synchronicities. It is when you, the observer, feel there is more to an experience than the surface meaning. This is the key to recognizing something as an awake dream: when your heart recognizes an event as out of the ordinary, special, or possibly containing more meaning than only the surface meaning.

Sometimes the awake dream will manifest through the spoken word, such as a song on the radio or a piece of the conversation of a passerby just at the right time. An awake dream may also manifest as the written word, such as a billboard, license plate, or bumper sticker on a passing car. God can and will use just about anything to deliver the message to you. The common denominator of recognizing something as an awake dream is that it catches your attention and stands out to your consciousness. It gives that feeling of "what was that all about?" or "the timing of that was interesting, is there more to it?"

Most of the time an awake dream will relate to your immediate thoughts and actions. When you perceive an awake dream ask yourself, what was I just doing or thinking about? Are you considering looking for a new job or are you struggling with a relationship? If no answer comes, let it go for the time being. It is not worth spending all day on.

An important point to mention is awake dreams are not as dependable as inner communication or knowingness. The biggest danger with awake dreams is getting too "mental" trying to decipher them. For the most part you should not make a major life decision based on a single awake dream, or nighttime dream for that matter. They should merely confirm what your heart already knows to be true. You are Soul and Soul knows truth. Your "truth detector" trumps all — awake dreams included. If everything and every sign is pointing you to take a certain direction, but your heart is drawn somewhere else, follow your heart! (This definition is found in my book "The Pearl of Dream Study")

Beach House — The name for the classroom/sanctuary at the Guidance for a Better Life retreat center.

Consciousness — An individual consciousness is that state of awareness lived in daily. One part of this state involves the physical awareness relayed by the physical senses. The other part of one's daily state of awareness is independent of physical senses and involves one's spiritual awareness. It takes effort to go beyond basic survival and gain higher states of both physical and spiritual consciousness. Each individual has a different state of consciousness, but there are general levels that can be recognized. See the Key "Growth of Consciousness" (page 73) for an explanation of the various levels of consciousness.

Coworker — One who serves God through His Prophet, a servant of God. The focus is on doing God's will when serving, not the coworker's own personal will.

Daily Bread — Daily Bread is a poetic name for daily spiritual nourishment. We believe it is our responsibility to stay spiritually nourished. When Soul is nourished it becomes fortified, more active, and we recognize Divine communication more clearly. When Jesus said "give us this day our daily bread," he meant daily spiritual nourishment, not physical bread. An example of this in the Bible, when Jesus was tempted by the Negative Being during his forty day fast to turn stones into bread, Jesus said "Man shall not live by bread alone, but by every word that proceedeth out of the mouth of God." The Word of God IS spiritual nourishment. Once an individual has this understanding of "daily bread," it can be found throughout scripture.

Receiving daily spiritual nourishment, "our daily bread," is critical for spiritual success. This can be achieved by singing HU, reading scripture, praying, dream study, demonstrating gratitude for our blessings, being in a living Prophet's physical or inner presence, or listening to his words. The sacred experiences shared in the section of this book "Traveling the Heavens" are only possible when Soul has been spiritually nourished consistently over time.

Devil — Devil and Satan are common names for the negative power, which exists to contribute to Souls' growth of maturity and consciousness. The Devil is a master of illusion, but ultimately has no power over Soul, unless one gives it over. Soul is strengthened by learning to resist the negative power's temptations and to not buy into the lies. Staying spiritually nourished through prayer, singing HU, and being in Prophet's presence spiritually or physically will help one to not fall prey to lies and illusion.

Divine — See "The Divine"

Dreams — Dreams (both daytime dreams - see "Awake Dreams," and night-time dreams) are a source of Divine guidance. In the Bible "an angel of the lord came, in a dream" is stated several times. Usually the part "in a dream" is forgotten. Much wisdom can be gained by learning to invite, recall, and understand your dreams. My book "The Pearl of Dream Study" is very complete and easy to understand.

Eck — Another name for Holy Spirit and the Light and Sound of God. It flows from the Ocean of Love and Mercy on the twelfth Heaven creating and sustaining all life. Soul is made of the Light and Sound of God.

God's Prophet — There is always a Prophet of God residing in the physical world. Each of these Souls in a physical embodiment is chosen and raised up by God. Former Prophets have prepared and conditioned the soon-to-be Prophet over multiple lifetimes. God ALWAYS has one primary Prophet at any given time in history. This is a long and unbroken line of God's Prophets. Prophets' words and teachings come directly from God, our Heavenly Father. **Prophet is the Master Key that unlocks the deeper meanings hidden within all the other Keys.** He activates and unleashes their value by helping you integrate and make them operational in your life.

In the Bible Jesus said he would ask his Father to send a Comforter. "And I will pray the Father, and he shall give you another Comforter that he may abide with you forever." John 14:16 KJV The original Greek word used for Comforter was "Paraclete." Paraclete implied an actual physical person who helps, counsels, encourages, advocates, comforts, strengthens, and sets free. "Comforter" **is only one aspect** of the original meaning.

God had Prophets before Jesus and Christianity and will continue this line of teachers. The Bible includes historical accounts of many Prophets prior to Jesus. Some Prophets are extra-special spiritually, such as Jesus who was also the Father's Son. Each of God's Prophets has a special mission given to them by God. Each usually has the highest God Consciousness on Earth during their time. God's Prophet is given spiritual authority directly from God. This authority includes, but is not limited to, sharing God's Light and Sound and taking Souls into the Heavens, to God's Temples of Learning, and Home to God Himself. It also includes teaching God's eternal truths, speaking on behalf of, healing, protecting, and passing on the blessings and Grace of God.

All of God's Prophets are also here to lift up Souls in consciousness, as high as possible for each individual Soul. God wants His children to know His ways and His Love. He sends Prophets to teach His ways and truth, and for those who are ready, bring them HOME.

There are two aspects of God's Prophet, an inner spiritual Prophet and an outer physical Prophet. The inner Prophet can teach us through dreams, intuition, spiritual travel, inner communication, and his presence. The outer Prophet also teaches through his discourses, written word, videos, and his presence. Having an inner and outer teacher brings great benefit and tremendous opportunity to grow. Prophet is always with us spiritually on the inner. Prophet points to and glorifies the Father.

Hand of God — In this book "Hand of God" usually refers to God's Prophet. (See "Voice of God")

Heavenly Worlds — The Heavenly Worlds are those worlds of Spirit beyond the physical realm and physical senses. When Soul leaves the Earth after Its current physical incarnation, Soul goes to the Heavenly World best suited for Its continued growth, depending on Its actions while incarnated. There are many levels or planes in Heaven. It's not as simple as "Heaven and Hell." Soul and Its unique growth, lessons, actions, level of consciousness, and deeds vary widely, so God has created many Heavens for Soul to continue Its journey between physical lifetimes. In time most Souls will return to Earth, incarnating into a new physical body, to continue Its journey to become spiritually more mature, learning to give and receive love, and to serve God.

The testimonies "Truth Uncovered" on page 91, "Journeys to the Fifth Heaven" on page 319, and "Escorted to the Heavens" on page 369 cover additional information about God's various Heavens, also called planes or mansions.

Hell — The idea of Heaven above and hell below is false — all the inner spiritual worlds are "above" the Earth plane. Hell is found in certain "difficult" or "uncomfortable" areas of the first Heaven above Earth, often referred to as the Astral plane. Hell is different for different people, depending upon what they need to learn. Hell is NOT FOREVER, nor does Soul find themselves there for little transgressions — we all make mistakes. Soul may find themselves there for a time, but God loves Soul and always gives Soul another chance to learn from Its errors.

HU — An ancient name for God, and when sung becomes a love song to God. HU has existed since the beginning of time and is available to all regardless of religion. It is a pure way to express your love to God and give thanks for your blessings.

Inner Vision — Our physical body has physical eyes to perceive what is around us physically. We also have, as a spiritual being Soul, inner spiritual vision. Soul can see past the physical into the worlds of Spirit. This can be experienced in a dream, a spiritual contemplation, and sometimes during waking life. (See "Spiritual Eye")

Inner Worlds — The spiritual worlds beyond the physical. They may be safely visited in dreams, spiritual travels, and contemplations when guided by Prophet. (See "Heavenly Worlds")

Jesus — The literal Son of God who incarnated and physically walked the Earth teaching his Father's ways while in the role of God's Prophet. Earth always has a living Prophet to teach God's ways as promised by Jesus.

Karma — Every deed has consequences whether they be considered good or bad. Karma is simply an accounting system for our deeds, positive and negative. Karma is a blessing because it helps us to become more mature by helping us learn from our actions, attitudes, and thoughts.

Language of the Divine — The first step in learning to confidently follow Divine guidance is being able to recognize it in the first place. Divine guidance comes in countless ways, from the dramatic to the very subtle; we call this the "Language of the Divine."

Light and Sound of God — See "Spiritual Light and Sound"

Negative Passions of the Mind — These passions include fear, anger, guilt, worries, lust, greed, excessive attachments, and vanity. (See page 22)

Ocean of Love and Mercy — A poetic name for the Home of God. A vast expanse of Spiritual Light and Sound. All life, love, and Spirit flows from the Ocean creating, sustaining, and nourishing all the worlds below. Most fortunate are those who have had the blessing of being escorted there spiritually, as Soul, by Prophet.

Paraclete — Implies an actual physical person who helps, counsels, encourages, advocates, comforts, strengthens, and sets free. "Comforter" is only one aspect of the original meaning. (See "God's Prophet")

Passions of the Mind — See "Negative Passions of the Mind"

Prophet — In this book Prophet and God's Prophet are interchangeable. (See "God's Prophet")

Reincarnation — Our physical body lasts a single lifetime. Soul however, is eternal, meaning it lives forever. Soul will incarnate into a new physical body to reside on Earth for a time, continuing Its journey home to God by becoming more mature, learning more about giving and receiving love, and serving the Lord. You have one life as Soul, but many physical lifetimes. (See "Soul")

Reunion — An advanced eight-day spiritual retreat held at Guidance for a Better Life retreat center each summer.

Soul — Our real and eternal self is called Soul. As Soul we are literally an individualized and eternal piece of God's Voice, the Holy Spirit. More specifically, the Holy Spirit is made of God's Light and Sound, which is actually God's Love. **As Soul we are made in the image of God.** As an individual and uniquely experienced Soul you have free will, intelligence, imagination, opinions, clear and continuous access to Divine guidance, and immortality. **As Soul we have an innate and profound spiritual growth potential, way**

beyond the spiritual growth of what our physical selves alone can accomplish.

Soul is eternal, with no beginning or end. When living on Earth Soul needs a physical body to reside within. One might call our physical bodies "earth suits" for Soul. While our physical bodies eventually wear out, Soul never wears out, but moves to higher worlds after leaving a particular physical body permanently. **We do not "have" a Soul, we "are" Soul that has a body. This is a major change in consciousness and it takes time to absorb, accept, and eventually live this core truth. Experiencing yourself as Soul is the essential foundation for extraordinary spiritual growth.**

Soul innately wants a relationship with Its Maker, God. Soul is destined to eventually become part of God's team as a coworker with God (a servant of God) through God's Prophet. Singing HU (an ancient name for God and when sung becomes a love song to God) and other spiritual exercises nourish and strengthen Soul. **As Soul gains strength over the mind we begin to operate more as Soul, then Soul influences our decisions and choices for the better, thus growing both closer to God and creating a more abundant life while here on Earth.**

When operating as Soul we have a higher spiritual consciousness than our physical self. **When we speak of our higher self, we are referring to Soul. With the help and guidance of God's Prophet, Soul has an unlimited potential to grow into higher and higher states of consciousness.** When we stay spiritually nourished, receiving our daily spiritual bread, and recognize our true selves as Soul, we make better choices in life. Then both our daily life improves and our relationship with God grows. The spiritual wisdom we gain during our earthly incarnation can be taken to the other worlds when we translate. As Soul we can keep our relationship with God and God's Prophet in the next world. We can take our spiritual progress and wisdom with us.

When we speak of our lower self, or little self, we are referring to our physical body and physical mind. Compared to Soul our lower self is very limited and mortal. **As Soul we have access to far more wisdom and intelligence than even the smartest physical mind. Our goal is to allow Soul to influence our daily behavior and**

decisions. This brings abundance, joy, peace, clarity, and love. Only Soul can explore the Heavens or visit the Abode of God with Prophet, not the temporal physical self.

Soul is that part of us made in the image of God that knows God best, is selfless, wants to bless others, and can more truly, fully, and deeply love their neighbor and God, as we have been commanded to do. Soul has been around forever. Being created long ago it has developed wisdom and experience way beyond intellect. Soul knows what is best for us, better than the mind. Soul is very receptive to the Holy Spirit because it is made from an individualized piece of the Holy Spirit. **When Soul and our mind work together in the way God intended our life blossoms. The Spiritual Keys will lead to Soul and the lower self working together the way God intended, and abundance will follow!**

Spiritual Ear — See "Spiritual Eye"

Spiritual Eye — Also known as the Third Eye and is located between the two eyes. During contemplations this is where one may see God's Light. Also known as Spiritual Ears, this is where one sees, hears, or perceives inner spiritual experiences.

Spiritual Food — See "Daily Bread"

Spiritual Keys — Spiritual Keys are like nuggets of spiritual truth that provide a road map to a richer and fuller life. They are a set of Divine principles, which help us make better decisions in all areas of our lives. Spiritual Keys, if understood and integrated into daily life, can help us build a more abundant life. The Keys are like seeds that if watered and nurtured will bloom into something profound and bear "fruit" in your life and the lives of those you love.

These Keys can also bring us closer to God and His Prophet, which is the foundation of an abundant life. Some Keys tune us into the Divine so we can receive guidance or experience God's Love directly. Other Spiritual Keys are like spiritual laws, and like the law of gravity they work whether one knows of them or not. Being aware of these is a huge advantage. Some Keys bring spiritual wisdom. Other Keys help us travel through life more smoothly and in balance, while helping us avoid unnecessary troubles and challenges. Many of these Keys help us to grow in our ability to both give and receive love.

Spiritual Light and Sound — Spiritual Light and Sound are the twin aspects of the Holy Spirit. They both originate from God at His Abode on the twelfth Heaven; most often distributed to Souls through His Prophet. God's Light and Sound is God's Love.

Spiritual Nourishment — See "Daily Bread"

Sugmad — An ancient and very sacred name for God. Whenever we travel to the Abode of God, at the twelfth Heaven, we sing this name. It is the name for the supreme God, the Heavenly Father.

The Divine — Refers to God, His Holy Spirit, and Prophet.

Third Eye — See "Spiritual Eye"

Truth Detector — Soul has what I call a "Truth Detector." God built into Soul the ability to know truth, even when the mind is not convinced. Remember, Soul can accept and adapt to change faster and more comfortably than most minds. As Soul becomes nourished and more active in our lives, this ability to recognize truth when it is heard or read improves. This valuable gift from God must be protected to remain properly calibrated. If I hear someone share an untruth or misinformation during my retreats, even if unintentional, I quickly provide a correction. If I do not, then others may assume what they heard is truth, and letting that happen can damage truth detectors or student's trust in themselves. Having confidence in one's truth detector is vital.

Vision Rock — Rock outcropping on retreat center property with a stunning view.

Voice of God — Within the Heavenly realms the Voice of God, or the Holy Spirit, manifests itself in a wide range of spiritual light and sound. The Voice of God is a deep well of spiritual light and sound (which is God's Love) and guidance to draw from as you go about your life. You are never alone — the Voice of God is always with you trying to help guide you through the challenges of life and manifest more joy and happiness. The problem for most folks is life is busy and full of distractions making it hard to "hear" those gentle whisperings. To experience the Voice of God in any form is a profound blessing. God's Prophet is a concentrated aspect of the Holy Spirit, which is also called the Voice of God.

Guidance for a Better Life
Our Story

My Father's Journey

God always has a living Prophet on Earth to teach His Ways and accomplish His will. My father, Del Hall III, is currently God's true Prophet fully raised up and ordained by God Himself. He was not always a Prophet, nor did he even know what a Prophet was, but God had a plan for him like He has for all of His children. Over many years through many life experiences, God had begun to prepare my father for his future assignment, mostly unbeknownst to him.

Prophet Del Hall III

Everything he experienced in his life from the joys to the sadness helped prepare him for his future role as Prophet.

My dad grew up in California and was a decent student but a better athlete. He received an appointment to the United States Naval Academy in Annapolis, Maryland where he later met my mother. They were married two days after he graduated and received his commission as an officer. After a short tour on a Navy ship deployed to Vietnam, he went to flight training school and became a Navy fighter pilot. While attending flight school in Pensacola, Florida he also earned a Master of Science Degree and had the first of his three children, a son. After flight school he was stationed in a fighter squadron on the east coast, where he and my mom began investing in real estate, adding to their family with the birth of two daughters. Following this tour of duty he was assigned as a jet flight instructor in Texas, after which, his time in the Navy was finished. He was a natural pilot and loved his time in the sky, but it was time to move on.

So far in life he had no real concern for, or even thought much about God, religion, or spiritual matters in general. He lived life fully. He raised his family. He traveled. He invested and became an entrepreneur starting and growing highly successful businesses in diverse fields ranging from real estate to aerospace consulting. Years before however, a seed had been planted when God's eternal teachings were introduced to him in his late teens, and while it did not show outwardly, the truth in these teachings spoke to his heart. My dad might not have been giving much thought to God up to this point in his life, but God was definitely thinking about him and the future He had planned for him. Like an acorn destined to become a mighty oak, the seed that lay dormant in his heart would someday be stirred to life. Through all his life experiences, both "good" and "bad," God would be preparing him for his future role as His Prophet.

When God decided it was time, He called my dad to Him. He did this by shutting down the world of financial security my dad had built. Over a period of two years all of his businesses were wound down and dissolved. What seemed like security turned out to be an illusion. Financial success had not provided true security. He now had failed businesses and a failing marriage and was trying to fix things without God's help, principles, or guidance. As painful as this time in his life was, it was yet another step towards the glorious life of service awaiting my father. God was removing him from the world my dad had created and furthering him along his path to his future role as Prophet.

After his marriage ended and his businesses wound down, he started fresh by going out west to give flying lessons near Lake

Mead, Nevada. While living in Nevada my dad was reintroduced to the eternal teachings of God he first learned of as a teenager twenty-three years earlier, and though they resonated with him at the time, his priorities were different back then. Now, his serious training could begin. He started having very clear experiences with the Holy Spirit and noticed there was a familiarity with these teachings and experiences. He embraced the long hours of instruction, which often lasted until sunrise, and was receptive to the personal spiritual experiences he was given. This began an intense period of study and desire for spiritual truth that continues to this day. Some of his most profound and meaningful experiences during this time were with past Prophets of old. They came to him spiritually in contemplations and dreams. He learned of their roles in history and how they were raised up and ordained by God directly. He began to realize they were training him but was not clear why. A few times his experiences led him to believe he was in training to be a future Prophet. However, that revelation made no sense to him because he felt he was an imperfect person who made mistakes and had failures. He thought of the past and current Prophets of God as perfected Souls, not imperfect like he felt he was. Why would God choose him for such a role? He did not feel qualified.

Besides being introduced to God's teachings while he was out west, my father was blessed to meet his current wife Lynne. Returning to the East Coast, my father and Lynne moved into a small cabin on land he had acquired before his businesses shut down. This was a major change in his life, but it felt deeply right within him. He began to remember a desire to live like this as a child; from early childhood my dad found clarity and peace in nature. He had forgotten about this until now, but God had not and made this dream a reality. In addition to being their home, these beautiful, three-hundred-plus acres of land in the Blue Ridge Mountains would eventually become the location for the Guidance for a Better Life retreat center. The perfection of my father's experiences from earlier in his life in real estate, providing the land for his next step in life, speak to the perfection of God's plan. One of many many examples I could list.

For many years my dad took wilderness skills courses around the country. He specialized in the study of wild edible and medicinal plants, tracking, and awareness skills, and authored articles for publication. Inspired to help folks feel more comfortable in the outdoors, my dad and Lynne began the Nature Awareness School in 1990. Classes were focused on teaching awareness and the primitive living skills needed to enjoy the woods and survive in them if necessary. An amazing thing happened within those first few years though; students began to experience aspects of God in very personal and dramatic ways. Somewhat like my dad's experience out west, they found that stepping away from their daily routine and the hustle of life, if even for a few days, created space for Spirit to do Its work. Whether they were enjoying the beauty of the Virginia wilderness and tranquility of the school grounds or relaxing by the pond, he found students' hearts opened, and they became more receptive to the Divine Hand that is always reaching out to Its children. More and more the discourse during wilderness classes shifted to the meanings of dreams, personal growth, finding balance in life, and experiences the students were having with the Voice of God in Its many forms. An increase of spiritual retreats was offered to fulfill the demand and over time became the predominant class offerings; the wilderness survival skills classes eventually fading away completely. The name "Nature Awareness School" seemed to be less fitting for what was actually being taught now and in February 2019 my father changed the name of the retreat center to Guidance for a Better Life.

Throughout this time my father's training and spiritual study continued. My father reached mastership and was ordained by God on July 7, 1999 but he was still not yet Prophet, more was required. On October 22, 2012, twenty-five years since his full-time intensive training had begun, God-ordained him as His chosen Prophet, and He has continued to raise him up further since. God works through my father in very direct and beneficial ways for his students. Hundreds and hundreds of students over the past thirty years have received God's eternal teachings through my father's instruction and mentoring. They have had personal experiences with the Divine which have transformed and greatly blessed their lives. My father's greatest joy is being used by God as a servant to share God's ways and truths with thirsty Souls and hungry seekers. In addition to mountain-top retreats, my father continues to spread God's ways and teachings that so greatly blessed his life and the lives of his loved ones in many ways.

The book you hold in your hand is but one of more than a dozen titles we have co-authored. These incredible testimonies of God's Love are being shared in print, eBook, audio, YouTube videos and podcasts in hopes of blessing others.

Maybe you are at a turning point in your life and looking for direction. Maybe you have a knowing there is more to life but not sure what that might be or how to find it. Or, maybe you are simply drawn to what you read and hear in our stories. God speaks to our hearts and calls each of us in many different ways. Like my father's journey demonstrates, it doesn't matter where you started or the twists, turns, or seeming dead-ends your life has taken; God wants us to know Him more fully, and for us to know our purpose within His creation. He wants us to experience His Love regardless of our religious path or lack thereof. He always has a living Prophet here on Earth to help us accomplish His desire for us — to show us the way home to Him and to experience more abundance in our life while we are still living here on Earth. God's Prophet today is my father, Del Hall III. You have the opportunity to grow spiritually through God's teachings which Prophet shares. His guidance for a better life is available for you — please accept it.

Written by Del Hall IV

My Son, Del Hall IV

My son, Del Hall IV, joined Guidance for a Better Life as an instructor after fifteen years of in-class training with me, his father. He helped develop the five step "Keys to Spiritual Freedom" study program and facilitates the first two courses in the program: Step One "Tools to Recognize Divine Guidance" and Step Two "Understanding Divine Guidance." Del also teaches people about

Del Hall IV

the rich history of dream study and how to better recall their own dreams during the "Dream Study Workshops," which he hosts around the country. He is qualified to step in and facilitate any of my retreats should the need arise.

Del is also Vice President of Marketing and helps with everything required to get the "good news" from Guidance for a Better Life out to hungry seekers: everything from book publishing, blogging, podcasts, and other social media outlets. He is co-author and book cover designer for many of our, thus far, fourteen published books.

My son loves the opportunity to work on creative projects for Guidance for a Better Life. From a very early age he has been an artist and loved creating artwork in multiple mediums. He was accepted into gifted art programs in Virginia Beach, Virginia and then after high school graduation he attended the School of the

Museum of Fine Arts in Boston. He is now a nationally exhibited artist and his paintings of the Light and Sound of God are in over seventy-five public and private collections. One of the greatest joys of the painting process for Del is using his paintings as an opportunity to share with others the inspiration behind them, God's Love and his experiences with the Light and Sound of God, the Holy Spirit, in contemplation and in waking life.

Del lives on the retreat center property in the Blue Ridge Mountains of Virginia with his wife and my three grandchildren whom they homeschool. He loves woodworking, tending to his vegetable garden, pruning his fruit trees, and helping maintain the beautiful three-hundred acres of retreat center property for students to enjoy. There is always something that needs attention on the land and Del is always up to the challenge. He loves to travel and spends his free time enjoying this beautiful country with his family in their RV.

My son has had multiple brain surgeries starting when he was seventeen years old for a recurring brain tumor. He credits God for surviving and thriving all this time when most with his condition do not. He looks to the sunrise every day with gratitude for yet another chance at life. With that chance he desires to help me share the love and teachings of God that have so blessed our lives. I pray to God daily thanking Him for my son's good health.

Written by Prophet Del Hall III

Articles of Faith

Written by Prophet Del Hall III

1. We believe in one true God that is still living and active in our lives. He is knowable and wants a relationship with each of His children. He is the same God Jesus called FATHER, and is known by many names, including Heavenly Father. God wants a loving personal relationship with each of us, NOT one based upon fear or guilt.

2. The Holy Spirit is God's expression in all the worlds. It is in two parts, the Light and the Sound. It is through His Holy Spirit God communicates and delivers all His gifts: peace, clarity, love, joy, healings, correction, guidance, wisdom, comfort, truth, dreams, new revelations, and more.

3. God always has a chosen living Prophet to teach His ways, speak His Living Word, lift up Souls, and bring us closer to God. God's living Prophet is a concentrated aspect of the Holy Spirit, the Light and Sound, and is raised up and ordained by God directly. His Prophet is empowered and authorized to share God's Light and Sound and to correct misunderstandings of His ways. There are two aspects of God's Prophet, an inner spiritual and outer physical Prophet. The inner Prophet can teach us through dreams, intuition, spiritual travel, inner communication, and his presence. The outer Prophet also teaches through his discourses, written word, and his presence. Prophet is always with us spiritually on the inner. Prophet points to and glorifies the Father.

4. God so loves the world and His children He has always had a long unbroken line of His chosen Prophets. They existed before Jesus and after Jesus. Jesus was God's Prophet and His actual SON. God's chosen Prophets are considered to be in the "role of God's Son," though NOT literally His Son. Only Jesus was literally His Son. Prophets were sometimes called Paraclete. The Bible uses the word Comforter, but the original Greek word was Paraclete, which

is more accurate. Paraclete implied an actual physical person who helps, counsels, encourages, advocates, comforts, and sets free.

5. Our real and eternal self is called Soul. We are Soul; we do NOT "have" a Soul. As Soul we are literally an individualized piece of God's Holy Spirit, thereby Divine in nature. We are made of God's Light and Sound, which is actually God's Love. As an individual and uniquely experienced Soul you have free will, intelligence, imagination, opinions, clear and continuous access to Divine guidance, and immortality. As Soul we have an innate and profound spiritual growth potential. Soul has the ability to travel the Heavens spiritually with Prophet to gain truth and wisdom, and grow in love. Soul exists because God loves it.

6. We believe Soul equals Soul, in that God loves all Souls equally and each Soul has the same innate qualities and potential. Soul is neither male nor female, any particular race, nationality, or age. All Souls are children of God.

7. We believe in one eternal life as Soul. However, we believe Soul needs to incarnate many times into a physical body to learn and grow spiritually mature. Soul's journey home to God encompasses many lifetimes. A loving God does not expect His children to learn His ways in a single lifetime.

8. We believe Soul incarnates on Earth to grow in the ability to give and receive love.

9. We believe God is more interested in two Souls experiencing love for one another than in their sexual preference.

10. It is God's will that a negative power exists to help Soul grow spiritually through challenges and hardships, thereby strengthening and maturing Soul. We are never given a challenge greater than our ability to find a solution. Soul has the ability to rise above any obstacles with God's help.

11. We study the Bible as an authentic teaching tool of God's ways, in addition to books and discourses authored by a Prophet chosen by God. We know the original Biblical writings have been

altered in some cases by incorrect translations and political interference throughout the ages. God loves each of us regardless of our errors. We do not believe in God's eternal abandonment or damnation. He would never turn His back to us for eternity.

12. Karma is the way in which the Divine accounts for our actions, words, thoughts, and attitudes. One can create positive or negative karma. Karma is a blessing used to teach us responsibility. We do not have to earn God's Love, He loves us unconditionally.

13. We do not believe that a child is born in sin, though the child may have karma from a former life. Karma, God's accounting system, explains our birth circumstances better than the concept of sin.

14. We believe that a living Prophet, including Jesus, can remove karma and sin when necessary to help us get started or to grow on the path to God. However, it is primarily our responsibility to live and grow in the ways of God, thereby not creating negative karma and sin.

15. There are four commandments of God in which we abide: First — Love God with all your heart, mind and Soul; Second — Love your neighbor as yourself. We believe the Third is, "Seek ye first the Kingdom of God, and His righteousness." We believe this means that it is primarily our responsibility to draw close to God, learn His ways, and strive to live the way God would like us to live. God's Prophets are sent to show His ways. We believe our purpose, the Fourth Commandment, is to become spiritually mature to be used by God to bless His children. Becoming a co-worker with God is our primary purpose in life and the most rewarding attainment of Soul.

16. We believe all Souls upon translation, death of the physical body, go to the higher worlds, called Heavens, Planes, or Mansions, regardless of their beliefs. The way they live life on Earth and the effort made to draw close to God impacts the area of Heaven they are to be sent. Those who draw close to a Prophet of God receive special care. We know of twelve distinct Heavens, not one. The primary abode of the Heavenly Father is in the twelfth Heaven,

known as the "Ocean of Love and Mercy." We can visit God while we still live on Earth, but only if taken by His chosen Prophet and only as Soul, not in a physical body.

17. We believe prayer is communication with God and is an extreme privilege. God hears every prayer from the heart whether or not we recognize a response. Singing an ancient name of God, HU, is our foundational prayer. It expresses love and gratitude to God and is unencumbered by words. Singing HU has the potential to raise us up in consciousness making us more receptive to God's Love, Light, and guiding Hand. After praying it is best to spend time listening to God. Prayer should never be rote or routine. We desire to trust God and surrender to His will rather than our own will.

18. We believe it is our responsibility to stay spiritually nourished. When Soul is nourished and fortified it becomes activated and we are more receptive and have clearer communication with the Divine. We believe when Jesus said "give us this day our daily bread," he meant daily spiritual nourishment, not physical bread. This can be done by singing HU, reading scripture, praying, dream study, demonstrating gratitude for our blessings, being in a living Prophet's physical presence, or in his inner presence, or listening to his words.

19. We believe TRUTH has the power to improve every area of our lives, but only if understood, accepted, and integrated into our lives.

20. We believe God and His Prophet guide us in our sleeping dreams and awake dreams as a gift of love. God's Prophet teaches how to understand both types of dreams. All areas of our lives may be blessed by the wisdom God offers each of us directly in dreams.

21. Gratitude is extremely important on our path of love. It is literally the secret of love. Developing an attitude of gratitude is necessary to becoming spiritually mature. Recognizing and being grateful for the blessings of God in our lives is vital to building a loving and trusting relationship with God and His chosen Prophet.

A relationship with God's Prophet is THE KEY to everything good and a life more abundant.

22. We believe in being good stewards of our blessings. We recognize them as gifts of love from God and make the effort to have remembrance. Remembering our blessings helps to keep our heart open to God and builds trust in God's Love for us.

23. We believe in giving others the freedom to make their own choices and live their lives as they wish. We expect the same in return.

24. We believe the Love and Blessings of God and His Prophet are available to all who are receptive. If one desires guidance and help from Prophet, ask from the heart and sing "Prophet." He will respond. One does not need to meet Prophet physically to receive help. To be taught by Prophet it is best to attend a retreat with him in the physical. However, much can be gained by reading or listening to his teachings.

25. We have a responsibility to do our part and let God and His Prophet do their part. This responsibility brings freedom. Our goal is to remain spiritually nourished, live in balance and harmony, and serve God as a co-worker. Anything is possible with God if we do our part. We pray to use our God-given free will in a way that our actions, thoughts, words, and attitudes testify and bear witness to the Glory and Love of God.

26. We believe there is always more to learn and grow in God's ways and truth. One cannot remain the same spiritually. One must make the effort to move forward or risk falling backward. To grow in consciousness requires change. Spiritual wisdom gained during our earthly incarnations can be taken to the other worlds when we translate, and into future lifetimes, unlike our physical possessions.

Contact Information

Guidance for a Better Life is a worldwide mentoring program provided by Prophet Del Hall III and his son Del Hall IV. Personal one-on-one mentoring at our retreat center is our premier offering and the most direct and effective way to grow spiritually. Spiritual tools, guided exercises, and in-depth discourses on the eternal teachings of God are provided to help one become more aware of and receptive to His Holy Spirit and the abundance that awaits. With this personally-tailored guidance one begins to more fully recognize God's Love daily in their lives, both the dramatic and the very subtle. Over time our mentoring reduces fear, worry, anxiety, lack of purpose, feelings of unworthiness, guilt, and confusion; replacing those negative aspects of life with an abundance of peace, clarity, joy, wisdom, love, and self-respect leading to a more personal relationship with God, more than most know is possible. We also offer our YouTube videos, our podcast, and more than a dozen inspirational and educational books.

Guidance for a Better Life

P.O. Box 219

Lyndhurst, Virginia 22952

(540) 377-6068

contact@guidanceforabetterlife.com

www.guidanceforabetterlife.com

"A Growing Testament to the Power of God's Love One Profound Book at a Time."

SPECIALIZED TOPICS

Whether you wish to reconnect with a loved one who has passed, understand how you too can experience God's Light, improve your marriage, or learn how to understand your dreams, these incredible books have you covered.

TESTIMONIES OF GOD'S LOVE SERIES

God expresses His Love every day in many different and sometimes subtle ways. Often this love goes unrecognized because the ways in which God communicates are not well known. Each of the books in this series contains fifty true stories that will help you learn to better recognize the Love of God in your life.

JOURNEY TO A TRUE SELF-IMAGE SERIES

This series includes intimate and unique stories that many readers will be able to personally identify with, enjoy, and learn from. They will help the reader transcend the false images people often carry about themselves — first and foremost that they are only their physical mind and body. The authors share their journeys of recognizing and coming to more fully accept their true self-image, that of Soul — an eternal child of God.